The Grammar of Silence

The Grammar of Silence
A Reading of Marguerite de Navarre's Poetry

Robert D. Cottrell

The Catholic University of America Press
Washington, D.C.

Copyright © 1986
The Catholic University of America Press
All rights reserved
Printed in the United States of America

LIBRARY OF CONGRESS CATALOGING IN PUBLICATION DATA
Cottrell, Robert D.
  The grammar of silence.

  Bibliography: p.
  Includes index.
  1. Marguerite, Queen, consort of Henry II, King of
Navarre, 1492-1549–Criticism and interpretation.
2. Christian poetry, French–History and criticism.
1. Title.
PQ1632.C68 1986   841'.3   85-12734
ISBN 0-8132-0615-4

For J.E.C., A.A.C., A.E.C.

Contents

Preface

The poems of Marguerite de Navarre (b. 1492–d. 1549) are a *terra incognita*, a vast and somewhat forbidding linguistic terrain that has attracted relatively few exegetes and so remains largely uncharted and unmapped. They are mainly devotional works, many of which Marguerite composed in her carriage during the numerous trips she made across France in her capacity as Queen of Navarre and sister of Francis I, or in one of the convents to which she habitually retired to meditate and pray. The poems describe the anguish and joy of the Christian wayfarer who seeks to negotiate the ladder of perfection (*scala perfectionis*) and to attain the final stage of mystical ecstasy (*unio mystica*). They express a longing for union with God, a desire to efface difference, a yearning for a spiritual state in which everything in the world is perceived as a signifier whose referent is always Christ, the one and only signified. Composed in the Augustinian-Dionysian tradition that equates the Johannine *logos*, or the Word, with silence (It transcends human discourse), Marguerite's poems confront with relentless persistence the problem of finding a language capable of signifying "Divine Silence,"[1] the generator of all discourse.

This book is called a grammar because it studies the parts of speech and the syntax of that "language." It tries to classify the ways in which Marguerite's texts encode and produce meaning. At the same time, it is a reading or decoding of Marguerite's poems that ends up re-encoding in the folds of a second text whatever significance is disclosed in the course of that reading. The second text, which is *my* text, will in turn be subjected

---

1. These words are by Dionysius the Areopagite, *On Divine Names and the Mystical Theology*, ed. C. E. Rolt (1920; rpt. New York: Macmillan, 1951), p. 88. Shortly, we shall discuss Marguerite's considerable debt to Dionysius.

(perhaps) to a reading and a decodement that will produce yet another text, another encodement. This process is coextensive with the operation of the Word in the world, for in the tradition that informs Marguerite's poetry, creation is viewed as a series of texts that, together, constitute God's Book. Each discrete text is a metaphor (*translatio*) for Christ the Text, the *Verbum* that was in the beginning.

I have not attempted to examine in detail every one of Marguerite's poems. I do, however, analyze all the long, important poems as well as a good number of the short, relatively minor ones. In a sense, Marguerite's poetry is an extension of the spiritual and linguistic concerns that are enunciated in her correspondence with Briçonnet, Bishop of Meaux, who for four years (1521–24) served as her mentor and counselor. Traces of Briçonnet's vocabulary and thought are visible in all of Marguerite's poetry. Part One of this study, begins, therefore, with an examination of the Briçonnet-Marguerite correspondence, which reveals the context within which Marguerite's poetry takes shape. The investigation of this correspondence is followed by readings of Marguerite's first two long poems, "Dialogue en forme de vision nocturne" and "Petit Oeuvre dévot et contemplatif," both of which were probably written during the years she was in constant contact with Briçonnet. Although Marguerite did not include these early works in the three collections of poems published during her lifetime (*Le Miroir de l'âme pécheresse* [The Mirror of the Sinful Soul], 1531; *Marguerites de la marguerite des princesses* [Pearls by the Pearl of Princesses], 1547; *Suyte des marguerites* [Continuation of the Pearls], 1547), they are important signposts that orient us with great accuracy toward what is central in her poetry.

Part Two deals with images of pictorial representation, with metaphors of sight and insight, and is entitled "The Iconic Text." It opens with an examination of "Le Miroir de l'âme pécheresse," the first poem in Marguerite's first collection of poetry and a work that retained its privileged position in the *Marguerites*, where it is also the first poem. In subsequent units of Part Two, I discuss individual poems, most of which were included in the *Marguerites*. Generally, I present the poems in chronological order, or at least in what is presumed to be their chronological order, for it is difficult to date with precision several of Marguerite's works. In a few instances, I group together two or more poems that share the same thematics or the same problematics, as in the case of Marguerite's last poem, "L'Art et usage du souverain mirouer du chrestien," which I discuss along with "Le Miroir de l'âme pécheresse."

In Part Three, I investigate several of Marguerite's most important poems, each of which is emblematic of a "closed system" as that phrase is used in cybernetics and modern communication theory. These works were all written during the last few years of Marguerite's life. Most were composed after 1547, the year Francis I died and Marguerite, for all intents and purposes, withdrew from the Court. Many of them remained unpublished until the end of the nineteenth century.

This book consists, then, of a series of readings. A reader who is interested in a particular poem can turn to the pages in which that work is examined and find a discussion that is largely self-contained. At the same time, however, and in a paradoxical way, I have sought to give my text an inner consistency and logic of such persuasiveness that it can only be read as a single whole, each part emending and modifying what precedes and what follows. My model for this has been Marguerite. Although each of her poems is a discrete work, every one is so clearly a rewriting of a single pre-existing text that they gain immeasurably by being read as one opus whose rhythms and chromatic modulations are subtle maneuvers intended always to direct the reader's gaze beyond the text to Christ, the *Verbum* in which the end as well as the beginning of every text is inscribed.

Because Marguerite's poems are all signs pointing to God and the reign of charity, they are, in a sense, "repetitious." They always say the same thing, for, from Marguerite's Evangelical perspective, there is only one thing to say. Insofar as my text consists of readings that try to capture (or produce) the significance of Marguerite's poetry, it duplicates the "repetitiousness" of her text. But Marguerite's "repetitiousness" is not (at least in theory) the "Superfluity of Words" that Thomas à Kempis warned against.[2] It is not a gratuitous redundancy that dissipates meaning. Rather, it is a loving duplication of the kind that Kierkegaard meant when he declared that man's speech is always a "repeti-

2. *The Imitation of Christ* (London: J. M. Dent, 1960), I.10, p. 14.

tion" of God's speech, a sign of the inexhaustible fertility of the Word reproducing Itself and renewing Its unique meaning in an endless flow of language.

Marguerite concludes her prologue to the *Marguerites* with an exhortation to "lecteurs de bonne conscience" [readers of good conscience]. She counsels them to "prendre la patience" [have patience] and to "lire du tout ceste oeuvre" [read all of this work], adding: "Et n'en prenez seulement, que le bien" [And do not take from it anything but the good]. This advice seems simple, but it demands much of the reader. Taking my cue from Marguerite, I, too, address my book to "lecteurs de bonne conscience." I hope that they will have the patience to read it all the way through and that, their reading done, they will retain only the good they may have found in it.

Throughout this book, quotations are given as they appear in the editions used, except that in the case of sixteenth-century texts I resolve abbreviations and change consonantal *i* and *u* to *j* and *v* respectively. All translations are my own unless otherwise indicated. They are utilitarian and are intended to help readers who may wish to use them to understand better the original. My discussions of Marguerite's poems are always based on the French text. Occasionally I have not translated short phrases composed of cognates. All quotations from Scripture are taken from the Jerusalem Bible.

I
Reading Aright

I

Mary and Martha

Early in June 1521, Marguerite d'Angoulême, twenty-nine-year-old sister of Francis I and wife of the Duke of Alençon, wrote the following letter to Guillaume Briçonnet, Bishop of Meaux, thus initiating a correspondence that was to last for some four years:

Monsieur de Meaulx, congnoissant que ung seul est necessaire, m'adresse à vous pour vous prier envers luy vouloir estre par oraison moien qu'il luy plaise conduire selon la saincte volonté Monsieur d'Alençon qui, par le commandement du Roy, s'en va son lieutenant general en son armée que, je doubte, ne se departira sans guerre. Et, pour ce que la paix et la victoire est en sa main, pensant que, oultre le bien publicque du royaulme, avez bon desir de ce qui touche son salut et le mien, vous emploie en mes affaires et vous demande le secours spirituel. Car il me fault mesler de beaucoup de choses qui me doivent bien donner crainte. Et encores demain s'en va ma tante de Nemours en Savoye. Parquoy, vous faisant les recommandations d'elle et de moy et vous priant que sy congnoissez que le temps fust propre que maistre Michel peult faire ung voiage, ce me seroit consolation que je ne quiers que pour l'honneur de Dieu, le remectant a vostre bonne discretion et la scienne. La toute vostre Marguerite.[1]

Monsieur de Meaux, knowing that only one thing is needed, I address myself to you to ask you to have the kindness to entreat Him to lead, in accordance with Divine Will, Monsieur d'Alençon, who, by the King's command, is leaving to be Lieutenant General in the King's army, which, I fear, will not fail to see combat. And, so that peace and

---

1. Guillaume Briçonnet-Marguerite d'Angoulême, *Correspondance*, ed. Christian Martineau and Michel Veissière, I (Geneva: Droz, 1975), 25. Volume I covers the years 1521–22 and Volume II, which was published in 1979, the years 1523–24. Henceforth, quotations from the *Correspondance* will be identified in the text by volume and page number.

victory will be his, believing that you, in addition to the public good of the kingdom, have a keen interest in whatever touches on his welfare and on mine, I am engaging you in my affairs and ask you for spiritual help. For I must participate in many things that make me very apprehensive. And tomorrow my aunt de Nemours is leaving for Savoy. For these reasons, I send you her greetings and mine, and request that, if you consider the time appropriate, you allow Master Michel to come and visit me. This would be for me a comfort, which I seek only for the glory of God. I leave the matter to your discretion and to his. Your devoted Marguerite.

In this letter, Marguerite uses the diplomatic skills for which she was famous among foreign ambassadors at the French court.[2] Cunningly fashioned, the letter is composed of two distinct themes. The dynamics of the text is determined by the pressures and tensions that result from the uneasy contiguity of these two themes, one of which can be identified with the biblical figure of Mary, the other, with that of her sister, Martha.

The story of Mary and Martha is inscribed in the first line of the letter by means of the words "ung seul est necessaire," which, according to Luke 10.42, were said by Jesus in response to a remark by Martha. (The Vulgate reads "unum est necessarium.") Martha complained that while she was busy with the household chores Mary "sat down at the Lord's feet and listened to him speaking" (Luke 10.39). Jesus answered Martha saying, "Martha, Martha, you worry and fret about so many things and yet few are needed, indeed only one. It is Mary who has chosen the better part; it is not to be taken from her." By introducing this Scriptural passage into its own discourse, Marguerite's text becomes charged with a significance that is related to the opposing viewpoints of Mary and Martha.

The biblical quotation appears in a participial phrase ("congnoissant que ung seul est necessaire"), the subject of which is not at once apparent. That is to say, the grammatical framework

2. See Pierre Jourda, *Marguerite d'Angoulême, Duchesse d'Alençon, Reine de Navarre (1492–1549): Etude biographique et littéraire* (Paris: Champion, 1930), pp. 43–78. Jourda cites a communiqué in which the Venetian ambassador noted that Marguerite was privy to "tutti li secreti" [all the secrets] pertaining to matters of diplomacy and should be treated with extreme deference and circumspection (p. 61). See also Lucien Febvre, *Autour de l'Heptaméron: amour sacré, amour profane* (Paris: Gallimard, 1944). During the early years of Francis I's reign, Marguerite often served as hostess at official functions, replacing Francis' wife, Claude.

of the text does not permit the reader to identify immediately the subject of "congnoissant." It does, however, give him textual signs by which he can discern two different subjects. Because he is reading a letter, the reader anticipates the voice of an addresser who speaks to an addressee.[3] He is inclined to assume that "I" is the subject of "congnoissant." Nevertheless, there is another sign that points to a different subject. Since it is Mary who "knows that only one thing is needed," the subject of "congnoissant" ought to be Mary. The next words of the letter ("m'addresse à vous") establish the fact that the subject of "congnoissant" is "I," or Marguerite herself. Such is the power of the biblical allusion, however, that the image of Mary does not fade. It fuses with that of Marguerite; the figure who sits at the Master's feet, knowing "that only one thing is needed," is Marguerite-cum-Mary.

Instead of confirming the link between Marguerite and Mary, the text, however, immediately sets about to weaken it. In the biblical text, Mary says nothing. She "sat down at the Lord's feet and listened to him speaking." She listens but does not speak. Silence is one of her essential attributes. Speaking, however, is one of Martha's. It was Martha, "distracted with all the serving," who approached Jesus and said: "Lord, do you not care that my sister is leaving me to do the serving all by myself? Please tell her to help me." The Marguerite who writes to Briçonnet, enumerating the burdens she bears, asking him for help and engaging him in conversation, is more like Martha than Mary. Although the opening words of the letter suggest that Marguerite resembles Mary, the text now suggests that Marguerite is closer to Martha. Like Martha, Marguerite "worries and frets about many things." The next several lines of the letter make clear what these things are.

Marguerite asks Briçonnet to pray for her husband, who has recently been appointed commander of the army in Champagne. If fighting were to break out (and she fears it will), the good of the kingdom depends on a decisive victory by her husband's forces. She explains to Briçonnet that she is writing to

3. Emile Benveniste has pointed out in "Le Langage et l'expérience humaine," *Problèmes de linguistique générale* (Paris: Gallimard, 1966) that as soon as *I* appears in language *you* is implied. In the case of a letter, the reverse is equally true: as soon as *you* appears, *I* is implied.

him because she knows that he is interested in the welfare of the state. Ingratiatingly, she adds that she knows that he is also interested in her own welfare.

Briçonnet had good reason to be interested in Marguerite's welfare. He was deeply involved in politics, and his fortune rode on that of the royal family.[4] Marguerite was writing to a political ally as well as an ecclesiastic of distinction. Although her letter opens on a note of Christian piety ("ung seul est necessaire"), the first two of the five sentences that constitute the letter (these two sentences actually make up more than half of the text) stress the political side of their relationship. The vocabulary points to affairs of state: "par le commandement du Roy," "lieutenant general en son armée," "guerre," "paix," "victoire," "le bien publicque du royaulme." The notion to which all of these terms lead is contained in the word "salut": "Et, pour ce que la paix et la victoire est en sa main [Marguerite's husband], pensant que, oultre le bien publicque du royaulme, avez bon desir de ce qui touche son *salut* et le mien, vous emploie en mes affaires et vous demande le secours spirituel."

In the linear progression of the text, "salut" first means "welfare," in the sense of physical well-being. This is the first definition that Cotgrave (*Dictionarie of the French and English Tongues*, 1611), gives for *salut*: "health, safetie, soundnesse, good plight." Reinforcing the resolutely pragmatic and political tone of the letter, Marguerite insinuates that there is a close relationship between her welfare and that of Briçonnet, whose support she would like to elicit in those matters of special interest to her ("vous employer en mes affaires").

The words "secours spirituel," which conclude the sentence, compel, however, a reinterpretation of "salut." They indicate a

---

4. On Briçonnet, see Febvre, *Autour de l'Heptaméron* and his "Le cas Briçonnet," in *Au coeur religieux du XVIème siècle* (Paris: S.E.V.P.E.N., 1957), pp. 145–71. See also Henry Heller, "The Briçonnet Case Reconsidered," *The Journal of Medieval and Renaissance Studies*, 2 (1972), 223–58, and Michel Veissière, "Guillaume Briçonnet, abbé rénovateur de Saint-Germain-des-Prés (1507–1534)," *Revue d'Histoire de l'Eglise de France*, 40, No. 164 (1974), 65–84. The literature on the reforms Briçonnet instigated at Meaux is extensive. See Augustin Renaudet, *Préréforme et humanisme à Paris pendant les premières guerres d'Italie, 1494–1517* (1916; rpt. Paris: Librairie d'Argences, 1953), and Henry Heller, *Reform and Reformers at Meaux*, Diss., Cornell University, 1969. See also Henry Heller, "Marguerite de Navarre and the Reformers of Meaux," *BHR*, 33 (1971), 271–310; Heller, Introduction to Briçonnet-Marguerite *Correspondance*, I, 16–24; Pierre Imbart de la Tour, *Les Origines de la Réforme* (Paris: Hachette, 1914), III.

change of emphasis in the text. Marguerite is no longer (or not only) asking an old political ally for support in a cause dear to her; she is also asking a vicar of Christ, as any troubled and penitent Christian might, for spiritual guidance. Indeed, the plea for spiritual succor is more urgent, more pressing, than either the formulaic request that Briçonnet pray for Alençon as he goes off to war or Marguerite's insinuation that she and Briçonnet work together to their mutual benefit. In light of the end of the sentence, "salut" has a richer meaning than it had when it first appeared in the linear flow of the text. In addition to meaning "health, safetie, soundnesse, good plight," "salut" also means (and Cotgrave gives this definition next) "salvation." It is this latter meaning that, in sympathetic vibration with "secours spirituel," is now heard in the text. Located at the center of the text, "salut" is a pivotal word, containing within itself both the notion of "good plight" (which was Martha's concern) and that of Christian salvation (Mary's concern). The text has in fact pivoted on the word "salut." It has changed its thrust and altered its message. The reader's attention has shifted from Alençon's physical safety to the psychic state of the narrator and her need for "secours spirituel."

Marguerite explains explicitly why she needs spiritual counsel: "car," she says in the next sentence, "il me fault mesler de beaucoup de choses qui me doivent bien donner crainte." Fear, then, or anxiety, is at the root of her request for guidance. Loneliness, too, for Marguerite continues by saying that not only is her husband leaving shortly, but her aunt, Philiberte de Savoie, will conclude her visit on the following day, leaving her alone. After having asked Briçonnet for "secours spirituel," which presumably he could provide in letters, Marguerite urges him to send Michel d'Arande to her for a visit so that, we are led to believe, Briçonnet's counsel will be reinforced by conversation with one of his associates. "Ce me seroit consolation," the letter ends, "que je ne quiers que pour l'honneur de Dieu, le remectant a vostre bonne discretion et la scienne."

Originating in anxiety, this letter reveals a desire to resolve tension and distress. As a psychological document, it is of considerable interest. But it is something more, too. Situated at the beginning of Marguerite's *oeuvre* (as far as can be determined she wrote no literary texts prior to 1521) it functions as a paradigm, for it establishes a pattern that is duplicated in an astonishing number of her major poems. Time and time again her poems open on a note of conflict and apprehension. At the beginning of most of her longer poems, the narrator is, like Marguerite-cum-Martha, unhappy, distraught, and troubled. He—or, more frequently, she—is a "navire loing du vray port assablée" [ship grounded far from its true port] (La Navire), a "feuille agitee de l'impetueux vent" [leaf shaken by the impetuous wind] (La Navire), a wayfarer lost in "le buisson de tribulation" [the thicket of tribulation] (Le Petit Oeuvre), a wanderer whose "coeur . . . n'ha de plaisir une goutte" [heart has no pleasure at all] (La Coche) [The Coach].

The relatively few literary historians who have commented on Marguerite's poetry have usually suggested that Marguerite's anxiety was provoked by the stresses and strains of her intense political activity at Court and by her presumably unhappy first marriage. Often they intimate that Marguerite turned to writing in an effort to assuage a womanly heart bruised by the rough game of politics and by a supposedly gruff husband.[5] Such con-

5. On December 2, 1509, at the age of seventeen, Marguerite married Charles, Duke of Alençon. Her sixteen-year marriage to the Duke was childless, and historians have assumed that Marguerite suffered from her barrenness. (Alençon died in 1525. In 1527, Marguerite married Henri d'Albret, King of Navarre, and the following year gave birth to her first child, Jeanne, who would be her only child to live to adulthood.) Historians have also insinuated that a woman of Marguerite's sensitivity and intelligence would have found the soldierly Alençon an incompatible husband. Michelet, for example, calls Marguerite a "veuve de coeur dans son triste mariage" [a widow in her heart in her sad marriage]. Histoire de France (Réforme), in Oeuvres complètes (Paris: Flammarion, 1978), VII, 336. Jourda affirms that Marguerite's first marriage "n'a pas procuré à la soeur du Roi les satisfactions qu'elle était en droit d'en attendre" [did not give the King's sister the satisfactions she had a right to expect]. Marguerite d'Angoulême, p. 65. Febvre is more cautious. Admitting that Alençon was not handsome, he notes that there is no reason to think that Marguerite's marriage was any more unhappy than other royal marriages. Autour de l'Heptaméron, p. 28. Christine Martineau-Génieys claims that after the birth of Jeanne, Marguerite had a second child who died in infancy, two or three children who were stillborn, and several false pregnancies and miscarriages. Evidence for all but the first of these claims is weak. Le Thème de la mort dans la poésie française de 1450 à 1550 (Paris: Champion, 1978), p. 525.

The feverish imagination of two nineteenth-century commentators generated another explanation for Marguerite's "crainte," one so outlandish and unsubstantiated by the facts that it deserves mention only as a curious example of the grotesque distortion to which a text can be subjected. In the introduction to his edition of the Nouvelles lettres de la reine de Navarre, addressées au roi François Iᵉʳ, son frère (Paris: Renouard, 1842), F. Génin distorts Marguerite's rather confused and linguistically awkward first letter to Francis by seeing in it a confession of an incestuous love for her brother. Génin affirms that Marguerite was saved from "une voie criminelle" (p. 10) [a criminal road] by Francis' indifference. Marguerite's letter to Francis was probably written in 1521. Since her

jectures, vaguely condescending and unsupported by convinc-
ing evidence, fail to do justice to the source of Marguerite's creative energy. Although her poems often seem to be couched in
the autobiographical mode, they allude only rarely to precise
events or situations in her life. They do, however, refer with obsessive frequency to the two events that, for a spirit as deeply
Christian as was Marguerite's, are the two most important events
in history, indeed, in a sense, the only two historical events
of any significance: the fall of mankind through Adam's disobedience, and the redemption of mankind through Christ's suffering on the cross. Recounting the Christian's effort to attain
mystical union with God, her poems trace the soul's journey as
it strives to overcome fear and despair. Hers is the vision of a
Christian who, profoundly conscious of the fallen state of man,
is sustained by a faith in the redemptive power of the cross that,
if at times sorely tested, remains unshakable.

Such was Mary's faith as she sat at Christ's feet listening to His
words, her whole being focused on His message, her speech-
lessness contrasting sharply with Martha's querulous loquacity.
Indeed, Mary's rapt silence is a sign of her closeness to the Truth,
for, in the words of the *Imitation of Christ*, a book Marguerite
surely knew well, the Truth "speaketh within us without the
Noise of Words."[6] Mary knew that in order to hear God we
must first still the incessant babble of words. Marguerite knew

---

first letter to Briçonnet is dated June 1521, Génin declares that Marguerite's anxiety is a
manifestation of the guilt provoked by her monstrous passion.

   Michelet seized on the dramatic potential of this situation, but altered the scenario so
as to make Francis the more aggressive of the two parties. He tells us that as a cruel
diversion Francis pressed his demands on Marguerite with such insistence and urgency
that she, struck by "l'horreur . . . d'une situation si nouvelle" (op. cit., p. 340) [the horror of a situation so new], was forced to flee from her brother. Like Génin, Michelet sees
in Marguerite's correspondence with Briçonnet an attempt to expiate a guilty love by
means of mysticism. After examining all the evidence, Jourda states that the story of an
incestuous love between Marguerite and Francis is pure fiction. *Marguerite d'Angoulême*,
p. 64.

   6. Thomas à Kempis, *The Imitation of Christ* (London: J. M. Dent & Sons, 1960),
II:2, p. 76. Although the following two studies, the first of which was a pioneering
work, have been partly superseded, they can still be consulted for comments on the presence of Thomas à Kempis in Marguerite's thought: Abel Lefranc, "Les Idées religieuses
de Marguerite de Navarre d'après son oeuvre poétique," *Bulletin de la Société de l'histoire
du protestantisme français*, 46 (1897), 7–30, 72–84, 137–48, 295–311, 418–42; Eugène
Parturier, "Les Sources du mysticisme de Marguerite de Navarre: à propos d'un manu-
scrit inédit," *Revue de la Renaissance*, 5 (1904), 1–16, 49–62.

this too, but her way was not to be Mary's.[7] Too troubled, anxious, and fretful, too Martha-like to remain silent, she speaks
tirelessly, creating a poetic opus of substantial proportions. At
the same time, however, seeking to emulate Mary, she strives to
fashion a language that is somehow the equivalent of silence. In
her attempt to elaborate a poetic discourse that is comparable to
Mary's muteness, she was profoundly influenced by Briçonnet,
for the concept of language as a signifier of silence was one of
the central ideas in the lengthy letters he wrote to Marguerite in
response to her request for spiritual guidance. To clarify that
concept, we turn to Briçonnet's letters.

7. From the time of Augustine and Gregory, Mary typified the contemplative life
and Martha the active. For a discussion of the two lives, see Dom Cuthbert Butler, *Western Mysticism: The Teaching of SS. Augustine, Gregory and Bernard on Contemplation and the
Contemplative Life* (1922: rpt. London: E. P. Dutton, 1951), esp. pp. 200–214; see also
Eugene F. Rice, *The Renaissance Idea of Wisdom* (Cambridge: Harvard University Press,
1958), pp. 30–57. Since the true contemplative life could be lived only by monks who
had withdrawn from the world, another category of life was needed that would permit
"active" people to participate to some degree in the insights provided by contemplation.
This third kind of life came to be known as the "mixed life." Although Briçonnet generally elevates Mary over Martha, on one occasion he observes that both Mary and Martha
honor their guest: "Marthe soliciteuze et fort empeschée, combien qu'elle solicitast
Marie, qui vacquoit au necessaire, à luy aider, n'estoit pourtant contraire à sa soeur ne
repugnante, car leur ouvraige tendoit à une fin: pour honorer leur bon hoste," II.62
[Martha, who was busy and had so much to do that she asked Mary to help her with
what had to be done and to assist her, was not, however, opposed to her sister or hostile
to her, for their work tended toward the same end: to honor their good guest], letter
dated September 15, 1523.

2

Briçonnet's Response

THE AUGUSTINIAN SLANT

In accepting Marguerite's request to serve as her spiritual mentor, Briçonnet recognizes the fact that he is being asked above all to lighten the burden of fear that seems to oppress his correspondent's spirit. "Madame," he says in the middle of his first letter, "la cause du secours par vous requis est, comme m'escripvez, que vous meslez de pluseurs choses qui vous doivent bien donner crainte. Qui a foy, esperance et amour a son seul necessaire, en est hors et n'a besoing d'ayde ne secours" (I.28) [Madame, the reason you ask for help is, as you write, because you are involved in many things that frighten you. Anyone who has faith, hope and love has the one thing that is needed; he is beyond fear and does not need help or guidance]. Briçonnet's strategy is to focus Marguerite's attention on the one thing that is needed. By commenting at length and in a variety of ways upon the Christian's love for Christ and God's love for His creation, Briçonnet strives throughout his correspondence to undo the Marguerite that resembles Martha and to nourish with spiritual sustenance the Marguerite that yearns to be like Mary.

Using one of the most venerable and far-reaching metaphors in Christian thought, Briçonnet suggests that the world is a text[8] that, if read properly, reveals only one message: the reign of charity. Christ is inscribed in the world, and it is the duty of the Christian exegete to read and reread the text before him until the meaning that *must* be there is fully revealed. Thus, in a sense, fear results from misreading the world. To dispel her

---

8. On the *topos* of the world as a book, see E. R. Curtius, *European Literature and the Latin Middle Ages*, trans. Willard R. Trask (Princeton: Princeton University Press, 1953), pp. 319–26.

anxiety, Marguerite must learn to *see*. That is to say, she must learn to *read* correctly. She must become skilled in the praxis of interpretation. To assist her toward this end, Briçonnet provides her with an illustration of exegesis by using her own letters as texts on which he writes exegetical commentary. He shapes his letters within the terms provided by Marguerite herself. He probes the words of her letters, turning them this way and that, searching for clues, looking for meanings. He picks up the expressions and images she uses in her letters and repeats them, sometimes over and over and throughout several letters, extracting from them ever more significance.[9] Ultimately, Briçonnet's exegesis of Marguerite's letters becomes an interpretive exercise designed to metacommunicate the principles of hermeneutics, which he proposes to Marguerite as a means of consolation.

The hermeneutics that Briçonnet practices in his letters to Marguerite is derived mainly from Augustine.[10] In one of the most famous passages in the *Confessions*, Augustine tells how, as a young pagan teacher of rhetoric, he was reluctant to accept Christianity because the style of the Bible differed so markedly from that of the books written by the pagan philosophers—notably Cicero—whom he had been accustomed to consider the great dispensers of wisdom. Christianity and philosophy were incompatible, he thought, because the styles of the Bible and Cicero were so divergent. Then, while listening to Ambrose's allegorical interpretations of the Old Testament, Augustine gradually came to the realization that Christianity and philosophy, the Bible and Cicero, are not necessarily irreconcilable. "I began to believe," he noted, "that the Catholic faith, which I had thought impossible to defend against the objections of the Manichees, might fairly be maintained, especially since I heard one passage after another in the Old Testament figuratively ex-

---

9. In a letter dated June 1523 (II.36–37), that is to say, two years after the first exchange of letters, Briçonnet remarks that Marguerite's letters generate or "fecundate" his own. If Marguerite's letters may be said to generate Briçonnet's, it is equally true that Briçonnet's letters are one of the main sources from which Marguerite draws the major themes of her poetry.

10. That Briçonnet does not refer specifically to Augustine is not surprising, for, like many of the early Evangelicals, he tends to avoid as much as possible direct allusion to patristic texts, preferring to cite Scripture as the only sacred text. On Briçonnet's hermeneutics, see Glori Cappello, "Per la storia dell'ermeneutica biblica nel 1500: Guglielmo Briçonnet," *Storiografia ed ermeneutica* (Padova: Editrice Gregoriana, 1975), pp. 293–304.

plained."[11] Showing the young and ardent pagan rhetorician "how to interpret the ancient Scriptures of the law in a different light," Ambrose "lifted the veil of mystery and disclosed the spiritual meaning of texts which, taken literally, appeared to contain the most unlikely doctrines" (*Conf.* VI.4.115–16). In short, Ambrose taught Augustine how to read allegorically; he taught him that meaning is revealed by a figurative, not a literal, reading of the text.

Once converted to Christianity, Augustine espoused the exegetical mode of thought that had been decisive in his own conversion. Given his passionate nature and thirst for an absolute, it is not surprising that he extended Ambrose's allegorization of the Old Testament to a theory of figurative reading that would in fact permit the Christian to see everything in the world as a written code that must be translated into spiritual truth.[12]

In his elaboration of the insight he had derived from Ambrose's figurative reading of the Old Testament, Augustine was led to a consideration of language as a vehicle of signification within the context of Christian epistemology. His concept of linguistic phenomena is grounded on the Ciceronian distinction between *res* and *signa*, i.e., between things and the words that signify them. "All doctrine," Augustine declares, "concerns either things or signs, but things are learned by signs. Strictly speaking, I have called a 'thing' that which is not used to signify something else."[13] Things, then, are self-referential and do not

11. Saint Augustine, *Confessions*, trans. R. S. Pine-Coffin (Penguin Books, 1961), V.14, p. 108. Further references to this work will be cited in the text as *Conf.*, followed by book number, chapter and page.

12. See Richard McKeon, "Rhetoric in the Middle Ages," in *Critics and Criticism*, ed. R. C. Crane (Chicago: University of Chicago Press, 1952), pp. 260–96; Joseph Anthony Mazzeo, "St. Augustine's Rhetoric of Silence: Truth vs. Eloquence and Things vs. Signs," in *Renaissance and Seventeenth-Century Studies* (New York: Columbia University Press, 1964), pp. 1–28; Stanley E. Fish, *Self-Consuming Artifacts* (Berkeley: University of California Press, 1972), pp. 21–43; Eugene Vance, "Saint Augustine: Language as Temporality," in *Mimesis: From Mirror to Method, Augustine to Descartes*, eds. John D. Lyons and Stephen G. Nichols, Jr. (Hanover and London: University Press of New England, 1982), pp. 20–35. The following two books treat extensively various linguistic problems related to Augustinian hermeneutics: Nancy S. Struever, *The Language of History in the Renaissance* (Princeton: Princeton University Press, 1970); and especially Marcia L. Colish, *The Mirror of Language: A Study in the Medieval Theory of Knowledge* (New Haven: Yale University Press, 1968).

13. *De doctrina christiana*, I.2, trans. D. W. Robertson, Jr., *On Christian Doctrine* (Indianapolis: The Bobbs-Merrill Co., Library of the Liberal Arts, 1958), p. 8, henceforth cited in the text as DDC. See B. Darrell Jackson, "The Theory of Signs in St. Au-

signify other things. Furthermore, they exist prior to the signs that signify them.

After defining things, Augustine takes up the matter of signs. If the Pauline concept of seeing not the letter but the spirit[14] was strongly colored by Plato's belief that material, sensory, and temporal existence may be contrasted with spiritual, intellectual, and eternal being, the definition that Augustine gives of the sign recalls Aristotle's belief that signs do indeed signify things accurately, that they provide reliable knowledge of things that already exist.[15] "A sign," Augustine affirms, "is a thing which causes us to think of something beyond the impression the thing itself makes upon the senses" (DDC II.1.34). He continues by saying that there are two kinds of signs: natural and conventional. Smoke, for example, is a natural sign that signifies fire. The track made by a passing animal is another natural sign, as is a sad or wrathful countenance. Such signs, however, do not interest him. He declares abruptly that he does not intend to discuss them further but rather to consider the problem of conventional signs, which he defines as "those which living creatures show to one another for the purpose of conveying, insofar as they are able, the motion of their spirits or something which they have sensed or understood. Nor is there any other reason for signifying, or for giving signs, except for bringing forth and transferring to another mind the action of the mind in the person who makes the sign" (DDC II.2.34–35). Banners and military standards are conventional signs, as are the gestures of actors. Far more important, however, are words. Augustine ob-

---

gustine's *De Doctrina Christiana*," *Revue des études augustiniennes*, 15 (1969), 9–49; R. A. Markus, "St. Augustine on Signs," *Phronesis*, 2 (1957), 60–83. Both of these articles also appeared in *Augustine: A Collection of Critical Essays*, ed. R. A. Markus (New York: Doubleday Anchor, 1972), pp. 92–147 (Jackson), 62–91 (Markus).

14. This concept permeates Paul's epistles. Briçonnet and Marguerite alluded with particular frequency to two passages by Paul: "But now we are rid of the law, freed by death from our imprisonment, free to serve in the new spiritual way and not the old way of a written law" (Romans 7.6); "[God] is the one who has given us the qualifications to be the administrators of this new covenant, which is not a covenant of written letters but of the Spirit: the written letters bring death, but the Spirit gives life" (II Corinthians 3.6). Briçonnet wrote, for example, to Marguerite: "La vraie clef de l'intelligence de l'Escriture Saincte est l'esperit et non la lettre, car, comme dit saint Pol: 'Littera occidit, spiritus vivificat'" (II.14) [The true key to the understanding of the Holy Scripture is the spirit and not the letter, for, as Saint Paul said: "The written letters bring death but the Spirit gives life"].

15. Colish, *The Mirror of Language*, pp. 63–72.

serves that "words have come to be predominant among men for signifying whatever the mind conceives if they wish to communicate it to anyone" (DDC II.3.35–36). In fact, all conventional signs are "like so many visible words" (DDC II.3.35). These remarks are of primary importance for the Augustinian theory of signification, for Augustine has in effect reduced all signs to the category of verbal signs.

Contrary to things, which are self-referential, words, then, point not to themselves but to things beyond. This distinction, however, begins to crumble as Augustine's thought slips from the confines of classical rhetoric and moves toward the Christian perception of charity. Words, Augustine notes, are obviously things themselves. If they were not, they could not exist, for "that which is not a thing is nothing at all" (DDC I.2.35). The difference between word and thing becomes blurred. For example, wood, stone, and cattle are, strictly speaking, things; that is, they do not signify something beyond themselves; "but not that wood concerning which we read that Moses cast it into bitter waters that their bitterness might be dispelled, nor that stone which Jacob placed at his head, nor that beast which Abraham sacrificed in place of his son" (DDC I.2.8). For the wood that Moses cast into the waters to sweeten them was a sign of the Cross, itself a sign of the Crucifixion, which in turn is a sign of Christ's love for mankind; the stone that Jacob used as a pillow is a sign of the firmness of Christ on whose love all Christians may rest; and the ram that Abraham sacrificed in place of his son is a sign of Christ's sacrifice of Himself for the love he bore to mankind. Here Augustine is speaking not within the limits of classical rhetorical theory, but within the context of his vision of Christian reality. Over and over he stresses the fact that everything in Scripture—indeed, everything in creation—points to charity, which is identical to Christian truth. "Scripture," he says, "teaches nothing but charity" (DDC III.10.88). The distinction between things and words tends to disappear. Things become signs of the single reality that informs all of creation: that of love of God and love of one's neighbor through Christ. And since signs, as we have seen, are essentially verbal, things become words that the Christian must read in such a way that he will arrive at an interpretation pointing to the law of love.

In a fundamental way, then, signification is linguistic. Augustine *scripturalizes* the whole of creation. In great part, medieval culture owes its tendency to view the world as a text written in cipher to Augustine's reduction of the Ciceronian categories of *res* and *signa* to the single category of language.

If man's present knowledge and expression of God are based on language, it is, Augustine asserts, because human speech has been "redeemed" through the Incarnation, the cornerstone of his linguistic epistemology.[16] Two Scriptural passages are crucial for an understanding of the correlation between the Augustinian theory of sign as word and Christian faith. The first is John's affirmation (I.1) that God is the Word: "In the beginning was the Word: the Word was with God and the Word was God" (*Deus erat Verbum*). John's statement is all the more powerful because the identification of the divine will with the Word is not restricted to the New Testament but goes back to the Wisdom Books of the Old Testament and Apocrypha.[17] The second passage, also from John (I.14), complements the first: "The Word was made flesh, he lived among us, and we saw his glory." To the extent that human speech is created by man, it is a faulty instrument incapable of revealing knowledge about divine reality. God, however, overcame the inadequacy of human speech by uniting divinity and humanity in the Word made flesh. In Christ, God speaks to man. Furthermore, the Incarnation, by renewing the faculties of man, by making all of them (including speech) *christiforme*, to use one of Briçonnet's favorite words, enables man to communicate with God by means of words. By becoming flesh and dwelling among us, the Johannine *logos* affirmed the existence of a covenant between speech and knowledge. Indeed, It continues to affirm this covenant, for the Incarnation is not so much an historical event as an ever-occurring event in the life of each Christian. The fact that the Word became words guarantees the congruence of the structure of language and that of reality. Augustine explains this concept, central to his epistemology, in a passage from his sermons on the Psalms:

Before you perceived God, you believed that thought could express God. Now you are beginning to perceive Him, and you think that you

---

16. Colish discusses the "function of redeemed speech" in Augustine, pp. 45–67.

17. See D. P. Walker, *The Ancient Theology: Studies in Christian Platonism from the Fifteenth to the Eighteenth Century* (Ithaca: Cornell University Press, 1972), p. 4.

cannot express what you perceive. But, having found that you cannot express what you perceive, will you be silent, will you not praise God? . . . Honor is due Him, reverence is due Him, great praise is due Him. . . . 'How,' you ask, 'shall I praise Him?' I cannot now explain the small amount which I can perceive in part, through a glass darkly (*in aenigmate per speculum*) . . . All other things may be expressed in some way; He alone is ineffable, Who spoke, and all things were made. He spoke, and we were made; but we are unable to speak of Him. *His Word, by Whom we were spoken, is His Son. He was made weak, so that He might be spoken by us, despite our weakness.* (my emphasis) [18]

The Pauline coloration of this citation is both obvious and significant. In his epistle to the Corinthians (I Corinthians 13.12), Paul had written: "Now we are seeing a dim reflection in a mirror; but then we shall be seeing face to face." Augustine made of this passage the central metaphor of Christian epistemology. He recast the faculty of human speech into a Pauline mirror in which man can see a (partial) reflection of God.

Even when he evokes the rapt silence of the soul that has transcended creation, that has passed beyond human language and moves, lovingly, toward the Word, Augustine uses verbal terms. In his famous account of the mystical experience he shared with his mother Monica, Augustine defines a knowledge of God that transcends human speech; silence becomes God's supreme mode of expression. In that joyful state, the soul "hears" His silence.

Suppose, we said, that the tumult of a man's flesh were to cease and all that his thoughts can conceive, of earth, of water, and of air, should no longer speak to him; suppose that the heavens and even his own soul were silent, no longer thinking of itself but passing beyond; suppose that his dreams and the visions of his imagination spoke no more and that every tongue and every sign and all that is transient grew silent— for all these things have the same message to tell, if only we can hear it, and their message is this: We did not make ourselves, but he who abides forever made us. Suppose, we said, that after giving us this message and bidding us listen to him who made them, they fell silent and he alone should speak to us, not through them but in his own voice, so that we should hear him speaking, not by any tongue of the flesh or by an angel's voice, not in the sound of thunder or in some veiled parable (*per aenigma similitudinis*), but in his own voice, the voice

---

18. *Enarratio in Psalmum XCIX*, 6, *Corpus Christianorum*, 39, 1396–97. Cited in English by Colish, op. cit., pp. 34–35.

of the one whom we love in all these created things; suppose that we heard him himself, with none of these things between ourselves and him, . . . ; suppose that this state were to continue . . . so that this single vision entranced and absorbed the one who beheld it . . . would not this be what we are to understand by the words *Come and share the joy of your Lord*? Matt. 25.21 (*Conf.* IX.10.148)

All those things that, during the Christian's earthly life, serve as cognitive channels between man and God eventually fall silent. In the final analysis, God is beyond words. As earthly life must cease before spiritual life can be fully realized, so speech must be stilled, for it cannot represent the eternal Godhead, the Word, in Whom meaning and being, expression and existence, are identical and simultaneous. All language, the literally as well as the metaphorically verbal, is folded back into the Word, which transcends all linguistic phenomena and must be represented as a "heard" silence.

Language, or speech, operates, of course, through the senses. As an instrument of cognition, it is limited by the fact that it originates in man's physical nature, which, within the Platonic framework Augustine adopted, is "lower" than man's spiritual nature. Furthermore, Augustine stresses that man's physical nature, unlike his spiritual nature,[19] is not made in the image of God. The Incarnation itself was a descent from the spiritual into the physical, from silence into speech. We have seen that this descent, however, opened a channel that permitted a reverse movement, an ascent from the physical back to the spiritual, from speech back to silence. Indeed, the Incarnation was God's way of opening a path whereby man could ascend to Him. Augustine represents the Christian's transformation in Christ, his ever-increasing perception of reality and his ascent toward God, as a journey through words to a translinguistic vision of God and of all things in God.

Despite the inevitable limitations of speech, Augustine's epistemology is grounded on the belief that language, redeemed through the Incarnation, is our only (though ultimately an inadequate) means of knowing God. Typifying "the Christian orator

---

19. For Augustine's most explicit discussion of these matters, see *De trinitate*, X–XII, trans. Stephen McKenna (Washington: The Catholic University of America Press, 1963).

who interprets his vocation as an apostolic expression of the Word,"[20] Augustine valorized language while at the same time using it in such a way that in the end it denies its own substantiality and, in an act of self-effacement, points beyond itself to the reality (*res*) it imperfectly represents.

THE MECHANICS OF SIGNIFICATION

Writing within a tradition that exploited biblical metaphors, Briçonnet in his first letter to Marguerite compares God to food and drink.[21] God is the "viande divine" [divine meat], the bread and water that sustain man. "Plus on en gouste," Briçonnet declares, "plus on le desire, et par impacient desir serchez secours et ayde pour combattre le grand geant d'amour insuperable" [The more one tastes it, the more one desires it, and with impatient desire you look for help and aid to combat the great giant of insuperable love]. God is also fire, "le feu d'amour" [the fire of love] that liquifies the heart, transforming "la terreistreté . . . en divinité" (I.27) [worldliness into divinity]. Of the many metaphors in Briçonnet's correspondence, those of fire, water, and food are perhaps the most persistently used and intricately embellished.

Of these three, the one that Marguerite uses most often is that of food. In a letter written to Briçonnet shortly after January 8, 1522 (the exact date cannot be determined), she notes that she has received the letters in which he developed the images of fire and water. She now longs for the "manne" he has promised her:

Le temps est sy froit et le coeur sy glacé que l'eaue chaulde ne le trèsardant feu ne peuvent desgeller sa froide duretté. Car, comme insatiable, après avoir eu, par la bonté de Dieu, eaue et feu pour resister au temps et à sa soif, dont à luy seul le blasme s'il n'y a proufité, crye maintenant à la faim desirant viande doulce et de substance. Parquoy esperant son amandement par la grace du Tout-Misericordieux, suis contraincte vous prier n'avoir regard à la peine que par cy devant avez prise, mais, subvenant à sa necessité, luy envoier la manne, pour passer plus fortement ce desert et demander au Tout-Puissant grace de la

---

20. Colish, *The Mirror of Language*, p. 81.
21. On alimentary metaphors in the Bible, see Curtius, *European Literature* . . . , pp. 134–36.

bien gouster, faisant fin à ceste, après estre à voz devotes prieres recommandée.

Vostre gellée, alterée et affamée fille.

Marguerite. (I.132).

The weather is so cold and the heart so frozen that neither hot water nor fiercely burning fire can melt its cold hardness. For, I am like someone who, after having had by God's goodness water and fire to withstand weather and hunger and having only himself to blame if he did not take advantage of them, cries out now in hunger, craving delicious meat and food. Therefore, hoping for a change for the better by the grace of the All-Merciful, I am forced to beseech you not to take into account the trouble you have already gone to; but I ask that you, heeding the need, send manna so that I can cross this desert with greater strength, and that you ask the All-Powerful to grant me the favor of savoring it fully. I conclude this letter after having commended myself to your devout prayers. Your frozen, parched, and famished daughter. Marguerite.

Briçonnet did not answer this request in his letters of January 17, January 20, or January 30, which are all quite short. He did, however, respond in the long, rich letter of February 5. This letter is Briçonnet's clearest statement of his theory of hermeneutics, which is in effect the "manna" he offers the famished Marguerite.

The letter opens with the following pseudo-sentence, which, because it lacks a principal verb, seems to serve as a title: "Le superexcelent et supereminent seul necessaire par l'excessive bonifiante amour et amoureuse bonté, penetrant et conservant toutes creatures, viviffiant les capables de vie en se donnant manne vivifiante et mortiffiante" (I.138) [The superexcellent and supereminent one and only necessity through extreme benevolent love and loving benevolence, penetrating and preserving all creatures, vivifying those capable of life by offering itself, vivifying and mortifying manna]. Developing the common biblical paradox that death is the beginning of life ("Lequel est pain de vie, qui donne la mort que vie accompaigne, par vie mortiffiant et par mort vivifiant en vie veritable et vraie vie vivante," I.138) [Which is the bread of life, which gives the death that accompanies life through mortifying life and through vivifying death into genuine life and true living life], Briçonnet observes that after the soul has been cleansed and purged of all terrestrial elements in the "ardente fournaise d'amour divine" [burning fire of divine love], it yearns, "impaciente de fain" [impatient with hunger] for "la viviffiante manne en laquelle gist et est sa perfection et aliment, qui est vray pain de vie" (I.138) [for the vivifying manna in which abides and is his perfection and sustenance, which is the true bread of life].

The biblical source from which the image of manna is derived is the account in Exodus 16 of the manna that God sent to the children of Israel as they wandered in the wilderness. To support his statement that the purified soul hungers for the bread of life, Briçonnet adheres closely to his model and retells the biblical story, which he introduces with the words: "Et pour l'intelligence est à presupposer ce qui est escript en Exode XVIᵉ chappitre" (I.139) [And for an understanding of this, one has only to read what is written in Exodus, Chapter 16].

Having completed his lengthy paraphrase of Exodus 16, Briçonnet, in the time-honored tradition of preachers, begins to comment on the sacred text. Quickly, however, he turns his thoughts away from the text to an explanation and a justification of the praxis of exegesis itself. "Madame," he begins, "Monsieur saint Pol nous instruict que ne debvons entendre ce passaige litteralement ains eslever l'esperit à la vraye manne, le doulx Jesus, que serchez sy songneusement en demandant (après feu et eau) manne qui soit mortiffiant vostre coeur pour le vivifier en luy, qui est vostre vie" (I.139) [Madame, Saint Paul instructs us that we must not interpret this passage literally but raise our spirit to the true manna, sweet Jesus, whom you seek so earnestly, asking (after fire and water) for the manna that can mortify your heart in order to vivify it in him who is your life]. Indeed, in I Corinthians 10.1–4 Paul had referred to Exodus 16, interpreting the sea through which the Israelites passed as a sign of Christian baptism and the manna they ate as a sign of spiritual food, i.e., Christ. Providing a brief but powerful Christian reading of Exodus 16, Paul had discovered in these verses signs of the two basic Christian sacraments, Baptism and the Eucharist. Not content with a simple allusion to Paul's succinct exegesis of the Old Testament passage, Briçonnet now furnishes an exegesis of the Pauline text. Commenting on the first two verses of I Corinthians 10 ("I want to remind you, brothers, how our fathers were all guided by a cloud above them and how they all passed through the sea. They were all baptised into Moses in this cloud and in this sea."), Briçonnet says that, "Monsieur sainct Pol, vaisseau d'election," wished to "designer par la nuée et le passaige de la mer Rouge le sacrement de baptesme, auquel est donné le Sainct Esperit, signiffié par la nuée, ablation et mortifficacion de peché par la mer" (I.139) [Saint Paul, chosen vessel, designated by the cloud and the crossing of the Red Sea the sacrament of Baptism, in which man is given the Holy Ghost, signified by the cloud, the cleansing and the mortification of sin by the sea]. Briçonnet continues by explaining that verses three and four ("All ate the same spiritual food and drank the same spiritual drink . . .") meant that "tous ont mengé une mesmes viande spirituelle et beu ung mesmes bruvaige, parlant non de la materielle manne et de l'eaue de contradiction, qu'il feist yssir de la roche après le deuxiesme coup de sa verge mais de la spirituelle manne, qui est le vray corps du doulx Jesus et de son precieulx sang espandu en perfusion et plenitude de grace" (I.140) [all ate the same spiritual meat and drank the same drink, speaking not of the manna made of matter and of the water drawn from stone, water which he made gush out of the rock after the second blow of the rod, but of spiritual manna, which is the true body of sweet Jesus and of his precious blood spilled in abundance and the fullness of grace]. Concluding his discussion of I Corinthians 10, Briçonnet cites verse 11 ("All this happened to them as a warning, [the Vulgate reads: "Haec autem *in figura* contingebant illis"] and it was written down to be a lesson for us . . ."). He interprets Paul's comment as "signiffiant le tout avoir esté baillé *en figure* (my emphasis) aux Juifz et escript pour nostre instruction" (I.140) [signifying that everything was given in symbols to the Jews and written down for our instruction].

Having finished his commentary on Paul's text, Briçonnet explains to Marguerite how a biblical text is to be read. "Eslevez donc vostre esperit," he counsels, "et entendez que la manne, dont dessus est parlé, de laquelle ont par quarante ans vescu les enfans d'Israel, representoit par figure la verité des viandes qu'ilz trouverrent en la terre de promission" (I.140) [Lift up your mind and understand that the manna of which we spoke above and which sustained the children of Israel for forty years represented symbolically the truth of the sustenance they found in the promised land]. A text, he says, must be read not literally but spiritually. "Où est le coeur chrestien," he asks rhetorically, "qui ne peult comprendre la volunté spirituelle et celeste représentée par la corporelle" (I.140) [Where is the Christian heart that cannot understand the spiritual and divine will represented by the corporal]. With his assertion that the physical "represents" the spiritual, Briçonnet introduces the concept of the world as a text composed of *figura* or signs whose referent is always God. He provides Marguerite with a way of reading, i.e., a way of seeing, that is applicable not only to Scripture but to that larger text which is the natural world created by God. It is the privilege and duty of a Christian to translate what he sees into that which he does not see. The believer is counseled to "see through" the world that is present to his senses, for the sensible world is merely a text that "represente par figure la verité." The innumerable *figura* that the Christian perceives with his carnal eyes must be translated into the single, indivisible truth, which he can discern only with his spiritual eyes. All *figura*, everywhere and at all times, point to the one living truth that informs all of creation: Christ, who signifies the reign of charity.

For Briçonnet as for Augustine, all the signs and ciphers that constitute the texts of the world signify a single, pre-existent truth that lies beyond them. All signifiers lead to one signified (*res*), which, however, cannot be adequately designated by any single signifier. Furthermore, the perception or experience of *res* is, in a profound sense, a denial of the reality of the single cipher, for as the spiritual eye discerns the signified, the sign itself is consumed, or to use the words Briçonnet uses for this process, annihilated and pulverized.

Briçonnet's example of this process, which we may call the mechanics of signification, is the meat and manna that sustained the children of Israel. As they began to eat, they said: "'Quelle viande esse icy!'" (I.141) [What meat is this]. Briçonnet explains what kind of meat it was: "Elle n'estoit chappon, faisant, perdrix, becasses, allouette ne aultre viande, et toutesfois en elle se trouvoient en coincidence tous goustz telz que l'on voulloit" (I.141) [It was not capon, pheasant, partridge, woodcock, lark or other meat; and yet they found coinciding in it all these tastes, such as they wished for]. As the famished Israelites ate, the meat they devoured ceased to be that which we designate by any of the various words signifying meat. It was, in Briçonnet's words, "une viande innominable, car elle estoit toute viande de tous noms et de nul nominable" (I.141) [a meat without a name, for it was every kind of meat with every name, but it could not be called by any name]. To the extent that the meat signified Christ, it was quite literally beyond words because the experience of divine love is ineffable. Love, Briçonnet says, is "par nature" (I.141) incapable of being expressed fully in human language. Once again he supports his thesis by paraphrasing Paul, who said that Scripture reveals to us "the things that no eye has seen and no ear has heard, things beyond the mind of man" (I Corinthians 2.9).

By a series of subtle associations, Briçonnet links the concept of "figure," "representation," sign, to that of corporeality. Like all physical matter, which must be pulverized before the divine reality inscribed within can become visible to the spiritual eye, signs must be consumed before the signified (and there is only one) can become manifest. All signs collapse into "le seul signe de vie: amour et charité de Dieu et de son prochain" (I.143) [the only sign representing life: love of God and of one's neighbor].

For Briçonnet, love is inseparable from the effacement of self. To love Christ is to wish to be united with Him. This union can be accomplished only by the annihilation of self.[22] "Amour se veult et desire joingdre à son seul necessaire" [Love wishes and seeks to join the only thing needed], Briçonnet notes, explaining that "bien eureulx est qui [dont] le coeur est attainct au vif, et, hors de soy, vivant en luy, abismé et aneanty" (I.27) [blessed is he whose heart is pierced and, outside himself, lives in him, engulfed and annihilated]. As fire melts wax, so love of Christ dissolves the heart ("liquefie le coeur," I.28). The experience of dissolution by the fire of love is, however, inexpressible. Silence alone can signify this love, for "langue humaine n'est a ce suffisante ne l'entendement (et fut il angelicque) à le comprandre" (I.27) [human language is incapable of this; nor can intelligence (even if it is that of angels) comprehend it].

Having noted in his early letters to Marguerite the inadequacy of speech, Briçonnet returns to this matter in the letter of February 5 and makes the problematics of language the focus of his discussion. His concept of language is derived mainly from Dionysius the Areopagite's *On Divine Names and the Mystical Theology*. Compiled in the sixth century and attributed (falsely, as we now know) to the Dionysius whom Paul converted at

---

22. The "dying" metaphor is common in mystical literature. See William Ralph Inge, *Christian Mysticism* (1899; 8th ed. London: Methuen & Co., 1948), p. 115.

Athens, the writings of the Pseudo-Dionysius acquired virtual canonic status that lasted until well into the Renaissance.[23] They contributed significantly to the integration of Platonism and Neoplatonism into Christian theology, a process Augustine had already done much to promote. Following the Pseudo-Dionysius, Briçonnet establishes a distinction between the human word, which is a sign, and the divine word, which is *res*. By "divine word" Briçonnet means the Johannine *logos*, or God as Word. He notes that God is the "Tout-Verbe, . . . infinie, superceleste, eternelle" [All-Word, infinite, supercelestial, eternal]. Language is derived from the *Tout-Verbe*: "Les autres verbes, que appellons parolles, sont finies, procedent et sont de l'infini seul Verbe, auquel, par lequel et pour lequel ilz sont et subsistent. Et, comme en la manne judaïcque tous goustz particuliers estoient, laquelle estoit tout goust, aussy tous aultres verbes et parolles sont au superceleste Tout-Verbe, comme en leur source et vraye fontaine, dont ilz sont deryvéz" (I.148) [Other words, which we call speech, are finite; they proceed and come from the infinite, single Word, in which, by which, and for which they exist and subsist. And just as all distinct tastes existed in the Jewish manna, which was every taste, so all other words and languages exist in the supercelestial All-Word as in their source and true spring, from which they are derived]. *Parolles* contain a trace of the Johannine *logos*. This trace, however, is too slight to enable them to serve as adequate signifiers of the *Tout-Verbe*. "Lequel [le Tout-Verbe] est de tous verbes et parolles nominable et de nul; car il n'est nom qui soit le sien et n'y a point de raison qu'il soit plus nommé d'un nom que d'aultre et n'est nom qui le puisse nommer, car chacun nom est particulier et propre à chacune creature et il a tout nom, comme createur de toutes creatures qui sont finies, et infinitude ne se peult nommer" (I.148) [The All-Word has the names of all words and languages and of none of them; for it has no name of its own and there is no reason for it to be called by one name rather than another; no name exists that can name it, for each name is dis-

23. On the Pseudo-Dionysius see D. P. Walker, *The Ancient Theology*, pp. 5–6, 80–84. On the influence of the Pseudo-Dionysius on Briçonnet, see H. Heller, "Marguerite de Navarre and the Reformers of Meaux," op. cit., pp. 271–310 and Glori Capello, "Neoplatonismo e riforma in Francia: dall'epistolario tra Guglielmo Briçonnet e Margherita di Navarra," in *Logica e semantica ed altri saggi*, ed. Carlo Giacon (Padua: Antenore, 1975), pp. 139–82.

tinct and suitable for a particular creature, and it has every name, being the creator of all creatures who are finite; infinitude cannot be named].

Briçonnet's distinction between *parolle* and *Tout-Verbe* may strike a modern reader as remarkably close to the Saussurian distinction between *parole* and *langue*. Indeed, there is a conceptual similarity between the binary principle of *parolles/Tout-Verbe* and that of *parole/langue*. For Saussure, *langue* is a language system that has no tangible existence but that is the totality of linguistic possibilities at any given moment. *Parole*, on the other hand, is individual speech and thus a partial actualization of some of the potentialities of *langue*. Following the Pseudo-Dionysius, who wrote that God is "a Word beyond utterance, eluding Discourse, Intuition, Name, and every kind of being,"[24] Briçonnet notes that because the *Tout-Verbe* is beyond speech man cannot name it; and yet, since the *Tout-Verbe* is the totality of all linguistic possibilities, all the names man may wish to apply to it are equally appropriate (as they are equally inappropriate). In the following paragraph, Briçonnet discusses the problem of naming God. At the same time, he introduces other themes into this text, orchestrating them all in such a way as to make this passage particularly important:

Madame, les noms que donnons à Dieu sont noms selon noz inclinations, desirs, passions et affections. Et tel que l'homme est au dedans, il baille les noms à Dieu. S'il est encoires en la fange de peché, y prenant plaisir, il appelle Dieu terrible, plain d'ire et couroux. S'il est hors de peché, nouvellement reduict et repenty, le dict misericordieux, debonnaire, piteux. S'il a quelque temps cheminé en la voie des commandemens de Dieu, tendant à vertu et honneur de son bien aymé Jesus, l'ayant quelque peu gousté, l'appelle bon, beau, saige, lumiere, puissant, verité, raison, esperit, sapience et telz noms par lesquelz il experimente que Dieu, par sa grace, se communicque en son ame. S'il est plus spirituel, l'appelera foy, esperance, son amour, sa vie, son tout. Et qui plus hault vollera, laissant les terres et penetrant les cielz, incomprehensible, infini, eternel et qui jà sera par excellente et ravissable grace hors de soy ne pourra plus le nommer, le contemplant en silence de coeur oultré et feru d'amour, sans parler, sans le contempler, pour

24. Dionysius the Areopagite, *On Divine Names and the Mystical Theology*, ed. C. E. Rolt (1920; rpt. New York: Macmillan, 1951), p. 53. Further references to this work will be cited in the text as *Div. Names* followed by page number.

l'offuscacion des lumineuses tenebres, esquelles pour l'excelente et tout surmontant lumiere, son entendement est obtenebré, absorbé et noyé. Et quant au monde se trouvant incensible, mort, cruciffié, le abhominant et à luy abhominable, vivant en son amour, qui est Dieu, sans propres actions, dementé et aliené de soy, souffrant par doulce passion, sentant le doulx ouvrier ouvrant en luy sans luy, car les oeuvres qu'il luy plaist y faire sont sur l'homme par admirables attouchemens et doulcereux attiremens, qui, desamparant l'esperit du corps sans separacion, le congnoissant, sans congnoistre, Tout, et son rien au Tout abismé (I. 150).

Madame, the names we give to God are names according to our inclinations, desires, passions and feelings. And depending on how man is within, so he applies names to God. If he is still in the filth of sin, finding pleasure in it, he calls God terrible, full of rage and anger. If he is outside of sin, newly returned to God and repentant, he calls him merciful, gentle and compassionate. If he has for some time moved along the way of God's commandments, going toward the virtue and glory of his beloved Jesus, having tasted him a little, he calls him good, beautiful, wise, light, powerful, truth, reason, spirit, knowledge and such names by which he proves that God, by his grace, reveals himself to his soul. If he is more spiritual, he will call him faith, hope, his love, his life, his all. And anyone who flies higher, leaving earthly things and entering the heavens, incomprehensible, infinite, eternal, and who, by surpassing and consummate grace, is already beyond the self, will no longer be able to name him, contemplating him in the silence of the heart pierced and struck by love, without speaking, without beholding him, because of the darkening of the luminous shadows, coming from the surpassing and overwhelming light, and his understanding is obscured, absorbed and drowned. And with regard to the world, finding himself insensible, dead, crucified, hating it and hateful to it, living in his love, which is God, not determining his own actions, grieved and alienated from himself, suffering the sweet Passion, feeling the sweet workman working in him without him, for the works he likes to make are on man, by means of admirable strokes of the hand and gentle enticement, which, disengaging the spirit from the body without separation, knowing it, without knowing, All, and his nothingness engulfed in All.

In addition to discussing the names we give to God, this paragraph suggests the course the Christian must follow if he is to approach Christ. The Christian's journey is represented as a progressive cleansing of the soul. Briçonnet stresses the dynamic aspect of the process by which the soul becomes evermore *chris-tiforme*. As the soul is purged of the filth and dross that are inseparable from terrestrial existence, it moves, in characteristic Platonic-Augustinian fashion, to ever higher and more luminous spheres. Of particular interest, however, is the fact that the various stages of this journey are signified by changes in the Christian's speech. The soul's reorientation is marked and, in a sense, made manifest by a linguistic evolution that is in fact a shift from *parolles* to *Tout-Verbe*. As the soul becomes increasingly *christiforme*, *parolles* are absorbed into the *Tout-Verbe*. Ultimately, individual utterance ceases to exist, and *parolles* are folded back into the *Tout-Verbe*, a kind of metalanguage, which, although itself the origin of all speech, must be represented as silence. Within this conceptual framework, silence is meta-discourse.

Each of the stages of the Christian's journey upward from "la fange de peché" [the filth of sin] to "les cielz" [the heavens] is characterized by a particular type of speech or discourse. The language that a Christian uses is a sign of the stage he has attained. Briçonnet conceptualizes the Christian life as a Platonic ladder, each rung of which is a spiritual stage whose external manifestation is speech of a distinctive kind. As the Christian climbs to a higher rung, he kicks away the one he has just left, discarding the lower level for the higher. Since the Christian is, as Augustine says, a "reader," his upward progress is marked by the effacement of each successive reading. For Briçonnet, exegesis is the method by which the Christian negotiates the rungs of the ladder. The locus of the Christian experience is thus not the text but the mind that comprehends the higher (more spiritual) rung of the ladder and pulls itself up toward it.

The ladder that the Christian climbs rests on the text. Each successive reading is a step away from the text and toward the spirit that the words conceal. But like the leaves of certain plants that reveal their fragrance only when they are crushed, words disclose their higher meaning only at the expense of their lower form. They are like seeds that fall into the fertile mind of the reader; their inner truths can be disclosed only if the outer husk disintegrates.

Several times in his letters to Marguerite, Briçonnet uses the image of the seed to suggest the process of progressive illumination that exegesis effects in the Christian soul. The image has a venerable history.[25] In the *Phaedrus* (277A), Socrates had referred to words as seeds that are used up in the very act of being spoken. Despite the Platonic resonances in his text, Briçonnet depends mainly on the Bible for his discussion of words as seeds. Synthesizing two ideas that appear in different passages in the Bible, he presents the Christian life as a process of textual effacement. The first of these passages is Christ's parable (Matthew 13.3–8, Mark 4.3–20, Luke 8.5–15) of the sower who sowed his seed in such a way that some fell by the wayside, some upon a rock, some among thorns, and some on good ground. Only the seed that fell upon fertile ground bore fruit. When asked by His disciples to explain the meaning of His parable, Christ answered (in Luke 8.11): "The seed is the word of God" (*Semen est verbum Dei*). Although Luke clearly identifies the seed with *verbum* (Mark says, more obliquely, "What the sower is sowing is the word"), none of the first three apostles points out that the seed must burst before the plant can grow. This idea appears, however, in the fourth Gospel. Contrary to Matthew, Mark, and Luke, John did not relate the parable of the sower. But he did use the image of the seed. In John 12.24, Christ foretells His death, saying: "I tell you, most solemnly, unless a wheat grain falls on the ground and dies, it remains only a single grain; but if it dies, it yields a rich harvest."

In his first synthesis of the parable of the sower and the words of Christ in John 12.24, Briçonnet notes that the material substance of the Christian's body will one day be "convertie, transmuée, abismée et absorbée en la toute-puissante divinité" (I.83) [converted, transmuted, engulfed and absorbed in the all-powerful divinity]. He reminds Marguerite in his letter of December 22, 1521, that "il a fallu que le grain de froment, le doulx Jesus, qui estoit tumbé en la terre virginalle, mourut pour apporter grant fruict" (I.83) [it was necessary that the wheat grain, the sweet Jesus, which had fallen on virgin earth, die in order to yield a rich harvest]. Some ten days later (December 31, 1521), Briçonnet returns to this idea and tells Marguerite: "Le grain mis en terre n'est vivifié s'il ne meurt premierement ne le coeur aussy susceptible de telle semence. Il fault mourir à soy, au monde et à tout plaisir, à finitude aussi, pour estre cappable de infinitude

---

25. See Dorothy Koenigsberger, *Renaissance Man and Creative Thinking* (Hassocks, Sussex: The Harvester Press, 1979), pp. 136–38.

savourer" (I.122) [The grain laid in the earth is not awakened to life unless it dies first; nor is the heart any more favorable to such seed. One must die to oneself, to the world and to all pleasure, to finiteness too, in order to be able to savor infiniteness]. His most important synthesis of the two biblical ideas occurs, however, in the conclusion to his letter of February 5, 1521. Since the seed is the word of God and because Christ is God's word, the seed (Christ) and the word are, at one level of conceptualization, identical. The seed must perish so that the plant can live; Christ must die so that man can live; the word, that is to say, discourse and exegesis, must cease to sound aloud so that the *Tout-Verbe*, which is the same as love, can resound silently in man's heart.

Interpretation culminates in love. Briçonnet's argument, however, is circular, for interpretation is impossible without the illumination provided by love. Nothing is more foreign to Briçonnet's thought than the notion of exegesis as an intellectual exercise characterized by ingenuity and cleverness. The key to a correct reading is the understanding that results from the interpreter's love of God. Correct exegesis is not possible without the operation of the law of love in the interpreter. Love, which Briçonnet identifies as "la consummacion, perfection et abreviacion de la loy evangelicque" (I.150) [the consummation, perfection and summation of the evangelical law], is both the beginning and the end of all "reading." In one sense, exegesis or reading is merely an instrument that, when handled in the spirit of love, can assist others in their search for truth. The soul that burns with the fire of divine love has no need of such a tool.[26] Like Mary, but unlike Martha and Marguerite, such a soul already possesses the one thing that is needed. Silent and unmoving, it remains in loving contemplation of Christ.

Briçonnet's analysis of the relationship between speech and the *Tout-Verbe* contains a concept of the text that has profound implications for his own work as well as for Marguerite's poetry. The text is a tool, an instrument that is used to fashion something else and then discarded. Composed of words, each of which contains a trace of the *Tout-Verbe*, the text is a sign that

---

26. Augustine wrote: "A man supported by faith, hope, and charity, with an unshaken hold upon them, does not need the Scriptures except for the instruction of others. And many live by these three things in solitude without books" (DDC I.39.32).

points not to itself or its own artifices but to reality, i.e., Christ. It aspires to its own annihilation just as words, striving to deny themselves, seek to be reabsorbed into silence. It tries to draw the reader away from the literal meaning, which Briçonnet calls *Rien* [nothing] and to lead him to the spiritual meaning, which he calls *Tout* [All]. Only if it overcomes its textuality and becomes a kind of blank page or mirror can the text reflect a reality that is other than itself.

Briçonnet's letters illustrate various stylistic devices by means of which a text can try to erase itself and deny its own textual or material presence. Most of these devices come from the Pseudo-Dionysius, who, in his search for the silence immanent in words, rejected the formal beauty of the classical literary style. He favored crudeness in grammar and vocabulary. He also advocated the use of gibberish, for he believed that nonsense can lead the soul away from the *Via Affirmativa* (the sphere of dogmatic theology) and guide it down the *Via Negativa* (the sphere of mysticism), which is the most direct road to the Godhead. Henry Heller has pointed out the Pseudo-Dionysius' fondness for seemingly inappropriate images:

Dionysius expressly sanctioned the use of rhopographical images, i.e., images of insignificant objects, odds and ends, and rhypological images, i.e., images of low and sordid things. They were to be used, according to his teaching, to conceal mysteries from the vulgar, to shock and awaken the spirit into religious awareness, and purposely in order to suggest how far removed man's ordinary understanding was from a genuine comprehension of the essence of a wholly transcendent God.[27]

In some ways Briçonnet carried the Dionysian strategy further than the Pseudo-Dionysius himself had done. Briçonnet's comparisons are often more strained, his syntax more contorted, his allegories and paradoxes more farfetched than those of the Pseudo-Dionysius. The sentence that opens Briçonnet's letter of January 20, 1522, for instance, is opaque in the way matter unilluminated by the spirit is opaque: "L'abisme qui tout abisme

27. "Marguerite de Navarre and the Reformers of Meaux," p. 274. Heller borrowed the terms "rhopographical" and "rhypological" from art history. Both refer to Greek mosaics that depict common objects. The former is applied to works that depict small, insignificant objects, such as a pebble or a gnat. The latter is applied to works that show objects considered to be vulgar or base, such as a fingernail paring or an apple core. See Charles Sterling, *La Nature Morte de l'antiquité à nos jours* (Paris: Tisné, 1952), p. 11.

previent pour en le desabismant l'abismer en abisme sans l'abismer, auquel abisme est fons sans fons, voie des errans sans
chemin ne sentier, qui les desvoiéz retire d'erreur pour abissale-
ment les desvoier en voie abissale, abissallement desvoiant, et
plus desvoie moings desvoie" (I.134) [The abyss that engulfs
everything averts, by not engulfing it, engulfing it in the abyss
without engulfing it, which abyss is the bottomless bottom, the
way of wanderers without road or path, which leads wayfarers
without a way from error in order to lead them engulfingly from
the way into the engulfing way, engulfingly leading them from
the way, and the more it leads from the way the less it leads
from the way]. The same tone is maintained throughout the
letter. Entrapped in a morass of words that reflect each other, the
reader may well abandon any effort to "understand" the text.
And that is the point. The letter is not meant to be "understood" in the usual sense of the word. It is designed to prepare
the soul for experiencing God. It is "about" the sterility of reason (the word *sterilité* appears near the end of the letter) and the
"vray aneantissement, qui est la voie sans voie et lumiere sans
lumiere" (I.135) [true annihilation, which is the way without a
way and light without light]. By its opaqueness, its repetitive-
ness, its "unintelligibility," Briçonnet's letter is designed to "humiliate" the reader. "Je vous supplie, Madame," Briçonnet concludes, "n'en soiez point ingrate, en vous humiliant de plus en
plus vers l'abisme de toute humilité, par simplicité, verité et
puretteé de vostre coeur" (I.135) [I beg you, Madame, do not be
ungrateful, and humble yourself more and more toward the
abyss of total humility, by simplicity, truth, and purity of your
heart]. The humility that Briçonnet would like Marguerite to
experience is the first stage in the soul's experience of Christ.

Heller has pointed out that Briçonnet was capable of writing
prose that is unaffected, forceful, and lucid.[28] Indeed, Briçonnet's sermons are composed in a style appropriate to the *Via Affirmativa*. But this is not the style of most of his letters to Marguerite. They are designed to do violence to their recipient, to
begin the process of pulverization and annihilation that will ultimately be taken over by the fire of love. The letter of January 20,
1522, for example, aims to paralyze reason, to still discourse, to
transcend language. The constant hum of words becomes the

28. Ibid., 278.

semantic equivalent of silence. By silencing reason, the text performs the function of readying the reader for the experience of love.

For reasons that are not clear, Marguerite and Briçonnet stopped writing to each other in 1524. But Marguerite had taken Briçonnet's message to heart. More than twenty years later, ill, despondent, and knowing that she would soon die, she alluded over and over to ideas and actual phrases in the letters she had received years before. Either she had kept the letters and reread them toward the end of her life or—and this is even more remarkable—she had read them so thoroughly in the 1520s that she was able in the late 1540s to cite them from memory. In any case, the spirit of Briçonnet is everywhere apparent in Marguerite's poetry. His letters sharpened Marguerite's religious sensibilities, whetted her desire to possess the "one thing that is needed," and, perhaps most important of all, provided her with a poetics that, suiting her talent and temperament, permitted her to find her own distinctive poetic voice.

3
Catechistic Discourse

A NOCTURNAL VISION

Marguerite wrote her first two major poems, *Dialogue en forme de vision nocturne* and *Petit Oeuvre dévot et contemplatif*, either during the years she was corresponding with Briçonnet or shortly thereafter. Critics generally agree that the *Dialogue* was probably written first.[29] Be that as it may, the *Dialogue* was written shortly after Marguerite's eight-year-old niece, Charlotte, daughter of Francis I, died of rubella. Marguerite had been at Charlotte's bedside during the last thirty days of the child's illness and was with her when she died on September 8, 1524.

In a letter dated September 15, Briçonnet sought to console Marguerite. This letter remained unavailable to scholars until 1970 when Christine Martineau and Christian Grouselle published it for the first time.[30] In their commentary, they compare the letter with Marguerite's *Dialogue*, concluding that Briçonnet's letter was the direct source of Marguerite's poem. Furthermore, they point out that after the first 350 lines or so (the poem consists of 1293 lines), Marguerite borrows heavily from the earlier letter of August 31, 1524, that Briçonnet had written to her to console her after the death of Claude de France, Charlotte's mother, who had died on July 26 of the same year.

The *Dialogue* was not included in the first collection of Mar-

---

29. Hans Sckommodau is the exception for he believes that the *Petit Oeuvre* preceded the *Dialogue*. See his edition of *Petit Oeuvre dévot et contemplatif. Neuedition und Versuch einer Erklärung* (Frankfurt am Main: Vittorio Klostermann, 1960). *Analecta Romanica. Beihefte zu den Romanischen Forschungen.* Heft 9, p. 21.

30. "La Source première et directe du Dialogue en forme de vision nocturne: la lettre de Guillaume Briçonnet à Marguerite de Navarre, du 15 septembre 1524. Publication et commentaire," *BHR*, 32 (1970), 569.

guerite's poetry, which was published in 1531 under the title of *Le Miroir de l'âme pécheresse*. It appeared, however, perhaps without Marguerite's approval, as the opening poem in one of the various editions of *Le Miroir* that came out in 1533. Some fourteen years later when Marguerite prepared what she intended to be the definitive collection of her poetry (*Marguerites de la marguerite des princesses* and *Suyte des marguerites de la marguerite des princesses*, both published in 1547), she chose not to include the *Dialogue*. Whatever her reasons for excluding the poem, the *Dialogue* provides a remarkably suitable entry into Marguerite's poetic *oeuvre*; first of all, it catechizes the reader by instructing him in the principles of Evangelical doctrine, which constitutes the ideological ground on which much of Marguerite's poetry rests; secondly, it directs the reader's attention in a particularly forceful way to certain strategies that are of special importance in Marguerite's poetics.

After composing a poem, Marguerite was in the habit of directing one or more of her secretaries to copy it. In these manuscript copies, the poems are seldom titled. Since Marguerite paid little attention to the details of publishing her work, it would appear that the titles to most of her poems were selected by an editor at the time of publication. *Dialogue en forme de vision nocturne* is a case in point. The manuscript contains four rondeaux that deal with the death of Charlotte and a long, untitled dialogue between Marguerite and the soul of her departed niece.[31] Published in 1533 under the title by which we now know it, the poem opens with three of the rondeaux (a total of 39 lines) before moving into the dialogue proper, which consists of 1253 additional lines written in *terza rima*.[32] Whether by Marguerite or by an editor, the title of *Dialogue en forme de vision nocturne* is an integral part of the reader's experience of the text and must be deemed an essential member of the textual body. It informs the reader not only that the poem is a dialogue but that the particular conversation recorded in the text is represented as having occurred in a dream.

The 1533 edition identifies each of the two speakers by print-

31. On the manuscript copy, see Hans Sckommodau, *Die religiösen Dichtungen Margaretes von Navarra* (Cologne: Westdeutscher Verlag, 1955), p. 63–64.

32. The *Dialogue* has been published twice since 1533: Carlo Pellegrini, *La prima opera di Margherita di Navarra e la terza rima in Francia* (Catania: Battiato, 1920); *Dialogue en forme de vision nocturne*, ed. P. Jourda, *Revue du seizième siècle*, 13 (1926), 1–49.

ing, as in the text of a play, her name before the words she
speaks. In his edition, Jourda follows the 1533 edition in this regard and identifies each speaker. The first rondeau is introduced
with the words "La Royne de Navarre à l'âme de ma dame
Charlote sa nièpce"[33] [the Queen of Navarre to the soul of the
lady Charlotte, her niece]; the second, with the words "L'âme
de madame Charlote respond" [the soul of Lady Charlotte an-
swers]; the third, with the words "La Royne de Navarre repli-
que" [the Queen of Navarre responds]. Thereafter, each voice is
designated as being either that of "la Royne de Navarre" or that
of "l'âme de madame Charlote." Thus the text has a graphic dimension that is not without importance in preparing the reader
to perceive the poem in terms of a dramatic presentation.

Charlotte's spirit appears to the sleeping Marguerite and, in
response to her aunt's questions, assures her that she is happy
now that she has been reunited with Christ. Prodded by Marguerite's repeated questions, Charlotte, the catechist, explains to
the exceptionally troubled catechumen the doctrine of the true
faith, which affirms that the death of the body is the beginning
of everlasting joy. Everything in the poem bears directly on this
concept. Suspicious of literary niceties and embellishments designed to charm the unwary reader (in her vocabulary, to charm
is to deceive), Marguerite moves simply and bluntly to the heart
of the matter. Presented in the form of a murmured nocturnal
conversation that takes place in Marguerite's troubled dreams,
the poem is edged with night, with the blackness of despair that
is forced to recede momentarily before Charlotte's words but
that remains, threatening, just beyond the confines of the poem's
circumference.

The poem opens with a voice that rises imploringly and ur-
gently. "Repondez moi" [Answer me], it pleads at the very beginning of the text. These two words—the first two in the
poem—indicate what will be the fundamental stance of the narrator throughout Marguerite's poetry. The "I" in her poems (although we shall call the "I" Marguerite, we refer of course to
the persona contained within the poem) is a seeker after an-

33. In 1533, Marguerite had been married to the King of Navarre for some six years
and would of course be referred to as the Queen of Navarre. She composed the poem,
however, two years before her marriage to Navarre. In a manuscript copy that antedates
the first edition, Marguerite is identified as "Madame la duchesse," abbreviated several
times to "Madame L. D." See Jourda edition, 5.

swers. The voice that opens the *Dialogue* emerges out of the chaos of unformed linguistic matter and, by imploring an interlocutor to respond to its request, establishes dialectic as the dominant discursive mode in Marguerite's poetic work.

The first rondeau makes clear what the narrator desires:

```
 1        Respondez moy, o doulce ame vivante,
          Qui par la mort qui les fols espovente
          Avez esté d'ung petit corps delivre,
          Lequel huyt ans acomplyz n'a sceu vivre,
 5        Faisant des siens la vie trop dolente;
          Dictes comment en la court triumphante
          De nostre Roy et Père estes contente,
          En declarant comme amour vous enyvre:
                              Respondez moy.
10        Las! mon enfant, parlez à vostre tante
          Que vous laissez après vous languissante,
          Fort désirant que peine à mort me livre!
          Vie m'est mort par désir de vous suyvre:
          Pour soullager ma douleur véhémente,
                              Respondez moy.[34]
```

Answer me, O sweet living soul, who, by death, which frightens the foolish, have been freed from a little body that after eight years did not know how to go on living, making life too sad for those close to it; tell me about how you are happy in the triumphant court of our King and Father, saying how love intoxicates you: answer me. Alas! my child, speak to your aunt, whom you have left behind after you, languishing, strongly desiring that grief might deliver me over to death! Life is death to me because of my desire to follow you; to lighten my intense sorrow, answer me.

Marguerite asks for a description of the joy and love that overpower the soul that has been united with Christ. The *unio mystica*, which Charlotte now experiences, contrasts with Marguerite's "douleur véhémente." Two distinct and antithetical states of being are posited: one is terrestrial or corporeal, the other, heavenly or spiritual. The former is temporal and destined to perish; the latter is eternal and can be fully realized only

---

34. Quotations of the *Dialogue* are from the Jourda edition and are identified by verse number.

when the body dies. However, within the Christian context ("Anyone who loses his life for my sake will find it." Matthew 10.39), the terms "life" and "death" become referentially ambiguous as one shifts from an earth-bound perspective to that of transcendence.

Line 3 refers to the soul that has been freed from the body. Few images appear more often in the work of Christian mystics than that of the body as a prison from which the captive soul is released by death. The potency of the prison metaphor results largely from the fact that it allows two dialectical visions of the world to converge. In the prison metaphor, the Platonic concept of the soul as imprisoned in the body is assimilated with the Pauline antithesis *carnalis/spiritualis*. Being of a deeply dualistic cast of mind, Marguerite returns over and over to the ambiguous bond that links body and spirit and exploits the prison metaphor to convey an essential aspect of her religious experience.

In his consolatory letter of September 15, 1524, Briçonnet had assured Marguerite that the imprisoned soul greets death, the liberator, with joy. The Christian soul, he tells her, desires nothing more eagerly than the arrival of death, for when death comes the prison walls collapse and the freed soul, radiant and jubilant, joins Christ. Indeed, the Pauline theme of *cupio dissolvi* ("I want to be gone and be with Christ," Philippians 1.23) runs through the Briçonnet-Marguerite correspondence and gives doctrinal support to the yearning for annihilation and pulverization. When Briçonnet writes that "ce monde est prison" (II.265) [this world is a prison], his intent is not to inform Marguerite of something she does not know but to sooth and calm by repeating, as in a litany, certain time-worn expressions so deeply rooted in the Christian conscience that, having incantatory power, they may trigger a response that heals. "Le prisonnier, qui en prison pleure, se esjouit en liberté" (II.263) [The prisoner, who weeps in prison, rejoices in freedom], he observes. "Autre chose n'est mort que liberté et unyon avec le desiré, doux et amiable espoux" (II.264) [Death is nothing else but freedom and union with the desired one, sweet and gracious husband].

With the sentence I have just cited, Briçonnet introduces in his letter of September 15, 1524, another metaphor that permeates the work of Christian mystics: the soul is a bride who ardently desires to be united in marriage with Christ the bridegroom. The Scriptures sanction the concept of the Church joined in marriage with Christ. Christian thinkers from the time of the earliest Fathers on seized upon this image as a particularly forceful expression of the soul's union with God.[35] Briçonnet repeats the familiar *topos* when he speaks of the "unyon du vray espoux" or of the "unyon d'amour." His language, however, is not always so chaste. He makes the carnal connotations of the marriage metaphor much more explicit than most of his fellow Renaissance churchmen do: "L'espouze endormie entre les bras de son espoux, qu'elle a longuement cherché et desiré, et l'ame fidelle par extatique ravissement unie au debonnaire Jesus, ne prendroient plaisir d'estre esveillées de leur savoureux dormir" [The bride asleep in the arms of her husband, whom she sought and desired for a long time, and the faithful soul united with gentle Jesus by an ecstatic ravishment would not take delight in being awakened from their savory sleep]. He speaks of "le doux Jesus desmesurement embrazé" [sweet Jesus exceedingly enflamed] and of "ses espouses abismées en douceurs indicibles" [his wives engulfed in indescribable sweet pleasures].

Marguerite often uses the marriage metaphor to convey the joy of the *unio mystica*. In the *Dialogue*, Charlotte, who died at the age of eight, speaks of her mystic marriage with Christ:

151   Mais mon Espoux m'a faict plus grand honneur
       De me prendre en ma virginité,
       Sans que péché ayt regné en mon cueur.

But my Husband did me greater honor by taking me in my virginity, without sin having reigned in my heart.

She tells Marguerite how the soul can best prepare itself to meet the Bridegroom. Certain points of Evangelical doctrine are elaborated with special care: a Christian does not need saints to

---

35. The metaphor is developed in the Song of Songs, in Paul's epistles, and in the Apocalypse. Dom Cuthbert Butler notes, however, that the prevalence of the metaphor in mystical literature is due largely to Bernard, for whom it was a central concept. *Western Mysticism*, p. 110. Butler reminds us (p. 97) that there runs through much mystical literature a twofold allegorical interpretation of the Bridegroom and Bride: "(i) the Bridegroom is Jesus Christ and the Bride is the Church—this is in accordance with St. Paul and the Apocalypse; but (ii) when the bride is the soul of the devout individual man, the Bridegroom is not Jesus Christ in His Humanity, but the Divine Word, the Logos, the Second Person of the Holy Trinity—in more than one place He is called 'the Bridegroom-Word,' 'Verbum Sponsus' (*Cant.* lxxiv. 3)."

intercede for him (346); the question of free will is so knotty that it should not even be discussed (496); since God's grace is a gift, it is independent of merit (547); good works cannot assure the Christian of receiving grace, although if he is illuminated by faith, he will do good works (556–65). After explaining these points of doctrine, Charlotte then tells Marguerite that they are unimportant and that the Christian should not concern himself with doctrinal matters. The Christian's essential duty is to love Christ. All else will follow if one obeys the law of Love.

Throughout the long catechistic discourse that constitutes the major part of the poem, Charlotte insists on the necessity of renouncing ". . . père et mère / Amyz, parentz, plaisir, richesse, honneur" (220–21) [father and mother, friends, relatives, pleasure, wealth, honor]. Reason must be rejected in order for the soul to flourish: ". . . raison sera destruicte / Pour commencer l'âme à édifier" (269–70) [reason will be destroyed so that the soul can begin to rise up]. Eventually, even the soul will be consumed in love:

> . . . .
> L'âme et l'esperit fault mourir par amour,
> Qui jusques à là ne lairra sa poursuyte;
>
> Amour n'aura ne repoz ne sesiour,
> 275   Tant qu'il aura nature anneantie,
> Raison, âme, esperit sans retour.
>
> Amour est feu, qui la piquante ortye
> Noircist, seiche, eschauffe et enflamme,
> Tant qu'en cendre l'ayt toute convertie.

The soul and the spirit must die through love, which, until that is achieved, will not abandon its pursuit; love will have no rest or leisure until it has annihilated nature, reason, soul, spirit, irrevocably. Love is fire that blackens the pointed nettle, dries, heats and ignites it until it is converted into ashes.

The Christian must abandon his "propre volonté" (719) [own will] as well as his desire to understand. "Ne desirez plus avant en sçavoir" (865) [do not wish to know more], Charlotte admonishes Marguerite.

The essential insight Charlotte tries to convey to Marguerite is that Christ is all. The corollary is that the self is nothing. This insight is profoundly *self*-destructive because it requires renouncing the perceptual and conceptual categories that permit the self to exist or, rather, that cultivate the illusion of independent existence. The self must cease to assert its independence. Behind Charlotte's dismissal of doctrinal matters is the message that Marguerite must learn to abandon those ways of thinking, seeing, and speaking that sustain the illusion of independence.

As Charlotte elucidates one point of doctrine after another, Marguerite typically answers with a "je le croy bien; mais . . ." (160) [I do believe it; but . . .]. She believes; nevertheless she raises objections, asks questions, requests clarification. After Charlotte has delivered a particularly lengthy disquisition on the importance of mortifying the heart, Marguerite replies with the following verses, which, on first reading, may appear to be an appropriately devout response but which provoke the ire of Charlotte:

> Puis que *j*'entens que *mon* seul créateur
> Est *mon* Saulveur, *mon* Advocat et Juge,
> *Je* n'auray plus par deffiance paour.

> 475   Faire de luy *mon* appuy et refuge,
> Pour *me* tirer de la mer des péchéz,
> Tant mortelle qu'il n'est pire déluge.

> Et quand *j*'auray *mes* péchéz arrachéz,
> *Je* planteray les vertus en *mon* âme
> 480   En lieu des maulx, qui y sont sy cachéz. (my emphasis)

Since I understand that my only creator is my savior, my advocate and judge, I will no longer be afraid through distrust. I will make him my support and refuge so that he can pull me from the sea of sins, so fatal that there is no worse flood. And when I have torn out my sins, I will plant virtues in my soul in the place of the evils that are so hidden there.

Charlotte expresses her displeasure with Marguerite's comments:

> 487   Ne congnoissez vous que avez mal dit?
> Car en vous n'est mettre fin à la guerre
> De vos péchéz, si dieu n'y met respit.

Do you not realize that you have spoken evilly? For it is not in you to put an end to the war of your sins if God does not put a stop to it.

In other words, Marguerite erred grievously in declaring that *she* was going to do this or that, for by repeating with irritating insistence "je" and "mon" she was in fact expressing confidence in her own independence. Her words reveal how far she is from the spirit of Christ, for she asserts rather than effaces self. "N'ayez le cueur orgueilleux, sot ne dur, / Mais humble et doux" (399–400) [Do not have a proud heart, foolish or hard, but humble and gentle], Charlotte chides before launching into an explanation of the transformation that grace effects in the heart. Marguerite, who naturally (the word is double edged) resists her own undoing, asks what she must do to merit grace. Charlotte answers that she can do nothing. Even the good an individual does is the result of the will of God manifesting itself through mankind and cannot be viewed as augmenting the merit of the individual. The self is incapable of doing good. Everything it does is evil, for the self *is* evil:

568   Si vous avez vouloir de faire bien
             C'est le vouloir de dieu, car le seul vostre
             Est vouloir mal, quant riens n'y a du sien.

If you have the will to do good, it is God's will, for your will alone is evil when nothing of his is in it.

Having been told that whatever she chooses to do will be evil, Marguerite says that she will do nothing:

580   Je seray donc sans faire nul ouvrage
             Croyant en dieu, espérant qu'il fera
             Sa volunté, s'il veult, en mon courage.

I shall then remain without performing any works, believing in God and hoping that he will do his will, if he wishes, in spirit.

Marguerite's words annoy Charlotte, who scolds her by pointing out that even in declaring she will do nothing she has in fact affirmed her ability to act or not to act and thus insisted upon the invidious distinction between self and Christ.

586   Mais vous allez, sans cesser, au contraire,
       Car en voz faictz vous mesmes vous cerchez,
       Voire et en lieu seulement pour vous plaire.

But you constantly go to the opposite of the truth, for you look for
your deeds in yourself, and indeed there only to please yourself.

What Charlotte asks Marguerite to do is to learn to perceive and
speak in such a way that all traces of *self*-consciousness will be
effaced. She urges Marguerite to cast off those habits of thought
and speech that preserve the individual's dignity by implying
his independence. Marguerite's inquiries, her misunderstandings
and hesitations mirror the reluctance of the self to acquiesce in
its own destruction.

Desire is an attribute of a self that is not yet united with Christ.
Originating in a sense of lack, it creates (or confirms) a distinction between self and the object of desire, that is to say, Christ.
The insight that God is all dissolves this distinction. The self
that is united with Christ ceases to exist independently. It no
longer desires; it begins to enjoy. Charlotte expresses an essential aspect of this self-dissolving insight when, in the second
rondeau of the *Dialogue*, she stresses her contentment. "Je suis
icy belle, claire et luysante, / Pleine de Dieu et de luy jouys-
sante" (19–20) [Here I am beautiful, bright and shining, full of
God, joyous in him]. Like Marguerite, Charlotte uses the first
person pronoun. There is a difference, however, between her use
of "je" and that of Marguerite. When Charlotte, who is "pleine
de Dieu" says "je," it is the voice of Christ we hear, for Charlotte's self has been absorbed into Christ. When Marguerite says
"je," the voice we hear is that of the self as yet unassimilated
with Christ. Charlotte's marked preference for the verb *être*,
which she uses repeatedly throughout the *Dialogue*, is another
indication of her identity with Christ, who is eternally present.
On the other hand, Marguerite's frequent use of verbs in the
various past tenses and in the future tense reveals her link with
temporality and thus her separation from Him.

In the third rondeau, the speaker is again Marguerite. But this
is not the languishing Marguerite who, in the first rondeau, had
wanted to die. Touched by Charlotte's joy, Marguerite now appropriates Charlotte's vocabulary and pitches her voice so as
to repeat the girl's song of contentment. "Contente suis d'ung

grand contentement / Que m'asseurez avoir entièrement" (27–28) [Content I am with a great contentment that you assure me of possessing fully]. Maintaining the same rapturous tone, Marguerite concludes the first of the two stanzas that make up the rondeau with the following lines:

32   Mon esperit contemple incessamment
        Dieu joinct à vous inséparablement,
        Pour me garder de me desconforter:
        Contente suis.

Unceasingly my spirit contemplates God, who is joined inseparably to you, in order to keep me from being sad: content I am.

Her joy does not last beyond the limits of the first stanza. In the next line, which opens with the disjunctive "mais," the self re-asserts its presence, affirming separation from Christ:

35   Mais mon vieil corps lié sy longuement
        A vostre sens, ne se poeut nullement
        Jusqu'à la mort de son dueil déporter.

But my old body attached so long to the thought of you can in no way be free from grief until death.

Like most of Marguerite's poems, the *Dialogue* dramatizes the dilemma of a self that longs for the experience of Christ as all but resists the experience of self as nothing. In her poetry, Marguerite tries to find a poetic form and a language capable of translating this dilemma. The spiritual or psychological problem becomes a poetic problem. Writing in the tradition of the Pseudo-Dionysius and Briçonnet, she seeks to manipulate language in such a way that it will undermine discursive forms of thought and thus weaken reason and the will, two of the pillars that support the self in its illusion of independence. She seeks to render superfluous the mode of discourse of which the poem is an example. The peculiar force of a poem by Marguerite depends on the reader's awareness that the form and language of the work are designed to subvert the very notion of poetic discourse. In a sense, a poem by Marguerite is a statement on the impossibility of poetry in the same way that the Christian's insight that Christ is all is a denial of the autonomy of the self without which there would have been no insight in the first place.

YOURSELF YOU MUST DISSOLVE

But how can the self experience a *self*-dissolving insight? By what strategies can the poet translate this insight into texts that are vehicles through which the reader can experience a comparable insight? The *Dialogue* provides us with an initial—and partial—answer to these questions, which are central to Marguerite's poetic *oeuvre*. The simplest way to state Marguerite's answer as she works it out in the course of the *Dialogue* is to say that a Christian experiences desire and enjoyment alternately. At times, he *desires*, thereby affirming the illusory independence of the self. At other times, he *enjoys*, thus "tasting" (to use one of Briçonnet's words that Marguerite borrows) the beatific pleasure of the *unio mystica*. The oscillation between these two states leads in the text to a poetics of tension between desire and enjoyment.

That it is the Christian's duty to be joyful is a commonplace in religious handbooks.[36] The Scriptures in fact stress the notion that a man in whom dwells the spirit of truth experiences a joy indescribably greater than that known by other men. In John 15.11, Christ, after reminding His disciples to keep His commandments, says: "I have told you this so that my own joy may be in you and your joy be complete." Paul informed the Corinthians that he was writing to them not to dictate the terms of their faith but to help them know joy (II Corinthians 1.24). But it was Augustine who codified the concept of Christian happiness and passed it on to later generations of believers.

After distinguishing between things and signs, Augustine proceeds in rhetorical fashion to make distinctions within the category of things. "Some things," he observes, "are to be enjoyed, others to be used, and there are others which are to be enjoyed and used" (DDC I.4.9). As he begins to develop his thought, Augustine eliminates the third kind of thing, for he makes it clear that things cannot be enjoyed and used simultaneously. This being so, at any moment a particular thing must be

---

36. See *Medieval Handbooks of Penance*, ed. John T. McNeill and Helen Gardner (New York: Columbia University Press, 1938).

either a thing to be enjoyed or a thing to be used. He notes that "those things which are to be enjoyed make us blessed" and "those things which are to be used help and, as it were, sustain us as we move toward blessedness in order that we may gain and cling to those things which make us blessed" (DDC I.4.9). He warns against the dangers of wishing "to enjoy those things which should be used" (DDC I.4.9). To seek enjoyment in things that should in fact be used will "impede and sometimes deflect" (DDC I.3.9) our course so that we may be altogether prevented from obtaining those things which are to be enjoyed.

But what are those things that should be enjoyed? Augustine's answer is unequivocal: "The things which are to be enjoyed are the Father, the Son, and the Holy Spirit" (DDC I.5.10). Basing his thought on the Pauline distinction between the letter and the spirit, Augustine declares that "we should use this world and not enjoy it, so that the 'invisible things' of God 'being understood by the things that are made' [Romans 1.20] may be seen, that is, so that by means of corporal and temporal things we may comprehend the eternal and spiritual" (DDC I.4.10).

Things, then, can never be enjoyed for themselves, unless one is willing to call God a thing. For his part, Augustine hesitates to apply the word "thing" to God, pointing out that God, rather than being a "thing" Himself, is "the cause of all things, or both a thing and a cause" (DDC I.5.10). Joy in things other than God is, in Augustine's words, "a perverse sweetness" that alienates us from "our country [i.e., Christ] whose sweetness would make us blessed" (DDC I.4.10). Augustine conceives of the *via Christi* as a gradual process of seeing in "things" signs of the reign of Christ. Since the Christian can enjoy things to the extent that they are signs of Christ, his journey is marked—in theory, at least—by an ever increasing experience of joy. Tracing the same itinerary, Marguerite's poetry reveals, however, the painfulness of the journey. "Fleshy" desire may tease the Christian away from contemplation of the truth, which alone can be enjoyed. It may propel him toward things that elicit from him an unworthy and misplaced love. In Marguerite's poems, there is a careful distinction between the desire to know Christ and the actual experience of joy that comes from knowing Him. Although the wish to be undone and to experience the joy of the *unio mystica* is a proper Christian desire, it is, like all desire, an impulse of the self. Marguerite's desire in the rondeau that opens the *Dialogue* is in sharp contrast to Charlotte's *contentement* in the succeeding rondeau.

After evoking Charlotte's release from the prison of the body ("d'ung petit corps delivre," 3) [freed from a little body], Marguerite says she also wants to die: "Fort désirant que peine à mort me livre!" (11) [Strongly desiring that grief might deliver me over to death!]. *Livre* echoes *delivre*, provoking unexpected resonances across the surface of the text. The prefix *de-* has two functions. It can make the word on which it is grafted an antonym of the root word, as in form/deform. Or it can reinforce the meaning of the root word, as in denude. Occasionally, as in the case of *delivrer*, a *de-* word can be both a synonym and an antonym of the base word. Intensifying the meaning of *livrer*, *delivrer* can mean submission or surrender. (Cotgrave's definition is "to yeeld over unto.") But it can also mean the opposite, that is to say (citing Cotgrave again), "to free, loose, release, rid from." The peculiar effectiveness of the *livrer/delivrer* dialectic at the beginning of the *Dialogue* lies in the fact that the unstable enigmatic relationship between these two words parallels at the linguistic level the Christian's perception (which Marguerite seeks to render) of the paradoxical relationship between life and death. For if life and death are antonyms, in the context of mysticism they may be synonyms. To submit to death (*livrer*), which is Marguerite's wish, is in fact identical to deliverance from the body (*delivrer*) and marks the beginning of a joyful life with Christ. The text effaces the difference between life and death. Words tend to lose their referential meaning and to become signs that, in their semiotic process, point to a figurative or spiritual meaning.

Throughout the *Dialogue*, Charlotte is shown as having already arrived at the destination toward which Marguerite is moving. "Je suis quiete de toute adversité / Que pelerins mondains ont à porter" (134) [I am released from all the hardships worldly pilgrims have to bear], Charlotte says with satisfaction. Charlotte's principal concern is to make certain that Marguerite does not take a wrong turn and go astray. For there are two ways—the wrong one ("chemin esgaré," 1197) and the right one. The wrong way is that of the self. The right way is that of Christ, who declared in a statement that reverberates throughout Marguerite's poetry, "I am the Way, the Truth, and the Life. No one can come to the Father except through me" (John 14.6).

Charlotte reminds Marguerite that in order to reach the Father, who is the source of all enjoyment, she must follow the way of Christ:

805   Il est vie, et verité et voye;
       Par luy qui est Voye, nous fault passer,
       Et Verité à Vie nous convoye.

He is life, and truth and the way; through him, who is the Way, we must pass, and Truth accompanies us to Life.

The alliterations and assonances in the French, which in this respect is closer to the Latin (*Ego sum via, et veritas, et vita*) than is the English, help to establish the fact that *vie*, *verité*, and *voye* are identical in Christ.

Originating in Christ's own words, the metaphor of a way allows the Christian to structure his spiritual experience in a specific manner. The analogy with a physical journey invites him to experience Christ within a conceptual framework of spatial and temporal progress. The literary form best able to express a step-by-step advance toward a desired goal is narrative. Beginning at a particular time and place, a narrative recounts a sequence of related events. It traces out a forward motion along a temporal-spatial axis. To express her vision of the Christian life as a pilgrimage toward God, Marguerite depends heavily on narrative. The *Dialogue* opens with Charlotte's appearance in Marguerite's dream and ends with her return to heaven. Furthermore, Charlotte's doctrinal message is presented within the context of an account of her journey to the "celeste édifice" (253). Using the Platonic image of a ladder to symbolize the Christian way, Charlotte emphasizes the importance of steady, purposive progress toward the final destination.

Numerous small narrative units are inserted within the broad narrative framework of the poem. Recounting her experiences along Christ's way, Charlotte, for example, tells Marguerite of the fate of the two ladies, *Espoir* [Hope] and *Foy* [Faith], who accompanied her on her journey. They led her up to the doors of paradise and then died at the moment she entered heaven. From their death, however, *Charité* was born. In a sentence that draws attention to the phonic similarity between the word *Charlotte* and *Charité*, Charlotte says, "Contente suis d'elles, car en moy ont engendré Charité" (1216–17) [I am happy with them, for they have engendered Charity in me]. Charlotte's little tale is an elaboration of one of the most familiar of Paul's statements: "There are three things that last: faith, hope and love [*caritas*]: and the greatest of these is love" (I Corinthians 13.13). At the end of the first book of *On Christian Doctrine*, Augustine had interpreted Paul's words in a passage that is close in spirit to the allegory of *Espoir*, *Foy*, and *Charité* that Charlotte narrates in the *Dialogue*:

But the vision we shall see will replace faith, and that blessedness to which we are to come will replace hope; and when these things are falling away, charity will be increased even more. If we love in faith what we have not seen, how much more will we love it when we begin to see it? And if we love in hope what we have not attained, how much more will we love it when we have attained it? Between temporal and eternal things there is this difference: a temporal thing is loved more before we have it, and it begins to grow worthless when we gain it, for it does not satisfy the soul, whose true and certain rest is eternity; but the eternal is more ardently loved when it is acquired than when it is merely desired. (DDC I.38.32)

In the *Dialogue*, Marguerite dramatizes I Corinthians 13.13 by turning faith, hope, and love into allegorical figures. Augustine's association of desire with temporal things on the one hand and satisfaction with eternity on the other hand is central to Marguerite's vision of the Christian's journey, which proceeds along an axis from desire to enjoyment.

That Marguerite changed the word order of faith, hope, and love, putting *Espoir* first and then *Foy* and *Charité*, is curious and worth examining. Augustine had kept the word order of the Vulgate: *fides*, *spes*, *caritas*. There are no requirements of prosody that can explain Marguerite's word order, which seems to have been deliberate because it appears more than once in the *Dialogue*. The allegory of *Espoir*, *Foy*, and *Charité* is told by Charlotte, who tries to lighten Marguerite's grief. The order of *Espoir*, *Foy*, and *Charité* is determined by a concept of the psychological process by which despair can be overcome. Hope is the first step. As Marguerite uses the word, hope is somehow self-generated within the human soul. It is therefore lower on a graduated scale of spiritual qualities than faith, or *Vive Foy* as she often calls it, which is a gift of God. *Vive Foy*, this "don que Dieu baille / A ses amyz" (1126–27) [gift God gives his friends], is the penultimate station that a Christian reaches before arriving at his final destination. In Marguerite's vision, *Espoir*, *Foy*, and *Charité* each mark a step along the Christian's way, which, within this small allegory as within the whole of the *Dialogue*, is interpreted as a progression of sequential events, that is to say, as narrative.

In his study of Marguerite's religious poetry, Hans Sckommodau devotes considerable effort to answering the complaint of earlier critics that the longer poems are badly constructed.[37] He argues that the *Dialogue* and the *Petit Oeuvre* as well as later works are carefully plotted in accordance with a trinitarian principle. Calling attention to the frequency of tripartite construction throughout the *Dialogue*, he points to stanza 292–94, which he reads as a paradigm of the whole poem.[38] In this stanza, Charlotte speaks of "les Esleuz qu'il [Christ] luy a pleu choisir" (291) [the Chosen whom it pleased him to select], and describes what we may call the mechanics of salvation, that is, the process by which Christ prepares a soul to make it worthy of being "unie au Chef" (333) [united with the Head].

292   Seicher les faict [le Christ les faict seicher]
          par tribulation,
      Les eschauffant par claire congnoissance.
      Il les brusle par sa dilection.

He dries them up by tribulation, warming them by clear understanding. He burns them by his love.

Three stages are involved in this process; the elected are first *seicher*, then *eschauffer*, and finally *brusler*. This is the process of annihilation or pulverization of which Briçonnet spoke repeatedly and which mystics often referred to as *mortificatio*. It reduces the self to its true state, which Marguerite (following Briçonnet) identifies as *Rien*, and then returns the spirit to God or *Tout*. The verbs that indicate how Christ prepares a soul for salvation are complemented by nouns that describe the soul's condition in each of the three stages. From *tribulation* the soul proceeds to *congnoissance* and then advances to *dilection*.

Sckommodau has pointed out that these three stages corre-

37. *Die religiösen Dichtungen* . . ., p. 74.
38. Ibid., p. 77.

spond to the three steps of the *scala perfectionis* that symbolized for mystics the process of achieving union with God: *purgatio, illuminatio, perfectio*. Briçonnet alludes often to the three stages of the *scala perfectionis*, metaphorizing them into three illnesses that man must endure: the "maladie purgative"; the "maladie illuminative," which "allume la chandelle de congnoissance" [lights the candle of understanding]; and the "maladie perficiente," or assimilation with God (I.74). Once again the importance of the Pseudo-Dionysius in the mystic tradition can scarcely be overemphasized, for it was he who, in his *De Ecclesiastica Hierarchia*, defined with precision this tripartite process, associating with each of the three stages a particular sacrament.[39] The first stage, purgation or purification, is reached by the sacrament of Baptism, during which the initiate dies in a symbolic mystical rite and is reborn in Christ. Marguerite's reordering of the Pauline *fides, spes, caritas* would seem to be along the line of the *scala perfectionis*, *Espoir* corresponding to the first stage and *Foy* and *Charité* to the next two respectively. Marguerite saw them as sequential whereas Paul had not. The second stage is the Eucharist, during which, according to the Pseudo-Dionysius, the initiate is united with Jesus. The final stage, perfection or union, is the mystical act of Chrism by which the initiate, having been anointed with Christ's oil of joy, becomes transformed into Him.

Although in one sense the three stages are progressive and sequential, the first stage is not abandoned when the Christian experiences the second, nor the first two when he experiences the third. The Christian never "moves beyond" the purgative life, for he never attains a state in which confession and contrition are no longer necessary. Nor does he ever progress beyond the illuminative stage of life, which represents man's attempt to reach God through the dialectical process. The unitive or contemplative stage, which is that of identity with Christ, is both a consummation and an annihilation. The Christian's experience of this stage will be a continual approximation of the ideal of *unio*. In fact, *perfectio*, which Marguerite calls *dilection* in the *Dialogue* (294), is not so much a stage as an infinite Becoming.

39. There is no English translation of *De Ecclesiastica Hierarchia*. There is, however, a good French translation: *La Hierarchie ecclésiastique* in *Oeuvres complètes du Pseudo-Denys l'Aréopagite*, trans. Maurice de Gandillac (Paris: Editions Montaigne, 1943). The Pseudo-Dionysius' discussion of *purgatio, illuminatio* and *perfectio* is in Ch. 1, pp. 245–51.

That the *tribulation*, *congnoissance*, and *dilection* of stanza 292–94 in the *Dialogue* correspond to the purgative, illuminative, and unitive life of a Christian is clear. Sckommodau argues, however, that the poem is a firmly constructed *scala perfectionis*. The first two hundred and forty lines, he says, constitute the proem; lines 240–341 are the *purgatio*, lines 342–672 the *illuminatio*, and lines 673–1293 the *perfectio*. These divisions are rather too rigid and arbitrary. Seldom is there a clear sense of a break at the point he indicates. Within the confines of Charlotte's narrative, there is obviously a sense of progression toward the *perfectio* because she is recounting a journey that she has already completed. But Charlotte's account is a dream that Marguerite has while asleep. For Marguerite herself, there is no progress at all, only an occasional "I understand" spoken in response to Charlotte's sharp questions. At the end of the poem, Marguerite is still in *purgatio*. The concluding stanza of the *Dialogue* emphasizes her unabated grief:

1291   Et moy, faisant ma lamentation,
         En ce mal plein de tribulation,
         Laissée m'a vivante piz que morte.

And I, continuing my lamentation, in this sorrow full of tribulation; she left me alive but worse than dead.

One feature of the *Dialogue* has often been noted by critics. Like the *Petit Oeuvre* and *La Navire*, it is composed (except for the opening rondeaux) in *terza rima*. The only French poem written in *terza rima* before the *Dialogue* was a work by Saint-Gelais.[40] Sckommodau stresses the tripartite nature of the rhyme scheme that Marguerite chose for her first two long poems. The *terza rima* is intimately associated with the *Divine Comedy*, a work little known and appreciated in France during the first half of the sixteenth century. Marguerite obviously knew Dante, for she mentions him by name in her work. In her longest poem, *Les Prisons*, her debt to Dante is large and direct. She also alludes to him several times in the *Petit Oeuvre*. In much of her poetry, however, the presence of Dante is not so immediate. Ex-

---

40. Jourda, ed. of *Dialogue* . . ., 2. See L. E. Kastner, "History of the terza rima in France," *Zeitschrift für französische Sprache und Literatur*, 26 (1904), 241–53.

cept for *Les Prisons* and the *Petit Oeuvre*, similarities between Marguerite's work and the *Divine Comedy* are due less to the direct influence of Dante than to a certain sharing of Christian *topoi* and narrative strategies.[41]

The *terza rima* served Marguerite's purpose (as it served Dante's). It is peculiarly suited to evoke a journey, for it is progressive, moving regularly and predictably from one rhyme to another. But if there is progress, there is also backsliding. For every two steps forward there is one step backward. This pattern of steady but laborious progress, marked by continual backsliding which, however, is never severe enough to annul forward movement, is an apt expression of the Christian's way from *tribulation* through *congnoissance* toward *dilection*.

Still, the very concept of progression, which is translated formally by narrative, is vexing. Augustine describes the "cleansing" of the mind (in effect, the *purgatio*) as "a journey or voyage home" (DDC I.10.13). No sooner does he use this metaphor, however, than he takes it back, for he observes in the next sentence: "But we do not come to Him who is everywhere present by moving from place to place" (DDC I.10.13). As Augustine implies, the danger of the journey metaphor is that it suggests a correlation between physical and spiritual place. Christ had said "I am the way," but Augustine enjoins us to read His words correctly and to reject the notion of spatial movement as well as that of time, without which no journey, at least in the "fleshy" sense of the word, can be accomplished. So important is this point that he returns to it several times within the space of a few pages. The road we travel is not, he says, "a road from place to place but a road of the affections" (DDC I.17.16) that was blocked by original sin, preventing us from reaching Him. Christ's crucifixion removed this obstacle, and we can now return to God. Clarifying in yet another passage his concept of the journey metaphor, Augustine notes: "Thus He is said to have

41. Pellegrini stressed Marguerite's debt to Dante and Petrarch. See Pellegrini, *La prima opera di Margherita di Navarra e la terza rima in Francia*, op. cit., and "Riflessi di cultura italiana in Margherita di Navarre," in *Tradizione italiana e cultura europea* (Messina: Anna, 1947); Henri Hauvette, "Dante dans la poésie française de la renaissance," in *Etudes sur la Divine comédie* (Paris: Champion, 1922), pp. 144–87; Jourda, *Marguerite d'Angoulême*, pp. 372–73; Sckommodau, *Die religiösen Dichtungen . . .*, p. 49. Robert J. Clements, "Marguerite de Navarre and Dante," *Italica*, 18 (1941), pp. 37–50 points out that all of Marguerite's allusions to Dante are to the first five cantos of the *Inferno*. He argues that the influence of Dante on Marguerite has been exaggerated.

come to us, not from place to place through space, but by appearing to mortals in mortal flesh. *He came to a place where He was already*, for He was in the world, and the world was made by Him" (DDC I.12.14). On the rational level of comprehension the sentence "He came to a place where He was already" makes no sense at all. It is an affront to logic and to all our normal processes of reasoning, which take us from one point to another in sequential fashion. While seeming to announce spatial displacement ("He came . . ."), the sentence in fact denies the sequential implications contained in the verb "came" and declares, contrary to all logic, that He *arrived* at the place He had never left. There is a sense, then, in which the Christian never *progresses* toward Christ, for to follow Christ's way is to have already arrived at the destination. Desire and enjoyment are con-fused (welded together) and con-founded (mixed together, from Latin *confundo*). We touch here upon one of the Pseudo-Dionysius' most important contributions to the mystical tradition: his elaboration of the concept of God as both transcendent and immanent. To the extent that we perceive God as being transcendent, we cross over to Him; but to the degree that we view Him as being immanent we cannot move toward Him, for He is inseparable from ourselves. For the Pseudo-Dionysius, God's transcendence and immanence are the same fact. This means that in one sense motion and rest are the same thing. Because our "fleshy eyes" require signs, the emblem best able to signify the Christian way is not a straight line moving from here to there but a circle, which has neither beginning nor end.[42]

How can narrative relate the spiritual experience of the followers of Christ except by frustrating the reader's desire to follow a clearly delineated progression toward a conclusion? How

---

42. We shall return to the notion of circularity. Koenigsberger, p. 127, discusses the inadequacy of a straight line to represent Cusanus' concept of knowledge, derived in part from that of the Pseudo-Dionysius: ". . . Cusanus used his unusual immanent and transcendent deity to make the concept of knowledge non-directional. Men might descend to God at the essence of things or rise up to him; they could reach out to God and move in to him. For, God is both the essence and end of all things; in the cosmos He is centre and circumference, all in all and all all at once. In this case the knowing process is not just a simple ascent from particulars to conclusions, nor is it an ascent moving away from the particulars of experience to an inner psychic territory of spiritual insight. Instead it runs a curious zig-zag course between the senses and the various capacities of the mind, from particulars to conclusions, from conclusions to desire, from desire to perfected notions, from the multiplicity of these notions to a further desire for simplicity."

can it convey the truth except by refusing to trace out a path that leads, like the words on the page, "from place to place"? How can narrative deny the notions of linearity and sequentiality to which it owes its existence and, by turning the reader away from itself, metacommunicate the true meaning of Christ's words "I am the way"? These questions are implicit in the conversation between Marguerite and Charlotte in the *Dialogue*. They become the focus of concern in Marguerite's next poem, *Le Petit Oeuvre dévot et contemplatif.*

4

Spiritual Exercises

The *Petit Oeuvre* was not published until the twentieth century. Using a manuscript that is in the Bibliothèque Nationale, Eugène Parturier prepared an edition of the *Petit Oeuvre* that appeared in 1904.[43] Since no title is indicated in the manuscript, Parturier called the poem *Récit de la conversion*. He was apparently unaware of the fact that another manuscript of Marguerite's poem existed in the Bibliothèque de l'Arsenal. In 1960, Sckommodau published a critical edition of the poem based on the Arsenal manuscript, which differs in a number of ways from the copy in the Bibliothèque Nationale. In the Arsenal manuscript, the poem bears a title that is written on the first page in red ink: *Petit Oeuvre dévot et contemplatif / composé par la royne de Navarre*.

The poem is a first-person account of a laborious journey. Traveling through desert and forest, the narrator (once again we shall call her Marguerite) was overcome by despair and fell to the ground. After some time, she heard in her heart a voice urging her on. She lifted her head and saw a man who gave her a crucifix (61–62). She contemplated Christ's image for some time and then, raising her eyes, noticed on her right a large wooden cross. Embracing it, she acknowledged the errors of her past life and underwent an experience analogous to the *illuminatio* experienced by mystics. Restored in spirit, she continued on her journey, determined to follow the way of the cross. The road led

43. *Revue de la Renaissance*, 4 (1904), 108–114, 178–90, 273–80. For a discussion of the manuscripts of the *Petit Oeuvre*, see Sckommodau's edition: *Petit Oeuvre dévot et contemplatif*, op. cit. Quotations of the *Petit Oeuvre* are identified by the line numbers given in the Sckommodau edition.

out of the barren desert and threatening forest into a broad, pleasant meadow, identified as "la plaine de consolation" (153) [the meadow of consolation]. At this point, her heart was pierced with love and she fell to her knees to worship the cross, which, being both far and near, was the same one she had seen earlier. (The present verb tense now replaces past tenses in the text.) After completing her prayer (230–430), Marguerite realizes that she has not yet reached her destination. Although she does not want to leave the cross behind, she feels she is too weak to carry it. Hearing a sound, she turns and notices a figure "portant / Croix en travail et merveilleuse peine" (418–82) [carrying a cross with great effort and in extreme sorrow]. Filled with pity, she recognizes Christ, who says to her: "Viendrez vous pas?" (540) [Will you not come?]. Marguerite answers that she will follow Him. Thereupon, she takes up the three crosses she must bear: the black cross of repentance, the white cross of patience, and the red cross of compassion. Keeping her eyes on Him who passes on ahead, she vows to continue on her way, which is now identical with His way.

The *Petit Oeuvre* has a distinctive structural feature. The verse form used throughout most of the poem's 593 lines is the *terza rima*. Fourteen lines, however, do not follow this pattern. Lines 115–119 form a quatrain (*a b a b*) that interrupts momentarily the flow of tercets. Beginning again in line 119, the tercets proceed without further interruption until lines 440–443, which make up another quatrain (*a b a b*). Tercets are reinstituted in line 444 and continue until the final stanza of the poem. In Sckommodau's edition, the last stanza is printed as if it were a sestet (558–593). The rhyme scheme is *a a b a a b*, which means that the sestet can be viewed as being composed of two tercets. These tercets do not, however, conform to the metrical form of the *terza rima*.

Interrupting the regular rhythm of the tercets, the quatrains divide the text into three parts, of which the first two end in quatrains and the third in a sestet. The quatrains draw attention to the poem's architectural design, to its form. They invite an interpretation that will "explain" their presence in the text. One might argue, for example, that they mark critical moments in Marguerite's journey. In the tercets just before the first quatrain, Marguerite, in a paroxysm of mystic fervor, embraces the cross, which is spotted with the bright red drops of Christ's blood. Beginning with the words "O que l'heure court tost . . ." (115) [O how time flies quickly], the quatrain signals the *illuminatio* that Marguerite experiences as she kneels and weeps before the cross. It represents a moment of suspension in the narrative flow of the text. Following the quatrain, the text resumes its normal course, and Marguerite gets up and continues on her journey. The second quatrain, too, would seem to mark a particularly important moment in the poem. The heart of the *Petit Oeuvre* is the long prayer, or *oraison*, of seventy-one stanzas that begins in line 230 with an adoration of the cross ("O digne bois . . .") [O worthy wood] and ends with the quatrain of lines 441–43. To make sure that the reader sees in the quatrain the conclusion of the prayer, the first line of the tercet that follows it stresses the fact that the *oraison* is now over: "Contraincte fuz de finir ma harengue" (444) [I was forced to conclude my oration]. According to this reading, the quatrains, then, mark moments of intense mystical experience.

A more careful reading, however, reveals that other moments of *illuminatio* and intense mystical experience are expressed in *terza rima*. Even in the case of the first quatrain, it could be argued that Marguerite begins to relate her illumination in the tercet that precedes the quatrain and then continues her account of that experience throughout the two tercets that follow the quatrain. The narrative line and the journey metaphor are not clearly picked up again until tercet 125–27. Although the appearance of the quatrain calls attention to a particular moment in the text, the significance of that moment is not clear, for the message conveyed in the quatrain is conveyed with equal force in the two succeeding stanzas, which are tercets. As for the second quatrain, the final couplet ("Le vous offrant, Seigneur, tout à present / Par vraye amour et bonne voulenté.") [Offering it to you, Lord, here and now through true love and a willing heart.] does indeed suggest the end of a prayer, but only because we *know* it is, thanks to the first line of the next stanza. Throughout the course of the prayer, several lines suggest the beginning of a conclusion: "Bref, je ne veulx avoir autre desir" (320) [In brief, I do not wish to have any other desire]; and, even more powerfully, "Doncque, Seigneur, . . ." (365) [Therefore, Lord, . . .]. In each of these cases, the text raises an expectation it does not fulfill. The real conclusion of the prayer, however, does not begin with *bref* or *doncque*. It announces its presence by a sign (the form

of the quatrain itself) of such uncertain meaning that the reader
does not know he has read the end of the prayer until the next line
tells him so. In short, the poem's most striking formal feature—
the division of the text into three distinct parts—loses importance for the reader as he moves through the poem.

This reduction of the poem's formal design to insignificance is
part of the work's message: the things we see with carnal eyes
become inconsequential when seen with spiritual eyes. By sub-
verting the meaning that the graphics of the text imply, the
poem urges the reader to abandon his confidence in the faculty
of sight and invites him to replace it with the blindness of insight. It is significant that the tercets are interrupted by quatrains rather than by couplets or five-line stanzas. Both the
number three and the number four have precise symbolic meanings. Originating in the Pythagorean notion that the physical
world is composed of four elements (fire, water, earth, and air),
the tetrad was a symbol of the physical world[44] whereas the triad
was a symbol of God. In the quatrains, Marguerite reflects on
her temporal condition. Signifying the flesh, the quatrains are
submerged in the flow of tercets, which are a graphic representation of the trinitarian principle and symbolize the spirit that
pulverizes the world of physical forms.

Subversion of its form is not the only strategy the text uses to
lead the reader away from the physical world and toward God,
whom the Pseudo-Dionysius defined as "Formlessness Itself"
(*Div. Names* 89).[45] It undermines the vocabulary of spatiality
and temporality implicit in the metaphor of a journey. Subvert-
ing its own narrativity, it asks the reader to turn away from the
interpretative direction suggested by the journey metaphor and
to take to heart Augustine's insight that Christ's way "is not
a road from place to place but a road of the affections" (DDC

---

44. On the significance of the number four and the Pythagorean tetrad, see S. K.
Heninger, Jr., *The Cosmographical Glass. Renaissance Diagrams of the Universe* (San Ma-
rino, California: The Huntington Library, 1979), pp. 99–106. See also Vincent Foster
Hooper, *Medieval Number Symbolism* (1938; rpt. New York: Cooper Square Publishers,
Inc., 1969), pp. 83–84.

45. The Pseudo-Dionysius observes: "Now if the Good is above all things (as indeed
It is) Its Formless Nature produces all-form; and in It alone Not-Being is an excess of
Being, and Lifelessness an excess of Life and Its Mindless state is an excess of Wisdom,
and all the Attributes of the Good we express in a transcendent manner by negative
images."

I.17.16). To see how this is so, we must examine the text in greater detail.

The *Petit Oeuvre* opens in the allegorical mode:

1   Au grant desert de folle accoustumance,
        Dans le buisson de tribulation,
        En la forest de peu de congnoissance,

        Pourmenee par jeune affliction,
        Puis ça puis là laissant la seure sente,
5   M'arresta court consideration

        En me disant: "Tourne ailleurs ton entente,
        Car tu n'as pas tenu le chemin seur,
        Là ou tu doys affermer ton actente."

10   Alors senty un tremblement de cueur
        En regardant l'aspreté d'un buisson,
        Dont le pencer renouvelle la peur.

        Quant j'entendiz que sonnoit la leçon,
        Je congneuz bien que trop avant j'estois
15   Ou de l'entrer j'obliay la façon.

        Mon oeil partout et loing et pres gectois,
        Mais remede ne voyois d'en saillir,
        Dont en regret plus avant me mectois.

        Branches, ronces prindrent à m'assaillir,
20   Et espines me picquerent si fort
        Que je sentiz ma force deffaillir.

        A l'heure feiz de terre reconfort
        M'y laissant cheoir, pour mon appuy la pris,
        En desirant secours ou brefve mort.

In the great desert of foolish habit, in the thicket of tribulation, in the forest of little understanding, led along by fresh affliction, I was straying, now here, now there, from the sure path when a thought made me stop short, saying to me: "Turn your mind elsewhere, for you have not kept to the sure road, there where you ought to walk firmly." Then I felt a trembling in my heart while looking at the sharpness of a thorny thicket, the thought of which renews my fear. When I heard the message, I realized I had strayed too far or had forgotten how to reach the path. I looked around everywhere, far and near, but saw no solution, and so, with regret, continued onward. Branches and brambles set about attacking me, and thorns stuck into me with such force that I felt my strength failing. Then, letting myself fall, I made the earth my solace; I used it as my support, desiring assistance or quick death.

Echoes of Dante reverberate throughout the first few pages of Marguerite's poem. The metrical form is, of course, that of the *Divine Comedy*. Occasionally, Marguerite's lines are paraphrases of lines in Dante's poem, as, for example, line twelve which is Marguerite's rendering of "Chel nel pensier rinnova la paura" (*Inferno* I.6). Like Dante, Marguerite moves through a landscape whose features are allegorical representations of the world through which the soul must pass.

As a mode of discourse, allegory has certain characteristics that are important in Marguerite's text. Quintilian provided the classical definition of allegory:

Allegory, which is translated in Latin by *inversio*, either presents one thing in words and another in meaning, or else something absolutely opposed to the meaning of the words. The first type is generally produced by a series of metaphors [46]. . . . On the other hand, that class of allegory in which the meaning is contrary to that suggested by the words, involves an element of irony, or, as our rhetoricians call it, *illusio*. [47]

In allegory, then, the words say one thing and point to something else. This is the basic definition of metaphor. Indeed, in early books on rhetoric, allegory tended to be viewed as an extended metaphor. [48] What the words "say" is the first, or literal, meaning (Marguerite was lost in the woods.) and what they "point to" is the second, or allegorical, meaning. It follows that allegory is inherently temporal, for allegorical meaning is produced by the reader's perception of a meaning that is different

46. *Institutio oratoria*, Loeb Classical Library (Cambridge, Mass.: Harvard University Press, 1967), 8, 327 (VI.44).

47. Ibid., 8, 333 (VI.53).

48. For a general discussion of allegory, see Angus Fletcher, *Allegory: The Theory of a Symbolic Mode* (Ithaca: Cornell University Press, 1964), pp. 1–23. See also Northrop Frye, *Anatomy of Criticism* (1957; rpt. New York: Atheneum, 1965), pp. 89–91 *et passim*.

from and posterior to the literal meaning. Paul de Man has called our attention to this essential aspect of allegory. "In the world of allegory," he observed, "time is the original constitutive category."[49] Speaking of the relationship between the allegorical sign and its meaning (the signified), he notes that "if there is to be allegory, [it is necessary] that the allegorical sign refer to another sign that precedes it."[50] Thus, in line eight of the *Petit Oeuvre* allegorical meaning is produced when we see in the words "chemin seur" a sign that refers to an anterior sign, i.e., Christ's way. "The meaning constituted by the allegorical sign," de Man continues, "can consist only in the *repetition* (in the Kierkegaardian sense of the term) of a previous sign with which it can never coincide, since it is the essence of this previous sign to be pure anteriority." Designating a distance in relation to the sign to which it refers, allegory "establishes its language in the void of this temporal difference. In so doing, it prevents the self from an illusory identification with the non-self, which is now fully, though painfully, recognized as a non-self."[51]

Marguerite's poem opens at the moment in which the self becomes aware of its distance from Christ. When the narrator addresses herself with the words "Tu n'as pas tenu le chemin seur," she is allegorizing her journey, seeing in it a sign that refers to another sign (Christ's way) with which it cannot coincide. The *Petit Oeuvre* is a spiritual exercise by means of which Marguerite strives to make her way coincide with Christ's. At the level of linguistic discourse, this effort is translated into an attempt to replace allegorical speech, which is the language of distance and difference, with a speech that postulates the possibility of identity and coincidence.

Because the fundamental element in the production of allegorical meaning is time (the allegorical meaning *follows* the literal), allegory always tends toward narrative. The reader perceives the events that succeed each other in narrative as being sequential and, consequently, as stretching out along a line that moves forward through time. Since nothing can move forward

49. "The Rhetoric of Temporality," in *Interpretation: Theory and Practice*, ed. Charles S. Singleton (Baltimore: The Johns Hopkins Press, 1964), p. 190.
50. Ibid.
51. Ibid., p. 191.

unless there is a place to move to, space is the second essential element in narrative. In fact, the reader's perception of narrative depends on his ability to situate events in time and space. The language of narrative tends, therefore, to be emphatically referential.

A striking feature of the first 180 or so lines of the *Petit Oeuvre* is the precision and insistence with which the text establishes temporal and spatial relationships. As the poem opens, we see Marguerite, who is "pourmenee par jeune affliction" (4). "Puis ça puis là laissant la seure sente," (5) she stops. The first twenty-four lines of the poem are filled with adverbs and conjunctives that link events together in a tightly sequential fashion, fixing the narrative as a linear, diachronic axis. The progressive, forward-moving pattern of the *terza rima* provides a metrical underpinning to the linear thrust of the narrative. Marguerite's progress in the first part of the poem is marked by continual stops and starts. Stopping suddenly with the realization that she is not on the right road (6), she feels faint (23), recovers somewhat (25), and, raising her eyes (49), hails a passerby (53). Momentarily the narrative line passes to the stranger, who approaches (57) and then begins to speak to her. Marguerite does not relate the passerby's words (the man may well represent Briçonnet), but does say that "il eut à moy long propoz et langaige / Tout en vertuz" (58–59) [he spoke to me at great length, all in goodness]. Before leaving, he gives her a crucifix on which is painted "l'ymaige vraye de pure charité" (62) [the true image of pure love]. He continues on his journey (74). Marguerite, however, remains where she is, meditating on the meaning of the crucifixion (76–78). Looking up (82), she sees a cross and tries to move toward it (96). She falls to her knees (109) and embraces it (110). Somewhat restored, she gets up (126) and continues on her way (127). The text here draws attention to her progress: "Lors je marchay" (131) [Then I walked]; "Je m'advançay pour saillir lors du terme" (134) [I moved forward then to leap beyond the road]; "De cheminer feiz si bien mon debvoir" (137) [I made it my duty to walk]. Arriving in the "plaine de consolation" (144), she feels her heart filled with love and, falling silent, prostrates herself on the ground before Him (183).

As well as being situated at a particular time along the temporal continuum of the narrative line, each of these stops and starts occurs in a place that is made specific by the presence of discrete objects. A desert, a thicket, a forest, branches, brambles, and thorns fill the landscape in which the first event of the poem takes place. The birds and plants that flourish here are cruel and baneful. The pilgrim cannot survive in such a place. "Passay des nuictz et jours si longuement / Que la frisson de la fievre m'en dure" (37–38) [I passed so many long nights and days that I still tremble with fever]. The objects that fill the space in which succeeding events occur are specified with equal care. The passerby to whom Marguerite speaks is characterized by his "voix vive" (49) [lively voice], which is phonetically very close to *foi vive* [living faith]. The crucifix becomes, of course, a privileged object within the landscape of the poem, looming ever larger until it merges into the shape of "ung grant arbre en forme d'une croix" (89) [a large tree in the form of a cross]. This cross, which is the focus of Marguerite's attention, is particularized by the drops of blood with which it is spotted. Here Marguerite's language is remarkably graphic. The bright red spots that "decorate" (104) the huge cross are like pearls. As the description continues, the tree becomes a kind of *meraviglia* in the sense that art historians use the word to designate the finely executed artifacts that were meant to please and astound wealthy Renaissance patrons.[52] The word "merveille" in the next line ("Si je plouray, ce n'est pas de merveille," 105) [If I wept, it was no wonder] underscores the response that the cross provokes in the viewer. By presenting the cross as a concrete object that can be seen with the carnal eyes, the text stresses the *out-thereness* of the crucifixion. By virtue of its conspicuous referentiality, the language of the first part of the *Petit Oeuvre* creates the temporal and spatial dimensions essential to allegory and narrative.

As well as being referential, language in the opening section of the *Petit Oeuvre* is conspicuously *self*-referential. It refers back to itself repeatedly, pointing out its own distinguishing features, one of the most important being the regular displacement of monologic by dialogic discourse. The first-person narrative is often interrupted by another voice, that of the narrator's heart or of a second person. The words of the "other" voice are almost always presented in direct discourse. They are introduced with a phrase such as "En me disant" (7) [Saying to myself], which

52. For a discussion of *meraviglie* in art, see John Shearman, *Mannerism* (London: Penguin, 1967), pp. 144–46.

calls attention to the shift from monologue to dialogue. Whereas the referentiality of the language serves to affirm the presence of the world of discrete things (the world we usually think of as "real"), the self-referentiality of the language affirms the presence, or reality, of discourse.

There is a delicately plotted concordance between the self-referential language at the beginning of the *Petit Oeuvre* and the narrator's search for Christ. Since Christ lives in the heart, we can find Him only through a process of increasing self-awareness. *Purgatio*, the starting point of the Christian's journey, is basically the soul's gradual recognition of its own true nature.[53] The paradox is that this process of self-recognition leads the soul away from the physical world that is evoked by means of referential language, away from texts marked by self-referentiality. Increased awareness of self, which leads to the realization that Christ lives in man's heart, makes it more and more difficult for Marguerite to represent the *via Christi* as a journey from place to place along an axis of spatiality and temporality. To the self that moves toward illumination, space and time are elements that appear more and more illusory.

As Marguerite becomes increasingly aware of the presence of Christ, narrative becomes an inadequate mode through which to express her experience. The insufficiency of narrative is translated in the text by the frequent and ever longer halts that mark the pilgrim's laborious advance along the road depicted in the first part of the *Petit Oeuvre*. When the "I" stops moving forward, the language of the text can no longer spread out along the spatial and temporal axis of narrative. It must "turn elsewhere" ("tourne ailleurs"), as Marguerite specifies as early as line seven. Where it eventually turns is revealed to the reader little by little.

In line forty-six, Marguerite announces abruptly that she hears a voice in her heart: "Car dans mon coeur j'ouyz raison qui dist: . . ." [For in my heart I hear reason saying . . .]. This voice addresses her directly, urging her to continue her journey.

---

53. Joseph E. Milosh, *The Scale of Perfection and the English Mystical Tradition* (Madison, Wisc.: University of Wisconsin Press, 1966) observes that "the beginning of the soul's progress comes with its realization of its own nature" (p. 89). Butler calls Purgation "that process of self-discipline and reformation and readjustment of character which is the necessary preparation for entry into the higher degrees of the spiritual life." *Western Mysticism*, pp. 27–28.

At this point in the text, the passerby appears. He is a kind of John the Baptist announcing the imminent arrival of Christ. The fact that he appears to Marguerite at all indicates the spiritual progress she has made, for he can appear only to those who have been prepared by the experience of *purgatio* to receive Christ. Marguerite does not relate the stranger's words. She does tell us, however, that "il eut à moy long propoz et langaige / Tout en vertuz" (59) [he spoke to me at great length, all in goodness]. She then adds the words: "mais le taire en est beau" (59) [but it is well to be silent about it]. Marguerite assures us that the man's "parler" was "si saige et vertueux, / Qu'il esclarcit tenebres d'ignorance" (68–69) [so wise and virtuous that he lightened up the shadows of ignorance]. "L'ouyr parler," she insists, "me fut si prouffitable / Qu'il fut cause si depuis valuz mieulx" (71–72) [To listen to him speak was so profitable for me that if I have been worth more since, it was because of him].

If Marguerite does not record the man's words, it is because his "parler," however encouraging it may have been, is less precious than the "ymaige" he gave her. His true gift to her, the consequences of which are revealed in the course of the poem, is the understanding that words fall silent before the image. The text that would express Christian truth must deny discourse (both in the sense of reason and of speech) and seek to become an icon. Overwhelmed by this insight, Marguerite remains motionless and speechless. Although "l'ymaige" she holds before her is a kind of text, she does not "read" it. She "contemplates" it, which is an altogether different matter.

Marguerite does not remain silent for long. "Ma voix haulsay, faisant humble request / Au Dieu" (83–84) [My voice rose up, making a humble request to God], she writes. She now addresses her words not to the reader who sees the text with carnal eyes but to God. As the text shifts momentarily away from narrative to what Augustine calls "true eloquence" (DDC IV.1–6.117–24), i.e., prayer, there is a sudden change in verb tenses. Verbs in the past tenses are for a moment replaced by verbs in the present tense (87–88). This change is not permanent. In verse eighty-nine, the narrative line begins again, and verbs in the past tenses reappear. The reader has, however, seen the direction in which the text will move, that is to say, away from narrative and toward prayer.

Although narrative is resumed, it now focuses on Marguerite's attempt to approach the large cross she sees before her. More explicitly than elsewhere in the poem, the narrative at this point reflects the unfolding of desire. The climactic *illuminatio* results in another turning inward toward self, which is represented at the level of discourse by a halt in narrative thrust and by the intrusion of dialogue:

128   Tout à part moy, dans mon cueur, je disoye:
       "Ny pour mourir de travail et de peine
       N'auray repoz que hors d'icy ne soye."

Secretly to myself, in my heart, I kept saying: "In order not to die of effort and grief, I will have no rest until I am out of here."

In the next line, the narrative starts up again with renewed force ("Lors je marchay"), and Marguerite, "par le moyen de la croix" (138) [by way of the cross] makes her way out of the desert and through the forest, arriving at the "plaine de consolation" (153). In a sense, this is as far as the narrative line of the poem can take her. Moving forward on a spatial and temporal axis through language whose referential fixity is reinforced by the rhetoric of self-referentiality, narrative reaches an impasse. Wishing to talk to Him about herself, Marguerite prepared a speech she intended to deliver before the cross (179–81). As she approached the cross, however, she fell silent. Marguerite's silence signals a crisis in narrative discourse. Beginning in tercet 182–84 and continuing throughout the next three tercets, the text reorients itself and compels language to serve a function different from the narrative function it had served in the first 184 lines of the poem:

       Parquoy pensay et feiz tout mon discours
180   De remonstrer mon tant piteux affaire
       Et m'advancer, puis que mes jours sont cours.

       Mais je ne sceuz autre chose que faire
       Fors prosterner à terre mon visaige;
       Car joye et dueil par amour me font taire.

185   Ung peu apres, reprins force et couraige
       En la vertu de celluy qui m'a fait
       Parler françois et laisser mon ramaige.

> D'un langaige nayf, non contrefaict,
> Partant de cueur, qui n'eust peu supporter
190 Amour sans mort, l'a celee en effect,
>
> A haulte voix, pour me reconforter
> Je diz ung peu, non tout ce qu'elle chante;
> Plus ne la peuz sans parler supporter.

Thereupon I reflected and prepared my whole speech to show my pitiable state. And I moved forward, since my days are short. But I was not able to do anything except prostrate myself facedown on the ground; for joy and sorrow make me fall silent through love. After a little while, I regained strength and took heart in the virtue of him who made me speak French and led me out of the wood. In a natural language, not counterfeit, coming from the heart, which, being unable to bear love without dying, had concealed it, I spoke out loud, a little to comfort myself, not saying everything that love was singing in my heart; no longer could I bear this love without speaking.

Before the cross, language is inadequate. Silence alone, which the Pseudo-Dionysius called the negative image of speech, can represent the Christian's experience of Christ's way.[54] With line 184 ("Car joye et dueil par amour me font taire"), the language that had served up to this point in the poem ceases to be operative. Parturier and Sckommodau were both disturbed by a certain syntactical imprecision in the next two stanzas (185–190).[55] The grammatical armature of these sentences is less secure than the demands of logic would require. But the meaning is clear: the demise of the old, inadequate language is followed by the birth of a new language that is better able to transmit the experience of charity. A reader who, like Augustine, delights in transform-

---

54. Cf. Bovelle's statement, written in 1501: "Le silence parle, et les voix se taisent" [Silence speaks, and voices become silent]. Cited in Marguerite de Navarre, *Chansons spirituelles*, ed. Georges Dottin, TLF (Geneva: Droz, 1971). p. xlvi. Dottin reminds us that Zwingli banished from the religious service all prayers that were read aloud and replaced them with silent prayer (p. xlvi). The medieval English contemplative, Walter Hilton, in *The Scale of Perfection*, ed. Evelyn Underhill (1923; rpt. 1948, London: J. M. Watkins) speaks of three "manners of prayer." The first is "prayer of speech made specifically of God as is the *Pater noster*" (1.26, p. 46). The second manner is also "by speech, but it is not by any certain special saying" (1.29, p. 49), by which Hilton means that the soul, "wounded with the sword of love," now finds its own words. Dispensing with words altogether, "the third manner of prayer is only in the heart without speech, by great rest and softness of the body and of the soul" (1.32, p. 53).

55. Parturier, op. cit., 184. Sckommodau, *Die religiösen Dichtungen . . .*, p. 52.

ing textual "flaws" into virtues (DDC II.6.37–38), may be inclined to see in this syntactical confusion a reflection of the linguistic chaos that results from the destruction of an old language. Out of this destruction, however, a new language arises. What Marguerite has done here is to transfer to language the Pauline notion, repeated often by Briçonnet, that Christ's crucifixion marks the death of the old man (Adam) in us and the birth of the new (Christ).

The new language will be "nayf, non contrefaict" and will come from the heart, which expresses its love in song. It is not clear whether the pronoun "elle," which is the subject of "chante," is the cross or love, but it does not matter because the two are synonymous. Marguerite's heart is so filled with love that she can no longer remain silent. The language she now speaks is, however, radically different from the discursive language that dominated the first part of the poem:

> "Bien que indigne suis, et telle me sente,
> De lever l'oeil en hault pour regarder
> Vostre bonté tant grande et excellente,
>
> Si viens à vous et ne m'en puis garder
> Tout maintenant. . . .

195

Although I am unworthy—and feel myself so—to raise my eyes to look upon your goodness, so great and excellent, I cannot stop myself from doing it now. . . .

The dominant verb tense in the rest of the poem is the present tense, which fixes the temporal framework of the last four hundred lines of the text. Christ *is*, and a text designed to reflect Him will make little use of verbs in the past tenses, for they suggest a human organization of time that is totally meaningless to Him who is outside time. He is also outside space, and, as we might expect, Marguerite's language loses some of its referentiality. Words designed to reflect Christ do not refer us to precise places or to the physical things that occupy space. They do not create a world that we are accustomed to call real. In the mystical tradition within which Marguerite wrote, Christ alone is real; the world of the flesh is illusory.

The rhetoric of self-referentiality, too, almost completely disappears from the text, which no longer comments directly on its own strategies. This lack of self-awareness is one of the characteristics of the "langaige nayf" that Marguerite will speak throughout the rest of the poem. The echoes of Dante in the first part of the *Petit Oeuvre* now take on new significance. They had helped to define the text as literary artifact, as "letter" as opposed to "spirit." The text's rejection of language that is "contrefaict" is also a rejection of its status as literature. Only twice in lines 184–593 does the text allude to its own discourse. In each case, it notes that language is unable to express the love that fills the Christian's heart (277 and 446). *La parolle* cannot represent the *Tout-Verbe*. Marguerite continues speaking, however, but only after making it clear to the reader that her words now refer to Christ and not to the physical world, which she no longer mistakes for reality.

Sentences and stanzas that, in the first part of the poem, had been syntactically linked with conjunctives, now follow each other paratactically as in a litany. "O digne bois, o venerable fust" [O worthy wood, o venerable staff], begins tercet 230. The next tercet begins with the words "O doulx arbre" (233) [O sweet tree]. A distinctive feature of the next several stanzas is the use of anaphora, a rhetorical device that consists of repeating the same word at the beginning of successive clauses. Anaphora is complemented by what one might call pseudo-anaphora, or the repetition of a synonym at the beginning of successive phrases. Thus consecutive stanzas begin with the words "Treshaulte palme" (242) [Very tall palm tree], "Doux olivier" (245) [Sweet olive tree], "Rosier" (248) [Rosebush], "O verd ramel" (251) [O green bough], "O grenadier" (254) [O pomegranate], "O boys tressec" (257) [O wood so dry]. Having connotations that extend beyond formal rhetoric, anaphora is peculiarly suited to Marguerite's purpose at this point in her poem. Cotgrave's first definition of anaphora is "an ascension of the planets from the East, by daily course of the firmament." His second is "a figure called Repetition, when two verses begin with one word." In addition to these meanings, anaphora also means the Eucharist. Etymologically, anaphora contains the idea of motion back up to an original source, for it is derived from Greek *ana*, meaning "up" or "back," and *pherein*, "to carry." Whether it is used to designate the Eucharistic service whereby the Christian is reunited with Christ, or the apparent ascension of planets in the

sky, or the repetition of words used "back up" in the text, anaphora always connotes some kind of upward motion. Anaphora
appears in Marguerite's text when language loses its referential
fixity, when narrative, which may be conceptualized as extending along a syntagmatic axis, ceases to be an adequate mode of
expression. The text changes direction and begins to move
along a vertical, or paradigmatic, axis. Declaring that her language will henceforth be "nayf, non contrefaict," Marguerite
indicates the new direction that the text will take by stressing ascending movement. The use of anaphora is a strategy by
which she redefines the Christian way as an ascent.

In the stanzas that follow the anaphoric verses mentioned
above, the text continues to stress verticality. Addressing Christ,
Marguerite says, for example: "Par ta haulteur chaucun te voit
et mire" (260) [Because of your height everyone can see you and
look at you]. When Christ speaks near the end of the poem, He
tells those who would follow Him that His way is upward:

> Ne vueillez plus à peché devaller,
> 535   Je vays devant montant; or suyvez moy,
> Et a peché vous fault voille caller:
>
> Tout au plus hault je planteray le may.
> . . . .

Desire no longer to go down to sin; I go before you, ascending; follow
me; and you must let sin float away from you. At the highest point, I
shall set the stake.

Nevertheless, after the long prayer that ends in line 443, there is
a momentary return to narrative. The journey metaphor is re-
introduced with the following verses:

> Mais je n'y puis demeurer à loysir,
> Car le brief temps que j'ay, et long voyaige
> 455   Du despartir font du regret desir.

But I cannot remain here in idleness, for the little time I have and the
long journey transform my regret at leaving into desire to be gone.

Verbs slip back into the past tense as Marguerite resumes her
way. But the syntagmatic thrust of narrative is openly subverted,

first by the non-referentiality of the language, which fails to articulate sequentiality, and second by the constant intrusion of verbs in the present tense, which disrupt temporal flow and deny progress.

Pausing in her journey, Marguerite makes a statement that illuminates the problems of narrative language:

> Mon cueur, mon corps, mon esperit refait
> 460   Sont par elle [the cross]. Bref, si jamais riens vaulx,
> Elle seulle en est cause en effect.

My heart, my body, my spirit are remade by the cross. In short, if ever I am worth something, it alone is in effect the cause.

Reality has a double structure. It has a surface level on which cause and effect are matters of sequence and contiguity. Narrative discourse can adequately represent this level. But reality also has a deeper (or higher or more profound) level on which the accidents of time and space are incidental to true causality, which is the Word, or as Marguerite says, the Cross. Revelation of the Word through the Cross is both the cause and effect of the reality that Marguerite desires. And this reality *is*. It *is* in the "nowness" of the present, that is to say, in the "nowness" of the text. One cannot progress toward it because it informs the structure of everything. It is God, of whom Paul wrote: "All that exists comes from him; all is by him and for him" (Romans 11.36). The closest language can come to representing It (or Him) is through negative images, that is, through language that on one level establishes an axis of cause and effect, of progress, and then on another discredits its own rhetoric and denies all claims to sequentiality. Only a text whose language is antiprogressive can convey some notion of the reality that is God. The very tenuousness of the narrative line that appears after the long central prayer serves to emphasize the fact that narrative represents the surface level of reality. As the poem draws to a close, narrative disappears, leaving in its stead an antiprogressive mode of discourse designed to expose the deeper level of reality.

The poem ends in jubilation. Throughout the final stanzas, Marguerite sees in Christ an *exemplum*, a paradigm that will henceforth be her model. "A l'exemple de ses vertuz, tout droit! / Que sur chemin nous laisse pour montjoye!" (570–71) [Following the example of his virtues, straight onward! May he keep us on the road, for his sake, our joy!]. She uses the word *chemin* two more times in the next few lines. At the beginning of the poem, she had admonished herself to turn from the wrong way. "Tourne ailleurs ton entente" (7) [Turn your mind elsewhere], she had told herself. To illustrate this turning away from the wrong way, the text reduces its syntagmatic thrust and organizes its language along a paradigmatic axis. The final image of the poem is of "celluy qui fut, est, et sera sans per" (590) [he who was, is, and will be, without peer], a line that echoes Revelations 4.8 ("He was, he is and he is to come."). Marguerite locates Christ's way outside time and space, in a perpetual "now"[56] that is situated, to cite the concluding words of the poem, "en nostre cueur . . . nunc et semper" (593) [in our heart . . . now and always]. The final words of the poem are in Latin, which, unlike French, exists beyond the limitations of time and space. To express the soul's joyful union with Christ the paradigm, Marguerite's text moves "beyond" French and into Latin, the language *sans per* that, within the economy of the poem, is the paradigm of linguistic performance.

"QUICKEN THINE HEART BY PRAYER"[57]

Christ's way is that of the revealed Word operating within the heart. As long as the *Petit Oeuvre* moves along the syntagmatic axis of narrative and allegory, we read the poem in terms of a journey from place to place. But when the text abandons the syntagmatic for the paradigmatic way, our perception of the poem changes. No longer are we constrained to experience the text as a road along which we travel. Rather, we are now invited to see it as a place, a site, a temple (the last word of the title, *contemplatif*, contains the idea of temple) in which the devout can contemplate the revealed Word, which is always present, *nunc et semper*. If the language of narrative and allegory is determined by the

---

56. Meister Eckhart spoke of the *Now* moment, which contains all time within the present: "To say that God created the world yesterday or tomorrow would be foolishness, for God created the world and everything in it in the one present *Now*. Indeed time that has been past for a thousand years is as present and near to God as the time that is now. . . ." *Meister Eckhart*, trans. Raymond B. Blakney (New York: Harper and Brothers, 1941), Sermon 25, "Get Beyond Time," p. 214.
57. The words are by Walter Hilton, *The Scale of Perfection*, 1.25, p. 43.

experience of temporality, that of prayer is controlled by the experience of Christ as ultimate reality. It is not surprising that Marguerite, in an attempt to remain as long as possible in the temple of contemplation, wrote a number of poems in which the language of diachrony, of narrative and allegory, is reduced to a minimum. Such a poem is the *Oraison de l'âme fidèle, à son seigneur Dieu*, which may be thought of as an elaboration of the prayer that occupies the central place in the *Petit Oeuvre*.

Unlike the *Dialogue* and the *Petit Oeuvre*, the *Oraison de l'âme fidèle* was published in the 1547 edition of the *Marguerites*. According to Jourda, it was probably written before 1531, but for reasons we do not know it did not appear in the 1531 or 1533 editions of *Le Miroir*. A longer poem than either the *Dialogue* or the *Petit Oeuvre* (it has some 1500 lines compared to the 1293 of the *Dialogue* and the 593 of the *Petit Oeuvre*), the *Oraison* is followed in the first edition of the *Marguerites* by a second *Oraison*, which is called *Oraison à nostre Seigneur Jesus Christ*, a poem of some 500 lines that had first been published in *Le Miroir* (1531). The combined length of these two *Oraisons* gives particular prominence to the concept of prayer in the *Marguerites*.

The opening lines of the *Oraison de l'âme fidèle* describe a universe composed of two elements, spirit and matter.

> Seigneur, duquel le siege, sont les Cieux;
> Le marchepied, la terre, et ces bas lieux;
> Qui en tes bras encloz le firmament,
> Qui es toujours nouveau, antique et vieux,
> Rien n'est caché au regard des tes yeux. (p. 77)[58]

Lord, whose throne is the heavens, whose footstool, the earth and these low places; you who enclose the firmament in your arms, who are always new, ancient and old; nothing is hidden from the glance of your eyes.

In terms of sixteenth-century cosmography, Marguerite's description is not exceptional. Most books of the period that deal with cosmography contain diagrams showing the cosmos as a

---

58. Many of the poems in the *Marguerites* have not been reedited in modern editions. All citations from *Oraison de l'âme fidèle, à son seigneur* and *Oraison à nostre Seigneur Jesus Christ* are identified by page number in *Marguerites de la marguerite des princesses* (1547; rpt. The Hague: Johnson Reprint Corporation, 1970), Vol. 1.

pyramid with God at the topmost point and the earth at the base of the triangle.[59] Indeed, this cosmographical model was a convention and reflected the formula high/good:low/bad that resulted in part from the vulgarization of Platonic thought and from Augustine's concept of spiritual progress as a meditative ascent toward increasing awareness of Christ.

Combining Platonic and Christian notions in the syncretistic way typical of the Renaissance, Marguerite declares at the beginning of *l'Oraison de l'âme fidèle* that God ". . . formoit les Cieux par sa Parole, / Le feu et l'air, la Terre, et l'eaue tant molle" (p. 79) [made the heavens by his Word, fire, air, earth and water that is so soft]. In the diagrams that adorned Renaissance books on cosmography, Christ was often assimilated to the Platonic demiurge, who, as explained in the *Timaeus* (7.59.32B–C), created the four elements. The distinctly Christian aspect of Marguerite's depiction of God as the *opifex optimus*, or supreme creator, is the identification of the Johannine *logos* as the creative force. Ascribing paradigmatic status to the *Tout-Verbe*, Marguerite declares that God is an author: "O Jesus Christ . . . Tu es l'amy et le sage inventeur / De tirer Rien à son Tout et autheur" (p. 103) [O Jesus Christ . . . You are the friend and the wise inventor, to draw Nothing to its All, and author]. More striking is her assertion that He is a book: "Ce D I E U . . . / O, qu'il est cloz devant noz yeux ce Livre!" (p. 105) [This God, O how closed he is before our eyes, this Book!]. God is a text we cannot read until It is translated into Christ, the "tresvive Parole" (p. 106) [living Word], the "Verbe chair" (p. 107) [Word flesh]. Because Marguerite likens God's creation of the world to the production of a book, we may see in the opening lines of the *Oraison* not only a cosmographical model but also a model designed to reveal something of the morphology of the text.

The first two verses of the poem seem to fix the setting by establishing a space (high/low) that we can comprehend in terms of our experience of the empirical world. Lines three and four, however, subvert the referentiality of the preceding two verses and tell us that the concepts of spatiality and temporality

---

59. For a study of Renaissance works that deal with cosmography, see Heninger, *The Cosmographical Glass*, op. cit. See also Claude-Gilbert Dubois, *La Conception de l'histoire en France au XVIe siècle 1560–1610* (Paris: Nizet, 1977), Ch. 1, "La Création du monde."

that we bring with us from the world we call "real" are not operative here. For space, as we normally experience it, is an area within which there can be movement from one place to another. In line three, Marguerite stresses God's coincidence with His creation, which the reader is invited to experience in terms of closure ("en tes bras encloz") and containment. Since nothing exists outside God, there can be no "place" beyond this enclosure. Thus, in the world of the poem, there is only one place. At the beginning of the *Oraison*, Marguerite defines both God's creation and her own, i.e., the text, as temples, or spaces in which the divinity is always present. Time is as meaningless a concept in this world as space, which is what Marguerite says in line four.

In the context of the *Oraison*, "high" ("les Cieux") and "low" ("ces bas lieux") do not function referentially but paradigmatically. The division of the universe into a spiritual element on top and a material element on the bottom is a graphic representation of the dialectic between "I" and "thou" that is at the heart of the poem. "High" represents the "Seigneur," the addressee, whereas "low" stands for the speaker. And yet the thrust of the text is to deny this dialectic and to efface the difference between "I" and "thou." Once more we see the double structure of reality. The "I," representing the surface level of reality, is enfolded within the "thou," that higher level on which all the accidents of time and space are incidental to true causality, the *Tout-Verbe*.

The first four lines of the poem provide, then, a model that shows the self contained within Christ, whose timelessness and joy the "I" shares. In the text that extends throughout the hundreds of lines that follow, the speaker seeks to effect her union with Christ not by moving from place to place but by increasing her awareness of Christ's presence. The fact that Christ is present everywhere, *nunc et semper*, means that "les Cieux" and "les bas lieux" do not refer to points within a spatial continuum but to degrees of awareness of His presence in the world and in the heart, for the "I" contains the "thou" just as surely as, from a different perspective, the "thou" contains the "I."

Marguerite speaks of the self's union with Christ as a "mutation / De nous en toy" (p. 87) [mutation from us into you]. This transformation entails an effacement of the self, which Marguerite evokes in images of pulverization and liquefaction. Annihilation, whose equivalent in the spiritual life of the Christian is humility, is a necessary prelude to awareness of Christ's presence. When she comes to speak of the actual experience of the *unio*, Marguerite dwells on the mystery of the mutation of the "I" into the "thou" in an extended passage that begins:

> Ta grand' Amour, ô Pere et Createur,
> Quand tu l'uniz à nostre pesanteur,
> Nous fait saillir en la vie eternelle:
> Du centre embas jusques à la hauteur,
> Tu fais voler la facture, au facteur,
> Par la vertu de ta treslegere aesle:
> C'est ton Amour, dilection, et zele
> Dont tu remplis ceste celeste masse,
> En l'eslevant par divine estincelle
> Legerement, maugré sa terre basse.
> 　　Ta grand' beauté, ta clarté, ta lumiere,
> Nous vient chercher au fonds de la taniere,
> Pour convertir en beauté la laideur.
> Ceste union par tresdouce maniere
> Oste de nous ceste forme premiere
> Du vieil Adam, son feu et son ardeur,
> Sy laid et ord que c'estoit grand' hydeur:
> Mais par Amour est sy bien effacé
> Et nous repaintz et couvertz de splendeur,
> Que soubz beauté est Adam trespassé.　　(pp. 87–88)

Your great Love, O Father and Creator, with which you infuse our heaviness, thrusts us into eternal life; you make what you have created fly up from the center to the top, to the Maker, by the power of your very light wings; your love, affection, and zeal, with which you fill this celestial mass, raises it up lightly (despite its low earthiness) by a divine spark. Your great beauty, your brightness, your light, comes searching for us in the depth of our den in order to convert ugliness into beauty. Very gently this union takes away from us the first form of old Adam, his fire and his ardor, so ugly and filthy that it was hideous; but by love it is so well effaced and painted over and covered with splendor that the Adam in us died under beauty.

Neither temporality nor spatiality is a constitutive element in this mutation. Love "nous fait *saillir* en la vie eternelle." It provokes an instantaneous change. To express this change, Marguerite uses the image of flight, a flight so rapid that the reader is not allowed to perceive it in either temporal or spatial terms. "Mutation / De nous en toy" cannot be allegorized as a journey.

Indeed, the journey metaphor is of limited usefulness in a text that denies spatiality and temporality from the outset. It appears in the *Oraison* only when Marguerite wishes to subvert the notion of wayfaring as a journey through time and space. In the first part of the *Petit Oeuvre*, hardship and toil had been the wayfarer's lot. One could argue that the emphasis Marguerite had placed on constant effort and struggle allied her briefly with an ethical stance that would soon come to characterize Protestantism.[60] We may speculate that Marguerite excluded both the *Dialogue* and the *Petit Oeuvre* from the *Marguerites* because she sensed in these two early poems a certain reformist bias that no longer reflected her faith. In any case, she uses Christ's statement "Je suis la vraye voye" (p. 97) [I am the true way] for a significantly different purpose in the *Oraison* than in the *Petit Oeuvre*. What this purpose is becomes clearer when Marguerite addresses the following words to Christ:

> Tu es la voye et le chemin tresample
> Par ou l'on va au grand celeste temple;
> Car nul n'y peult par autre voye aller.
> Aux pelerins tu es mis pour *exemple*,
> *Et celuy là qui mieux t'ayme et contemple,*
> *Est plus avant, et mieux en sçait parler.*
> Pource qu'aux tiens desire reveler
> Ta volunté; à fin que chacun voye
> Le droit chemin, n'as pas voulu celer,
> Mais leur as dit, Je suis la vraye voye.   (p. 97, my emphasis)

You are the way and the very wide road by which one goes to the great celestial temple; for no one can go there by another way. You have been sent to pilgrims as an example, and he who loves you best and contemplates you is farther along and knows better how to talk about you. You wish, therefore, to reveal your will to those who belong to you. So that each one can see the straight road, you have not tried to conceal it but have said to them, I am the true way.

---

60. Calvin provided a solid theological underpinning to the work ethic. See, for example, his pages "On Christian Liberty" in *On God and Political Duty*, The Library of Liberal Arts (Indianapolis: The Bobbs-Merrill Co., 1956), pp. 33–34.

Marguerite does not depict the Christian as a traveler who strives to reach a destination. The way has become, in Augustine's words, a road of the affections, and the Christian, instead of moving from one place to another, contemplates with love the paradigm (*exemple*) that God has set before his eyes. Emptying the journey metaphor of the notion of progress and effort, Marguerite makes it plain that Christ's way cannot be conceptualized as a road the Christian must negotiate. Rather, the Way is awareness of Christ's presence in the eternal now that is God's time. The more one loves God the closer one is to Him and the better one can talk about Him.

The Marguerite of the *Oraison* does not press onward as did the Marguerite of the first part of the *Petit Oeuvre*. In fact, the speaker of the *Oraison* assumes the posture of one who prays; she remains motionless and waits: "Je la [Christ's glory] contemple à part moy à loisir, / En attendant qu'il te plaise choisir / Mon coeur . . ." (p. 108) [I contemplate it secretly and leisurely, waiting until it is your pleasure to choose my heart]. From the beginning of the poem, timelessness is expressed by the strategies we noted in the prayer section of the *Petit Oeuvre*. The verbs in the *Oraison* are mostly in the present tense as befits a poem designed to affirm the eternal presence of Christ in the human heart. "Christ," Marguerite tells us emphatically, "n'ha demain ne hyer; / Car son temps est toujours prest et present" (p. 115) [Christ has no tomorrow or yesterday; for his time is always at hand and present]. As we saw in the prayer that makes up the central section of the *Petit Oeuvre*, anaphora is an especially effective rhetorical figure to express the idea of duration within a continuous present. Throughout the first three pages of the *Oraison*, Marguerite makes extensive use of anaphora, depending on this particular kind of repetition to bear the message that Christ, to borrow from the Scriptures, is "the Alpha and the Omega . . . who is, and who was, and who is to come" (Revelations 1.8). Verses are assembled into blocks that form anaphoral patterns: lines 6–9 all begin "Au fonds"; lines 11–16, "Plus que"; lines 21–25, "Plus que"; lines 34–37, "Qui." Interwoven among these blocks of verses are single lines (4, 10, 20, 30, 31) that all begin with the words "Qui es" or "Qui est," thus constituting a kind of anaphoral counterpoint. The combined effect is to focus the reader's attention on a presence that is perpetually duplicated.

On the level of discourse, the pulverization of the self by God's "feu consommant" (p. 88) [consuming fire] and the effacement of the difference between the "I" and the "thou" translates as a displacement of the syntagmatic by a paradigmatic axis. There are bits of narrative material scattered throughout the *Oraison* (the verbs, as we might expect, are in the past tense), but they are so brief and discontinuous that they do not succeed in establishing a narrative axis in the text. The first narrative fragment in the poem begins in line 51 and continues for six lines before it disappears:

> Seigneur, Cuyder a voulu entreprendre
> De ta hauteur, sens, et puissance entendre,
> Et deviser de tes graces et biens:
> Mais il auroit besoing premier d'apprendre
> Que c'est de luy, et dedens soy descendre;
> Lors trouveroit que s'il est, il est Riens.   (p. 79)

Lord, Presumptuousness decided to try to understand your eminence, thought and power, and to talk about your grace and goodness; but he ought to learn first what he is and to descend within himself; then he would discover that to the extent that he is, he is Nothingness.

Indeed, several times in the course of the poem, the allegorical figure of *Cuyder*, man's presumptuous pride in self and the Christian's most cunning enemy, tries to speak and assert his narrative voice.[61] Often he is assimilated with another allegorical figure, that of the "old Adam" in us. No sooner does *Cuyder* begin to speak than the text conspires to silence his voice ("O, le Cuyder, il vous fault icy taire," p. 79) [O, Presumptuousness, you must be silent here]. *Cuyder* represents human reason and man's propensity to think along the lines of cause and effect. Marguerite addresses him contemptuously as *Rien* or "fange et fiens" (p. 79) [filth and dung]. He is ejected repeatedly from the poem, which is called an *oraison*, a word that may be read as a homonym of *hors raison*.[62] *Cuyder* requires a syntagmatic axis

---

61. On the theme of *Cuyder* in the work of Marguerite, see Raymond Lebègue, "Le Cuyder avant Montaigne et dans les Essais," *Cahiers de l'association internationale des études françaises*, 14 (1962), 275–84. See also Sckommodau, *Die religiösen Dichtungen* . . ., p. 93.

62. On the word *raison* in Marguerite's works, see Henri Vernay, *Les Divers Sens du*

along which to manifest itself. "L'homme souvent se mue et change tant" (p. 90) [Man often transforms himself and changes so much], says Marguerite, contrasting human inconstancy with the permanence of the paradigmatic figure of Christ, whom she addresses with the words, "Immuable es, ferme, stable, et constant" (p. 90) [You are immutable, firm, stable and constant]. In the *Oraison*, narrative, the mode of discourse that expresses man's changeability, is always a sign of error.

The rejection of narrative is of a piece with the denial of the distinction between "I" and "thou," man and Christ, a distinction that exists on the surface level but not the higher level of reality. The idea of transcendence, whose forward thrust is most adequately expressed by narrative, is replaced by that of immanence. Indeed, belief in God's immanence informs every aspect of the *Oraison*. "Dieu tout en tous, de tous la vie et l'estre" (p. 81) [God, all in all things, the life and being of all things] is a principle that Marguerite states early in the poem and that constitutes its underlying theme. If in other works (as, for example, the *Dialogue* and, to some extent, the *Petit Oeuvre*), Marguerite portrays God as transcendent, in the *Oraison* she emphasizes, as the Evangelicals tended to do, His immanence. She points out that it is inaccurate to say that "we" love "Him," for Christ, being love, is both the cause and effect of love, both lover and beloved. As we submit to Him, we experience love by virtue of the fact that we become Christ-like. But the love we feel does not originate in us but in Him who lives in our heart ("Tu es en nous vivant," p. 97) [You are alive in us]. Emanating from Him, love is reflected back to Him:

> O vray Amy, nous ne t'aymons donc point,
> Mais si en nous tu es par Amour joint,
> Ton Amour t'ayme, te glorifie, et loue.   (p. 87)

O true Friend, we do not, therefore, love you; but if you are joined to us by Love, your Love loves you, glorifies you, and praises you.

God is the loving *Tout-Verbe* that endlessly repeats itself. Only by yielding to the discourse of love can we experience "ceste mutation / De nous en toy" [this mutation of us into you].

The *Oraison* is the third poem in the *Marguerites*. It follows a short (for Marguerite) poem that bears a long title: *Discord estant en l'homme par la contrarieté de l'Esprit et de la Chair, et paix par vie spirituelle* [The Discord that exists in man because of the opposition of Spirit and Flesh, and peace through spiritual life]. Having the formal features of a medieval *débat*, the *Discord* is based on the Pauline antinomy of flesh and spirit. One Pauline text is particularly important: Romans 7. In this epistle, Paul contrasts "the new spiritual way" with "the old way of the written law." Paul's main theme is man's propensity for sin. In a verse that Augustine often cited, Paul sees the essence of man's dilemma in his inability to resist the "law of sin" despite his wish to follow the "law of God." "I fail to carry out the things I want to do," wrote Paul, "and I find myself doing the very things I hate" (Romans 7.15). Man's spirit is always at war with his flesh. This is the human predicament that Marguerite portrays in the *Discord*. "Vivre nous faut estans toujours en guerre" (p. 72)[63] [We have to live being always at war], she writes. Because "les humains n'ont possibilité / Pouvoir guarir ceste fragilité" (p. 73) [humans do not have the possibility of being able to cure this frailty], the "bataille obstinée / [qui] Est dedans l'homme" (p. 73) [obstinate battle that is in man] will not cease before the spirit is freed from the body. Nevertheless, we can enjoy the peace of which the title speaks even before the ultimate triumph of the spirit if we have faith in the "Verbe Divin, J E S U S   C H R I S T Salvateur, / Unique filz de l'Eternel autheur" (p. 73) [Divine Word, Jesus Christ the Savior, only son of the eternal author]. In anaphoric verse, Marguerite says:

> L'homme est par Foy fait filz du Createur:
> L'homme est par Foy juste, saint, bienfaiteur:
> L'homme est par Foy remis en innocence:
> L'homme est par Foy, Roy en C H R I S T regnateur;
> Par Foy avons l'Esprit Consolateur
> Uniz au Pere, et au Mediateur:
> Par Foy j'ay C H R I S T, et tout en affluence.   (pp. 73–74)

63. Page references are to the *Marguerites* (Johnson Reprint Corporation), Vol. 1.

Man is by Faith made son of the Creator: man is by Faith just, holy, a kind friend: man is by Faith restored to innocence: man is by Faith King in Christ the ruler; by Faith we have the Spirit, the Comforter, and are united with the Father and with the Mediator: by Faith I have Christ and everything in abundance.

Faith in Christ is a sign of "vie spirituelle" as distinct from "vie charnelle." But, Marguerite asks, "Qu'appellez vous vivre charnellement? / Qu'appellez vous spirituellement?" (p. 75) [What do you call living carnally? What do you call living spiritually?]. Explaining that the spiritual life does not mean a life without sin, for that is impossible, Marguerite notes that he who would follow the spirit must direct his *thought* toward Christ.

> Je dy vivre Spirituellement,
> Cil qui vers D I E U a mis son pensement,
> Fiance, et Foy; dont vient la Charité.   (p. 75)

I say that he lives spiritually who has directed toward God his thought, confidence, and faith; from this comes Love.

It is surely not by accident that in the first edition of the *Marguerites* the *Oraison* follows the *Discord*. In the *Discord*, Marguerite identifies contemplation (*pensement*) as the central activity in a life that is "directed by the Spirit" (Galatians 5.25). Responding to the *Discord estant en l'homme*, the *Oraison* illustrates the praxis of contemplation. Indeed, the *Oraison* is an elaborate and remarkably successful attempt to metacommunicate about what it means to be "guided by the Spirit" and to avoid "yielding to self-indulgence" (Galatians 5.16), or, to quote the words that Marguerite used to translate this Pauline message, to "vivre spirituellement," not "charnellement," or "temporellement" (p. 76), or "bestialement" (p. 76).

In the fifth chapter of his epistle to the Galatians, Paul had assured his readers that the Spirit brings "love, joy, peace, . . ." whereas the Flesh leads to "fornication, gross indecency and sexual irresponsibility; idolatry and sorcery; feuds and wrangling, jealousy, bad temper and quarrels; disagreements, factions, envy; orgies and similar things." Marguerite develops this contrast in the *Oraison*, calling the spirit "l'interieur homme" (p. 94) and the flesh "l'exterieur lien" (p. 93) [the exterior bond].

The fundamental distinction between a man who lives in accordance with the law of the spirit and one who obeys the law of the flesh is that the soul of the former is "contente et pleine" [content and full] while that of the latter writhes continually in the "tourment du desir" (p. 91) [torment of desire]. In its quest for "biens, honneurs, et plaisirs" [wealth, honors and pleasures], "desir bruslant" (p. 95) [burning desire] is oriented toward the future. The only instances of the future verb tense in the *Oraison* are in the evocation of the world of the flesh. Striving always to transcend the present, the flesh "ne fait rien que courir / Apres le bien" (p. 95) [does nothing but run after pleasure]. Marguerite projects desire along a syntagmatic axis that accommodates time and space and seems to lead to the future. But the flesh has no future. Thus the man who is consumed by desire rushes down a road that leads nowhere; or rather, that leads to death. "Desir, courroux, le mettront au cercueil" [Desire, anger, will put him in the coffin], writes Marguerite, thereby stressing the vanity (Latin *vanus* means "empty") that characterizes the life of a man who mistakes "ceste fange moite" (p. 97) [this moist mud] for reality.

Repeating a strategy she had used in the *Dialogue*, Marguerite introduces the concept of enjoyment in the *Oraison* to convey the essential quality of a life that is consonant with the way of the spirit. In a rhapsodic passage that begins "O Dieu d'amour, ô tresparfait amant" (p. 90) [O God of love, O very perfect lover], she evokes the joy that man experiences as he is enfolded in Christ:

> Car le plaisir d'ouyr la melodie
> Du son tresdoux de ton divin parler,
> Le rend content, sy fort qu'il ne maudie
> Nul bien dehors, ou plus ne veult aller.   (p. 90)

For the pleasure of hearing the melody of the very sweet sound of your divine speech makes him content and so happy that he is not jealous of the pleasures of the world, nor does he wish any longer to go to them.

All desire vanishes from the heart, and the man who lives in the world of the spirit, enjoying what he has, does not wish to be elsewhere.

In one sense, Marguerite's vision of the *unio* is the projection

of human wishes and ambitions onto God. Marguerite describes
the world of the spirit as a state in which human desires have
been satisfied. The joy the Christian experiences in his union
with Christ is presented in terms of the pleasure he derives from
eating and drinking:

> Qui a gousté, ô Pere, de ta main
> La grand' douceur, de ton celeste pain,
> De son desir ha satisfaction:
> De joye il est, et de plaisir sy plein,
> Que d'autres biens n'ha plus ne soif ne faim;
> Car en toy seul prend consolation.
> Mais ceste faim par grand' dilection
> De tous les jours en manger, ne tarit:
> Plus il en prend, plus croist l'affection
> D'avoir du pain, sans lequel il perit.   (p. 92)

Anyone who has tasted, O Father, from your hand the great sweetness
of your celestial bread has his desire satisfied; he is so full of joy and
pleasure that he no longer is thirsty or hungry for other pleasures; for
in you alone he finds consolation. But, because of great love, this hunger to eat of it every day does not disappear; the more of it he takes, the
more he longs for this bread, without which he would perish.

Marguerite here presents the *unio* in imagery that Northrop Frye
calls "apocalyptic."[64] Explaining that "the apocalyptic world,
the heaven of religion, presents, in the first place, the categories
of reality in the forms of human desire,"[65] Frye points out that in
the Book of Revelation all the biblical images of desire "are
brought into complete metaphorical identification" through the
figure of Christ. He is All, or, as Marguerite says over and over,
Tout. "Tout est sy Tout," she writes, "que l'on n'y sçauroit
mettre, / Ny adjouster, ny tirer, ny omettre / Chose qui soit"
(p. 104) [All is so All that one could not put anything there, nor
add anything, nor take away, nor leave out].

But whereas the Book of Revelation presents the apocalypse
as a future reality, Marguerite presents her apocalyptic vision as
a representation of the world as it is here and now for the man
who lives in the Spirit. Marguerite's apocalypse is essentially a

64. *Anatomy of Criticism*, op. cit., p. 151.
65. Ibid., p. 141.

reformulation of Eckhart's *Now* moment. What the Book of Revelation says will be, Marguerite says already is, for Christ is within, not outside, the world. There is no time or space beyond Him, who is identical with His creation, God's text. Living spiritually means living in a world in which time and space have been collapsed back into God, who, in words that Marguerite cites more than once in the *Oraison*, revealed Himself to Moses with the phrase, "I Am who I Am" (Exodus 3.14). We, Marguerite declares, are nothing but letters in His book: "Tu Es qui Es, Nous rien, fors le recueil / Que tu en fais comme puissant facteur" (p. 95) [You are who you are, we, nothing, except for the welcome that you, like a powerful creator, extend to us]. But just as there is no book without letters, so God is dependent on us. He does not stand beyond His creation. In the figure of Christ, He is immanent in His work.

The *Oraison de l'âme fidèle* is followed by the relatively short *Oraison à nostre Seigneur Jesus Christ*, which is a meditation on the inability of language to represent Christ. Borrowing from the Pseudo-Dionysius, Marguerite says that language cannot name God. In a sense, however, His name, which we may call the *Tout-Verbe*, is immanent in all names (the *Verbe*). We can therefore use any name to signify Him.

> Vostre nom est sy grand et admirable,
> Que naturel esprit, ou raisonnable
> Ne vous sçauroit nommer parfaitement:
> Tous noms avez, estant innominable.   (p. 137)

Your name is so great and wonderful that the natural or rational mind cannot name you perfectly; you have all names, being unnameable.

Reflecting on the linguistic problems involved in naming God, Marguerite concludes that silence is the language best suited for praising the Divinity. She is, however, dependent on language to express this insight and so does not immediately fall silent. She continues speaking for some two hundred lines before returning in the last fifty lines of the poem to the notion of the inability of language to translate the Spirit.

> De vous dire, mon D I E U, mon Pere, et Roy,
> 275   Ce que vous seul sçavez trop mieux que moy,

A moymesmes je sçay que je fais tort:
Car vous louer ne puis comme je doy,
Ne mercier des biens que je reçoy,
Ne confesser le mal, qui me remord:
280   Satisfaire ne puis à nul effort,
Ne parvenir par mon labeur au port
De la grace; par laquelle je croy,
Que sauverez tous ceux, qui par la Foy
Ont mis en vous leur fiance et confort.
285   Nully fors vous, n'a acomply la Loy;
Nostre ouvrage est de si mauvais aloy,
Que le meilleur est mauvais, sale, et ord;
Parquoy voyant, que fin, rive, ne bort
En vostre bien, ny en mon mal, ne voy,
290   *L'impossible de vous louer bien fort*
Loue en taisant, ce que bon j'apperçoy.
          Aveuglez moy de vostre grand' lumiere,
Dont mon esprit ne congnoit la matiere,
Forme, ou façon congnue au regard sien:
295   Mais les effectz, sont en telle maniere,
Qu'au plus profond de sa fosse et tasniere,
Voit que d'elle procede tout son bien:
De la clarté, si, comment, et combien:
Elle est grande, lors il n'y entend rien.
300   Et plus se rompt de ses yeux la barriere:
Et plus il ha de regarder moyen,
Plus il confesse son regard terrien
Indigne à voir ceste clarté entiere,
Le vouloir voir, c'est volonté trop fiere;
305   Mais d'absorber en soy ce qui est mien
Par ses doux rayz, je vous en fais priere,
Pour deslier mon obstiné lien.
          Mon long parler, trop inutil, mal sonne,
Veu le propos, sy digne que personne
310   N'est suffisant pour soustenir le faix:
Congnoissance me commande et ordonne
De regarder d'impossible la bourne,
Que nul esprit subtil, leger, ou fraiz
N'a sceu passer, tant ayt il bon relaiz.
315   Pour estre donc du nombre des Parfaitz,
A la bonté de vous, mon D I E U, retourne;

Qui au pecheur grace pour grace donne:
Car regardant mes pensees, ditz, et faitz
Chose qui soit je n'y voy d'oeuvre bonne:
320   Mais verité vostre oeil de pitié tourne
A nous tenir la promesse de paix,
Par Charité, qui tout peché pardonne.
En cest Foy ferme et seure me taiz;
Et pour penser, *le parler j'abandonne.*   (pp. 145–47, my
emphasis)

To tell you, my GOD, my Father and King, what you alone know
better than I; in myself I know that I am wrong; for I cannot praise you
as I ought to, nor thank you for the riches I receive, nor confess the
evil that gnaws at me; I cannot satisfactorily complete any endeavor,
nor attain by my effort the port of grace, by which I know you will
save all those who through Faith have placed in you their confidence
and comfort. No one but you has fulfilled the Law; our work is of such
a bad alloy that the best is bad, dirty and filthy; therefore, seeing that I
do not see the end, the shore, or the limit of your good or of my evil,
and that it is impossible to praise you aloud with great force, I praise
by being silent the good I perceive.

Blind me with your great light, of which my mind does not understand the substance, the form, or the shape, recognizable by its appearance; but the effects are such that in the depth of its pit and burrow, the
mind sees that all its own good (if it has any, how it has it, and how
much) comes from it, from light. Light is great whereas the mind
understands nothing. And the more it pulls the bandage from its eyes
and the more it is able to see, the more it confesses that its earthly look
is unworthy to see all this light; the desire to see it is too proud a desire;
but to absorb into itself by its soft rays what is mine: that is what I pray
to you for, to untie the strong tie that binds me.

My long speech, utterly useless, does not ring true, considering the
subject, so worthy that no one is able to bear the burden. Understanding commands and orders me to look at the farthest border of the
impossible, which no mind, however subtle, light, or vigorous, has
managed to cross, even if it has advanced smoothly in stages. To be,
therefore, in the company of those who are perfect, I turn again, my
God, to your goodness, which gives the sinner grace for grace; for,
considering my thoughts, words and deeds, whatever these may have
been, I do not see any good work; but truth turns your eye of pity to us
to keep the promise of peace through Love, which pardons all sin. In
this firm and certain Faith, I become silent; and as for thinking, I give
up speaking.

Realizing that words connote differences and establish distinctions, Marguerite understands that the more she speaks the farther she moves from the Oneness that is Christ. With a note of exhaustion and frustration in her voice, she falls silent. In the course of the two *Oraisons*, she has learned that speech (*le parler*) is incompatible with the life of the Spirit. Once she has stopped *speaking*, however, she begins to *see*. In the last fifty lines of the *Oraison à nostre Seigneur Jesus Christ* there is a direct correlation between the cessation of speech and the beginning of sight. In the first of the three stanzas cited above (ll. 275–91), Marguerite confesses that her language is unable to praise Christ as He deserves to be praised. As this insight becomes increasingly powerful throughout the stanza, verbs of speech ("dire," l. 274 and "confesser," l. 279) are replaced by verbs of sight ("voir," l. 288 and "appercevoir," l. 291). The next stanza (ll. 292–307) is dominated by visual imagery. In the third and final stanza (ll. 308–24), the futility of speech is further underscored by allusions to the redemptive power of sight.

Marguerite's shift from the concept of word as sound to—as Thomas à Kempis put it—"word as light"[66] is of a piece with the shift in the *Petit Oeuvre* from a syntagmatic axis in part one of the poem to a paradigmatic axis in part two. The *Oraison* helps clarify the nature of this shift by describing it in terms of a change from "speaking" to "seeing." In Marguerite's texts, "speaking" is close to Aristotle's concept of *mythos* or plot whereas "seeing" is close to *dianoia* or thought. For Aristotle (*Poetics*, 1449b27–1450a19), *mythos* refers to the narrative line of a work and *dianoia* to its meaning. Northrop Frye has expressed with great clarity the distinction between the two:

The word narrative or *mythos* conveys the sense of movement caught by the ear, and the word meaning or *dianoia* conveys, or at least preserves, the sense of simultaneity caught by the eye. We *listen to* the poem as it moves from beginning to end, but as soon as the whole of it is in our minds at once we "see" what it means. More exactly, this response is not simply to *the* whole *of* it, but to *a* whole *in* it: we have a vision of meaning or *dianoia* whenever any simultaneous apprehension is possible.[67]

66. *Imitation*, 4.11, p. 212.
67. *Anatomy of Criticism*, pp. 77–78.

Marguerite's text demonstrates the difference between *mythos* and *dianoia*, between "speaking" and "seeing." The brief prefatory poem that opens the *Marguerites* warns us that we must direct our attention to *dianoia* rather than *mythos*: "Si vous lisez ceste oeuvre toute entiere, / Arrestez vous, sans plus, à la matiere" (p. 13) [If you read this work in its entirety, stop nowhere but at the substance]. We are advised to read the text in the same way a Christian reads the world, seeing everywhere and at all times the whole, i.e., Christ. By diminishing the importance of "le parler," the text invites the reader to experience the poem not as discourse that extends along a diachronic line but as an image (the "ymaige vraye" of the *Petit Oeuvre*) that conveys a sense of simultaneity and wholeness. Like most of Marguerite's poems, the two *Oraisons* aspire to be icons that transcend the limitations inherent in language (difference, distinction, in brief, the "Noise" of which Thomas à Kempis speaks) and reflect the reality of Christ's unchanging presence in the world. It is surely significant that Marguerite uses a visual image in the title of her first volume of poetry, *Le Miroir de l'âme pécheresse*, [68] which is also the title of the opening poem in the volume. In the *Marguerites*, *Le Miroir* retains its privileged position as the first poem in the collection. The "meaning" of Marguerite's poetry is intimately connected with the displacement of one perception (syntagmatic, diachronic, narrative) by another (paradigmatic, synchronic, reflexive), which the reader is invited to interpret as the image of a higher order of reality. This "meaning" is expressed powerfully in the mirror metaphor, the organizing figure in *Le Miroir de l'âme pécheresse*. We now turn to this poem, strategically situated at the beginning of both the 1531 and 1547 collections of Marguerite's poetry.

---

68. The complete title of the 1531 edition is: *Le Miroir de l'ame pecherresse, ouquel elle recongnoist ses faultes et pechez, aussi ses graces et benefices à elle faictz par Jesuchrist son époux. La Marguerite tres noble et précieuse s'est preposee à ceulx qui de bon cueur la cerchoient.* The 1533 edition of the same work has the following title: *Le Miroir de très chrestienne princesse Marguerite de France, royne de Navarre, duchesse d'Alençon et de Berry; auquel elle voit son néant et son tout.*

II
The Iconic Text

5
A Matter of Optics

"BY THY LIGHT SHALL WE SEE LIGHT"

The mirror metaphor holds a privileged place in Western literature.[1] A central image in the Platonic-Christian tradition, it is charged with a rich cargo of meanings. In the tenth book of the *Republic* (600E–601C), Plato compared art to a reflection of things. Since works of art are mere representations of appearances, which are themselves nothing more than imperfect reflections of ultimate reality, they are, Plato declared, of little worth. In the *Timaeus*, however, he used the mirror image in a more positive sense, for he noted that the lower orders of being reflect "as in a mirror" (71B) the higher reality that extends downward from God. Plotinus adopted this image and used it extensively in the *Enneads* (I.4.10) to convey the notion that the universals are not perceived directly but only in a reflector, be it language, reason, or matter.[2] The reflection of the universals in matter constitutes the mutable shadow-world that we in our folly and ignorance tend to confuse with reality. Later Greek and Latin writers who worked within the Platonic tradition often used the mirror metaphor to express their belief that the physical or material world is a reflected image of the archetypal forms.

Frequent in the work of classical authors, allusions to *specula* are also common in the Bible. The most famous instance of the

---

1. See Curtius, *European Literature and the Latin Middle Ages*, p. 336; Sister Ritamary Bradley, "Backgrounds of the title *Speculum* in Mediaeval Literature," *Speculum*, 29 (1954), 100–15; Frederick Goldin, *The Mirror of Narcissus in the Courtly Love Lyric* (Ithaca: Cornell University Press, 1967), pp. 5–15; Marianne Shapiro, "Mirror and Portrait: The Structure of Il Libro del Cortegiano," *The Journal of Medieval and Renaissance Studies*, 5, No. 1 (1975), 37–61, esp. 41–42.

2. See Paul Aubin, "L''Image' dans l'oeuvre de Plotin," *Recherches de science religieuse*, 41 (July-September 1953), 248–79.

mirror image in Scripture is Paul's "Now we are seeing a dim reflection in a mirror" (I Corinthians 13.12). We have already seen how Augustine, making of Paul's statement the fundamental metaphor of Christian epistemology, recast speech into a Pauline mirror capable of reflecting God. To the extent that a mirror permits us to glimpse the Truth, however partial and blurred, it is a precious epistemological tool. As well as reflecting God, however, a mirror may also reflect man's own image back to him and thus disclose his sinfulness. We touch here upon the ambivalent nature of the mirror metaphor. As Sister Ritamary Bradley observed in her seminal article on the use of the word *speculum* in medieval literature, the mirror image, at least from Augustine on, has had two basic connotations: a mirror may reflect a faithful image of what is, or it may serve as a paragon of what should be.[3]

Augustine made clear the dual nature of the mirror image. Seeing in Scripture a Pauline mirror in which man can discern God, Augustine linked beatitude with knowledge of the Bible. He referred to the sixth promise of beatitude, "Happy the pure in heart; they shall see God" (Matthew 5.8) and noted that the Scriptures have a twofold function. In the first place, they show the reader his own deformity and sinfulness by making him conscious of the distance that separates him from what God would have him be. "The mirror has set its writing before you," Augustine wrote; "it is read to you: 'Blessed are the pure in heart, for they shall see God'. The mirror is set forth in this reading; see whether you are yet so, then groan, that you may become so. *The mirror will disclose your face to you.* (my emphasis) As you will not see a flatterer in the mirror, so you will not wheedle yourself. Its brightness will show you what you are: see what you are."[4] At the same time, Scripture tells the reader what he should be (that is, pure of heart) and so provides a model of Christian virtue. Augustine explains in his *Confessions* that God, making allowances for our weakness and inability to comprehend Him directly, has given us the mirror of Holy Scripture (*speculum Scripturae*), in which we can read His will.

---

3. Bradley, op. cit., 100–101. See also Norbert Hugedé, *La Métaphore du miroir dans les épîtres de Saint Paul aux Corinthiens*, Thèse No. 157 (Neuchâtel: Delachaux et Niestlé, 1957).

4. *Enarratio in Psalmum CIII* (PL, XXXII, 1338). English translation by Golden, *The Mirror of Narcissus . . .*, op. cit., p. 5.

And who but you, our God, made for us the firmament, that is, our heavenly shield, the authority of your divine Scriptures? For we are told that *the sky shall be folded up like a scroll* [Revelation 6.14] and that, now, it is spread out like a canopy of skins, and these heavens are your Book, your words in which no note of discord jars. . . . There in the heavens, in your Book, we read *your unchallengeable decrees*, which *make the simple learned* [Psalms 18.8; 19.7]. . . .

Above this firmament of your Scripture I believe that there are other waters, immortal and kept safe from earthly corruption. They are the peoples of your city, your angels, on high above the firmament. Let them glorify your name and sing your praises, for they have no need to look up to this firmament of ours or read its text to know your word. For ever they gaze upon your face and there, without the aid of syllables inscribed in time, they read what your eternal will decrees. They read your will: they choose it to be theirs: they cherish it. They read it without cease and what they read never passes away. For it is your own unchanging purpose that they read, choosing to make it their own and cherishing it for themselves. The book they read shall not be closed. For them the scroll shall not be furled. For you yourself are their book and you for ever are. You allotted them their place above this firmament of ours, this firmament which you established to protect the weakness of your peoples here below, so that they might look up to it and know this work of your mercy which proclaims you in time, you who are the Maker of time. . . .

Those who preach your word pass on from this life to the next, but your Scripture is outstretched over the peoples of this world to the end of time. *Though heaven and earth should pass away, your words will stand* [Matthew 24.35]. The scroll shall be folded and the mortal things over which it was spread shall fade away, as grass withers with all its beauty; *but your Word stands for ever* [Isaiah 40.8]. Now we see your Word, not as he is, but dimly through the clouds, *like a confused reflection in the mirror* [I Corinthians 13.12] of the firmament, for though we are the beloved of your Son, *what we shall be hereafter has not been made known as yet* [I John 3.2]. . . . But, *when he comes we shall be like him; we shall see him, then as he is* [I John 3.2]. It will be ours to see him as he is, O Lord, but that time is not yet. (*Conf.* XIII.15.321–23)

Innumerable works throughout the late Middle Ages and Renaissance were called "mirrors." Few titles were more common than *Miroir de Mort, Miroir des nobles hommes de France, Mirouer des dames, Mirouer du monde, Mirouer de l'âme pécheresse tres utile et profitable, Miroir d'or de l'âme pécheresse, Petit mirouer de l'âme dévote*, not to mention Latin titles that used the word *speculum*. These books usually performed one of the two functions Augustine mentioned in relation to the mirror metaphor. Some of them reflect man's image back to him, revealing a creature that is base and sinful. Others disclose the image of man as God would have him be, pure of heart and filled with charity. In both cases, the same optical principle is in force: a relationship is established between an object (source) and its image (derivative). The object is defined as reality (and is thus superior), the image as mimetic reproduction (inferior). In those books in which man's image is reflected back to him, man himself is the object. He is posited as reality. The text is the mirror that reveals to him his fallen state. Since man is the source from which the image is derived, the framework in this case is anthropomorphic. The writer and the reader stand within a reality that centers man as the original of the reflected image. On the other hand, in the books that reveal the image of man as he has been redefined through the operation of the Incarnation, the underlying assumptions are fundamentally different. The illumination afforded by the Holy Spirit effects a complete redefinition of the terms of reference. No longer is man the reality whose image is reflected in the mirror/text. God, rather, is the source, and man, who has become *christiforme* through the operation of the Word, is now the image, the derivative, the reflection.

The richness and complexity of Marguerite's *Miroir* are due to the fact that the two functions of the mirror metaphor are both operative in the text. The double structure of reality is as vital a principle in this poem as in the *Petit Oeuvre*. At the beginning of the *Miroir*, reality is resolutely anthropomorphic. Marguerite herself is the source. The text reflects the image of the sinner that she is. The language that serves as the vehicle of this reflection is mainly referential. It evokes physical presence and does not immediately invite an allegorical or anagogic interpretation. Soon, however, it begins to acquire symbolic resonance. As it becomes increasingly anagogic, one level of reality gives way to the other. Christ is now identified as the source. Man, to the extent that he participates in the Incarnation, is seen as Christ's image. Man-seeing is transformed into man-seen, a being-in-Christ who is reflected in the eye of God as part of His divine creation. In other words, *Verbe* (*parole*) is folded back into *Tout-Verbe* (*langue*). In the *Miroir*, as in all her major poems, the linguistic problem Marguerite confronts is how to devise strategies whereby the *Verbe* of which the text is composed can efface itself and, by so doing, signify the *Tout-Verbe*, which can never be contained within the words on the page but which is the source of all speech. My reading of the *Miroir* will focus on these strategies.

The poem is preceded by an epigraph: "Seigneur DIEU crée en moy coeur net" [Lord God, create in me a clean heart]. In the margin of the 1547 edition of the *Marguerites*, this verse is identified as coming from Psalm 50, known as the *Miserere*, the most commonly used of the penitential Psalms. (In the Vulgate, which Marguerite used, the *Miserere* is Psalm 50. In most modern versions of the Bible, it is Psalm 51.) Indeed, the psalmist had written, "God, create a clean heart in me, put into me a new and constant spirit" (Psalm 51.10). The *Miserere* is a prayer of repentance in which the speaker first recognizes his iniquity and then asks God to cleanse his heart so that he will be able to sing the praises of the Lord. The song that rises from the purified heart exalts and reflects His righteousness: "My mouth will speak out your praise" (Psalms 51.15). Marguerite's *Miroir* retraces the pattern of spiritual progress outlined in the *Miserere*, which thus serves as a paradigmatic text.

The words "coeur net" assume particular significance on the first page of the 1547 edition of the *Miroir*. Cotgrave translates *net* as "neat, cleane, pure, cleere; spotlesse, unspotted; polished, smooth." The graphics of the page are such that the heart that has been cleaned and polished by God becomes the mirror announced in large type in the title. The text, which is of course the mirror, is metaphorically transformed into Marguerite's heart, which God, in answer to her prayer, purifies and polishes throughout the course of the poem.

The notion of a polished textual surface is repeated in the graphic play of the large and richly embellished capital letter O that opens the poem. The design of the letter O was undoubtedly the work of the printer or the engraver. Renaissance printers often transformed the first letter of a work or of a chapter into a design whose swirl of lines and configuration of forms provide an added visual dimension to the printed words.[5] The first letter

---

5. The impulse to embellish initial letters was a carry-over from pre-printing days. Lucien Febvre and Henri-Jean Martin point out that the earliest printers often engaged artists who had been accustomed to illuminating manuscripts. *L'Apparition du livre* (Paris: Michel, 1958), p. 84. On the function of illuminations in medieval texts, see Roger Dragonetti, *La Vie de la lettre au Moyen Age* (Paris: Seuil, 1980), pp. 52–61. On

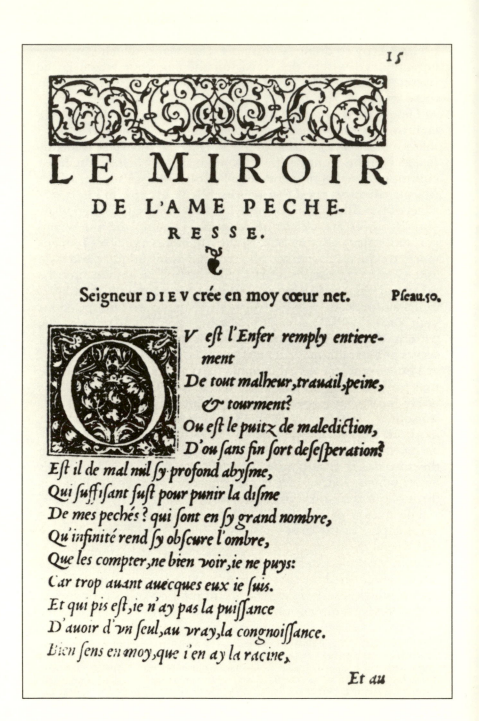

LE MIROIR
DE L'AME PECHE-
RESSE.

Seigneur DIEV crée en moy cœur net. Pseau. 50.

OV est l'Enfer remply entiere-
    ment
De tout malheur, trauail, peine,
    & tourment?
Ou est le puitz de malediction,
D'ou sans fin sort desesperation?
Est il de mal nul sy profond abysme,
Qui suffisant fust pour punir la disme
De mes pechés? qui sont en sy grand nombre,
Qu'infinité rend sy obscure l'ombre,
Que les compter, ne bien voir, ie ne puys:
Car trop auant auecques eux ie suis.
Et qui pis est, ie n'ay pas la puissance
D'auoir d'vn seul, au vray, la congnoissance.
Bien sens en moy, que i'en ay la racine,

                      Et au

in each of the poems of the 1547 edition of the *Marguerites* is treated in this way. The capital letter O at the beginning of the *Miroir* is a particularly powerful *figura*, for it reinforces graphically the organizing metaphor of the text, i.e., the mirror metaphor. It functions as a hieroglyph whose shape can evoke that of a mirror. From the beginning, the poem invites the reader to perceive the linguistic surface of the text as a mirror in which he, identifying with the "I" of the poem, sees his own image in that of the Christian supplicant who acknowledges the sinfulness of man. This is the perceptual framework I have called anthropomorphic, for man is the source whose image is reflected back to him by the clear polished surface of the page.

Simultaneously, however, the O functions within a radically different frame of reference. Perhaps the best way to clarify the letter O's second level of meaning is to turn to Geoffroy Tory's *Champ fleuri*. Published in 1529, *Champ fleuri* describes the shape of all the capital letters of the alphabet, relating their proportions to those of the human body and face. The descriptions are accompanied by illustrations in which each of the correctly formed capital letters is set in a finely executed design of considerable complexity. Tory's designs were frequently copied by French printers throughout the remainder of the sixteenth century. Jean de Tournes, the publisher of the 1547 edition of the *Marguerites*, used one of Tory's most characteristic patterns to decorate the O that opens Marguerite's *Miroir*: a floral design composed of the gracefully curved lines of acanthus leaves and flowers printed in white on a black background.[6]

As significant as Tory's designs and technical analyses are, another feature of his book is equally important. Alluding often to literary texts, Tory discusses the mystical and spiritual significance of each of the capital letters. Two letters, he argues, are of primary importance: capital I and capital O. All other capital letters are composed of shapes that are represented archetypally by I and O; that is to say, they are formed by various combinations of straight and curved lines. The letter I stands for the

---

the significance attached to the initial letter, see Dragonetti, Ch. 3, "La lettre initiale et l'initiative de la lettre," pp. 63–83.

6. For a detailed discussion of the designs that Jean de Tournes used in the books he published, see Albert Cartier, *Bibliographie des éditions des de Tournes* (Paris: Editions des Bibliothèques Nationales de France, 1937), 2 vols.

golden chain to which Homer refers (*Iliad* 8). In Tory's syncretistic explanation, it represents a Neoplatonic ladder that God
lowered to the Earth. It symbolizes the Way between God and
man. Capital letter O, on the other hand, stands for perfection
itself. It signifies God. "Il est certain en Geometrie," Tory observes, "que figure ronde, tant solide que non, est la plus capable, et la plus parfaicte de toutes"[7] [It is certain in geometry
that the round figure, whether solid or not, is the most capable
and the most perfect of all]. He notes that for the Greeks the
letter O signified Apollo or the sun. For Christians, however, it
represents "nostre vray Dieu et createur qui est le vray Soleil,
sans l'aide du quel, tout corps et tout esperit est toujours ebete
et inutile" [our true God and creator, who is the true Sun, without whose aid every body and every spirit is always dull and
worthless].

The notion that a circle can signify Christ is closely related to
the idea of *orbs doctrinae Christianae*, or the belief that Scripture
itself describes a circle and provides an exegesis of itself. It turns
back on itself and invites the reader to read it in such a way that
its obscurities, ambiguities, and contradictions are all resolved
into one clear, single, and unequivocal meaning, or *sensus*. Here
again Augustine's influence was crucial. Augustine saw in the
Bible a self-allegorizing text. Recognizing the fact that Scripture
contains obscure passages, he declared that apparent ambiguities
in the Bible result from the fallen state of language. God, however, makes use of the opacity inherent in fallen language to
counteract man's pride and to exploit the human hunger for
understanding. As Augustine put it:

Those who do not find what they seek directly are afflicted with hunger; those who do not seek because they have what they wish at once
frequently become indolent in disdain. In either of these situations indifference is an evil. Thus the Holy Spirit has magnificently and
wholesomely modulated the Holy Scriptures so that the clearer places
(*locis apertioribus*) present themselves to hunger and more obscure
places may deter a disdainful attitude. Hardly anything may be found
in these obscure places which is not found plainly said elsewhere.
(DDC II.6.8.38)

7. Geoffroy Tory, *Champ fleuri* (1529; rpt. The Hague: Johnson Reprint Corporation,
1970), n. pag. (Bk. 2, 29).

In other words, obscure Scriptural passages are designed to humiliate human arrogance. The reader must work out their meaning, which is not immediately apparent. To that end, Scripture contains "clear places" the reader can use to decode the obscure ones. Containing its own interpretive key, the Bible allegorizes itself. Because it is a reflexive text, it may be symbolized by a circle (*orbs doctrinae Christianae*).

The capital letter O at the beginning of the *Miroir* is a paradigm whose "rotondite," to borrow from Tory, "signifie toute entiere perfection." A figure of self-containment and perfect adequation, it emblematizes the Johannine *logos*. Augustine pointed out that "we cannot perceive the *logos* "without the aid of syllables inscribed in time." The Word must become a text before we can "read" it. Eventually, though, the text on which the syllables of human language are inscribed will, as Augustine says, quoting Revelations 6.14, be "folded up." Language will cease, and once again all things will be enclosed within His Word. The end will be indistinguishable from the beginning. Inscribed in time, Marguerite's texts strive to attain the perfect adequation that is signified by the capital letter O at the beginning of the *Marguerites*. They move back toward their beginning, searching for the silence that reigned before the Word was reflected in time by language.

Although Marguerite's poems tend to culminate in the experience of *illuminatio*, they open in darkness and fear. The very presence of language, which is a corrupted form of the Word, is a sign of obscurity and error. The voice we hear at the beginning of the *Miroir* is anxious and self-incriminatory. Disoriented, the speaker seeks first of all to get her bearings. The initial concern of the text is to determine spatial relationships. "Où est l'Enfer?" [Where is hell?] Marguerite asks in the opening words of the poem; "où est le puitz de malediction?" (p. 15)[8] [Where is the pit of malediction?]. If the location of hell could be determined, that of heaven would be immediately apparent, for the two constitute the opposite poles of the Christian universe. In fact, the reader has not advanced very far into the poem before he encounters a specific reference to the "treshault lieu, où est vostre [God's] demeure" (p. 22) [very high places where

8. Page references are to the *Marguerites* (Johnson Reprint Corporation), Vol. 1.

God's dwelling is]. Cosmographic matters continue to preoc-
cupy the speaker for several more lines until, in a flash of insight
that occurs during prayer, she realizes that hell is the earth insofar as it is unredeemed matter whereas heaven is the infinite.
Struck dumb by the insight accorded her, she decides to "laisser
le plaisir de la terre / Pour l'infiny, là où est paix sans guerre" (p.
24) [leave the pleasure of the earth for the infinite, there where
there is peace without war]. This resolution, dependent on a
clear understanding of the geometry of Christian space, marks
the end of the proem, which consists of some 260 lines out of a
total of nearly 1450. At the same time, it points to the nature of
Marguerite's enterprise in the rest of the poem. She will try to
rise above earthly concerns and to move toward God, an effort
that is expressed in the text through the displacement of literal
discourse by figurative discourse.

Language in the first forty or so lines of the *Miroir* is fallen
language. Symptomatic of the error, confusion, and darkness
into which mankind has plunged, it is the language of the "profound abysme" in which Marguerite finds herself at the beginning of the poem. We have seen that a marginal notation next to
the epigraph refers us to Psalm 50. A similar notation appears
next to line thirty-four, referring us to John 1. Beginning with
line forty-six, references to Scriptural passages follow one another in rapid succession. These marginal notations do not appear in the manuscript copies of the *Miroir*. Added by the editor
or printer of the 1547 edition of the *Marguerites*, they draw our
attention to the presence of the Word in human discourse. From
line forty-six on, nearly every page of the *Miroir* has at least
one—usually three or four—allusions to the Bible. Often Marguerite's verses are literal translations of Scripture. Sometimes
they are paraphrases of biblical passages. As more and more biblical citations and paraphrases appear in the poem, images of
light replace those of darkness and gloom. Effacing itself before
the presence of the Word, Marguerite's text becomes a clear, polished mirror that reflects God's text. The voice we hear in the
poem is no longer that of the distraught Marguerite but that of
God speaking to man through Scripture. Fallen language is redeemed through the presence of His Word, identical with the
operation of grace. Augustine had argued that "obscure places"
in the Bible are illuminated by "clear places" situated near them.
Augustinian hermeneutics consists of reading texts in such a way

that the "clear places" explain the "obscure places" so that, in the end, the distinction between one place and another is abolished. The biblical passages in the *Miroir* are "clear places" whose message of charity extends across the whole text and effaces the distinction made at the beginning of the poem between fallen language, allegorized as a "profound abysme," and God's Word, allegorized as a "treshault lieu." The *Miroir* traces the narrator's growing realization that the Johannine *logos* is located not beyond human speech in an inaccessible "treshault lieu" but rather within language itself.

The rhetoric of spatiality at the beginning of the *Miroir* is accompanied by a rhetoric of corporeality. In her desire to learn "où je suis, et pourquoi je labeure" (p. 17) [where I am and why I toil], Marguerite stresses a corporeal presence that occupies space. She calls herself "un corps remply de toute promptitude / A faire mal . . ." (p. 17) [a body filled with every proneness to do evil] and mentions her eyes, mouth, ears, nose, arms, and legs in language that is determinedly referential. Then in lines thirty-four and thirty-five she introduces the first specific allusion to Scripture since the epigraph: "Par sa clarté ma tenebre illumine" [By His light my darkness is made light], John 1.5. Only through His grace, she says, can her soul be freed from the oppressive presence of the body. Concerned with liberating her soul from the death to which her body seems to have condemned it, she turns to Christ as incarnated in Scripture. The operation of His grace is reflected in the text by the sudden and overwhelming infusion of biblical citations into the poem. Nine appear between verses forty-six and fifty-nine. Serving to illuminate the darkness of human speech, God's Word limits the referential significance of language. It reveals the spirit within the letter, which is the linguistic equivalent of the body, whose fate it is to perish. "It is the spirit that gives life, the flesh has nothing to offer," Christ told His disciples; "the words I have spoken to you are spirit and they are life" (John 6.63). The biblical citations inscribed in the text designate with increasing persistence a reality that denies corporeal presence. In referential terms, this reality is experienced as the pulverization of the flesh; in anagogic terms, as the effacement of the letter before the spirit.

Marguerite's attitude toward the body, that is to say, the letter, is ambiguous. At times she calls it "boue" [mud] and "fiens"

[dung] and speaks joyfully of its annihilation. But unlike those medieval mystics who utterly despised the flesh, she is conscious of the fact that the body is the only vehicle through which God can speak to man and reveal His presence. Although it is imperfect and destined to eventual annihilation, it has been redeemed by the Incarnation and so participates to some degree in the redemptive process, which Marguerite presents as a movement along an axis that leads from lower, fleshy forms to higher, spiritual ones.

Looking into the *speculum Scripturae*, which is immanent in her own text, Marguerite sees in the image of herself that is reflected back to her a sinner "qui soubz peché par Adam est vendu, / Et de la Loy jugé d'estre pendu" (p. 17) [who is sold under sin by Adam, and by the Law condemned to be hanged]. In the biblical allusions that mark the text at this point, the words of Paul dominate. The mirror she holds before her and in which she discerns the likeness of herself is a *speculum Beati Pauli*. The Pauline emphasis on man as a fallen creature is a determining factor in Marguerite's perception of herself. Stressing the inability of man to make his will conform with that of God, Paul wrote: "Instead of doing the good things I want to do, I carry out the sinful things I do not want" (Romans 7.19), a verse Marguerite renders in the *Miroir* as "ce que DIEU veult, je ne le puis vouloir: / Ce qu'il ne veult, souvent desire avoir" (p. 17). Throughout Romans 7, Paul affirms that the source of evil is the assertiveness of the individual will. Marguerite adopts this Pauline notion and makes it the cornerstone of her perception of the human predicament. In the *Dialogue*, Charlotte had explained that the individual will must be stilled before the heart can be receptive to Christ's message. The only way to still the will, she had continued, is to love God and neighbor. The Marguerite who scrutinizes her image in the *speculum Beati Pauli* that is inscribed in the *Miroir* knows this truth but cannot yet draw her eyes away from the reflection of herself as sinner. "En moy je sens la force de peché" [In me I feel the force of sin], she declares, metacommunicating her sinfulness by repeatedly using the first person singular pronoun throughout the whole of this passage.

"Qui sera ce, qui me delivrera" (p. 17) [Who will it be who will free me], Marguerite asks anxiously as she continues to peer with increasing despair at the image of sinfulness reflected back to her in the Pauline mirror. The text soon answers her question with unequivocal clarity. "Par JESUS CHRIST" (p. 18), it affirms, alluding to Romans 5.1 in which Paul says that "through our Lord Jesus Christ, by faith we are judged righteous and at peace with God." After identifying Christ as the agent of liberation, Marguerite remarks, however, that He cannot save her from her sinfulness unless she beckons to Him and invites Him to reveal His presence in her heart. The potential for deliverance is always present, but Christ requires a sign of the sinner's desire to receive Him before the operation of grace can be accomplished. That sign is a gesture of submission to His Word. He who would be saved from darkness and ignorance must suppress his own will. Humbling himself before the Savior, he must feel the "tout nouveau desir" (p. 18) [entirely new desire] that Marguerite feels in her heart. Marguerite's "new desire" is to see herself as she is within the context of Christian reality. In a paradoxical way, recognition of her sinfulness or, to express it somewhat differently, realization of her distance from Christ, is the first step toward Him. In the vocabulary of mystics, this step, the first in the *scala perfectionis*, is the *mortificatio*. Briçonnet repeated tirelessly to Marguerite that only through the process of *mortificatio*, which he described as a pulverization of the self, can one be born in Christ.

Declaring that her own will has grown proud, Marguerite says that she wants to "sentir en moy mortification" (p. 19) [feel in myself mortification]. She recounts her past sins and calls herself a "ver de terre tout nud" (p. 19) [naked earthworm]. She reduces the sinful self to the status of non-being. At the same time, however, she begins to construct a new self that will be constituted as a reflection of Christ. Her deepest wish, she tells Christ, is to "estre toujours avecques vous en croix" (p. 19) [to be always with you on the cross]. Christ responds by opening her "spiritual eyes" so that she can see Him. The process of identification with Him starts when Marguerite suddenly sees His image clearly and remembers that when she was baptized He promised to be with her always. At the level of discourse, Christ's image is revealed in the biblical quotations that fill the text. Scriptural passages had begun to appear in the text sometime before the *mortificatio* theme was introduced. The Word was already there (indeed the Word is always present everywhere), but Marguerite had not seen It. In the words of Paul, her eyes had been "unseeing" (Romans 11.8).

As soon as she sees Christ, Marguerite realizes that He has been with her since the day of her baptism, even though she may have failed to recognize Him. Seeing His image and appropriating His wholeness by identifying with Him is tantamount to being "born again" (John 3.3) in Christ. It is a reaffirmation of the original bond that was forged between herself and Christ when, as an infant, she had been consecrated to Him at the baptismal fount. The rebirth of which she speaks cannot be fixed in time and space. Indeed, through the operation of the Holy Spirit the Christian is constantly and continually being born again. Ideally, every moment of his life is experienced as a duplication, a re-presentation, of the eternally present moment (Eckhart's *Now* moment) during which he was united sacerdotally with Christ. Being reborn at every instant, the Christian is always at the beginning. There is a sense in which the Christian wayfarer is ever an infant, newly baptized and united with God. If Marguerite used the language of spatiality early on in the poem, it was for tactical reasons. Even as the self seems to move progressively toward that place where it will fix its being in Christ, the *Miroir*, like nearly all of Marguerite's poems, subtly subverts the notion of forward or temporal progression. Inviting the reader to look along a vertical or upward rather than horizontal or forward axis ("profound abysme," "treshault lieu"), it compels him to respond to the relentless pressure of Christ's imperative—"Follow me. I am the way."—and helps him resist the temptation to leave the single right road for the innumerable wrong ones. Marguerite's text traces a movement that is antiprogressive for it locates the Christian's goal *at the beginning*, in the symbolic union with Christ that is achieved in baptism.

The metaphor Marguerite uses to express identification with Christ, whose image she sees in the *speculum Scripturae* that is situated in her own text, is that of marriage.[9] Her soul is an "espouse" [wife] whose husband is Christ. The marriage metaphor

---

9. On Marguerite's use of the word "marriage" and on the institution of marriage in the sixteenth century, see Emile V. Telle, *L'Oeuvre de Marguerite d'Angoulême, Reine de Navarre, et la querelle des femmes* (Toulouse: Lion et Fils, 1937).

was often used by Briçonnet, who developed it at length in his letter of June 14, 1524, to Marguerite. Like most of the metaphors in Marguerite's poetry, it is derived from Paul, for whom conjugal union was a symbol of man's covenant with Christ (Ephesians 5.25–32). Thanking Christ for having married her, Marguerite notes that her soul is now reconstituted so as to reflect Him.

> Elle [son ame] pourette, ignorante, impotente,
> Se sent en vous riche, sage, et puissante,
> Pour luy avoir au coeur escrit le rolle
> De vostre Esperit, et sacree Parole.   (p. 22)

Needy, unknowing, weak, she feels herself rich, wise, and powerful in you, who wrote in her heart the text of your Spirit and the holy Word.

The convergence of specular, baptismal, and conjugal metaphors in Marguerite's account of the *mortificatio* points to a self that is constituted within what Lacan calls the Imaginary.[10] Originating in the "mirror stage" of infancy, the Imaginary is a category of being in which the "I," seeing in the Other "a salutary *imago*" and "an ideal unity"[11] it feels it lacks, tries to master its world by identifying with the Other. For Lacan, the human self is originally an alienated self. The unity of the Other, which the self tries to appropriate by the process of identification, is an unattainable ideal. Resembling a superego, this imaginary construct of the self is both an ideal and a persecutory agent, for it constantly reminds the self of its failure to *be* the Other. The process of identification whereby Marguerite reconstitutes the self as the Other (i.e., Christ) is duplicated at the level of discourse by the text's appropriation of Scripture. In the verses cited above, Marguerite alludes to Paul ("you are a letter from Christ, . . . written not with ink but with the Spirit of the living God, not on stone tablets but on the tablets of your living hearts," II Corinthians 3.3) and declares that she has appropri-

---

10. Jacques Lacan, "The Mirror Stage," in *Ecrits*, trans. Alan Sheridan (London: Tavistock Publications, 1977). For a succinct analysis of Lacan's concept of "le stade du miroir," see J. Laplanche et J.-B. Pontalis, *Vocabulaire de la psychanalyse* (Paris: Presses universitaires de France, 1967), pp. 452–54.

11. *Ecrits*, pp. 18–19.

ated Christ's Word. Discerning in the Bible an expression of the Johannine *logos*, Marguerite's text appropriates the wholeness and perfection that Scripture represents by absorbing into its own textual body His "sacree Parole," thus seeking to possess the *Tout-Verbe* by identification with God's Word.

But no sooner does Marguerite define self within coordinates that resemble the Lacanian category of the Imaginary than she begins to suggest a subsequent restructuring of self within an order that transcends the Imaginary and is analogous to the Symbolic. Superseding the Imaginary, the Symbolic is the category of being into which the human being emerges when he begins to acquire language. The Symbolic is a preestablished order (it existed prior to the birth of the self and is independent of the self) that, Lacan emphasizes, is structured like a language. Transcending the Imaginary order, the "I" now "finds itself" as a signifier within a system of symbolic (linguistic) exchange in human society. Obviously, the self is still *another*, but it is no longer the Imaginary other constructed on the illusion of resemblance. Rather, it is alienated in a symbolic system, i.e., language, that it shares with others.

The shift from the Imaginary to the Symbolic is identical to the change from an anthropomorphic frame of reference, according to which man is reality, to a conceptual framework in which man is merely the reflection of reality. In the first instance, language is essentially referential whereas in the second it is anagogic. The movement away from the Imaginary and toward the Symbolic is effected in the *Miroir* by contemplation of a particular Scriptural passage that is inscribed in Marguerite's text. Addressing His disciples, Christ said: "Anyone who does the will of my Father in heaven, he is my brother and sister and mother" (Matthew 12.50). In the course of reading this Scriptural passage (". . . en oyant, ou lisant / Les motz sacrez," p. 25) [hearing, or reading, the holy words], the "I" of the poem discovers that it no longer wishes to define itself exclusively in terms of the anthropomorphically limiting concept of "wife" (the desire to be Christ's wife is an *imaginary* ambition) but rather to assume Christ's qualities or His "name" in that *symbolic* realm in which being-like-Christ is itself defined and marked off as a particular role. Amazed at her own audacity as she prepares to appropriate the Symbolic, Marguerite says:

> Mais, Monseigneur, si vous estes mon Pere,
> Puis-je penser que je suis vostre Mere?
> Vous engendrer, vous, par qui je suis faite?   (p. 25)

But, Lord, if you are my Father, is it possible for me to think that I am your Mother? that I begot you, through whom I am made?

Assuring herself that Christ did indeed say that anyone who believes in Him is His brother, sister, and mother, Marguerite appropriates with exultation the name of "mother" (". . . par amour je vous ay engendré: / Donques sans peur, nom de Mere prendray," p. 26) [through love I begot you. Therefore I shall take the name of Mother without fear] and then the names of "sister," and "daughter." "O mon bon frere, enfant, pere, et espoux" (p. 29) [O my good brother, child, father, and husband], she says.[12] Aware that she can assume the "function" of mother, sister, daughter, and wife without claiming that she *is* in fact His mother, His sister, His daughter, or His wife, she says ecstatically, "Mon filz, mon DIEU, ô JESUS, quel language!" (p. 28) [My son, my God, O Jesus, what language!].

Part One of the poem, which makes up about one fourth of the text, concludes when Marguerite's words lose their referential meaning and become signs that point to the symbolic order of the *Tout-Verbe*. Part Two consists of four discrete narratives, each of which re-presents the self's experience of *mortificatio* and its rebirth in Christ. In the first narrative, the "I" is a daughter, in the second a mother, in the third a sister, and in the fourth a wife. Each of these passages has an identical structure, which is modeled on that of the first part of the poem. As the self in each narrative strives to establish an "identificatory" relation to Christ (the first thing it does is "identify" itself as daughter, mother, sister, wife), we see even more clearly than in Part One the aggressive tension inherent in a relation lived in the Imaginary order. In each case, the *imago* is a fiercely persecutory agent, a

---

12. Marguerite often concluded her letters to Briçonnet with an expression such as "Vostre gellée, alterée et affamée fille" (I.132) [Your cold, thirsty and famished daughter] or "Vostre pauvre, inutille mere" (II.33) [Your poor, useless mother]. Briçonnet responded by calling himself "Vostre inutil filz" (II.34) [Your useless son]. For the Pseudo-Dionysius, distinctions of the kind indicated by words like "mother," "father," "brother," "sister," "wife," and "husband" have no meaning when placed against the background of absolute infinity, which he called the Undifferentiated.

stern *alter ego* that provokes feelings of humiliation and inadequacy in the self. As soon as the self assumes its identity (in terms, of course, of the other), it "sees" its own sinfulness and delivers a self-accusatory tirade that reflects the experience of *mortificatio*.

Each mortific scene is a sustained narrative couched in allegorical language. Marguerite describes her filial relation to God by retelling the story of the prodigal son. (Being both masculine and feminine, the French words "l'enfant prodigue," which Marguerite uses, facilitate her identification with the wayward child whose misadventures Christ recounted in one of His most famous parables.) At the conclusion of her account of "l'enfant prodigue," she exclaims: "Mais voicy pis; Quelle mere ay-je esté?" (p. 31) [But here is something worse; what kind of a mother was I?]. She begins immediately to redefine herself as Christ's mother. Here she relates an allegory of her own devising. Sitting near the cradle of her infant son, Jesus, Marguerite fell asleep. As she slept, plunged into "la nuict d'ignorance" [the night of ignorance], her "grande ennemie," defined variously as "sensualité" and "bestialité," stole the child from its cradle and replaced it with a dead child of her own named "Péché" [Sin]. When she awoke and discovered what had happened, Marguerite was disconsolate. In a long lamentation, she refuses to accept "Péché" as her child and bemoans her failure to provide the maternal protection her son required. As in the first scene, she is painfully aware of what she has lost ("Perdu vous ay, qui m'est un dur remord, / Perdu vous ay, par ma faute, mon filz," p. 31) [I have lost you, which makes me bitterly remorseful; I have lost you, through my own fault, my son] and confesses her guilt and unworthiness.

In the third scene, Marguerite calls herself His sister and identifies with Miriam who, together with Aaron, spoke out against Moses (Numbers 12) and thus incurred the wrath of God. Foolishly, Marguerite criticized her brother ("J'ay estimé voz oeuvres estre vice," p. 35) [I thought your works were defective]. To punish her, God turned her into a leper, as He had done with Miriam. "En voyant mon visage," Marguerite says, "chacun congnust que n'avoir esté sage" (p. 36) [Seeing my face, everyone understood that I had not been wise]. Expelled from human society, she contemplates her sinfulness with horror. Overcome with remorse, she begs her brother to readmit her to His presence. He recognizes her submission and extends His love and welcome to the guilty penitent. "C'est trop, c'est trop, helàs c'est trop, mon frere" [That is too much, that is too much, alas, that is too much my brother], repeats Marguerite. "Point ne devez à moy sy grans biens faire. / J'ay fait le mal, vous me rendez le bien" [You ought not extend such great kindness to me. I did evil; you give me back good], she says as she vows never to leave His side or speak ill of Him again.

Before beginning the fourth scene, which is longer than the previous three combined, Marguerite summarizes the movement traced in the narratives she has just related. In each of the three stories, a sinner recognizes his guilt and experiences *mortificatio*. He then returns, cleansed, to Christ with whom, or more precisely, within whom, he had resided at some point prior to the beginning of the narrative. The fall into sin is thus identical to the fall into narrative. The cessation of sin marks the end of discourse. Summing up the first three allegories and at the same time announcing the final one, Marguerite says:

> Si pere a eu de son enfant mercy,
> Si mere a eu pour son filz du soucy,
> Si frere à soeur a couvert le peché;
> Je n'ay point veu, ou il est bien caché,
> Que nul mary, pour à luy retourner,
> Ayt à sa femme onc voulu pardonner.   (pp. 37–38)

If the father has had pity for his child, if the mother has had concern for her son, if the brother has concealed his sister's sin, I have not seen (if there is such a case, it is well hidden) the husband who was ever willing to pardon his wife so that she could return to him.

Fathers and mothers may forgive and provide for their children, brothers may cherish their sisters, but never, Marguerite affirms, has a husband pardoned his wife. In fact, husbands are far more prone to kill an erring wife than to forgive her. The kindest treatment that a guilty wife can expect from an offended husband is, Marguerite says, to be locked up in a tower or sent back to her parents where she will be scorned and despised for the rest of her life. Seeing herself now as Christ's wife, she marvels at His conduct, for among all other husbands He alone forgave His guilty wife and, accepting her back, enfolded her lovingly in His arms.

Parquoy, mon DIEU, nulle comparaison
Ne puis trouver en nul temps ne saison:
Mais par amour, qui est en vous sy ample,
Estes icy seul, et parfait exemple.   (p. 38)

For this, my God, I cannot find any comparison in any time or age;
but through love, which is so abundant in you, you are here the unique
and perfect model.

Like Paul, Marguerite speaks of Christ's love within the context of marriage. But unlike Paul, she was sensitive to the effects
of marriage on women. She tends to view marriage alternately
as a prison in which the woman languishes without hope and,
at the other extreme, as a metaphor for mystical union with
Christ. Accusing herself of having abandoned Christ the husband, she explains that she deserted Him for "l'Ennemy, et le
Monde, et la Chair" (p. 40) [the Enemy, and the World, and the
Flesh]. "J'aymois bien mieux à mon plaisir aller" (p. 41) [I pre-
ferred to go to my pleasure], she confesses. Relying on anaphora to convey the relentless pressure of shame, Marguerite repeats ten times the words "Laissé vous ay" [I left you], which
express the essence of her offense against Christ:

En diray je la verité? ouy.
Laissé vous ay, oublié, et fouy:
Laissé vous ay, pour suyvre mon plaisir:
Laissé vous ay, pour un mauvais choisir.   (p. 40)

Shall I tell the truth about it? Yes. I left you, forgot you and fled; I left
you to follow my pleasure; I left you to choose a bad man.

At this point in the narrative, Marguerite equates desertion of
Christ with a misreading of Scripture. Even though she had left
Him, Christ continued to speak gently and compassionately to
her. She, however, failed to understand His message of forgiveness. She read His words, but, because love was absent from her
heart, could not interpret correctly what He said.

Làs, tous ces motz ne voulois escouter;
Mais encores, je venois à douter,
Si c'estoit vous: ou si par adventure
Ce n'estoit rien, qu'une simple escriture.

> Car jusques là, j'estoye bien sy fole,
> Que sans amour lisois vostre parole.   (p. 43)

Alas, I did not want to listen to all those words; but still I began to wonder if it was you, or if by chance it was nothing but a mere piece of writing. For, up to that time, I was so very foolish that I read your word without love.

Then she read Jeremiah 3 ("Je vins à lire Hieremie," p. 44) and saw her own image in the prophet's depiction of a wife who left her husband and "prostituted [herself] with so many lovers" (Jeremiah 3.1). According to the letter of the law, Marguerite says, the wife merited punishment for her "prostitution and vices" (Jeremiah 3.2). Justice required that the husband denounce her and refuse to see her again. The law of justice, however, has been superseded by the law of love. Christ forgave His wife and took her back, saying:

> Mais toy, qui as fait separation
> De mon doux lict, pour fornication
> Avec autruy meschantement commettre,
> Et en mon lieu tes faux amateurs mettre,
> A moy tu peux toutesfois revenir.   (p. 44)

But you, who have kept away from my soft bed to commit adultery foully with another and to put false lovers in my place, you can nevertheless return to me.

Reunited with her loving husband, the wife, whose self is now restructured within the coordinates of the *Tout-Verbe*, speaks of the destruction of the willful self she once was and of her rebirth in Christ:

> O Charité, bien voy que vostre ardeur
> Icy defait, et brusle ma laydeur:
> Et me refait creature nouvelle,
> Pleine de DIEU, qui me fait estre belle.
> Ce, qui est mien, avez du tout destruit,
> Sans y laisser renommee ne bruit:
> En me daignant sy parfaite refaire,
> Que tout le bien, qu'un vray espoux peult faire

> A son espouse, vous l'avez fait à moy;
> En me donnant de voz promesses Foy.   (p. 47)

O Love, I see clearly that your ardor here destroys and burns up my ugliness; and remakes me a new creature, full of God, who makes me beautiful. That which is mine you have completely destroyed, without leaving behind renown or notoriety; deigning to remake me so perfect, you have done for me every good that a true husband can do for his wife, giving me the Faith that you promised.

Marguerite's statement that she has been remade in His likeness marks a perceptual shift away from the concept of self as reality, seeing its own (imperfect) image in God's Word, to that of self as a reflection of Christ, seeing His perfection in the polished mirror of the human heart. Consummation of the "union, qui est de l'ame au corps" (p. 55) [union, which is of the soul to the body] is symbolized by a bed, which, the reader understands, is the "place" the soul sought in the opening verses of the *Miroir*:

> Or ay-je donc, par vostre bonne grace,
> De l'espouse recouverte la place.
> Bienheureux lieu, place tant desirable,
> Gratieux lict, throne threshonnorable,
> Siege de paix, repos de toute guerre,
> Hault dais d'honneur, separé de la terre,
> Recevez vous ceste indigne personne.   (pp. 47–48)

Thus I have, by your good grace, regained the place of the wife. Blessed spot, place so desirable, gracious bed, most noble throne, seat of peace and repose from all war, high dais of honor, separated from the earth, receive this unworthy person.

Increasingly ecstatic, Marguerite speaks of that reversal of values according to which death as the world defines it becomes life in Christ:

> Amour, amour, vous avez fait l'accord,
> Faisant unir à la vie la mort.
> Mais l'union a mort vivifiee.
> Vie mourant d'amour verifiee,
> Vie sans fin a fait nostre mort vive.
> Mort a donné à vie mort naïve.

Par ceste mort, moy morte reçoy vie;
Et au vivant par la mort suis ravie.
En vous je vy; quand en moy je suis morte,
Mort ne m'est plus que d'une prison porte.
Vie, m'est mort; . . . (p. 49)

Love, love, you have brought them together, uniting death with life. But the union gives life to death. Life dying with love confirms that life without end has given life to our death. Death gave life a natural death. By this death, I, dead, receive life; and I am borne away to the living by death. In you I live; when in myself I am dead, death is nothing more to me than a door out of a prison. Life is death for me.

With this vision of Christ as the source of life ("O vray amant, de Charité la source," p. 65) [O true lover, the fountainhead of love] and that of her own heart, cleansed and pure, as the mirror in which He can see Himself, Marguerite concludes the last of the four allegories designed to trace the paradigmatic trajectory from *mortificatio* to *unio*.

In order to blot out the sinful self, or, more accurately, the sin of self, Marguerite uses in each of the four allegories the same strategies she used in the *Petit Oeuvre*. Sustained by the overtly allegorical nature of the language, a strong narrative thrust is established early on in each case. The experience of *mortificatio* is described in language that is referential and in verbs that are almost exclusively in the past tense. As she is cleansed of sin, Marguerite enters the order of being characterized by the "nowness" of Christ's presence. The syntagmatic thrust of narrative is subverted as verbs in the present tense supplant those in the past. Temporal flow ceases. The text no longer exhibits forward momentum. It does not move, as Augustine put it, "from place to place" because it is designed, ultimately, to express a vision in which there is literally no place outside Him. The narrative at the beginning of each of the four allegories is fashioned so as to represent the "wrong way," down which the reader, i.e., the deluded sinner, travels. By abandoning narrative, the text compels us to perceive as error our assumption that Christ, or "meaning," is "out there" at the end of a road. Marguerite's recognition of her sinfulness parallels our realization that narrative, which we thought was taking us forward, has in fact brought us back to the beginning.

The frustration we may experience while reading the *Miroir* is due in part to the fact that the long second half of the poem, that is to say, the part that follows the fourth allegory, goes nowhere from a narrative point of view. The text strives to deny the temporal and spatial flow apparent in the lines of print that advance across page after page. Our dilemma, however, is the dilemma the Christian confronts every moment of his life, for he is enjoined to keep his eye on the perfect whole, i.e., Christ, and not to confuse Christian reality with the illusory notions of time and space. Failure to *see* the whole results inevitably in misreading, which is as good a synonym as any for sin. The seemingly interminable second half of the *Miroir*, which depicts the ecstasy of the *unio* and the blindness of insight (". . . le Soleil d'une seule estincelle / Aveugle l'oeil," p. 66) [the sun, with only one spark, blinds the eye], is designed to instill in us the habit of reading correctly, that is, of seeing (to use Northrop Frye's words once again) not only *the* whole *of* the text, but *a* whole *in* it. Ultimately, the reader of the *Miroir* is invited to see in the poem the whole that was represented graphically on the first page of the text by that emblem of perfection and completeness, the letter O.

Comprehension of the whole is a perceptual mode that displaces both the Imaginary and the Symbolic. Working their way through these two categories, Marguerite's texts posit a category of the Real that lies beyond the other two. This third category I call the Iconic. In the sense most commonly used by linguists, an icon displays actual (not *imaginary*) resemblance between the signifier and the signified, as in a portrait that signifies the person that it represents not by arbitrary convention only but by resemblance.[13] The Imaginary, too, is based on resemblance (the mirror stage) but there is a conceptual difference be-

---

13. The concept of *icon* was introduced into linguistics by Charles S. Peirce, *Collected Papers*, III (Cambridge: Harvard University Press, 1933), par. 362, p. 211: "I call a sign which stands for something merely because it resembles it, an *icon*. Icons are so completely substituted for their objects as hardly to be distinguished from them. . . . So in contemplating a painting, there is a moment when we lose the consciousness that it is not the thing, the distinction of the real and the copy disappears, and it is for the moment a pure dream—not any particular existence, and yet not general. At that moment we are contemplating an *icon*." See Jonathan Culler, *Structuralist Poetics* (Ithaca: Cornell University Press, 1975), pp. 16–17; Paul Ricoeur, *The Rule of Metaphor*, trans. Robert Czerny (Toronto: University of Toronto Press, 1977), pp. 189–91. W. K. Wimsatt applied the word *icon* to literary texts in his *The Verbal Icon* (Lexington, Ky.: University of Kentucky Press, 1954).

tween it and the Iconic, for what the Imaginary *seems* to be the Iconic *is*. To the extent that relations are lived in the Imaginary order, the "I" identifies with the other, seeing a resemblance between itself and an other. In the Iconic order, however, the "I" and the "other" do not *seem* to be identical; they *are* identical. By way of illustrating this distinction further, we can say that in the Imaginary the "I" seeks (ultimately without success) to be the father; in the Symbolic it assumes the functions of the father; but in the Iconic it *is* the father. The Iconic, then, is a realization (in the sense of making real) of the integration anticipated in the mirror stage of infancy. He whose relations are experienced in the Iconic has no "self." And that is precisely Marguerite's point. What the world calls "real" is in fact unreal. Within the context of Christian revelation, what Lacan calls *imaginaire* turns out to be not imaginary but real, for the Christian *is* an other. The text that represents this perception is an iconic text.

Anticipating her fusion with Christ, Marguerite says:

> Et jouiray de vostre vision:
> Par qui seray à vous sy conformee,
> Que j'y seray divine transformee.   (p. 57)

I shall share your vision; by this I shall be so like you that I shall become divine.

As the future becomes an actuality, Marguerite uses verbs in the present tense and, affirming that she is forever joined to Him, declares that because Christ is All, the love she bears Him is a reflection of Himself, the source of love.

> . . . et en l'aymant,
> Par son amour sentz l'aymer doublement.
> Mon amour n'est pour l'aymer, mais la sienne
> En moy l'ayme, que je sentz comme mienne.
> Il s'ayme donc en moy; et par m'aymer
> Il fait mon coeur par amour enflammer.
> Par ceste amour il se fait aymer tant,
> Que son effect (non moy) le rend content.   (p. 65)

. . . and in loving him, I feel that by his love I love him doubly. My love is not for loving him, but his love in me I love, which I feel as if it were mine. He thus loves himself in me; and by loving me, he makes my heart burn with love. By this love he makes himself so loved that its effect (not I) makes him content.

As in an icon, the relationship between Marguerite, the signifier, the *Verbe*, and Christ, the signified, the *Tout-Verbe*, is that of resemblance or likeness. Becoming *christiforme*, the text secures its identity first in Scripture, then in Christ the Text, whose love (and Christ *is* love) it reflects endlessly.

But the word "become" is profoundly inaccurate. Responding to the whole that is in the poem, we see in the text an image (reflection) of Christian reality according to which the self does not "become" *christiforme* for it has been so ever since baptism, which antedates the beginning of the poem. *Mortificatio* does not lead in a sequential way to *unio*. On the contrary, it *signifies* the *unio*, for it is an indivisible part of the marriage with Christ that was consummated in the beginning. The meaning of the poem, its *dianoia*, is that the Christian always comes to a place where he is already. In a fundamental way, Christian reality can never be narrated; it can only be reflected. The poet and the reader merely trace out—one with the pen, the other with the eye—a pattern or paradigm that stood complete before they came to it. In its unfolding, the *Miroir* manages to subvert its forward momentum and impose itself on the reader's consciousness as a mirror that reflects the iconic figure of Christ, inseparable, the text would have us believe, from our own image.

And yet the poem does not behave quite in this way. The strategies I have outlined, all of which conspire to effect what we may call the iconization of the text, are no doubt part of Marguerite's poetic program. But the *Miroir* itself is both an enactment of that program and an exploration of its problematics. No sooner does Marguerite declare that she and Christ are one—or, to express the same phenomenon somewhat differently, that the *Verbe* and the *Tout-Verbe* are radically alike—than she begins to reflect on the difficulties inherent in expressing the *unio* in language. Indeed, the function of language is to establish distinctions of the kind that mystical ecstasy abolishes. Paul had called the language of ecstasy unintelligible (I Corinthians 14.2) for it transcends the *Verbe* and attains the *Tout-Verbe*, which must be represented as silence. Paul also remarked that the ecstatic spirit can speak only to God. It cannot speak to man or commit its speech to paper. This distressing fact underlies the problematics of Marguerite's poetry. Time and time again her texts, which are aware of their own internal tensions, end up confessing their unworthiness. The sense of frustratio and impotence we noted at the end of the *Oraison à nostre Seigneur Jesus Christ* is equally strong throughout the final pages of the *Miroir*.

> . . . . le puis-je bien escrire?
> Vostre bonté, vostre amour se peult elle
> Bien concevoir de personne mortelle?
> Et s'il vous plait un petit l'imprimer
> Dedens un coeur, la peult il exprimer?   (p. 66)

Can I write it down correctly? Can a mortal person really conceive of your goodness, your love? And if it pleases you to print a little of it in a heart, can the heart express it?

> . . . il ne luy [l'Esprit] est possible
> Dire que c'est d'amour.   (p. 67)

It is not possible for the Spirit to say what love is.

> Le dire donc n'est pas en sa puissance,
> Puis que du feu il n'ha la congnoissance;
> D'amour ne sçait bien au vray diffinir,
> Qui la cuydé toute en son coeur tenir,
> Bienheureux est, qui en ha tel excés
> Que dire peult, Mon DIEU, j'en ay assez.
> Qui l'ha en soy, il n'en sçauroit parler.   (p. 67)

To say it is therefore not in its power, since it has no knowledge of the fire; he who thought that he could keep love in his heart does not know how to define it truly; happy is he who has so much love that he can say, My God, I have enough. He who has it in himself is not able to talk about it.

Proclaiming its own worthlessness, the text enacts the experience of *mortificatio* on the level of discourse. It humbles itself and, confessing its grossness and baseness, declares itself to be "moins que riens" (p. 68) [less than nothing].

But, as we have noted, *mortificatio* is one with *illuminatio* and *unio*. Confession of worthlessness is a sign of worth. Marguerite is Christ's wife (as well as mother, sister, and daughter) precisely because she is also, but in accord with a different set of optical principles, a "ver de terre" [earthworm], a "chienne morte" [dead bitch], an "ordure de fiens" (p. 68) [filthy dung], "poudre et fange" (p. 70) [dirt and mud]. Marguerite's text, too, acknowledges its shame. The capital letter O that figures on the first page of the *Miroir* now reveals its essential duplicity, for as well as representing perfection it is the cipher, the arithmetic symbol that denotes nought. Within the O, All and Nothingness, Presence and Absence, or, in Marguerite's words *Tout* and *Rien* (p. 66), are fused into Christ, who is one and indivisible. By declaring the futility of its own discourse, Marguerite's text tries to efface the words of which it is composed and so enacts the cleansing process by which the heart is prepared to serve as a faithful reflector of His love.

The abolition of discourse is a constitutive feature of the *unio*. On the final page of the *Miroir*, Marguerite and her text ruminate:

> Il [Christ] est en nous, et trestous en luy sommes.
> Tous sont en luy, et luy en tous les hommes;
> Si nous l'avons par Foy, tel est l'avoir,
> Que de le dire en nous n'est le povoir.   (p. 70)

He is in us and we are all in him. All are in him and he is in all men; if we have him by Faith, this having is such it is not in our power to speak of it.

Since the first person is no longer distinguishable from the second and third persons, linguistic communication, which is grounded on distinctions, is impossible. Referring yet again to Paul's injunction to heed not the letter but the spirit, the concluding pages of the *Miroir* focus on the paradox that informs nearly all of Marguerite's poetry: metalanguage must and can exist even though it cannot be translated into discursive language. With proper authorial manipulation, however, a text, although it cannot contain the *Tout-Verbe*, can be polished and cleaned until it is so smooth, so "white," as Plato said of the realm of True Being (*Phaedrus* 247C), that it becomes a mirror capable of reflecting not only the sinful soul of the self but also the glory of the Johannine *logos*. If Marguerite continues to speak despite her awareness of the fact that her words cannot contain (delimit) His Word, it is because her texts represent an attempt to interpret the experience of life as an unending sacrament. "L'impossible me sera donques taire" (p. 68) [It will therefore be impossible for me to be silent], she says near the end of the *Miroir*: "trop d'ingratitude / Seroit en moy, si n'eusse rien escrit" [there would have been too much ingratitude in me if I had written nothing]. Her poetry is the result of a sustained effort to provoke in the Christian soul a reflection of the mystery of baptism, a mystery that abolishes time and space and permits the cleansed and reborn Christian to live in the eternal nowness of Christ.

A "correct" reading of Marguerite's texts, one that leads the mind away from the letter and toward the spirit, is tantamount to a cleansing of the reader's own soul. The true locus of the experience her texts enact is not the words on the page but the soul into which they flow, washing away all sinfulness. At the end of the brief prefatory poem that opens the *Marguerites*, Marguerite shifts the focus away from the text to the reader's heart, the site of Christ's kingdom:

> Mais vous, Lecteurs de bonne conscience,
> Je vous requiers, prenez la patience
> Lire du tout ceste oeuvre, qui n'est rien:
> Et n'en prenez seulement, que le bien.
> Mais priez DIEU plein de bonté naïve,
> Qu'en vostre coeur il plante la Foy vive. (p. 14)

But you, readers of good conscience, I beseech you, have patience and read all of this work, which is nothing; and do not take from it anything except the good. But pray God, full of spontaneous goodness, that he will plant the living Faith in your heart.

Ultimately the text asks the reader to perceive it not as an artifact but as a secular enactment of baptism, that is to say, a sign of oneness in Christ. And just as the sign that is baptism is ever operative in the Christian soul, so the experience that the text generates is, ideally, ever present in the reader's mind, contributing to his progressive illumination.

"ECCE HOMO"

By placing the *Miroir de l'âme pécheresse* at the beginning of her published work, Marguerite stressed the *speculum* tradition that informs much of her poetry. The fact that her last poem, *L'Art et usage du souverain mirouer du chrestien*, written shortly before her death on December 21, 1549, is also a "mirror" poem gives a powerful sense of closure to the whole corpus of her work. Circling back to its point of origin, her poetry situates the end in the beginning. *L'Art et usage*, which Raymond Lebègue calls "le second Miroir,"[14] has been published twice. It appeared first in Toulouse in 1552 under the title of *Le Mirouer de Jesus Christ crucifié* and then in Paris in 1556 as *L'Art et usage du souverain mirouer du chrestien*.[15] The poem has not been reprinted since. The 1556 edition was prepared by the priest Pierre Olivier, who explains in his preface that Marguerite gave him a manuscript copy of the untitled poem a few days before her death. The title of the poem in the 1556 edition is Olivier's.

L'Art et usage is an enactment of the experience the Christian undergoes as he contemplates the crucifix. Its 1400 decasyllabic lines are divided (by Olivier?) into a "proem" and sixteen clearly marked "chapters," each with an explanatory title (supplied by Olivier?). In the proem, Marguerite, the devout penitent, looks at the crucified Christ and is at first overcome by horror at the spectacle of the son of God nailed, like a thief, to the cross. The pathetic quality of the scene is heightened by the fact that God seems indifferent to His son's suffering, which Marguerite evokes in pain. Christ's anguish, Marguerite understands, is her own. She abolishes the difference between herself and Christ by identifying with the crucified figure on the cross. Suddenly, however, the disjunctive "mais" introduces a modulation that signals

---

14. "Le second Miroir de Marguerite de Navarre," *Comptes rendus des séances de l'Académie des Inscriptions et Belles-Lettres* (1963), 46–56.

15. Lebègue tells us that only one copy of the Toulouse edition is extant. Since he published his article, that copy has apparently disappeared. On the missing copy, see Lucia Fontanella, "Per una edizione del *Miroir de Jesus Christ Crucifié* di Margherita di Navarra," *Le Moyen français*, 3 (1978), 110. Only one copy of the 1556 edition is extant. It was published by Guillaume le Noir and is now in the Bibliothèque de l'Arsenal. I am grateful to the Bibliothèque Nationale for providing me with a microfilm of this copy. All citations are from this edition and are identified by page number (*recto* or *verso* indicated).

a change, not in the scene itself, but in the way Marguerite perceives, or "reads," the figure of the crucified Christ. Sharing His suffering, she also shares His joy. The crucifixion signifies triumph, not defeat.

In the brief first chapter, Marguerite says that pride, or the sin of self, is the chief obstacle to union with Christ. *L'Art et usage* illustrates the process by which the penitent Christian humbles himself, frees himself from pride, and so becomes *christiforme*. Chapters II to XII each describe a specific part of Christ's body. Marguerite anatomizes human suffering through an enumeration of the signs by which it is made manifest in Christ's body, beginning with the face and moving to the eyes, mouth, ears, hair, chin, arms, hands, and feet. As in a *blason*, each part of the body is personified and addressed directly. Each one is a mirror in which the Christian sees both himself and Christ. Marguerite "exercises" all five of her senses as she seeks to absorb into herself as much of His experience as possible. She touches His wounds, tastes His blood, smells His "odeur delectable" (p. 16ᵛ), sees His contorted arms and legs, and hears His words. Her goal is to bring her body in accord with His. Marguerite's method here resembles that proposed by Loyola. In his *Spiritual Exercises*, Loyola advised the Christian to develop each of his senses so as to be able to experience, through heightened sensual perception, the reality that is Christ.[16]

·In each chapter, Marguerite repeats the procedure she uses in Chapter II, which is devoted to a description of Christ's face. Apostrophizing His face, she calls it ugly: "Comme tu es pailliée et decrachée, / Pleine de sang, et bouffie et machée!" (p. 11) [How scratched and bespattered you are, full of blood, and swollen, and macerated]. The *laideur* she sees in the mirror before her is her own ugliness reflected back to her:

> En toy je voy ma laide maladie,
>
> . . .
>
> En te voyant, recognois estre en moy:
> Qui par raison doy estre comme toy,
> Devant Dieu suis laid et abominable.   (p. 11ʳ)

16. *The Spiritual Exercises of Saint Ignatius of Loyola*, ed. W. H. Longridge (London: A. R. Mowbray, 1919), "First Week, Fifth Exercise," p. 67 and "Second Week, Fifth Contemplation," pp. 85–94.

In you I see my ugly sickness; seeing you, I acknowledge what is in me; by rights I ought to be like you; before God I am ugly and abominable.

But just as Christ took upon Himself her sins and so made her clean and pure, so He takes upon Himself her ugliness, leaving her beautiful. In the last three lines of the chapter, Marguerite says that Christ's ugliness is beautiful (". . . la laideur en luy belle apperçoy," p. 11ʳ) [ugliness in Him I perceive as beautiful], for it is the source of her salvation. The distinction between ugly and beautiful is now no more valid than the distinction between self and Christ. Whereas in the opening verses of Chapter II Marguerite had looked into the mirror of Christ's face and seen the image of her own sinful self, in the final verses she looks into the same mirror and sees reflected back to her the image of Christ, with whom she is united and from whom she is indistinguishable. This conjunction of signified (self) and the signifier (Christ) marks the experience of *unio*.

Eucharistic imagery is particularly suited to descriptions of mystical union with Christ. Although present in the first twelve chapters ("source abondant', je viens à voz fontaines, / . . . Beuvant ce sang qui est tant doux et soef," p. 20ʳ) [plentiful springhead, I come to your fountains, drinking this blood which is so sweet and delicious], it is especially prominent in the four chapters (XII–XVI) that follow the graphic representation of Christ on the cross. Equally striking in these concluding chapters is the apocalyptic image of the Lamb in whose blood the Christian washes himself clean. Exhorting herself to wash in the blood of the Lamb, Marguerite says:

> Plonge toy donc en ce sang tant nouveau,
> Et te revest de ceste digne peau,
> Que pour toy vois ainsi deschiqueter,
> Faictz toy dedans si bien empaqueter,
> Que ton peché et toy ne soit plus veu,
> De l'oeil divin, alors seras receu,
> Tant seulement pour ceste couverture,
> En qui seras nouvelle creature.   (p. 25ᵛ)

Plunge therefore into this blood so new and dress yourself again in this worthy hide, which you see torn like this for you; wrap yourself in it

so well that your sin can no longer be seen by the divine eye; then you
will be received, only because of this covering, in which you will be a
new creature.

In that ultimate union with Christ to which Marguerite aspires,
she herself, by a reversal of perspective that is characteristic of
the *unio*, becomes the mirror in which God sees His own image:
". . . Dieu en mon visage / . . . [peut] voir son image" (p. 27ʳ)
[God can see His image in my face].

Having attained this degree of identity with Christ, Marguerite points out, as she does in so many of her poems, the
utter inadequacy of language:

> Le cueur qui est noyé en c'est abisme,
> N'en peut parler ny raconter la disme:
> Car le grand bien de c'est eau salutaire
> L'esbaït tant, qu'il est contrainct se taire.   (p. 28ᵛ)

The heart that is drowned in this abyss cannot talk about or report a
tenth of it. For the great goodness of this wholesome water so as-
tonishes it that it is compelled to be silent.

The admission that discourse is unable to contain her experience
signals the approach of the end of the poem and the cessation of
language. Although in one sense language cannot express the
unio, it can state the *desire* for union. Thus the passage in which
Marguerite says she cannot go on speaking is followed by a
prayer; "En toy me change, et me transforme en toy" (p. 31)
[Change me into you and transform me into you], Marguerite
entreats Christ, whose image she holds before her:

> Qui tout à toy sans rien perdre retourne:
> A toy me tire, et tout vers toy me tourne,
> Comme vapeur que le soleil attire:
> Me tire à toy, qui dedans toy me mire,
> Et ton amour va mon cueur attirant,
> Que tu transmue en toy en se mirant:
> Car seulement te regardant se pert:
> Mais se perdant en luy, en toy appert.
> Mon riens faictz tout, ô plaisant changement,
> Ou l'imperfaict gaigne si largement.
> . . .

> Faictz que soions un seul et non plus deux.
> Un cors, un cueur, une ame et un esprit:
> Tant que du tout, je soye Jesuchrist   (p. 31 $^{v-r}$)

Who takes everything back to yourself without losing anything; draw me to yourself and turn me directly toward yourself as the sun draws up vapor. Draw me to you, who see me within yourself; and your love is drawing up my heart, which you change into you as it beholds itself; for just in looking at you it loses itself. But losing itself in your heart, it appears in you. Make my nothingness everything; O joyful change, whereby the imperfect gains so greatly . . . Make us one and no longer two. One body, one heart, one soul and one spirit, so that in every respect I am Jesus Christ.

Translating by anaphora the *nowness* of her transformation into Christ, Marguerite opens the final movement of the poem with the words:

> Icy je pers de moy le souvenir:
> Icy me veux, pour tout jamais tenir.
> Icy je pers, ce que le monde loue:
> Icy je voy ses biens n'estre que boue
> Icy je boy le vin tout à loisir:
> Du vray plaisir, que passe tout desir.   (p. 32 ^{v})

Here I lose memory of myself; here I wish to remain forever. Here I lose what the world praises; here I see that its riches are nothing but mud; here I drink wine at my leisure: true pleasure, which surpasses all desire.

Fifteen of the next (and final) thirty-six lines of the poem begin with the word "icy," which, of course, designates place and thus answers explicitly the question asked ("Où est. . .?") in the first words of the *Miroir de l'âme pécheresse*. Designating Christ as the "place" where desire is resolved into contentment, *L'Art et usage* concludes with a vision of paradisiacal bliss:

> Icy l'espoux embrasse son espouse:
> Icy mon cueur dedans ce cueur repose.
> Et en sentant ceste union si forte,
> Icy amour mon cueur à Dieu transporte

L'as je le pers, et ne le voy rien plus
Vous qui lisés contemplés le surplus.
   F I N   (p. 33ᵛ)

Here the husband embraces his wife; here my heart rests in this heart. And feeling that this union is so strong, here love transports my heart to God; you have it; I lose it and no longer see it at all. You who are reading, contemplate the rest. The End.

Whether by chance or by design, the poem ends on page thirty-three. Aware that Christ died at age thirty-three, we can see in the 1556 edition of the poem a body whose physical, or fleshy, form is a graphic textual duplication of Christ's human form. To the extent that we see a "resemblance" (in Peirce's sense of the word) between the body of the text and the body of Christ, "we are," to cite Peirce again, "contemplating an *icon*."

Repeating the word "icy," the text points to itself as the place where God is worshipped purely ("Icy est Dieu adoré purement"), where man's heart joins Christ's ("Icy se faict du cueur au cueur l'approche"), where joyous hallelujahs resound forever ("Icy se dit tousjours alleluya"). Blinded by the vision that her text seeks to contain, Marguerite takes leave of the reader in the last two verses of the poem by transcending language. The linguistic consequence of Marguerite's "union si forte" with Christ is a restoration of the *Tout-Verbe*, which, in the tradition of the Pseudo-Dionysius, can only be known by its negative image, silence. But the *Tout-Verbe* is not only transcendent; it is also immanent. It informs all the words that extend across the surface of Marguerite's text. Indeed, the *Tout-Verbe* cannot exist without the *Verbe* to reflect It any more than the *Verbe* can exist without the *Tout-Verbe*, which is the referent of all words. Silence is a property of language. Words lead to silence, and, in an endlessly circular motion, silence leads back to words. At the end of *L'Art et usage* Marguerite exhorts the reader to contemplate "le surplus," meaning that which her words cannot express. But, by a curious irony from which there is no escape, "le surplus" is not situated outside the text. Like the *Deus absconditus*, it lies hidden "icy," enfolded within discourse. The signs pointing to the "surplus" that Marguerite would have us contemplate are embedded in her text itself. The last line of Marguerite's last poem sends us

back to the texts, which, elaborating a problematics of reflection, constitute a mirror that allows us to see both the image of
our own sinful souls and a representation of the *unio mystica* as
Marguerite envisioned it.

6

The Apocalyptic Vision

THE LAW OF PLEASURE

Marguerite did not attach much importance to generic distinctions of the kind that were beginning to interest Humanists. That certain of her poems are called *comédies* or *farces* distinguishes them less in terms of content than in terms of the form they assume on the printed page. Even this external and purely formal difference between the "poems" on the one hand and the "plays" on the other is somewhat arbitrary, for, as we have seen, in the 1533 edition of the *Dialogue* the name of each speaker is printed in the text, giving the poem the appearance of a script. Indeed, a dialogic impulse animates all of Marguerite's poetry, which is designed to establish or confirm a communicative circuit between the "I" and the "Thou," the self and Christ.

The first edition of the *Marguerites* contains four *comédies* that make up almost half of the volume (229 pages out of 542). All four are biblical plays reminiscent of medieval miracle or morality plays, which remained popular until they were condemned and banned by the Parlement de Paris in 1548.[17] Entitled *Comedie de la nativité de Jesus Christ*, the first play in the *Marguerites* retells the story of Christ's birth. In the second play, *Comedie de l'adoration des trois roys a Jesus Christ*, the three kings, various angels, God Himself, and several allegorical figures, including *Philosophie, Tribulation, Inspiration*, and *Intelligence Divine*, praise Christ and speak of the glory of His coming. The third, *Comedie des Innocents*, recounts the massacre of the Innocents. In *Comedie du desert*, the last of the four plays, Joseph, Mary, and Jesus cross the desert, protected from harm by angels. In addition

17. See Raymond Lebègue, *La Tragédie française de la Renaissance* (Brussels: Office de Publicité, 1954), p. 6.

to the four *comédies* that appear in the *Marguerites*, Marguerite wrote several other plays, which were published in the twentieth century by V. L. Saulnier under the title of *Théâtre profane*.[18] The main difference between the plays published in the *Marguerites* and those published in *Théâtre profane* is that the former are based on narrative material derived from Scripture whereas the latter are not.

Like most of her poems, Marguerite's plays culminate in a vision of union with Christ. Within the economy of her texts, the syntagmatic axis is nearly always supplanted by a paradigmatic axis that leads to a "place" inseparable from the paradigm of Christian joy and the iconic figure of Christ. Often Marguerite represents the place to which the "way" leads as a *locus amoenus*. In this chapter, I focus on the thematics of pleasure in Marguerite's texts. Because this thematics is especially prominent in the plays, I turn mainly to them, drawing into the discussion, however, other texts in which the *unio* is also formulated in terms of an earthly paradise.

The plot of *L'Inquisiteur* (1536) is direct and unequivocal in the way medieval morality plays tend to be. In the opening scene, the inquisitor identifies himself as a "docteur de la Sorbonne" (17)[19]. He condemns the Evangelicals, who are represented as a group of children. One other character appears in the play—the inquisitor's valet who, although he serves his master, is closer ideologically and psychologically to the children. In the second scene, the valet calls the inquisitor's attention to the children who are playing joyfully in the snow. They are indifferent to the cold that torments the shivering "docteur de la Sorbonne." Angered by his valet's obvious sympathy with the children, the inquisitor beats him and then prepares to leave, hoping to discover some bit of heresy he can ruthlessly suppress. Using the coarse, insensitive language that is his stock in trade, he says: "Je voys veoir s'il y a des vers / En quelque nez, pour les tirer" (87–88) [I am going to see if there are any worms in anyone, so that I can pull them out]. Accompanied by his chastened valet, he meets the children and begins to ask them questions. This interrogation is the heart of the play. Not in the least intimidated

---

18. Marguerite de Navarre, *Théâtre profane*, ed. V. L. Saulnier, TLF (Geneva: 1963).
19. Quotations from the "secular" plays are identified by line number in Saulnier's edition of *Théâtre profane*.

by the inquisitor, who alternately cajoles and threatens them, the children answer in metaphorical language, which their literal-minded interrogator cannot understand. However, Christ's message of love, which is exemplified in both the words and the behavior of the children, touches the valet's heart. He leaves his master and joins the happy, playful group of children. Soon the inquisitor himself, in a flash of insight, experiences the joy and inner conviction that accompany the operation of Grace. As his valet did before him, he goes over to the side of the children, a new convert to the religion of love.

Throughout much of the play, the inquisitor and the children are set in direct opposition to each other. He is old; they are young. He is surly and irascible; they are courteous and cheerful. He is cold; they are warm. When he tries to beat them with a cane whip to make them obey, they laugh and run away. Representing the Old Testament reign of law, the inquisitor also represents that larger principle of which the law, according to Freud, is a part, namely, the reality principle. The children, on the other hand, live outside the law, in a world governed not by discipline and work but by "vray plaisir et liesse" (194) [true pleasure and happiness]. Juxtaposed to the inquisitor, they embody the pleasure principle.

Time is the constitutive element in the inquisitor's world. His first words in the play are:

1   Le temps s'en va tousjours en empirant;
     L'on ne faict plus de religion compte.
     Nostre crédit (dont je voys souspirant)
     Se pourroict bien en fin tourner à honte.

The times go continually from bad to worse; no one pays heed any longer to religion. Our credit, which I look at longingly, could well turn to shame.

As in most of Marguerite's poetry, the linguistic mode that translates the concept of temporality is narrative. The inquisitor's speech is full of brief narratives. The children, however, reject narrative discourse. In fact, throughout much of the play they do not speak at all but sing. In *L'Inquisiteur*, as elsewhere in Marguerite's poetry, music symbolizes the language of a truth that cannot be contained in words.[20] The language of the children differs in yet another way from that of the inquisitor. In his opening monologue, the inquisitor uses the formal decasyllabic meter. To speak to his valet and the children, he uses the octosyllabic meter. Although the children, out of politeness, use the octosyllabic meter when they address the inquisitor, they use the pentasyllabic meter when they speak—or sing—to each other. The inquisitor's conversion to Evangelism at the end of the play is marked by his adoption of the children's pentasyllabic meter.

If time is constitutive of the reality the inquisitor illustrates at the beginning of the play, money is its most concrete symbol. Venality is the dominant trait of the inquisitor's personality.

> Quatre ans y a que suis Inquisiteur
> 20   De nostre foy, sans espargner personne.
> Je ne dys pas que, si quelcun me donne
> Ung bon présent pour rachacter sa vye
> (Mais que jamais à nully mot ne sonne)
> Qu'à le saulver promptement n'aye envye.
> 25   Mais à ung sot . . . il se laisse mourir
> Par ung tesmoing que lors je luy suscite,
> Et ne se veult par argent secourir,
> Comme raison à ce faire l'incitte.

For four years I have been the inquisitor of our faith, without sparing anyone. I do not say that if someone gives me a nice present to save his life (but never says a word about it to anyone) I do not promptly wish to save him. But a fool . . . he lets himself die because of a piece of evidence I get out of him, and is not willing to save himself through money, as reason incites him to do.

The inquisitor's vocabulary is full of financial terms such as "crédit," "argent," "acquérir," "proufictable," "gaing." The notion of financial gain is inseparable from that of time. Indeed, the inquisitor's main criticism of the children is that they waste time.

> Il vauldroit myeulx qu'à noz leçons
> 160   Feussent par leurs parens induictz,

20. Louis E. Auld, "Music as Dramatic Device in the Secular Theatre of Marguerite de Navarre," *Renaissance Drama*, 7 (1976), 192–217.

Qu'ainsi en jeux et en chansons
Passer leur temps; ilz sont séduictz.
Enfans, enfans, vous perdez temps:
Vous feriez myeulx d'estudier.

It would be better if they were made by their parents to do our lessons
rather than spending their time playing games and singing. Children,
children, you are wasting time. You'd do better to study.

The inquisitor's insistence on work and his belief that time is
money suggest that he embodies not only a theological reality
(anti-evangelical orthodoxy) but also an economic reality. He
represents the economic system that was embraced by the rising
bourgeoisie of the Renaissance, i.e., capitalism.[21] In his provoca-
tive book, *Rabelais au futur*, Jean Paris has argued that Rabelais
reflects the moral code of the bourgeoisie and the tenets of capitalism.[22] Marguerite's inquisitor, too, displays the dynamism of
the bourgeoisie, the class that, in its active pursuit of "gaing,"
was not only becoming increasingly conscious of itself but was
also transforming its own values into the dominant value system
of society. But whereas Rabelais, at least in Jean Paris' reading, is
an apologist of capitalism, Marguerite is suspicious of the value
system being codified by the bourgeoisie, holding that it is in-
imical to the Christian way.

The inquisitor's conversion marks the collapse of the binary
opposition that informed the first part of the play. Touched by
the children's songs, he wonders, like Nicodemus (John 3.4),
how an old man can be reborn: "Moy, qui suis vieillard devenu,
/ Puis je renaistre de nouveau?" (406–07) [I, who have become
an old man, can I be born again?]. His valet advises him to con-
sult the children. When he does, they tell him that he must "laisser Adam et son cuyder" (468) [leave behind Adam and his pre-
sumptuousness]. Understanding for the first time the biblical
injunction against pride, he says, "Je veulx estre enfant, non plus
saige" (478) [I want to be a child, no longer a wise man]. At this

21. See Henri Hauser, *Les Débuts du capitalisme moderne en France* (1902; rpt. Paris:
F. Alcan, 1931) and Richard H. Tawney, *Religion and the Rise of Capitalism* (London: Marray, 1929).

22. Jean Paris, *Rabelais au futur* (Paris: Seuil, 1970). The classic study on the economic code that informs Rabelais' work is Mikhail Bakhtin, *Rabelais and His World*,
trans. Helene Iswolsky (Cambridge: M.I.T. Press, 1968).

point, the old Adam in him dies. Illustrating Christ's statement that "anyone who does not welcome the kingdom of God like a little child will never enter it" (Luke 18.17), the inquisitor joins the children in their games.

Some of Marguerite's poems, e.g., *L'Art et usage*, present the *unio* as an experience so radically mystical that the self "becomes" Christ and the text, drawing closer and closer to the *Tout-Verbe*, announces its inability to go on. In *L'Inquisiteur*, the experience of the *unio* is presented differently. The play does not end with a vision of otherworldly bliss. Rather, it ends in a jubilant celebration of God's presence in a world redeemed by the Word. Expressing their joy, the children, joined by the inquisitor and his valet, sing and dance. "Plus en rien ne pense / Qu'à plaisir et joye," says the inquisitor. "Je saulte, je dance, / Et n'ay congnoissance / De ce que j'estoye" (495–99) [I no longer think about anything except pleasure and joy; I jump, I dance, and have no knowledge about what I was]. Stressing the fact that their joy is of this world, the text concludes with an invitation to supper. "Allons soupper," says one of the children, "la table est mise" (670) [Let's go have supper, the table is set]. Christ, of course, had spoken of the joy that the Word brings to the world: "I have told you this so that my own joy may be in you and your joy complete" (John 15.11). Paul and Augustine both stressed the joy of the believer whose heart is filled with Christ's presence. For the Evangelicals in general and Marguerite in particular, joy is the true expression of Christian truth. In *L'Inquisitor*, this joy is generated in the inquisitor's heart by a sudden perceptual shift resulting in the understanding that the world he thought was "real" is in fact not so, for God alone is real.

Dedicating his *Tiers Livre* to "the spirit of the Queen of Navarre," Rabelais calls Marguerite an "esprit abstraict, ravy et ecstatic" [abstracted soul, ravished in ecstasy], a disembodied spirit that lives in the firmament far from worldly cares. Rabelais' words may be an ironic comment on Marguerite's mystical bent. In any case, they do not describe the "I" that is present in most of Marguerite's poems. Her spirit was too troubled to have attained the serenity suggested by Rabelais. Furthermore, she knew that the Christian cannot reject the world without rejecting Him. To deny the body is to deny what Christ redeemed when He became flesh. Even more scandalously, it is to deny

Christ Himself, for His will operates through the flesh. Even in those texts in which Marguerite expresses a yearning for anni- hilation in Him, she creates a textual body, a fleshy form, that, embodying denial of the body, subverts her avowed rejection of matter and constitutes a redemption of corporeality mimetic of that effected by the Incarnation. Marguerite's spirit is less ec- static than ascetic, a word whose Greek root means not the rigid self-denial denoted by the modern word "ascetic" but exercise or practice, as in gymnastics. Marguerite's texts are ascetic in this sense; they are exercises, performances, reenactments of the most basic of all Christian performances, the embodiment of the spirit in flesh, which, thus redeemed, must be cherished.

Marguerite condemns wealth and the acquisitive spirit even more bluntly in another farce, *Trop, Prou, Peu, Moins* (1544) [Too Much, Much, Little, Less]. The allegorical figures *Trop* and *Prou* are rich but unhappy. *Peu* and *Moins* are poor but happy. Saying that he likes houses, good wine, and precious stones, *Trop* declares, "J'ayme grandes possessions" (142) [I love wealth and possessions]. He is driven by a desire to "bastir et acquerir" (165) [build and acquire]. However, he is never satis- fied and finds no pleasure in the things his money buys. *Peu* and *Moins*, on the other hand, have nothing and desire nothing; but they are always cheerful and contented. *Peu* is a shepherd and *Moins* is a laborer. They belong to one distinct socio–economic class whereas *Trop* and *Prou* belong to another. Throughout the play, the antithesis between the two pairs of allegorical figures is presented as an opposition between two social and economic classes. Other oppositions follow from this one. *Trop* and *Prou* call *Peu* and *Moins* "folz" (710) [foolish]. *Peu* and *Moins* accept the definition gladly, for, being "foolish," they are aligned with God, whose "foolishness is wiser than human wisdom" (I Co- rinthians 1.23). *Peu* and *Moins* are wise fools in the tradition of the Wise Fool *topos*, one of the most familiar of commonplaces in Renaissance literature.[23] In addition to being called "folz," *Peu* and *Moins* are called "petis" (710) [small], another term they ac- cept, for it aligns them with the small children who are welcome in heaven. The children in *L'Inquisiteur* express their "foolish-

23. On this *topos*, see Walter Kaiser, *Praisers of Folly* (Cambridge: Harvard Univer- sity Press, 1963), and M. A. Screech, *Ecstasy and 'The Praise of Folly'* (London: Duck- worth, 1980).

ness" in music, games and, occasionally, in baby-talk. *Peu* and *Moins* reveal their "foolishness" through laughter. As *Trop* says of them, "Ilz ne cessent de rire" (245) [They do not stop laughing]. Throughout the play, laughter is a sign of wisdom beyond human knowledge.

Nowhere in her work does Marguerite reveal with greater precision the gulf that separates human wisdom from Christian folly than in her last major play, *Comédie de Mont-de-Marsan* (1548). Following the death of Francis I on March 31, 1547, Marguerite spent four months grieving in the monastery at Tusson. Stopping in the city of Mont-de-Marsan, which is situated south of Bordeaux, she wrote the *comédie* to which she gave the name of the city she was visiting.

The richest of Marguerite's plays and the most complex from the standpoint both of ideological content and formal structure, *Comédie de Mont-de-Marsan* is a quartet for four female voices, each of which has an unmistakably distinctive timbre and coloration. The ladies are allegorical figures who embody four specific attitudes toward life. Each lady represents a cardinal point on the spiritual compass that Marguerite used to guide her along the *via Christi*.

The first voice we hear is that of the *Mondainne*, who opens the play with the arresting words: "J'ayme mon corps" (1) [I love my body]. Explaining that she can touch her body, which is lovely and fresh, she remarks scornfully that her soul, if in fact she has one, lies hidden within the flesh, invisible, unpalpable, altogether indiscernible. As for her body, "je le sens vivement" (8) [I feel it keenly], she notes. She is determined to devote herself exclusively to the pursuit of those pleasures the Bible calls "fleshy." Philosophically a materialist, the *Mondainne* represents one particular kind of sin. Another is represented by the *Supersticieuse*, who announces in her opening monologue that she is a pilgrim on her way to a holy shrine. Contemptuous of her body, which she mortifies constantly, she expects to acquire "gros mérites" (52) [great merit] by strict observance of all Church ritual. The confrontation between the *Mondainne* and the *Supersticieuse* is a duet reminiscent of the medieval *débat de l'âme et du corps* [debate of the soul and the body]. The *Supersticieuse* accuses the *Mondainne* of wallowing in sensual pleasure like a "porceau dans la fange" (99) [like a pig in filth] and reminds her that the body "n'est que charonge" (121) [is only carrion]. The *Mondainne* says that she does not care what happens to her body after her death so long as she can pamper it during her life.

With the entry of the *Sage*, the texture of the comedy becomes more intricate. In the monologue that opens the third scene (the play is composed of four scenes, each of which is dominated by one of the ladies), the *Sage* states her position with reasoned clarity:

> Dieu a bien faict ung tresbeau don à l'homme
> De luy donner *raison*, savez-vous comme?
> Comme à ung ange. Est-ce pas don honneste?
> Par la *raison* il assemble et assomme,

165
> Ayme et congnoist les vertus et les nomme:
> Par la *raison* il diffère à la beste;
> Dieu luy a mis en hault regard et teste
> Pour contempler ce qui est par sur luy:
> La beste en bas à la terre s'areste,

170
> Et l'homme en hault, dont vient tout son appuy.
> L'homme *raisonnable*
> Est faict agréable
> A Dieu et au monde;
> Dieu croid, ayme, adore,

175
> Loue, prie et honore:
> Là son esprit fonde.
> Quant à son prochain,
> Le bon cœur la main
> Mect à le servir.

180
> Ce qu'il doibt il paie,
> Et a tousjours joye
> A vertus suivir.

God gave a very beautiful gift to man in giving him reason; do you know to what degree? To that of an angel. Is it not a precious gift? By reason he assembles and calculates, loves and acquires knowledge of the virtues and names them. By reason he differs from the animals; God put his eyes and head on top of his body so that he can contemplate what is above him; the animal fixes its attention downward, to the ground, and man, upward, from whence comes all of his support. The rational man is agreeable to God and to the world; he believes in, loves, adores, praises, prays to and honors God. There his spirit is anchored. As for his neighbor, he puts his good heart and hand at his service. He pays what he owes, and is always happy to follow virtues.

The key word in the measured discourse of the *Sage* is *raison*. She is a *raisonneuse*. More importantly, she is an advocate of rational theology of the kind that was defended by (among many others) Raymond Sebond in his *Theologia Naturalis* (written in 1434–36 and published in 1484). The *Sage* mediates the disagreement between the *Mondainne* and the *Supersticieuse*. Both, she says, are mistaken: the former because she denies the reality of the spirit, the latter because she condemns the flesh and so fails to perceive the mystery of the Incarnation.

The *Mondainne* recognizes her error and becomes despondent. To save her from despair, the *Sage* gives her a copy of the Bible:

375   Pour vous metre toute à delivre,
       Je vous faictz present de ce livre:
       C'est la loy et vielle et nouvelle.
       En luy verrez ce qu'il fault faire
       Et qui pour vous peult satisfaire,
380   Pour vous metre en vie eternelle.

To free you completely, I give you as a gift this book. It is both the old and the new law. In it you will see what one must do, what can satisfy you and guide you to eternal life.

The *Mondainne* accepts the gift and says that she will read the Bible constantly so as to be sure that she will be saved. The *Sage* encounters more resistance and hostility when she undertakes to convert the *Supersticieuse*. Certain that she has found favor in God's eyes, the *Supersticieuse* is convinced that by renouncing ". . . accoustremens, / Festins, amours et instrumens" (432–33) [raiments, banquets, loves and instruments] she will attain her rightful seat among the elect. To combat such presumption, the *Sage* states flatly that no spiritual merit can be gained by punishing the body. She tells her that Christ is a husband who does not command His bride to mortify her flesh but to love Him. Eventually the *Supersticieuse*'s pride and vain-glory are overcome. The *Sage* gives her too a copy of the Bible and admonishes her to read both the Old and the New Testaments. The *Supersticieuse* confesses that she has never read the Bible and promises to do so. Addressing the two contrite ladies, the *Sage* points to the Bible that each holds in her hands:

> C'est le mirouer qui esclaire
> Voz cueurs, et puis qui les descouvre,
> 570 Grande joye j'ay de vous deux
> Veoir lire en ces livres si neufz,
> Que neufves serez en ceste euvre.

It is the mirror that lights up your hearts and then opens them up. I have great joy in seeing you two read these books so new that you will be new in this work.

The last of the four voices in the play is that of a shepherdess, identified as *la Ravie de Dieu*. The *Ravie* opens the final scene of the play with a song:

> 573 Helas! je languys d'amours . . .
> Helas! je meurs tous les jours.

Alas! I languish in love . . . Alas! I die every day.

Breaking off her song as if in deference to the three ladies who stand before her, she switches from her native language, music, to their alien tongue. However, by repeating the anaphoristic pattern of the opening melody, the verses she now speaks prolong in a subtle way the harmonics of the two lines that preceded them:

> 575 Qui vit d'amour a bien le cueur joieulx,
> Qui tient amour ne peult desirer mieulx,
> Qui scet amour n'ignore nul sçavoir,
> Qui void amour a tousjours rians yeulx.

He who lives in love has a truly joyful heart; he who has love cannot desire anything better; he who knows love knows everything there is to know; he who sees love has always laughing eyes.

The three ladies are startled by the *Ravie*'s words, which they find both incomprehensible and grotesque.

> La Mondainne
585   Oyez quel chant!
>   La Supersticieuse
>   Mais oyez sa parolle.
>   La Sage
> Ha! ce n'est pas langage d'une folle?

Listen to that song! Just listen to the words. Ah! is that not the language of a fool (or a simpleton)?

Indifferent to the unkind comments of the three ladies, the *Ravie* bursts once again into song, singing "La, la, la, la, la, la, la, la" (587). The dialogue that ensues throughout the rest of the comedy is, in a sense, a dialogue of the deaf. The three ladies understand enough of what the shepherdess says to realize that she is in love. But, exasperated by her refusal (or inability) to speak the language of rational discourse, they conclude that she is hallucinating or that she is an idiot ("Elle rayve ou est idiotte," 761). They decide to waste no further time with her. The *Mondainne* and the *Supersticieuse* are eager to start reading the Bible, and the *Sage*, who remarks that the *Ravie*'s words are utter nonsense ("Ces motz ne vaillent ung oignons," 923) [These words are not worth an onion], is convinced that the shepherdess is suffering from *dementia*. All three leave, and the *Ravie*, left alone, sings of her consuming love for her "ami."

Both the *Sage* and the *Ravie* embody principles that were important to Marguerite. The *Sage* understands that as a result of the Incarnation the flesh, rightly understood, is holy. When the *Mondainne*, recognizing her former errors, asks the *Sage* if man should cultivate the soul and neglect the body, the latter replies:

> Non, car l'ame tant seullement
> N'est l'homme; mais l'assemblement
> Des deux, hommes l'on doibt nommer.
315   Corps sans ames sont cadavers,
> Charongnes pour nourrir les vers,
> Qui de l'homme n'ont nul effect;
> L'ame sans corps ne peult veoir
> Et des euvres pert le pouvoir,
320   Dont elle n'est l'homme parfaict:

Mais l'ame au corps joincte et unie,
C'est l'homme: en ceste compaignie
De parfaicte confaction
Ceste union apporte vie:
325   Mais si l'ame est du corps ravie,
C'est mort leur separation.

No, for the soul alone is not man; but the assemblage of the two is what one ought to call man. Bodies without souls are corpses, carcasses to feed worms, having none of the properties of man. The soul without the body cannot see and loses the power of works; thus it is not a perfect man. But the soul joined and linked to the body, that is man. In this assemblage of perfect construction, this union brings life. But if the soul is taken away from the body, their separation is death.

Within the perimeters of Marguerite's faith, everything the *Sage* says is doctrinally correct. But her vision is confined to the letter of His word. The *Ravie*, on the other hand, incarnates the spirit; she embodies the actual experience of faith as distinct from its articulation in rational discourse that has hardened into doctrine. In the opening monologue of *L'Inquisiteur*, the inquisitor identifies the Evangelicals as readers of Scripture; but when they appear in the text, they are playful children, not diligent readers of the Bible. Marguerite's message is that they who hold in their hearts the spirit of His word need not concern themselves with the letter of His Book, for like Mary, they already have "the one thing that is needed."

In his edition of *Théâtre profane*, Saulnier wonders if Marguerite "was" the *Sage* or the *Ravie* (p. 262). The text cannot answer this question, at least not in any way except that of Rabelais' Trouillogan, who, when asked by Panurge if he should get married or not, responds, "Tous les deux" [both] and, when pressed further, "Ne l'un ne l'aultre" [neither one nor the other].[24] To the extent that Marguerite is the author of the text, she cannot be the *Ravie*, for a *Ravie* does not compose texts. Like the children in *L'Inquisiteur*, the *Ravie* is beyond the confines of language, just as she is beyond the kind of wisdom represented by the *Sage*. When the three ladies accuse her of

24. *Tiers Livre*, ed. Screech, Ch. 36, p. 251.

speaking the language of "une folle," they are right, but not in the way they mean. Like *Peu* and *Moins*, the *Ravie* is a wise fool. The Pseudo-Dionysius had discussed Paul's statement that "God's foolishness is wiser than human wisdom" (I Corinthians 1.25). "These words," he explained, "are true not only because all human thought is a kind of error when compared with the immovable permanence of the perfect thoughts which belong to God, but also because it is customary for writers on Divinity to apply negative terms to God in a sense contrary to the usual one" (*Div. Names* 147). Commenting further on the *Via Negativa*, the Pseudo-Dionysius noted that when Paul spoke of God's "foolishness" he used "in a higher sense the apparent strangeness and absurdity implied in the word [foolishness], so as to hint at the ineffable Truth which is before all Reason." Although "the human Intellect hath a faculty of Intelligence, whereby it perceives intellectual truths, yet the act whereby the Intellect communes with the things that are beyond it transcends its intellectual nature. This transcendent sense, therefore, must be given to our language about God, and not our human sense. We must be transported wholly out of ourselves and given unto God" (*Div. Names* 147). The Pseudo-Dionysius here makes a clear distinction between the *Via Affirmativa*, which he also called the Doctrine of Knowing, and the *Via Negativa*, or the Doctrine of Unknowing. While the former, which is the way of the *Sage*, permits the Christian to perceive "intellectual truths," only the latter, which is the way chosen by the *Ravie*, translates the experience of being transported out of self and given unto God. Marguerite's text illustrates the Pauline contention that "it was to shame the wise that God chose what is foolish by human reckoning" (I Corinthians 1.27). It enacts the humbling of human knowledge before Christian folly, that "Foolish Wisdom which hath neither Reason nor Intelligence" but is nevertheless "the Cause of all Intelligence and Reason" (*Div. Names* 148).

The appearance of the *Ravie* at the beginning of the last scene signals a directional change in the text of the kind we have seen in nearly all of Marguerite's works. In most of her longer poems, the protagonist, experiencing suddenly the reality of Christ's presence, abandons narrative discourse and adopts a linguistic mode in which narrative is reduced to a minimum. In *Mont-de-Marsan*, the strategy is different because the text has little narrative in the first place. The *Supersticieuse* is the only one of the ladies to use narrative discourse at all. She is a pilgrim and, not unlike the weary wayfarer at the beginning of the *Petit Oeuvre*, observes from time to time that "ce chemin long m'a aux piedz agravée" (47) [this long road has made my feet hurt]. Soon, however, she abandons narrative (if indeed remarks like the one just cited can be said to fall into the narrative mode of discourse) and begins to expound her theological views. The *Mondainne* has no use for narrative, for she lives in the immediacy of her body, in a kind of perverted Eckhartian *Now* moment. Since the text does not trace out the kind of narrative-induced syntagmatic axis we have seen in other poems, it cannot rely on conspicuous rejection of narrative to signal a shift from the lower to the higher level of reality. What it does instead is introduce in the text a foreign language (Latin *foris* means "outside"), a language that can be understood only by the residents of another place. Never at any moment in the last scene of *Mont-de-Marsan* do the three ladies understand anything that the *Ravie* says, or, rather, sings, music being the external mark of the foreignness of her language. The *Ravie* is a resident of the world of the spirit, the apocalyptic world, whereas the other three live in the world of the letter where rational discourse is the native language.

Music elevates the oral over the written, the voice over the graph. Since Latin *spiritus* means both breath and spirit, the *Ravie*'s song is a sign perfectly suited to the task of signifying the world of the spirit as distinct from the world of the letter, which is linked with writing. It might be objected that the *Ravie*'s song is transposed into writing which the reader "reads" rather than "hears." This is, of course, true, but can be answered in two ways. *Mont-de-Marsan*, as well as *L'Inquisiteur* and several other works in which voice is elevated over script, are plays. Indeed, most of them were performed. A performance of *Mont-de-Marsan*, during which the *Ravie* actually sings, would make it clear to the spectator-listener that the three ladies on the one hand and the *Ravie* on the other represent two distinct modes of communication, the first specific to the world of the letter, the second, to that of the spirit. Furthermore, the reader, recognizing all the signs in the text that tell him that he is reading a play, integrates this knowledge into his "reading" and recodes the text into a performative experience. Thus the *Ravie*'s music, although written into the text, differs from the language of the three ladies and escapes the logocentrism that tends to arise when a spoken language is transposed to written material.[25]

Neither *Trop, Prou, Peu, Moins* nor *Mont-de-Marsan* recounts a conversion as does *L'Inquisiteur*. The *Mondainne* and the *Supersticieuse* are persuaded by the *Sage* to read the Bible, but none of the ladies is converted to the religion of love represented by the *Ravie*. Interpreting literally what the *Ravie* says, they misunderstand her. The reader, however, experienced in the ways of metaphor, knows how to read correctly. He recognizes Christ in the "ami" whom the *Ravie* loves with an intensity that appalls the ladies, believing as they do that the shepherdess has lost her head over some unworthy shepherd. Not once in the play does the *Ravie* utter the words Christ or God. If the paradise of which she speaks (873) remains incomprehensible to the three ladies, the reader, progressing along the flow of the text, moves from the world of the *Sage* to that of the *Ravie*. At the end of the play, he finds himself alone with the *Ravie*, participating (to the degree that he submits to the power of her vision) in her experience of Christ's consuming love.

To metacommunicate Christ's love is the sole function of the *Ravie*'s language. The apocalyptic world that her song evokes is above all a place of pleasure. With its flowers ("Petite fleur belle et jollie, / Je scay bien que vous m'entendez," 646–47) [Little flower, beautiful and pretty, I know very well that you understand me], its music and its laughter, it is the classical *locus amoenus*:

> J'ay ce qui me peult satisfaire:
> Cherche ailleurs son bien qui vouldra,
> Jamais le mien ne me fauldra.
> Je n'ay nulle nécessité;
> 780   En voiant la diversité
> Des estoilles, des fleurs, des champs,
> En joye, en plaisir et en chants,
> Doulcement passe ma journée.

25. For a theoretical discussion of the communication that occurs during a theatrical performance, see Walter Rewar, "The Cybernetic Modeling of Performance," *Language and Style* (Spring, 1980), 282–93.

I have what can satisfy me; let anyone who would like search elsewhere for his riches; never will I have to look elsewhere for mine. I do not need to. Seeing the diversity of the stars, of the flowers, of the fields, I spend my day agreeably in joy, in pleasure and in songs.

When the *Ravie* says that she would rather possess the love of her "ami" than "ung grand tresor" [a great treasure], the *Sage* remarks reproachfully, "Vous estimez donc bien peu l'or" (768) [You therefore attach very little worth to gold]. The *Sage* embodies Freud's reality principle with particular force when she condemns pleasure and insists on discipline and labor:

> M'amie, vous n'estes pas née
785 > En ce monde pour rien ne faire:
> A *la loy* il fault satisfaire
> Qui commande *de travailler.* (my emphasis)

My friend, you are not born in this world to do nothing. One must obey the law that commands us to work.

The theological equivalent of "la loy . . . de travailler" is "good works." Marguerite did not rate "good works" high in the scale of Christian virtues, and neither does the *Ravie*. When the *Supersticieuse* comments that ". . . celle qui tousjours repose, / Nul bien ne luy peult advenir" (790–91) [to her who is always idle nothing good can happen], the *Ravie* answers by saying that he who already possesses "le bien" need not *work* for it; he can *enjoy* it. If the *Supersticieuse*, insisting on work and busyness, may be said to be of the same race as Martha, then the *Ravie*, whose singing makes the reader less aware of the meaning-producing aspect of the text and more conscious of its delight-producing function, must be thought of as belonging to the race that produced Mary, the adoring believer whose expressive silence Marguerite's text seeks to communicate through song.

Not content to let the argument about work drop, the *Supersticieuse* challenges the *Ravie*: ". . . monstrez-moy cestuy-là, / Auquel ne default quelque chose" (796–97) [show me someone who does not lack something]. The *Ravie's* response is significant:

> Ha! qui l'a, tient la bouche close
> Et ceste odeur là pas n'esventte.
> 800   Garde vous n'avez qu'il s'en vente
> Ny que ung seul semblant il en face.

Ah! he who has it keeps his mouth closed and does not breathe out that odor. You must not think that he is going to brag about it or only use it for show.

Silence, or (and it amounts to the same thing) a foreign language, is the sign of the apocalyptic world, which, to the extent that one can talk about it at all, is metacommunicated through the forms human desire assumes in a world that, ultimately, must be transcended.

A poetics of desire is expressed far more explicitly in *Mont-de-Marsan* than in *L'Inquisiteur*. Of the various forms that, in Briçonnet's words, "noz inclinations, desirs, passions et affections" (I.150) can assume, Marguerite opts in *Mont-de-Marsan* for *eros* to communicate the experience of the apocalyptic world. Given the multiple overtones of the word *love*, it is hardly surprising that Christian mystics exploited the vocabulary of what Briçonnet called "visceral" love in order to express the idea of ecstatic union with God. Indeed, such imagery may be found in Scripture itself. Furthermore, in the Neoplatonism that colored Christianity from the time of Augustine on there was an implicit justification for using the vocabulary of carnality to express the realm of the spirit. Neoplatonists elaborated at length the notion of a chain of being; matter, although it constitutes the lowest link in the chain, is still an integral part of the whole. In his letters to Marguerite, Briçonnet insists that "aymer est la consummacion, perfection et abreviacion de la loy evangelique" (I.152) [to love is the perfect consummation and summary of the evangelical law] and that "amour visceralle n'empesche la divine, mais y est conforme"[26] [visceral love does not hinder divine love, but is compatible with it]. He explains that the love we bear Christ fills us with pleasure, which he evokes in images of sensual delight (I.208).

In *Mont-de-Marsan*, Marguerite's presentation of "noz inclinations" is couched not in the unctuous terms Briçonnet favored

---

26. Cited by Saulnier in *Théâtre profane*, p. 271.

but in language that is powerfully evocative of erotic desire. Time and time again the *Ravie* (etymologically, she who has been ravished) speaks of the pleasure she experiences as she lies swooning "entre les bras" (853) [in the arms] of her beloved. At times, the intensity of her pleasure is such that it cannot be contained within the confines of coherent discourse. "Ho Ho y y on on on on" (915), she utters rapturously. Completely consumed by her love, the *Ravie* yearns to be killed or "assommer" (which is made to rhyme with "aymer," 1008) by her lover.

> Or t'esvertue,
> Amour, et tout soudain me tue.
> Puis, quant tu m'auras abatue,
> 1000 Me feras vivre.

Now use your utmost strength, love, and kill me suddenly. Then, when you have overthrown me, you will make me live.

The death Marguerite desires signals the *unio mystica* of the self with Christ ("A mon amy, unie et joincte," 875) [united and joined with my friend], the linguistic equivalent of which is the coalescence of the signifier and the signified, making language both impossible and irrelevant.

The *Mondainne*, the *Supersticieuse*, and the *Sage* all embody the principle Marguerite calls "la loy . . . de travailler" (the reality principle). All three ladies stress work. The *Mondainne* worked tirelessly to preserve and adorn her body:

> Je le pare et dore,
> Acoustre et decore
> De tous ornemens.
> Je le painctz et farde,
> 15 Remire et regarde
> Voire à tous momens.

I adorn it and cover it with gold, dress and decorate it with all kinds of ornaments. I color and paint it; I look at it and inspect it, indeed, at every moment.

The *Supersticieuse*, tired by the rigors of the pilgrimage she has undertaken, emphasizes the virtue of "good works" and effort. As for the *Sage*, she works hard to persuade the other two to accept her "reasonable" way of thinking. In the final scene, all three band together to dissuade the *Ravie* from persisting in her foolish ways. When they fail, they leave, declaring that they have wasted enough time and must get back to their study of the Bible. The "loy . . . de travailler" is ultimately illustrated in reading, a studious and purposeful activity that contrasts sharply with the effortless singing of the *Ravie*. At times, the *Ravie*'s words seem to echo those of the *Mondainne*, although in a different register. The *Ravie*'s joy is closer to the *Mondainne*'s delight in her body than to the *Supersticieuse*'s emphasis on endless effort and the *Sage*'s insistence on study. Expressing the intense pleasure she experiences in His arms, the *Ravie* declares:

850   Hellas, telle joye j'ay receue
        D'avoir sens et honneur perdu
        Pour luy, que mon cueur s'est rendu
        Entre ses bras, en sa puissance,
        Perdant de soy la congnoissance
855   Pour penser en luy nuict et jour.

Alas, I have received such joy in having lost my senses and honor for him that my heart yielded in his arms, losing awareness of itself in his power in order to think about him night and day.

Of the three ladies, it is the *Mondainne* who responds to the *Ravie*'s words, saying, almost as if to herself: "J'ay autrefois porté amour / A mon corps, à moy mesme seulle . . ." (856–57) [I used to be in love with my body, with only myself]. The *Ravie*'s words provoke in the *Mondainne* a recollection of the experience of pleasure that, visceral and carnal though it may have been, is closer to the rapture expressed by the *Ravie* than to anything experienced by the earnest *Supersticieuse* or the brisk, efficient *Sage*.

Within the economy of the play, the *Mondainne*'s formulation of pleasure precedes that of the *Ravie*. The *Mondainne* and, indeed, the *Supersticieuse*, too, submit to the reality principle embodied by the *Sage*. They progress from one stage of development to another, mirroring the maturing process that Freud defined in dialectical terms (pleasure principle/reality principle) and that Lacan described as an evolution from the Imaginary to the Symbolic. In the first three scenes, the text establishes a syntagmatic axis by recording the *Sage*'s success in persuading the *Mondainne* and the *Supersticieuse* to abandon their convictions and to accept her point of view. But, as we have noted, Marguerite posits a third and final stage that lies beyond the first two. The Christian experiences this last stage, the Iconic, as a transfiguration or transliteration of the first. Being a reenactment of the beginning, the Iconic is rendered in Marguerite's texts as a reformulation of the pleasure principle that, in the beginning, directed psychic energy toward immediate gratification and the desire for possession, both impulses being redefined and satisfied in the *unio mystica* of the Iconic stage.

Because the three ladies in the poem do not progress beyond the stage they have attained at the end of the third scene, evolutionary thrust is arrested at this point in the text. The syntagmatic axis of the text is broken, replaced in the last scene by the paradigmatic, iconic figure of the shepherdess. The reader, however, as distinct from the ladies in the text, continues to experience forward movement, for the act of reading the lines of print that flow across the page is inseparable from temporal and spatial displacement. And yet, because he sees in the *Ravie*'s expression of pleasure a reformulation of the primary principle in the development of the psyche, i.e., the pleasure principle, he experiences this displacement as a kind of circling back to the beginning. The text compels the reader (to borrow yet again the words Augustine used to define the essence of the Christian's journey) to come back to the place where he is already. The process whereby the reader returns to the beginning mirrors the process Christ evoked when He declared that we must become like little children before we can hope to enter the kingdom of God.

The *Sage* and her two companions are studious readers; the *Ravie* is not. Whereas the three ladies set off determinedly down the *Via Affirmativa*, believing wrongly that that road will lead to Christ, the *Ravie* negotiates effortlessly the *Via Negativa* and attains her goal. Ultimately, Marguerite's text subverts the very notion of reading (devotion to the letter). It seeks to duplicate the *Via Negativa* and, directing the reader away from discourse, invites him to see in the paradigmatic figure of the *Ravie* a revelation of the apocalyptic world to which every Christian aspires.

THE FLOWERING HEART

Marguerite presents the attributes of the apocalyptic world more graphically in the *Comédie du désert*, the last of her biblical plays, than in any of her other works. In the *Comédie du désert*, the various elements that constitute the apocalyptic vision come together to form a concept of bliss that finds expression in one of the most venerable and powerful images in Western literature—that of a garden. The *Ravie* in *Mont-de-Marsan*, joyful in her consuming love for Christ, may serve as a paradigm for the Christian. But except for one brief mention of a flower, the text does not describe the physical world in which she lives. Nothing in what the *Ravie* says suggests a correlation between her rapturous joy and the material or "fleshy" world around her. The paradise of which she sings is entirely within.

In one sense, of course, all paradises are within. One of Marguerite's messages is that only by a kind of reflexive movement away from the world of the flesh can we experience Christ, who is "written in our hearts" (II Corinthians 3.2). And yet there has always been a powerful impulse within the Christian tradition to seek in the material world a site that can serve as an incarnation of Eden, the paradigmatic place, which, Genesis 2.8 informs us, God made for man and which is our true homeland. Monastic orders, in particular, were founded for the purpose of establishing in the world places that would incarnate the *locus voluptatis* that Scripture (Genesis 2.10)[27] designates as man's first home. As Terry Comito has pointed out, "the whole pressure of Western monasticism is to extend a merely personal and interior reformation into the social world, to realize the city of God here below."[28]

Seeking in the last of her biblical comedies to represent paradisiac joy, Marguerite situates her characters in a garden, the main features of which are formulaic. Indeed, she chose the

27. "A river flowed from Eden to water the garden." In the Vulgate: "Et fluvius egrediebatur de loco voluptatis ad irrigandum Paradisum." The words "*de loco voluptatis,*" which modern versions, including the King James, do not adequately render, permit the assimilation of this *locus voluptatis* with the classical *locus amoenus*.

28. *The Idea of the Garden in the Renaissance* (New Brunswick, N.J.: Rutgers University Press, 1978), p. 41. Morton Bloomfield, "Joachim of Flora," *Traditio*, 13 (1957), p. 281, n. 36, has traced this emphasis back to the Pseudo-Dionysius' notion that the heavenly hierarchy is reflected in the earthly.

most familiar of the tropes and figures that, as early as the fifth century, had already come to signify the Christian earthly paradise.[29] For Marguerite, however, the true *locus* of Christian pleasure is the Word. The image of an Edenic site, which is developed throughout much of the play, is eventually absorbed into that of the book. In the *Comédie du désert*, reading is the fundamental metaphor for understanding God and experiencing joy. My discussion will gradually focus on the way this metaphor operates in the text.

The narrative kernel of the *Comédie du désert*, a play that is some 1500 lines long, may be found in Matthew 2.19–21 (the three other Gospels do not refer to this episode in Christ's life): "After Herod's death, an angel of the Lord appeared in a dream to Joseph in Egypt and said, 'Get up, take the young child and his mother with you and go back to the land of Israel, for those who wanted to kill the child are dead.' So Joseph got up and, taking the child and his mother with him, went back to the land of Israel." Marguerite's text does not actually trace the Holy Family's journey toward Israel. As the play opens, Joseph, Mary and the child have stopped for the night somewhere in the desert. Leaving momentarily his wife and child, who are resting, Joseph announces in the first speech of the play that he is going to search for food. Rejecting the *Supersticieuse*'s contempt for the flesh, Joseph declares that the mortal body must be attended to and nourished for the sake of the spirit that is enclosed within it. Being a work of "le grand Ouvrier" (p. 317) [the great Workman],[30] the body is precious and must be fed and cared for. On the other hand, Joseph also rejects the kind of idolatry of the body that was represented by the *Mondainne*. In a statement that we may legitimately read as another of Marguerite's attacks on the bourgeois mentality, Joseph makes it plain that he seeks only enough nourishment to maintain the body in good health. Condemning the impulse to accumulate more goods than one can actually use, he says that "du superflu nous n'avons nulle envie" (p. 316) [we have no desire for the superfluous]. He explains fur-

29. There is an extensive literature on this subject. See Curtius, pp. 458–62; A. Bartlett Giamatti, *The Earthly Paradise and the Renaissance Epic* (Princeton: Princeton University Press, 1966), especially pp. 67–83; Terry Comito, *The Idea of the Garden in the Renaissance*, pp. 25–50.

30. Page references are to the *Marguerites* (Johnson Reprint Corporation).

ther that it is not for ourselves that we attend to our body. In fact, since everything belongs to God, to speak of *our* body is to speak incorrectly. By caring for the body, we are really preserving His temple, for as Paul declared to the Corinthians, "you are [God's] temple" (I Corinthians 3.16), and again in another epistle, "your body is the temple of the Holy Spirit" (I Corinthians 6.19). In the first of Marguerite's biblical plays, *Comédie de la nativité de Jesus Christ*, a shepherd had repeated Paul's words:

> J'admire le hault Createur
> De toutes choses le facteur,
> Et duquel nous sommes le temple.   (p. 171)

I admire the mighty Creator, maker of all things and whose temple we are.

Another shepherd had said: "O Pasteur, que ce mot est doux, / Que ce hault Dieu habite en nous!" (pp. 171–72) [O shepherd, how sweet these words are, that this mighty God dwells in us!]. Joseph does not cite Paul as directly as do the shepherds in the earlier play; nevertheless, his words are Pauline in spirit. "Dedens nous il [God] oeuvre" (p. 317) [Within us He works], he says, noting that all our desires and thoughts are really tools through which God performs His will. All human impulses originate in "la Vie cachee / Soubs la Chair tachee" (p. 318) [the hidden life, stained under the flesh]. Joseph's opening speech, which is eighty-two lines long, moves quickly from an evocation of the desert that ostensibly constitutes the setting for the narrative content of the play to an affirmation of God's inwardness or immanence, a fundamental concept in all the works Marguerite chose to include in the *Marguerites*. In the opening lines of the poem the inner and outer worlds are so intertwined—indeed, the outer is viewed as an incarnation of the inner—that once the text begins to delineate a garden, the reader, conditioned to seeing in things an embodiment of "la Vie cachee," i.e., Christ, requires no prodding to discern in the *hortus* an image of the soul.

Concluding his speech (which functions as a prologue) with the words "Je laisse l'Espouse, / Laquelle repouse / Avec le Petit" (p. 319) [I leave my wife, who is resting with the baby], Joseph disappears from the text only to reappear near the end of the play, dejected and empty-handed, for he has not succeeded in finding food for his family. That is to say, he disappears from the text in the sense that he is not present in subsequent scenes, during which God speaks to Mary, the center of attention throughout most of the play. And yet the reader cannot forget that while the Blessed Virgin Mary (like that other Mary who sat at Jesus' feet listening to His words) is visited by emissaries from God in a kind of timeless "now," Joseph is wandering from place to place through the desert, living within the framework of human time. His arduous and fruitless journey, which is reminiscent of that of the narrator at the beginning of the *Petit Oeuvre*, is not recorded in the poem. Joseph's wandering, though, is inscribed in the text in the form of what Walter Rewar calls a "memory trace."[31] The syntagmatic axis, formulated distinctly in the first scene, is not really effaced by the second scene, during which God Himself speaks; it is retained in the reader's memory and informs his experience of the rest of the text. Furthermore, the reader, in whose memory the whole biblical narrative is firmly inscribed, knows that Joseph will return to his family and lead Mary and the child to Nazareth. The reader does not know whether this bit of narrative will appear in Marguerite's text, but he does know that it appears in God's text, of which Marguerite's is necessarily a part, the *Verbe* being always a part of the *Tout-Verbe*. Whereas in many of the texts we have examined thus far, a paradigmatic axis conspicuously replaces a syntagmatic axis throughout the second half of the work, in the *Comédie du désert* the strategy is different. After its initial formulation, the syntagmatic axis, which defines human time, is experienced by the reader through, to cite Rewar again, "memory inscription." If we may say that most of Marguerite's texts invite the reader to experience paradigmatic thrust after syntagmatic thrust, the *Comédie du désert* is so constructed that the reader can experience the simultaneity of the two axes, for here the paradigmatic is enclosed within the syntagmatic, timelessness embodied in time.

As soon as Joseph leaves, God Himself speaks, stressing His immanence in the world of time and things. He says: "Je ne suis

31. "The Cybernetic Modeling of Performance," op. cit., 288.

pas seulement amoureux, / Mais suis l'Amour" (p. 319) [I am not only full of love, I am Love], and then continues:

> . . . par qui le hault des Cieux
> S'est abbaissé jusques au profond centre:
> J'ayme m'amye [Mary] et pour le dire mieux,
> Je m'ayme en elle, et me voy en ses yeux.   (pp. 319–20)

. . . through whom the summit of the heavens came down to the deep center. I love my friend and, to express it better, I love myself in her, and see myself in her eyes.

Noting that Mary is the only perfect mortal, He announces that He wishes to transform the desert that surrounds her and the child into a *locus amoenus*, which is conflated of course with the Christian earthly paradise:

> En ce Desert, ou ilz seront long temps,
> Donner je veux plus plaisant passetemps,
> Qu'elle n'auroit en Ville ny Cité.   (p. 321)

In this desert, where they will be a long time, I wish to provide more pleasant ways of passing the time than she would have in a city or town.

Given the conspicuously allegorical mode of the poem, the reader is entitled to see in this desert a metaphor for terrestrial existence itself. Like a foreman assigning tasks to His various workmen, God directs *Contemplation* to appear before Mary and to give her a book, which, we soon learn, is the book of nature. Accepting her mission, *Contemplation* says: "Seigneur, je prens de ta main ce grand Livre, / Par qui pourra t'amye en toye vivre" (p. 321) [Lord, I take from your hand this great book, by which your friend will be able to live in you]. God then orders *Memoire* to take to Mary "ce Livre vieux," i.e., the Old Testament, the book through which His will ("vouloir") is disclosed to those who know how to discern the spirit that lies hidden behind "la lettre morte" [the dead letter]. *Memoire* assures God that Mary will find "un souverain plaisir" in "ce delicieux Livre . . ., antique et vieux" (p. 322) [great pleasure in this delightful book, ancient and old]. Finally, God calls before Him *Consolation*, whose charge is to present to Mary "ce petit Livre ouvert d'affection / Remply d'amour, et de dilection" (p. 323) [this little book opened with affection, full of love and friendship]. He gives the following specific directions to *Consolation*, emphasizing the fact that the New Testament is an incarnation of His Word ("vive Parole"):

> Ce petit Livre. . . .
> Luy feras voir, comme un Maistre d'eschole;
> En luy monstrant ceste vive Parole,
> Ce don promis, ce grand Emmanuel,
> Mon Verbe en chair, qu'Amour unist et colle,
> Elle en aura plaisir continuel.   (p. 323)

You will show her this little book, like a school master; when you show her this living Word, this promised gift, this great Emmanuel, my Word in flesh, which love unites and joins, she will have continual pleasure.

Having informed *Contemplation*, *Memoire*, and *Consolation* of their assignments, God then turns to the angels who are charged with the task of transforming the desert into a garden.

> Anges, allez en ce Desert destruit;
> Rejouyssez par harmonieux bruit
> Mere et Enfant: commandez de par moy,
> Aux arbres secz de leur donner du fruit,
> Et qu'un chacun ruisseau soit bien instruit
> D'offrir leur eaue à leur Seigneur et Roy,
> Tant qu'en ce lieu plein de tout desarroy,
> Ou rien n'y a, soit tout en abondance;
> Car ou je veux toucher du bout du doigt,
> Mon grand povoir se voit en evidence.   (p. 324)

Angels, go into this desolate desert; by harmonious sounds make the mother and child glad. In my name command the withered trees to give them fruit, and let all the brooks be instructed to offer their water to their Lord and King, so that in this place full of disorder, where there is nothing, everything will be in abundance; for wherever I wish to touch with my fingertip, my great power manifests itself.

The garden that the angels are directed to create is first of all a gift from God. Following a tradition that stresses God's fecundity and infinite creative energy,[32] Marguerite sees the act of creation as an outpouring of His love. God's overwhelming love suddenly blossoms into form, taking the shape of a flourishing garden. At the same time, of course, it blossoms forth into books, for since God is *Verbum*, His limitless love materializes (becomes matter or creation) in the form of texts.

The symbolic nature of the garden depicted in the *Comédie du désert* is suggested by the fact that from the many garden motifs that tradition had codified, Marguerite chose one above all others to carry the burden of her message—that of fruit. Responding to God's command, the angels, who are identified in the text as "anges chantans" [singing angels], lift their voices in song and say:

> Des arbres leur [Mary and the infant] porterons,
> Fruits pleins de saveur exquise;
> Des fleurs les consolerons,
> Et de l'eaue douce et requise.   (p. 324)

From the trees we will bring them fruit full of exquisite flavor; with flowers we will console them, and with the fresh water they need.

Later when they appear to Mary, they inform her that they are going to fill the desert with such "louenage" [praise] and "jubiliation" that it will be a more pleasant and fruitful place than Adam's paradise ever was. Marguerite is less interested in describing the garden than in recounting the actual fructification of the desert. She is concerned less to formulate a representation of the garden than to trace the process whereby the desert becomes a fruitful, lovely site. The agent of this transformation is God the Word, *Verbum*. From the Judeo-Christian account of creation, Marguerite retains the central fact that creation is a product of God's voice. (That God creates through speech is

---

32. The tradition has its roots in Platonism. Discussing the Platonic notion of creation, A. O. Lovejoy, *The Great Chain of Being* (Cambridge: Harvard University Press, 1936), speaks of the divinity's "self-transcending fecundity" (p. 49).

made clear in both the Old and New Testaments: "God said, 'Let there be light,'" etc., Genesis 1.3; in John 1.1 God is, of course, identified with *Verbum*.) We have already seen in one way or another the centrality of this notion to Marguerite's poetic enterprise as a whole. Whereas numerous writers dwelled longingly on the delights of the apocalyptic garden, often emphasizing, as did classical authors, social harmony, sensual pleasure, political peace, and economic security, Marguerite stresses instead the creative power of the word and its ability to make joy flourish in the erstwhile barren heart. Mary exhorts the "anges chantans" to move through the desert singing God's praises. The angels' songs are in fact hymns of praise. But they are also incantations of such dynamic force and creative energy that they provoke the transmutation whereby the desert becomes fertile. "Chantons," they sing, "tant que nul lieu n'ignore nostre voix" (p. 330) [Let us sing so that there will be no place where our voices are unknown]. Six angels (the number six is surely an allusion to the six days God spent creating the world[33]) then speak one after the other, their voices creating a progressively paradisiac garden around Mary and the child.

LE PREMIER ANGE.

Tous Arbres secz, ne soyez plus steriles,
Le Createur veult que soyez fertiles,
Donnans voz fruitz de tresbonne saveur.

LE SECOND ANGE.

Apparoissez dens ce Desert sans umbre,
Vous belles fleurs odorantes sans nombre,
Pour au jourd'huy recevoir grand'saveur.

LE TIERS ANGE.

Courez Ruisseaux, pres de la vierge mere;
Presentez luy eaue douce, non amere;
Honneur aurez quand de vous en prendra.

LE QUART ANGE.

O Miel tresdoux de la subtile mouche,
Viens toy monstrer pour consoler la bouche
Porte du Ciel dont chacun apprendra.

---

33. Hopper, *Medieval Number Symbolism*, points out that the number six meant earthly (but not divine) perfection, p. 86.

LE V. ANGE.
Serpens, Dragons, et Bestes venimeuses,
Eslongnez vous, et soyez gracieuses,
Sans faire mal à Mere ny Enfant.
LE VI. ANGE.
Tygres, Lyons, et furieuses bestes,
Baissez icy voz forces et voz testes;
Car resister contre eux Dieu vous defend.   (pp. 330–31)

(1) All you withered trees, be no longer fruitless; the Creator wishes you to be fruitful, producing fruit that tastes very good. (2) Appear in this shadowless desert, you beautiful, innumerable, fragrant flowers, to receive today a wonderful scent. (3) Flow, brooks, close to the virgin mother; offer her sweet water, not bitter; you will be honored when she takes some from you. (4) O very sweet honey from the cunning bee, come, show yourself; to console the mouth, bring from heaven that which everyone will understand. (5) Serpents, dragons, and venomous beasts, withdraw and be gentle, without harming the Mother or the Child. (6) Tigers, lions, and raging beasts, subdue your strength and bow your heads, for God forbids you to stand against them.

Just as God's creation was completed at the end of the sixth day, so the transformation of the desert into a garden is completed at the end of the speech made by the sixth angel. From this point on in the text, the paradisaic garden, the *locus* of Christian pleasure and jubilation, conflates with the figure of a book. Throughout the rest of the text, allusions to abundance and fruitfulness, derived from garden imagery, apply to textual copiousness and fecundity, for creation itself is now viewed as a text. This is in fact what *Contemplation* explains to Mary in a lengthy discourse that immediately follows the tercet of the sixth angel. Showing the Blessed Virgin the garden that the angels have just created, *Contemplation* says that she has been sent by God to help Mary read "ce beau grand Livre" [this beautiful and great Book] which she calls "Nature" (p. 331). Exhorting Mary to *look* ("Regarde, Dame," p. 332), *Contemplation* declares that "tout cecy est fait pour l'homme; / L'homme, pour Dieu," (p. 332) [All this is made for man; man, for God]. Throughout her speech, she repeats her imperative ("regarde," which is complemented by its synonym "voye"), directing Mary's attention to the orderliness of nature: "Or donc regarde comme / Tout va par ordre" (p. 332) [Just look how everything fits in place].

Curtius has pointed out that the *topos liber naturae* was widespread in Christian homiletics during the late Latin Middle Ages.[34] The "book of nature" and the "book of the creature" became staples in the metaphorics of philosophers and mystics during the thirteenth and fourteenth centuries and retained much of their power well into the Renaissance. In the *Imitation*, for instance, Thomas à Kempis wrote: "If only thy heart were right, then every created thing would be to thee a mirror of life and a book of holy teaching" (II.4). This is the tradition on which Marguerite draws. Emphasizing the apocalyptic nature of this garden, *Contemplation* identifies it specifically with Eden and informs Mary that had man not sinned he would still reside in the paradise that God prepared for him.

In her response to *Contemplation* (response more in the ecclesiastical sense of responsory than in that of reply, for the characters in the *Comédie du désert* do not so much answer each other as mark an advance along an axis leading to an ever greater perception of the Truth), Mary reinterprets "looking" and "seeing." She thus introduces a significant perceptual shift in the text. Heeding *Contemplation*'s counsel, Mary looks at the garden around her. She does not dwell, however, on the things she sees but rather on the living spirit of God whose presence she discerns behind the natural world, described as "masque et couverture" (p. 335) [mask and covering]. In other words, Mary does not see with the carnal eye but with "l'oeil de Foy" [the eye of Faith]. He who views the world with the eye of faith "laisse à part / L'exterieur, et tourne son regard / En toy, qui es son heritage et part" (p. 336) [leaves aside the exterior and turns his eyes toward you, who are his heritage and country].

Nowhere in her work is Marguerite closer to Augustinian hermeneutics than in Mary's disquisition on sight and insight. All the things of the natural world, Mary explains, are signs of God's presence. The usefulness of the book of nature is derived from the signifying function of its constitutive elements. Augustine had made a clear distinction between the things that are to be enjoyed and those that are to be used. He notes that the only things we can legitimately enjoy are "the Father, the Son, and the Holy Spirit, a single Trinity, a certain supreme thing common to all who enjoy it, if, indeed, it is a thing and not

34. *European Literature and the Latin Middle Ages*, p. 319.

rather the cause of all things, or both a thing and a cause" (DDC I.4.9–10). All things, with the exception of God, are to be perceived as tools that we should use in our effort to discern Him who informs everything and is both the source and object of all enjoyment. Mary does not display the slightest pleasure in the "things" that compose the garden around her. She sees them only to see through them, discerning the invisible in the visible. Speaking to God, she says:

> Tu es l'ouvrier de ce grand labourage,
> La vie aussi de tout arbre et fruitage:
> L'Estre et mouvoir
> De tout ce que l'oeil peult appercevoir,
> Soit verd, ou blanc, incarnat, bleu, ou noir.
> En terre et Mer
> L'on ne doit voir que toy, ny estimer.
> Tu fais fueillir, et fleurir, et germer,
> Et champs et bois,
> En tous lesquelz rien que toy ne congnois,
> En eux te voy, en eux j'entens la voix
> De ta puissance;
> Criant bien hault pour donner congnoissance
> Qu'il n'y a rien creé en ton absence.
> Car tout en tous
> Es et demeure.   (p. 334)

You are the workman of this great work, the life, too, of every tree and fruit, the Being and the mover of all that the eye can see, whether green, or white, pink, blue, or black. On earth and on sea, one ought not see or esteem anything but you. You make the fields and the woods leaf, flower, and grow; in all of them I perceive nothing but you, in them I see you, in them I hear the voice of your power; crying aloud to declare that there is nothing created in your absence. For you are and remain all in all things.

Reading the book of nature with the "eye of faith," Mary sees God in everything. Augustine had said that "to the healthy and pure internal eye He is everywhere present" (DDC I.12.13). To the extent that we "use" nature as Augustine would have us do and see in all things signs of God's presence, the world becomes once again the paradise that God created at the beginning of time. "Becomes" is, of course, the wrong word. God's paradise is here, now and forever, but we must learn to see it. The transformation from desert to garden does not occur in the natural world but in the eye that sees, that reads. He who reads creation with a carnal eye misreads, and so sees nothing but a desert. But he who reads the book of nature with a pure and healthy eye, with "l'oeil de foy," sees God everywhere. He comes to understand that the garden God made for him is situated not in the outer world but in the inward world of the heart.

In the *Comédie du désert*, the inwardness of the apocalyptic vision is suggested in esoteric terms that are likely to be discerned only by readers who are accustomed, as many Renaissance readers were, to attaching significance to the numerological patterns that can be discovered in a text. One of the most striking technical features of the *Comédie du désert*, and indeed of all the biblical comedies, is the diversity in both meter and rhyme schemes. Like oratorios, these comedies are composed of set pieces of contrasting rhythm and rhyme. Sckommodau has pointed out that *Contemplation*'s speech to Mary is composed of sixteen stanzas and a coda.[35] Mary answers in a speech made up of thirty-three stanzas and a coda. The number three figures prominently in several of Marguerite's poems, including the *Comédie du désert*. God sends three messengers to Mary. He also sends six angels. *Contemplation*, we recall, gives Mary the book of nature. In accepting the book, Mary demonstrates that she knows how to read it correctly. Although she makes no explicit reference to Christ, her discourse metacommunicates a christological view of nature by virtue of the fact that it has thirty-three stanzas. In her speech, Mary explains that to those who misread the book of nature the world is a desert but to those who read it with the eye of faith the world is a paradise. The correctness of her own reading is guaranteed by the fact that her words are infused with Christ's presence, which is represented by the number thirty-three.

After the departure of *Contemplation*, *Memoire* appears before Mary and, in a speech that is composed of sixteen stanzas and a coda, gives her a copy of the Old Testament. Accepting the book that is offered to her, Mary answers in a speech that repeats

35. Sckommodau, *Die religiösen Dichtungen . . .*, op. cit., p. 92.

the meter and rhyme of the discourse spoken by *Memoire*. But she adds one additional stanza. The result is that her response to *Memoire* consists of seventeen stanzas and a coda. The sixteen stanzas of *Memoire* plus the seventeen of Mary constitute, of course, a group of thirty-three stanzas forming a discrete unit that is set apart from the stanzas that precede and follow by a distinctive pattern of meter and rhyme. Once again numerology signals the rightness of Mary's reading of the Old Testament. By extending the pattern begun by *Memoire* to thirty-three stanzas, Mary permits the text to represent Christ's fulfillment of the Old Testament. Indeed, in the coda that terminates this block of thirty-three stanzas, Mary dwells on the fact that in reading the Old Testament she discovered the spirit of the New.

This grouping of stanzas into two units, each of which is composed of thirty-three stanzas, focuses the reader's attention (to the extent, of course, that he discerns these patterns) on Christ. *Consolation* arrives next and gives Mary a copy of the New Testament. *Consolation*'s speech and Mary's response form an intricate pattern in which the controlling number is no longer thirty-three but rather its root, the trinitarian number, three. The stanza in *Consolation*'s speech is composed of a *huitain* followed by two *sixains*. That is to say, each stanza is made up of three units. This stanza is repeated six times. Mary's answer is in the same stanzaic pattern, but doubled, making twelve stanzas, each of which is composed of a *huitain* and two *sixains*. The numerological patterning in *Consolation*'s speech and in Mary's reply surely represents an intentional effort by Marguerite to give the text a formal structure capable of metacommunicating the trinitarian principle. Mary's long discourse is a meditation on the mystery of the Trinity and the joy that fills the heart of the believer who reflects on the Incarnation. Her rapture reaches its highest degree of intensity when she realizes that faith actually engenders Christ, that the Savior is born in the heart of the believer:

> Qui croit comme moy
> Par tres vive Foy,
> Mere est du Sauveur;
> En son coeur l'engendre
> Mais qu'il puisse entendre

Sa grande faveur.
   Foy fait recevoir
Prendre et concevoir
Oyant Dieu parler.
Son enfant trescher
Son verbe fait Chair,
Qu'il ne fault celer.   (pp. 353–54)

Anyone who believes, as I do, by the true living Faith, is mother of the Savior; let him give birth to him in his heart, but let him understand the great favor. Faith makes one receive, take and conceive by hearing God speak. His beloved child, his word made flesh, which must not remain concealed.

Christological number schemes would seem to be the determining factor in the shape or form of large parts of the text. However, no allusions to this patterning or to the number three are made by *Contemplation*, *Memoire*, *Consolation*, or Mary. The inwardness of these patterns, all of which point to Christ, disclose the inwardness of the *hortus Christi*, which is situated in the heart rather than in the outer world of fleshy forms.

The text metacommunicates the inwardness of Christ in a second way. Giving Mary a copy of the Old Testament, *Memoire* retells briefly several of the principal episodes in Scripture: creation, the garden, Adam and Eve and the serpent, the flood, Abraham and Isaac, and David. The effect is nearly identical to that produced by the marginal references to Scripture in the *Miroir*. As we read *Memoire*'s speech, Marguerite's text recedes before a text that is both more authoritative and more familiar. In fact, by highlighting certain particularly well-known Old Testament scenes, Marguerite's text prods the reader's memory. The text that the reader "reads" is not the one hundred or so verses spoken by *Memoire* but the whole of the Old Testament as it is inscribed in his own memory. The function of *Memoire*'s words is not to affirm the presence of Marguerite's text as a literary artifact but to serve as a lens through which the reader can discover anew what he already knows, that is to say, what is already written in his memory.

Presenting the New Testament to Mary, *Consolation* explains that the parchment on which the Scriptural text is written is Christ's flesh.

> O Vierge, c'est le doux Livre de grace,
> Que Dieu par moy rend ouvert en tes mains;
> Tu ne seras jamais d'y lire lasse,
> Recongnoissant la peau du Saint des Saints
> Dont il est fait, pour à tous les humains
> Monstrer à cler l'amitié que leur porte:
> Tu y verras tout son secret (au moins
> Ce qu'il luy plaist que l'esprit en rapporte.)
>   La peau delicate
> Charité dilate
> Comme un parchemin;
> Et du doigt d'enhault
> Escrit ce qu'il fault
> Faire en ce chemin.   (p. 346)

O Virgin, it is the sweet book of grace that, opened, God puts into your hands through me; you will never tire of reading it, recognizing the skin of the saint of saints, of which it is made in order to show all humans clearly the affection he bears them; you will see there his secret (at least what he allows the spirit to report). Love stretches out the delicate skin like a parchment; and the finger from on high writes what one must do on this road.

As she begins to read, Mary realizes that "ce Livre d'amour plein" (p. 356) [this book full of love] is the true *locus voluptatis*, the site of all pleasure. A basic difference between the New Testament on the one hand and the book of nature and the Old Testament on the other was hinted at early in the play in the speech God addressed to *Consolation* when He commanded her to appear before Mary. Whereas the book of nature and the Old Testament were to be given to Mary so that she could "read" them ("Elle pourra lire à son beau loisir," p. 322) [She will be able to read at her leisure], the New Testament, "ce petit Livre ouvert d'affection / Remply d'amour, et de dilection" (p. 323) [this little book full of affection, full of love and friendship] was meant to be listened to. Responding to God's comment that the New Testament is His "vive Parole," His "Verbe en chair," *Consolation* says that she is eager to fly to Mary and give her ". . . ce Livre tant beau, / Dedens lequel elle t'oyra parler" (p. 323) [this very beautiful book, in which she will hear you speak]. She emphasizes further the auditory dimension of the book she is charged to deliver by noting that once Mary has heard the text speak, "son coeur chantera maint Cantique" (p. 323) [her heart will sing many hymns]. In antiphonal fashion, God picks up the image of music and, turning to the angels, says: "Anges, allez en ce Desert destruit; / Rejouyssez par harmonieux bruit / Mere et Enfant" (p. 324) [Angels, go into this desolate desert; by harmonious sounds make the mother and the child glad]. The de-emphasis on reading and the stress on listening represent the perceptual shift that other texts by Marguerite render in terms of a directional change away from a syntagmatic to a paradig-matic axis. The replacement of the Old Testament, with its em-phasis on historicity and sequentiality, by the New Testament signals a transcendence of "rational" discourse and of the lin-earity of logic. God's word operates in the world not by being seen or read but by being heard as it enters the heart and soul of mortal beings. *Logos* is transmitted through the literal reality of *parole* ("ceste vive Parole"). Revelation is spoken. To read cor-rectly is to hear the voice embodied in the text, an act tanta-mount to listening. As Jesus reminded the busy and talkative Martha, listening is the one essential activity.

The Mary of the *Comédie du désert* reads correctly when, look-ing at the texts given her, she hears a responsive echo in her own heart. Throughout the second half of the play, she sings psalms of praise and thanksgiving. Several of Marguerite's major poems end by stressing music. If we see all the poems of the *Marguerites de la marguerite des princesses* as a single poetic corpus, which they are, we cannot fail to note that in its published form Margue-rite's poetry concludes with a group of songs, the *Chansons spiri-tuelles*. These poems were meant to be sung. The first several of them are preceded by the title of the piece of music to which the text is to be set.[36] The two-volume collection of poetry Margue-rite published during her lifetime harbors in its textual folds allegories of itself. The *Ravie* and Mary are, among other things, allegorical figures that stand for *chansons spirituelles*, which are signs that point to the end of fleshy, or discursive, things and the permanence of *caritas*.

Early in the *Comédie du désert*, God sets in motion the process by which the desert will be made fruitful. He then becomes in-visible (at least to the carnal eye) throughout much of the play.

36. See *Chansons spirituelles*, ed. Georges Dottin, TLF (Geneva: Droz, 1971).

The scene shifts from His residence to the world of matter, which, if perceived rightly, is an embodiment of His will. At the end of the play, He reappears in His majesty, announcing that He is always present in the world and that everything that has happened is in accord with His plan. He reveals that Jesus, who in the context of the play is still an infant, will eventually die and in so doing conquer death. At this final point in the poem, the metaphors that have informed the text from the beginning fuse and harmonize. They combine to represent Christian bliss in terms of a paradisiac garden, fruitful and wonderfully fragrant. God calls Christ a sweet-scented flower and says that the believer's heart will burst into bloom. Striving to metacommunicate the flowering of the heart, the poem seeks a textual equivalent and finds one in music. God Himself enjoins us to raise our voices in song:

> O doux Esprits, si jamais me compleustes,
> Et desirants de m'obeïr vous feustes,
> Soyez joyeux; prenez voz instruments,
> Harpes, et Lucz, Orgues, Cymbales, Fluttes,
> Et racomptez comme charge vous eustes
> De rendre doux tous les quatre Elements. . . .
> Chantez qu'il fait bon en moy se fier.   (pp. 378–79)

O gentle spirits, if ever you have pleased me and been eager to obey me, be joyful; take up your instruments, harps, and lutes, wind instruments, cymbals, flutes, and tell how you were charged to make the four elements gentle . . . Sing that it is good to have faith in me.

The angels respond by announcing that they will sing God's praises everywhere. Each of the six angels sings in turn; the last two emphasize the fact that the Christian's song is continuous and uninterrupted:

> Le V. Ange
> Ciel, Terre, et Mer, sont tous pleins de ta gloire,
> Mais il en fault refreschir la memoire
> Incessamment par voix continuelle.
> Le VI. Ange
> De tous les biens qu'à l'ange aussi à l'homme
> As fait, Seigneur, dont nul ne sçait la somme,
> Louenge à toy en soit continuelle.   (pp. 379–80)

Heaven, Earth, and Sea are all full of your glory, but it is necessary to refresh constantly the memory by continual speaking. For all the good things you have done, Lord, for angels as well as for mankind, of which no one knows the full amount, let there be continual praise of you.

The life of a Christian is itself a psalm in which every element constitutes praise of the Creator. The text illustrates this notion in its conclusion by modulating once and for all into music. At the end of the *Comédie du désert*, all six angels join in singing a hymn. A marginal note in the text gives the name of the hymn tune to which the words are sung. The displacement of verbal by musical discourse is a textual mimesis of the flowering that Christ effects in the human heart.

THE PROBLEMATICS OF FINALITY

In the 1547 edition of the *Marguerites*, the *Comédie du désert* is followed by *Le Triomphe de l'Agneau*. The order of these two works is probably not accidental. The desert is a "wasteland" (Jeremiah 17.6) where man's faith is tested. To the extent that man remains faithful to God, "the wasteland rejoices and blooms" (Isaiah 35.1). Within the framework of the Christian model of reality, this flowering signals the triumph of the Lamb, the apotheosis of Christ. Thus *Le Triomphe de l'Agneau* completes the *Comédie du désert*. The journey undertaken by the Holy Family in the *Comédie* is concluded in *Le Triomphe*. The apocalyptic vision, which, in the *Comédie*, is rendered in terms of an Edenic garden and of music, is expanded in *Le Triomphe* to such an extent that the poem rivals the Book of Revelation in loftiness and grandeur of purpose.[37]

Though it is rooted in Revelations and the works of the Old Testament prophets, *Le Triomphe* owes certain of its features to Renaissance "triumph" poetry. As Henri Weber has observed, the Renaissance fondness for the "triumph" poem can be traced to Petrarch, whose *Trionfi* had inspired numerous imitations.[38]

37. H. P. Clive calls *Le Triomphe de l'Agneau* "le meilleur poème religieux de Marguerite" [Marguerite's best religious poem]. See Marguerite de Navarre, *Oeuvres choisies*, ed. H. P. Clive, I (Appleton-Century-Crofts, 1968), p. 19.

38. Henri Weber, *La Création poétique au XVIᵉ siècle en France*, I (Paris: Nizet, 1955), p. 649.

Adaptable to a variety of purposes, the "triumph" poem was used by sixteenth-century French poets to commemorate military conquests as well as spiritual victories. Following the model provided by Petrarch, the "triumph" poem glorifies an abstraction that is personified as a triumphant conqueror. Thus Love, Death, Time, and Fame frequently figure as undisputed masters of human destiny. Often the victor is shown returning from his exploits. He marches at the head of his army and is greeted enthusiastically by a cheering populace. Bringing up the rear of the procession is a group of illustrious foreigners, reduced to slavery by the conquering hero.

The Book of Revelation, the books of the Old Testament prophets, and "triumph" poetry have a feature in common that is central to Marguerite's *Triomphe*. They trace out a temporal unfolding. The biblical books that inspired *Le Triomphe* describe what has been and what will be. Using verbs in the past tense to show man his sinfulness and in the future tense to foretell what will happen to him, they fall under the sign of *Already-Not Yet* and firmly establish temporality as their principal axis. The main axis in "triumph" poetry, too, is temporal, for it recounts a procession that passes before the reader who is seated, as it were, in a reviewing stand, observing the spectacle that unfolds before his eyes. In "triumph" poetry, however, time is expressed not by means of the future verb tense but through narrative, which relates the unfolding of events sequentially along a linear axis. Like the prophetic books of the Bible, "triumph" poems come under the aegis of *Already-Not Yet*.

Comparing *Le Triomphe de l'Agneau* with *Le Miroir de l'âme pécheresse*, Jourda notes that "la composition [du *Triomphe*] est infiniment plus claire que celle du *Miroir*"[39] [the structure of the *Triomphe* is infinitely clearer than that of the *Miroir*]. Jourda is irritated by the *Miroir*, whose reflexivity and paradoxical nature seem to defy the laws of logic and sequentiality. Although he does not say so specifically, the reason he finds *Le Triomphe* "clear" and *Le Miroir* obscure is that the former is a narrative whereas the latter is not, at least not in the same unequivocal way. Narrative is marked by the precisely delineated progression that Jourda professes to see in *Le Triomphe*. He declares that the poem opens with a brief introduction, which is followed by

39. *Marguerite d'Angoulême*, p. 407.

three parts. According to Jourda, the first part concludes with an apostrophe to Adam, the second, with an apostrophe to the souls elected to reside with God, and the third, with an apostrophe to the great of this world, whom Marguerite urges to kneel before the king of kings. The text thus recounts "la lente montée [de l'Agneau]"[40] [the slow ascent of the Lamb], who arrives finally before God. The entire work concludes with the Lamb's glorious and triumphant entry into divine light, Its eternal abode.

Except for saying that each of the three parts ends in an apostrophe, Jourda does not indicate where the divisions he discerns in the text occur. In a general way, the poem does indeed relate the progression of the Lamb and so traces an axis that is narrative, or syntagmatic. The narrative line, however, is interrupted so often that it becomes problematic. Furthermore, there is a considerable amount of material in the text that does not fit tidily into one or another of Jourda's three parts. Each apostrophe trails off into a discussion that fails to enunciate the beginning of the succeeding part. The design that Jourda admires in *Le Triomphe* ("Le dessein du poème est très net: une introduction, trois parties, une conclusion.")[41] [The design of the poem is very clear: an introduction, three parts, a conclusion.] does not account for enough of the text to be a completely acceptable outline of the skeletal structure of the poem.

At the heart of *Le Triomphe* lies the mystery of the Incarnation. Embodied in the man Jesus, God lived in human (historical or narrative) time. But He also exists outside time, and so can be thought of as meta-historical. The problematic nature of narrative in *Le Triomphe* is a consequence of the text's attempt to duplicate the mystery of the Incarnation, that is to say, to embody meta-history in history.

The poem opens in the invocational-prophetic mode:

> Tous les Eslus et Souldars du Vainqueur,
> Tous vrays servants, qui n'avez en vain coeur
> Aux durs assaults de la cruelle guerre
> Que fait Sathan contre CHRIST sur la terre;
> 5   Tous les Signez et Bourgeois de Zion,

40. Ibid., 408.
41. Ibid.

> Vrays heritiers, enfans d'adoption,
> Assemblez vous pour chanter la victoire
> Du seul Agneau, tout revestu de gloire.
> Assistez luy dedens son capitole,
> 10   Tous bien ornez de la celeste estolle.
> Sans vous ne peult se parfaire la feste:
> Le membre doit aller où est la teste.[42]

All the elect and soldiers of the victor, all you true servants who do not in vain take heart in the fierce assaults of the cruel war Satan wages against Christ on earth, all those marked with his seal and citizens of Zion, true heirs, adopted children: assemble to sing of the victory of the only Lamb, all dressed in glory. Attend to him in his capitol, all attired in the divine stole. Without you this celebration cannot be completed. The limb must go where the head is.

Hearing the direct address of "assemblez vous" and "assistez," the reader constructs an "I" that, at this point in the poem, can be identified only as "the speaker." "The speaker" invites or, given the categorical quality of the imperatives, commands his listeners to raise their voices "pour chanter la victoire / Du seul Agneau." There is an analogy between the voice that spoke the world into being in Genesis and the voice at the beginning of *Le Triomphe* that calls out the names of the different categories of the Elect and so brings the text into being. Indeed, God's voice echoes throughout the beginning of *Le Triomphe*, for the opening lines allude repeatedly to Scripture. "Signez" evokes II Corinthians 2.22 as well as numerous passages in Revelations; "vrays heritiers, enfans d'adoption" echoes Romans 8.15–17; "la celeste estolle" comes from Revelations 7.9; "le membre doit aller où est la teste" repeats the words of Paul in Colossians 1.18 and Ephesians 1.22–23. Not only do echoes from the Bible resound throughout the opening lines of *Le Triomphe*. Other literary traditions, too, are mirrored in the text. The first rhyme of the poem (*vainqueur-vain coeur*) reminds us of the debt that Marguerite owes to the *grands rhétoriqueurs*. Echoes of Roman solemnity and, perhaps, of the high odic tradition of Pindar may be heard in line nine ("Assistez luy dedens son capitole"), which

42. Citations are taken from the Clive edition, op. cit. Further references to this work will be identified by line number in the Clive edition.

calls to mind the Roman practice of leading a conquering hero before the Capitol.

With Manichaean precision, line four identifies the two warring forces in the world: Satan and Christ. In the context of an invitation to attend a celebration commemorating "la victoire / Du seul Agneau, tout revestu de gloire," the verb "fait," in the present tense, is striking. Since the victory of the Lamb can be celebrated only if the "cruelle guerre" is already over, the use of the present verb tense, which suggests that the battle is still going on, creates an ambiguity and a seeming contradiction that we must account for in our reading of the poem. Explaining the paradox whereby what is past (the Lamb's victory) has not yet occurred (the war is not yet over, and so the Lamb has not yet emerged victorious) is the central task before us in our discussion of the problematics of narrative in *Le Triomphe*.

The first twelve lines of the poem invoke the presence of the faithful at the head of the procession that leads (will lead?) the Lamb before the celestial capitol. There may be a numerological allusion to the twelve disciples in the twelve-line invocation that opens the poem. Christ may be said to have existed always, beyond and outside time, but Jesus and the twelve disciples stand at the beginning of Christian narrative as it manifested itself in human time. Designed to narrate the victory of the Lamb, the text opens with twelve stately lines that call believers to their rightful place in the procession. The next twelve lines describe the "loups ravissants" (13) [plundering wolves] who make up Satan's band. Overpowered by Christ, they come at the end of the procession, "car il [leur] convient aller apres le maistre" (24) [for they should come after the master]. By saying that the defeated followers of Satan appear as captives at the end of the procession, the text suggests that the Lamb is *already* victorious. But since the battle between Satan and Christ is now being waged, the victory has *not yet* occurred. Evoking two registers of reality, the text unfolds as a gradual revelation of divine reality within human reality, or, to say the same thing the other way around, the collapse of human reality into the divine.

In the next fourteen lines, the "I," whose voice we have heard from the beginning of the poem, identifies itself as an author who, somewhat restive and anxious, prepares to embark on the creative adventure that will lead to the writing of the text we have already begun to read:

25   Je veux icy tes triomphes chanter,
      Verbe divin; vien donc me presenter
      Les doux accords de la musique haulte,
      Pour non avoir en mon chant quelque faulte.
      Je veux, Seigneur, exerciter ma plume
30   A tes grans loz, si ton esprit m'allume.
      Allume donc par ta splendeur illustre
      Mon bas penser, et me fais voir le lustre
      De celle noble et auguste couronne
      Qui ton saint chef richement environne.
35   Or, me fiant, Seigneur, de ta largesse,
      Et que seras ma conduite et addresse,
      Commenceray dire l'occasion
      Pourquoy tu prins de nous compassion.

I wish here to sing of your triumphs, divine Word; come then to grant me the sweet harmonies of lofty music so that there will be no flaw in my song. I wish, Lord, to use my pen for your great glory, if your spirit enlightens me. Enlighten, therefore, with your bright splendor, my lowly thought and make me see the light of this noble and majestic crown, which richly surrounds your saintly head. Now, Lord, having confidence in your generosity and that you will be my guide and leader, I shall begin to relate the circumstances that explain why you took compassion on us.

The "I" of *Le Triomphe* differs markedly from the "I" of the *Petit Oeuvre*. In the *Petit Oeuvre*, "I" is a persona (easily identifiable with Marguerite in particular and the Christian in general) whose experience of Christ is allegorized as a journey. The reader, whose steady advance across the pages of the text parallels the "I"'s progress toward Christ, accompanies the narrator, sharing in her experience. In *Le Triomphe*, the "I" disappears from the text after the passage cited above and does not reappear except for an instant in line 185. The "I" of *Le Triomphe* is not, at least not after line 38, a persona who moves within the text but rather a witness who assumes an authorial stance outside the text, recording as faithfully as possible a "revelation" that God has disclosed to her ("ton esprit m'allume"). Like the "I" at the beginning of Revelations, the "I" that introduces the narrative in *Le Triomphe* presents her text as a revelation accorded her by God.
    The story begins with Adam. He had three mortal enemies

who held him in bondage: *Loy*, *Péché*, and *Mort*. Of these three, *Loy* was the most powerful, for it brought in its train the other two. Temporal and spatial deictics[43] ("jadis," "après," "ainsi," "un jour," "là," "où") compel the reader to experience the text along a syntagmatic axis. Even more important in fixing the historical dimension of the text are the allusions to the Bible. We have seen that in certain of her texts Marguerite introduces long paraphrases of biblical passages. In *Le Triomphe*, she does not paraphrase extensively but rather alludes briefly and precisely to a few key biblical scenes that range from the beginning of the Old Testament to the New. These scenes appear in her text in the order in which they appear in the Bible. They establish a narrative axis that begins with Adam's creation and ends with the advent of Jesus Christ.

The reader's effort to progress along this familiar narrative axis is, however, repeatedly frustrated by allusions to Christ, which appear from the beginning of the narrative. Marguerite interprets events in the Old Testament as signs of Christ's timeless presence in the world. Within the coordinates of meta-history, Christ is the beginning and the end, consubstantial with all of creation. This Christian truth is signaled in the text by continual subversion of the biblical narrative, which, the reader of *Le Triomphe* knows, moves from Adam to Christ in an irresistible, linear fashion. By inserting repeated references to Christ in her retelling of the Old Testament, Marguerite compels the reader to see Christian truth (or meta-history) as ever present, informing all of history from the beginning of time to the end.

There is another way, too, in which the text frustrates the reader's desire to make headway along the axis of the Old Testament narrative. When the narrator reappears in the text in lines 183–85, sympathizing with "povre Adam," she starts the narrative all over again by retelling, but now in much greater detail, the circumstances of Adam's fall into sin. The reader, having progressed (in terms of the biblical narrative) to the story of Moses, must now go back to the beginning and start over. Repeatedly throughout the course of the poem, the reader is forced to regress (in terms of the familiar narrative) while he moves

---

43. On deictics, or "'orientational' features of language which relate to the situation of utterance," see Jonathan Culler, *Structuralist Poetics*, op. cit., p. 167.

forward through the text. In other words, the text does not allow the reader to experience it exclusively in terms of human time. Repetition and regression are strategies by means of which the text compels the reader to experience it in terms of another time, a time that stands still—in short, in terms of meta-history.

Despite the repetitions, the narrative eventually moves forward to that moment when Christ appears incarnate. This event occurs about one third of the way into the poem. Within the economy of the text, the reader does not experience the Incarnation as a conclusion. Indeed, the Christian does not experience Christ in this way. Christ is not situated at the end of human progress. He resides in the center of human time. The text illustrates the centrality of the Incarnation in Christian experience by situating it in the middle third of the poem, roughly from line 503 ("Or est venu ce beau Filz de Jessé") [Now this beautiful son of Jesse came] to lines 1037–38 ("Ainsi l'Agneau, de gloire couronné, / Monta . . ." [Thus the lamb, crowned with glory, ascended]. We can be even more precise and locate the center of this middle third between lines 800 and 854. In these fifty-four lines, the text relates the Passion. This is the center of the center, for it is through Jesus' suffering on the cross that man is liberated from *Loy, Péché,* and *Mort.* To the extent that we read Marguerite's text not narratively but iconically, we see that meaning radiates from the central core of the poem, informing both the first and last lines of the text with the message that the significance of history is to be found in the Passion.

The account of the Passion is preceded by a passage in which Christ declares that the New Testament has supplanted the Old. The text presents this "victory" of the New Testament over the Old as a sign that God's will has triumphed and that the reign of charity has at last arrived. In language reminiscent of the Song of Songs, the text describes "ce beau Paradis" (750) [this beautiful paradise] "où tout florist" (734) [where everything blooms] and in which the Bridegroom embraces His Bride. Once again Christian paradise is depicted as a *hortus conclusus.* Stressing a fundamental Evangelical belief, Marguerite notes that man does not gain admittance to this loveliest of gardens by good works but only by faith.

This description of paradise serves as a preamble to the text's account of Christ's Passion. Again the order of the scenes contradicts the reader's expectations. Paradise, or the *hortus conclusus* (literally, the *last* garden), ought to be situated, one feels, at the end of time, as in Revelations. It ought to follow, not precede, the Passion. By refusing to structure the narrative along the temporal axis anticipated by the reader, Marguerite undermines history further and highlights the meta-historical dimension of paradise, of the Passion, and of the text.

The Passion itself is presented differently in *Le Triomphe* than in *L'Art et usage du souverain mirouer du chrestien*. Whereas in *L'Art et usage* (also in the *Petit Oeuvre*) Marguerite gives a graphic description of Christ on the cross, in *Le Triomphe* she does not describe the crucified figure. Speaking from the cross, Jesus tells the readers that they too, like the Lamb, must be crucified in order to enjoy the bliss that awaits the faithful in paradise. Christ tells his Bride that she must be immolated just as He was.

> En outre, je vous dis,
> Espouse chere et noble, que tandis
> Qu'icy serez en ce monde pervers,
> 800 Voz ennemys par supplices divers
> Vous assaudront en telle cruauté,
> Qu'ilz rougiront vostre teinct et beauté
> De vostre sang coulant à grans ruisseaux,
> Et forgeront tortures à monceaux,
> 805 Mille tourmens pour emplir leur courage
> Et mettre à chef leur felonnie et rage.
> . . . .
> Cordes, liens, chaisnes, seps et cousteaux,
> Escorchement, desrompement, posteaux,
> Roues, tourmens, Chevaux, Lions, Serpens,
> La terre et l'eau, les flambes et les vents,
> 815 Rien n'y aura de ce que le Ciel coeuvre
> Que tout ne soit contre vous mis en oeuvre.

Moreover, I tell you, dear and noble wife, that while you will be here in this perverse world, your enemies will, by diverse torments, assault you with such cruelty that they will redden your complexion and beauty with your blood, which will run in great streams; and they will devise many kinds of torture, a thousand torments to crown their courage and to satisfy their felony and fury . . . Ropes, bonds, chains, irons and knives, skinning, breaking, stakes, wheels, torments, horses, lions, serpents, earth and water, flames and winds, there will be nothing under the heavens that will not be put to work against you.

The only way to become *christiforme* is to experience Christ's suffering, to live the Passion in an endless now. The crucifixion is not historical. It is meta-historical and signals the destruction of the shackles (*Loy*, *Péché*, *Mort*) that bind man to history. It is deliverance from narrative.

The rest of the poem is an account of the Lamb's arrival at Its celestial throne. This account is interrupted many times by lengthy segments of Old Testament narrative that take us back to the beginning of history with the story of Adam. The Old Testament, or history, is thus enclosed within Christian revelation. Other historical material is introduced as well. Marguerite enumerates the empires that have succeeded each other throughout the course of human time. All of "history" is enfolded in meta-history, represented by the Lamb. Time is contained within timelessness.

The Lamb entered the flow of time and allowed Itself to be crucified so that, by dying, It could subvert *Loy*, *Péché*, and *Mort*. Once again the central meaning—or, rather, the central ambiguity—of the text is conveyed by the shift from one verb tense to another. The Lamb's entry into time as well as Its immolation on the cross, which in one sense effectively ends human time, are rendered in the past definite verb tense:

> L'Agneau cy bas humblement s'abbaissa,
> Sa majesté pour quelque temps mussa,
> Et soubs la Loy obedience apprint,
> 1490   Tant que la mort execrable en gré print
> Et endura la honte de la Croix,
> Mourant, pendant comme infame en un bois.

The Lamb humbly lowered itself here below, hid its majesty for a time, and learned to obey under the law, to such an extent that it accepted willingly terrible death and endured the shame of the cross, dying, hanging like a criminal on a stake.

The next line begins with the disjunctive "pourtant" and marks a shift away from the past definite to the past indefinite. Moreover, as the text evokes the Lamb's elevation to a position of supreme authority, verbs shift again, passing through the subjunctive mood before settling into the present tense:

Pourtant ainsi l'a exalté le Pere,
Et a tollu de la mort l'impropere,
1495 En luy baillant planiere autorité,
Un nom aussi de telle dignité
A qui soit fait par tout le monde hommage,
A qui soit fait et d'oeuvre et de courage
Par tous les saintz deue recongnoissance,
1500 Comme à celuy qui ha toute puissance,
Qui tient la clef des celestes thresors,
Et comme il veult les dispense et met hors.

However, the Father then raised him on high, and took away the disgrace of death, giving him full authority and a name of great dignity, to which homage is rendered by everyone, to which due recognition is given in both deed and heart by all the saints, as to him who is all powerful, who holds the key of celestial treasures and can apportion and distribute them as he wishes.

By moving out of the narrative (past) verb tense into the non-narrative (present) tense, the text marks the end of the Lamb's story in terms of human time.

As do so many of Marguerite's texts when they signal a shift from a syntagmatic to a paradigmatic axis, the poem now modulates into prayer. For the next seventy-three lines (1509–1582), the Lamb begs the Father to pardon mankind. Recalling Adam's disobedience, which Its own death on the cross has redeemed, the Lamb begins Its prayer by reminding the "Pere Eternal" that Its task on earth, which was to illustrate (provide man a paradigm for) complete obedience, has been completed. Several times in its prayer, the Lamb speaks of Its conclusive victory over death. The finality that is stressed in the thematics of the text is underlined by the extensive use of the present tense, which situates the prayer in a *now* that contrasts sharply with the *then* of the Lamb's Incarnation. Superseding narrative, which is organized under the sign of *Already-Not Yet*, the Lamb's prayer is, like all prayer, composed under the atemporal sign of *Yes-Amen*.

Since time has been abolished, narrative ought to cease definitively, and in one sense it does, for we are near the end of the poem. As the Lamb concludes Its prayer, however, It reintroduces time into the text by moving from the present verb tense to the future. The concluding lines of the poem announce what *will* happen in human time:

1615   Or est ainsi sur son throne Royal
           Triomphamment cest Advocat loyal,
           L'Agneau, le Roy, le Redempteur, le filz;
           En attendant que du tout desconfitz
           Ses ennemys soubz ses piedz mys seront,
1620   Et ruez juz, de scabeau serviront;
           En attendant qu'une autre fois revienne
           Pour acomplir la promesse ancienne
           En ses Esluz, lesquelz suscitera:
           Ainsi tousjours sur tout triomphera.

Thus is the loyal Advocate triumphantly on his royal throne, the Lamb, the King, the Redeemer, the son; waiting until his enemies, completely destroyed, will be brought under his foot and, thrown down, will serve as his footstool; waiting until he comes again to fulfill the old promise made to his Chosen, whom he will raise up: thus always, and over every thing, he will triumph.

These lines are among the least triumphant in the poem. The repetition of "en attendant" expresses the yearning of the Christian who awaits the fulfillment of the promise made to him in the beginning, i.e., baptism. Ending with the word "triomphera," the poem projects the Lamb's victory into the future. But the future has already been; it lies in the past, at the beginning of the text where the triumph of the Lamb was celebrated. The end of the poem points to the *triomphe* announced in the title before narrative began to unfold.

If one re-reads *Le Triomphe* (the equivalent of re-reading is to remember the beginning after having read the end), one re-experiences the "victoire / Du seul Agneau" [victory of the only Lamb] described at the beginning of the poem. That experience follows one's previous reading of the poem and so is future in relation to the concluding lines of the text. The revelation that will be disclosed (*triomphera*) has already been divulged, and the reader arrives, in Augustinian terms, at the place where he is already. Like a pendulum designed to illustrate perpetual motion, *Le Triomphe* is an artifact constructed so as to generate a motion that leads ever back to its beginning, defining a movement that is circumscribed within its own perimeters and is, therefore, in a sense, ever still.

In commenting on the first thirty-eight lines of *Le Triomphe*, I pointed out that the narrator calls upon the faithful to raise their voices in song and praise. Referring specifically to the nature of her literary enterprise, Marguerite then says in a line I have already cited: "Je veux icy tes triomphes chanter, / Verbe divin; . . ." (25–26). A subsequent reference to "les doux accords de la musique haulte" (27) and to the narrator's wish that her song ("mon chant," 28) be flawless gives special prominence to music at the beginning of the poem. It was, of course, conventional in epic poetry to invoke the muse of poetry or the god of song in the first few lines of the work. In *Le Triomphe*, the references to song may indeed betray a certain desire on Marguerite's part to attain the elevated style associated with the epic form. But a reader of Marguerite's poetry hears other echoes in the allusions to music. In Marguerite's works, song marks the triumph of the spirit over the letter. It represents meta-history and the *Tout-Verbe* that is either not yet or no longer incarnated in the rational discourse of *Verbe*. As soon as Marguerite speaks about writing down her song ("Je veux, Seigneur, exerciter ma plume / A tes grands loz"), visual imagery replaces auditory images ("Allume donc . . . / Mon bas penser, et *me fais voir* le lustre / De celle noble et auguste couronne," 31–33, my emphasis). The displacement of the auditory by the visual is even more pronounced when the text begins its first sustained narrative movement. The embodiment of voice and song into a text that can be seen is a mimetic representation of the Incarnation. The text becomes an emblem of the body by means of which Christ was revealed to human eyes.

Beginning to narrate the subjugation of man by *Loy*, *Péché*, and *Mort*, the text urges the reader to look closely at these three enemies of mankind: "Voyons ces trois leur empire et povoir" (59) [See these three, their influence and their power]. By repeating the word *Chair*, the text stresses Satan's palpable presence in the material world. It directs the reader's attention to a world whose physical presence and *out-thereness* are conveyed in language that is essentially referential. Like the landscape depicted at the beginning of the *Petit Oeuvre*, the world dominated by *Loy*, *Péché*, and *Mort* is a terrifying place, inhabited by "dragons, et aspics, et viperes" (70) [dragons, asps, and vipers]:

65   Pres des deserts où gist la terre morte,
            Sans que nul fruit elle nourrisse ou porte,
            Et que jamais à ce ne fust induite,
            Où tout est sec comme cendre recuite,
            Où rien ne croit (ainsi disent noz peres). . . .

Near the deserts where the dead earth lies, without nourishing or
bearing any fruit, and which has never been induced to do so, where
everything is dry, like burned cinders, where nothing grows (as our
fathers say). . . .

The referential nature of the language is reinforced by the repetition of "où," whose specificity serves to define place. The single
most striking feature of this inhospitable terrain is a mountain,
"en langage Hebraïque / Nommé Sina, Agar en Arabique" (71–
72) [in the Hebrew language named Sinai, Agar in Arabic],
whose "teste" is "chauve, aspre, sterile et nue" (75) [summit is
bold, rugged, sterile and bare]. Mount Sinai strikes terror in the
heart of anyone who looks at it.

    Having evoked Mount Sinai, Marguerite retells the story of
Moses as recounted in Exodus 19. But she infuses the account
with a meaning that is foreign to—or, at least, only latent in—
the biblical text. As the summit of Mount Sinai is enveloped in
smoke and fire, the sky darkens, and groans are heard. "Cela
sembloit estre un ventre pesant / Prest d'enfanter" (105–106) [It
looked like a heavy belly ready to give birth], writes Marguerite
in a line Jourda condemns as a particularly striking example of
bad taste. "L'idée paraît bizarre de comparer la nuée qui couronne le Sinaï au ventre d'une femme enceinte" [The idea of
comparing the cloud that crowns Mount Sinai with the belly of
a pregnant woman seems bizarre],[44] he writes. Bizarre, perhaps;
but Jourda seems to miss the point. Marguerite is in fact describing a birth. What is being born amidst the wails of the
natural world is the written word. When the smoke clears from
the mountain, man sees before him a text, the incarnate form of
Loy. From this point on in the poem, the act of making visible,
which is the essence of the Incarnation, is rendered in terms of
producing a text. Henceforth, seeing is identical with reading.

44. *Marguerite d'Angoulême*, p. 411.

Governed by the notions of sequentiality, causality, differentiation, and specificity that are inherent in language, and informed by the concepts of beginning and end, the text manifests the "rigoreuse face" (84) [severe face] of *Loy*, which "jadis triomphoit" (43) [formerly triumphed]. As the embodiment of *Loy*, the text is both a sign and an instrument of oppression.

125   Au beau mylieu de ce divers prodige,
         Assise estoit la Loy, qui tous oblige,
         Monstrant l'escrit par plusieurs ans secret,
         Dit de peché chyrographe et decret,
         Portant, disant, requerant franchement
130   La mort de tous, si la lettre ne ment.
         Ho, quel decret à l'homme tant contraire!
         Quel obligé! *Qui le pourra deffaire?*
         O quel arrest! quelle dure sentence!
         Quel jugement, si de pres on y pense!
135   Il dit ainsi: Misericorde ouverte
         Estre ne doit, ne grace descouverte
         A ceux qui ont le peché par naissance.
         O bienheureux qui en aura dispense!
         Son vestement de sang tout coloré,
140   Le bort par tout tres richement doré,
         Puis par dessus escrit comme il s'ensuit:
         L'homme est maudit, qui franchement ne suyt
         Tous les sermons de la divine lettre,
         Et qui voudra un seul poinct en omettre.   (my emphasis)

Right in the middle of this strange wonder, Law was seated, which binds everyone, displaying the writing that was secret for many years, uttering decrees and judgments about sin, bringing, ordering, demanding plainly the death of all, if the letter does not lie. Oh, how hostile to man was such a decree! What an edict! Who will be able to destroy it? O what an order! what a hard sentence! what a judgment, if one thinks about it carefully! It said this: there must not be any pity granted, nor grace given to those who are marked by sin through birth. O happy he who will be exempted from it! Its garment colored with blood, the whole border richly gilded, and above was written as follows: That man is damned who does not follow, without halting, all the dictums of the divine letter and who will wish to omit any single point.

Who, Marguerite asks in line 132, will destroy *Loy*? Her question is tantamount to asking, Who will pulverize language? Who will undo the text, for, as Paul wrote, "the written letters bring death, but the Spirit gives life" (II Corinthians 3.6).

Marguerite's reader knows, of course, that Christ will save mankind from the rigor of the law. And, indeed, no sooner does Marguerite's text ask who will destroy *Loy* than the figure of Christ appears momentarily in the poem. According to Marguerite's account of what happened on Mount Sinai, God, shading His light so as not to blind Moses, appeared to the prophet in "quelque celeste umbrage / Où il [Moses] congneut du Filz de Dieu l'Image" (182) [a celestial cloud in which he [Moses] discerned the image of the Son of God]. Assimilating Moses with Adam and making of "povre Adam" the symbol of all mankind, Marguerite says in the next line:

> O povre Adam, quand tu vis telle monstre,
> Ton coeur fondoit comme la cire contre
> 185   Un ardent feu: j'en parle comme expert.

O poor Adam, when you saw such a spectacle your heart melted like wax in a burning fire. I am speaking as one who has much experience in these things.

Representing mankind before the Incarnation, Moses caught a glimpse of Christ. Marguerite altered the Old Testament narrative in order to demonstrate the presence of Christ in the world from the beginning of time. This scene also foreshadows Christ's eventual appearance in the world in human form. Nowhere in the Old Testament does anyone look upon God's face. The Old Testament God is exclusively a voice, never a countenance. He is heard, never seen. The New Testament, though, by giving corporeal form to the Divinity, invests the divine *logos*, or the Word, with a face. "The Word was made flesh, he lived among us, and we saw his glory" (John 1.14). In another passage, John reports that Jesus told His followers: "To have seen me is to have seen the Father" (14.9). Whereas the key word in Old Testament epistemology is *hear*, the New Testament reveals (*revelare* means to remove a veil and so expose to the eyes) another avenue to Truth: *sight*.

In much of Marguerite's poetry, Christ is represented as a visible figure incarnated in a human body and crucified on the cross. But, as Scripture makes clear, Christ is also enfleshed (to use an archaic but expressive word) in a textual body. Just as *Loy* is incarnated in the Old Testament, so Christ is embodied in the New. The combat between *Loy* and Christ is thus a struggle between two texts. However, since texts are dependent on a reader to give them their significance, the war between the Old text and the New is really a battle between two different modes of perception, two divergent "readings." Marguerite, by reading the Old Testament so that it reveals Christ's countenance at every step along the way, illustrates the victory of the Lamb even before her own text, in its linear, narrative flow, has reached the New Testament account of Jesus. Furthermore, her reading of the Old Testament serves as an example of how a Christian must see, or read, a text; he must read in such a way that the written word reveals its true meaning, which is always the Christian message of charity. To the extent that the written word incarnates *Loy*, it seeks to entrap the reader into believing that the physical world (both that beyond the page and that of the page itself, i.e., paper, ink, words, sentences) is real. But to the extent that the written word can be interpreted as incarnating Christ, it strives to situate reality outside matter and to draw the reader away from the page toward the immaterial spirit that informs the text. For the Christian, sight leads to the blindness of insight, which is signified by the undoing of the flesh. The "Verbe divin" that Marguerite invokes at the beginning of *Le Triomphe* becomes incarnate in Christ and is then immolated so that all who see (read) Him can be led back to the divine *logos*. It also becomes incarnate in Marguerite's text, which, seeking to emulate Christ the Text, tries to undo itself (the problematics of narrative) so that all who read it can be guided away from what they see with carnal eyes toward contemplation of the Truth, which is visible only to the spiritual eyes. Pulverization of the flesh, which allows us to be "conformes à l'Image / De son cher Filz" (443–44) [like the image of his dear Son], cannot be completely effected while the spirit remains captive in the body. Nor can it be perfectly duplicated on the page, for the text, despite its efforts to annihilate its own form cannot erase itself utterly from the page on which it is written. What it can do, however, is declare its desire for its own obliteration. Throughout *Le Tri-omphe*, the thematics of incarnation is countered by the thematics of effacement and pulverization.

Lines 445–502 present the Incarnation as the descent of the Word into human language. The "celeste autheur" (412) has just announced His decision to provide the faithful with a vehicle by means of which they can become like Christ. Marguerite then writes:

445   Or a voulu ce hault Seigneur des Cieux
          Par tel amour en eux ficher les yeux,
          Que pour l'arrest de son dire acomplir,
          Et pour iceux de ses vertus remplir,
          Pour mettre fin à sa volonté stable,
450   Son propre Verbe immortel, immuable,
          A delegué pour icy bas venir,
          Voulant par luy ses promesses tenir;
          Voulant qu'apres qu'il seroit descendu,
          Que son saint nom fust par tout estendu,
455   Et que des siens il assemblast l'Eglise,
          Qui luy seroit famille bien acquise;
          Voulant aussi que l'eternel propos
          Du grand Sabbat et celeste repos
          Fust conservé par un saint testament.

Now this lofty Lord of the heavens succeeded through such love in fixing his eyes on them so as to accomplish his decree and to fill them with his virtues. To put an end to his immobile will, he charged his own immortal, immutable Word to come down here, wishing to keep his promises through it; wishing that after he had descended, his holy name would be heard everywhere and would draw together the church of his own, which would be a very devoted family; wishing also that the eternal design of the great Sabbath and divine repose might be kept in a holy testament.

Marguerite stresses God's wish to fulfill (*accomplir*) His word and express His love for His own creation. Paradoxically, it is man who opens the way for God to demonstrate His love. At the beginning of both Revelations and *Le Triomphe*, man initiates speech by affirming his presence and by announcing his function as a witness ("I, John . . ."; "Je veux icy tes triomphes chanter"). Man opens the circuit of communication by calling

on God, who then answers in response. Only to those who seek
Him can God appear. As Matthew wrote in 7.7–8: "Ask, and it
will be given to you; search, and you will find; knock, and the
door will be opened to you. For the one that asks always receives
and the one who searches always finds; the one who knocks will
always have the door opened to him." In his discussion of the
Book of Revelation, Jacques Ellel says that "il ne faut pas dans
l'Ecriture supprimer la part de l'initiative de l'homme" [one
must not suppress in Scripture the role of man's initiative].[45]
Man's word is a preamble to God's. Unless man speaks first, God,
despite His longing to communicate with mankind, will remain
mute. By opening their works with a declaration of their faith in
Him, John and Marguerite activate, as it were, the Word. Responding to John, God spoke, saying: "Write down all that you
see in a book." All of the visions that fill Revelations have as
their true object the Word John "turned to see." In *Le Triomphe*,
the means whereby God fulfills His desire to put an end to His
immutability and separation from man depends on the Johannine definition of the Divinity as *Verbum*. To the family of faithful who have banded together to form His church, God gives
"un saint testament" (459) that will forever serve as a sign of His
love. His "eternel propos" will be incarnated in a Testament that,
being called New, will replace the Old Testament, identified as
"le vieil decret de la Loy" (463) [the old decree of the Law].

Jesus Christ is the "saint testament" that God gives to believers,
the text in which the Father enfleshes Himself and declares the
coming of the reign of charity and the victory of love over law.

> Ce Verbe donc tousjours victorieux,
> 470   Fort, tres puissant, permanent, glorieux,
> Par qui le Ciel en toute sa grandeur
> Print ornement, et figure, et rondeur,
> Vestu de chair, au combat s'appresta.

This Word, therefore, always victorious, strong, very powerful, permanent, glorious, by which heaven in all its grandeur takes on beauty,
and shape, and roundness, clothed in flesh, prepared for combat.

Embodied in Christ the Text, the Word attacks *Mort*, *Loy*'s
henchman and man's principal oppressor. Several brief narrative

---

45. *L'Apocalypse: architecture en mouvement* (Brussels: Desclée, 1975), p. 106.

passages describe how *Verbe* descended to the world of matter
and freed man from the prison in which *Mort* held him captive.
Its mission accomplished, the *Verbe* must submit to its own destruction. It is pulverized, "comme un vieil pot cassé" (492)
[like an old broken pot]. The destruction of the flesh, however,
liberates the spirit, which, in the form of the Lamb, now ascends
throughout the next 1600 lines of the poem, reversing the motion begun by the *Verbe*'s incarnation. To convey the meaning of
the crucifixion, Marguerite uses two familiar and unpretentious
images: that of an old pot that falls and breaks; and that of a
mustard seed that must be crushed in a mortar before its true
nature is revealed. John had supplied the second of these metaphors: "Unless a wheat grain falls on the ground and dies, it remains only a single grain; but if it dies, it yields a rich harvest"
(John 12.24). Without alluding specifically either to the crucifixion or the cross, Marguerite takes up John's metaphor and
uses it to express the notion that the incarnate form of the
"Verbe immortal" must perish before the generative and creative power contained within can be released:

> Pourtant tres bien ce Verbe est comparé
> Au grain de bled, lequel au champ aré
> 495 Porter ne peult aucun fruit ne proufit,
> S'il n'est avant du tout mort et confit.
> Semblablement la menue moustarde
> Sa grand vigueur dedens soy contregarde
> Autant de temps qu'il est en son entier;
> 500 Mais quand il est pilé dens le mortier,
> Incontinent à grand largesse sort
> Son naturel tant violent et fort.

However, this Word is compared very appropriately to a grain of wheat,
which in the tilled field cannot bring forth any fruit or profit if it is not
first completely dead and submerged. Similarly the little mustard seed
keeps its great vigor within itself as long as it is whole; but when it is
pounded in a mortar, its violent and strong nature comes out at once.

Upon its return to its celestial home, the Lamb, or the "Verbe
divin," is greeted by a choir of angels who retell in 113 lines the
story of the divine Word's incarnation and subsequent release
from the flesh. The angels exploit the metaphoric potential of the
word *Verbe* and present the history of the world as the coming-

into-being of a book. Before recording the angels' actual words, however, Marguerite warns the reader that "leur divine langue" (1183) [their divine language] cannot be adequately contained in "humaine parole" (1186) [human speech]. Once again the distinction between "langue" and "parole" has a Saussurian ring. "Toutesfois," Marguerite continues, "quelque umbrage [trace] / Ont peu suyvir de ce divin langage / Ceux qui par Foy aux cieux feurent ravis" (1187–89) [However, those who have been transported to the heavens by faith have been able to follow a trace of this divine language]. Faith allows the reader to discern in the text traces of the divine *logos*.

Declaring that the world is a materialization of the "Verbe tres saint, vive Image du Pere" (1205) [very holy Word, living image of the Father], which "fait tout soudain de son Rien comparoir / Le monde tout, et visible apparoir" (1209–11) [all at once brings forth out of its own Nothingness the entire world, and makes it visible], the angels relate the story of Adam, who, not content with God's "vive Parole" (1223), forged false gods and thus "tresbucha en telle cecité / Qu'il s'addonna à toute enormité" (1235–36) [stumbled into such blindness that he gave himself up to every kind of wickedness]. Longing to reestablish the circuit of communication with the creature He loved but who, now blinded by sin, could no longer see Him, God decided to make Himself manifest in the world in a form man could perceive. In the following passage, the text explains that, in accord with "l'expresse volonté / De l'Eternel" (1247–48) [the express will of the Eternal], the Incarnation is a "translation" of the divine Word into human language:

> Voyant ainsi la Chair se fourvoyer,
> [L'Eternel] Determina au monde t'envoyer,
> Sermon divin, Parole magnifique.
> Mais ton parler tres hault et mirifique
> 1255 A l'homme estant incongnu et estrange,
> L'Eternel dit pour sa gloire et louenge,
> Que toy qui es sa nayve diction,
> Serois traduit par incarnation
> En tel parler que le monde entendroit,
> 1260 Et que par toy le secret comprendroit
> Qui feut long temps en ton Livre celé,
> Lequel tu as pleinement deseellé.

Seeing the flesh thus going astray, He decided to send you to the world, divine Speech, magnificent Word. But your language, very lofty and wonderful, being unknown and strange to man, the Eternal One ordered for his glory and praise that you, who are his simple speech, would be translated by the incarnation into such language that the world would understand and, through you, grasp the secret that was for a long time hidden in your Book, which you have completely unsealed.

The *logos*, adapting itself to the limitations of human sight, became visible in a book, which Christ opened so that man could read and discover the Truth. Within the perspective of history, what man saw first was the book of *Loy*, which, Marguerite suggests, is a kind of abstruse grammar. Characterized by "maintes loix, langues et factions" (1283) [many rules, languages and divisions], the book of *Loy* allows—indeed, compels—man to exercise his eyes and so regain at least part of the vision that was lost at the time of the Fall. Not yet ready to "entendre . . . le parler tant elegant" (1273) [hear the elegant speech] of the "Verbe divin," man can, however, discern the letter, which is the coarse casing that contains the Word. Christ, who is consubstantial with the Father and so has no beginning or end, is present even in *Loy*, although, within the linear flow of history, man was at first unable to "read" Christ in the book of law. Christ's Incarnation was a "translation" (1258) that man could read. Complete understanding of the text in which the "Parole magnifique" is incarnated is possible, however, only in light of the crucifixion, which, paradoxically, is an effacement of the Book itself. Having identified the Incarnation as the embodiment of the divine Word in a text, Marguerite translates the crucifixion, too, into the language of textuality. Like the mustard seed that must be crushed before it can reveal "son naturel tant violent et fort" [its violent and strong nature], the text must be split open before it can disclose its essence and thus fulfill its mission.

In *Le Triomphe*, the process by which the text is broken open is identical with the act of reading. Marguerite tells us that the Lamb, symbol of submission to the divine will, unsealed ("a deseellé," 1262) the Book. Her metaphor for reading is breaking the seal of a scroll. She borrowed it from the fifth chapter of Revelations, in which John says that he saw on God's right "a scroll that had writing on back and front and was sealed with seven seals" (Revelations 5.1). When an angel proclaimed in a loud voice that only he who was worthy to open the scroll should step forward, the Lamb alone advanced. While the saints prayed, the Lamb opened the seals and allowed those who crowded around to see what was written on the scroll.

A seal is both an interdiction and a guarantee that the message enclosed is authentic. It is also a sign of appropriation. As long as a text remains sealed, it is the property of him who sealed it. As soon as it is opened, however, it belongs to him who broke the seal. Marguerite makes it plain that once a text is "opened," thus becoming the property of the reader, it is no longer located on the page but in the intuitive center of the self, where it is translated into the living language ("langage tout nouveau," 1606) [completely new language] of the heart. A text that is read becomes consubstantial with the reader, who may then re-utter it in a speech-act that is authenticated by the living presence of a second "reader." Marguerite here recasts Renaissance theories of imitation in a Christian mold. As a reader of Scripture, she absorbs the sacred text, which she then re-utters in her poems, imitating or reproducing the Bible. The reader of Marguerite's texts repeats this process. Of course, the reader need not compose literary artifacts to transmit the text he has read. A life, too, is a text whose signs can be read in the same way that the visible signs of a poem, i.e., words, can be read. Transmitted from heart to heart, the Word lives anew in every reader.

Or rather, the Word is re-uttered in the heart of every reader who *submits* to the text. The Christian reader does not scrutinize a text in an attempt to extract meaning from it. This was Martha's mistake when she questioned Christ. Nor does he impose meaning on a text. In fact, *he* does not penetrate the text at all; the text penetrates him. Marguerite stresses this point near the end of *Le Triomphe*. After delivering Its lengthy prayer before God and His host of angels, the Lamb falls silent. Marguerite then remarks: "Et penetra ce parler precieux / Jusques aux coeurs de ses feaux amys" (1606) [And these wonderful words penetrated the hearts of his faithful friends]. The imagery of submission, which abounds in *Le Triomphe*, is central to Marguerite's concept of reading. Only if the reader submits to the text (and Augustine reminds us that the whole of creation is a text whose visible signs point to the Word) can the divine *logos* penetrate the human heart, with which it then becomes consubstantial.

He who reads correctly, attending to the spirit and not the letter, effaces the "difference" between author and reader. He becomes, in the words of Mother Juliana of Norwich, "rightfully knitted and oned with Christ, the Divine Word."[46] As custodian of the Word, the reader is ultimately the *locus* of plenitude. He experiences apocalyptic fullness ("in him [Christ] you find your own fulfillment," Colossians 2.9), which is situated not at the end of human time but in the timeless *now* of the reader's heart. The ultimate message encoded in *Le Triomphe de l'Agneau* is that Christ achieves unending presence in the world by virtue of the contingent humanity of the reader, who in turn achieves eternal presence in God by virtue of the contingent divinity of Christ the Text.

46. *Revelations of Divine Love* (London: Kegan Paul, Trench, Trübner and Co., 1902), p. 143.

III
The Poetics of Love

7
The Rhetoric of Tears

FALLING CADENCE

Francis I became ill in mid-February 1547 and died several weeks later on March 31. During Francis' illness, Marguerite wrote several short poems, a few of which were included among the thirty-three poems that appeared at the end of the *Marguerites* (published later in 1547) under the title of *Chansons spirituelles*. In all, Marguerite wrote some forty-seven *chansons*. The fact that she included only thirty-three of them in the *Marguerites* suggests that the number thirty-three is intended to allude to Jesus' age at the time of His crucifixion.[1] The most quintessential, or "musical," of Marguerite's works, the *Chansons* were in many cases written to be sung to well-known hymns. Within the economy of the *Marguerites*, the *Chansons spirituelles* form a single poem only slightly longer than several other poems in the volume. Concerned with death, they account for the falling cadence that marks the conclusion of the *Marguerites*. Indeed, the last word of the thirty-third *chanson*, which concludes the volume, is "deffait" [undone].

The first of the *Chansons spirituelles* is entitled *Pensees de la Royne de Navarre, estant dens sa Litiere, durant la maladie du Roy. Sur le chant de, Ce qui m'est due et ordonné* [Thoughts of the Queen of Navarre, being in her carriage, during the King's illness. To the tune of "What is required and commanded of me"]. In the opening three stanzas, Marguerite returns to a double-

---

1. Fourteen unpublished *chansons* were copied down by a scribe in the manuscript called *Derniers Oeuvres*. In his modern edition of the *Chansons spirituelles*, Dottin gives all forty-seven poems, thus sacrificing the original configuration of the text to completeness. On the problem of the manuscripts, see Dottin, pp. vii–ix.

edged theme that runs through her poetry: although she recognizes the utter inadequacy of fallen language, she cannot remain silent; she is compelled by inner necessity to go on writing. Whereas for Humanists copiousness was a sign of man's fertile mind and inexhaustible creative energy, for Marguerite it signals an ontological flaw. Since the Fall, man has been condemned to language. Marguerite continues to speak, although she knows (or at least claims to know) that words are useless:

1   Si la douleur de mon esprit
           Je povois monstrer par parole
           Ou la déclarer par escrit,
           Onque ne feut sy triste rolle;
5   Car le mal qui plus fort m'affole
           Je le cache et couvre plus fort;
           Par-quoy n'ay rien qui me console,
           Fors l'espoir de la douce mort.

           Je sçay que je ne dois celer
10   Mon ennuy, plus que raisonnable;
           Mais si ne sçauroit mon parler
           Atteindre à mon dueil importable:
           A l'escriture véritable
           Defaudroit la force à ma main,
15   Le taire me seroit louable,
           S'il ne m'estoit tant inhumain.[2]

If I could show by word the sorrow of my spirit, or state it in writing, never would there be such a sad account; for the more forcefully misfortune wounds me, the more forcefully I hide and conceal it. So I have nothing that consoles me except the hope of sweet death. I know that I ought not conceal my grief more than is reasonable; however, my speech would fall short of my intolerable sorrow; the strength in my hand is not sufficient for a true written account; it would be laudable of me to remain silent if that did not seem to me to be so inhuman.

Declaring that she finds no solace in language, Marguerite asserts that her *chansons* are not linguistic structures at all. They rely not on the artificial code of language and textuality but on

2. I cite the *Chansons spirituelles* in the Dottin edition.

the natural code of tears, sighs, and sobs. Weeping is the non-linguistic discourse of the heart.

> Mes larmes, mes souspirs,[3] mes criz,
> Dont tant bien je sçay la pratique,
> Sont mon parler et mes escritz,
> 20   Car je n'ay autre rhétorique.

My tears, my sighs, my cries, of which I know so well the experience, are my speech and my writing, for I have no other rhetoric.

The poems in which Marguerite expresses the grief provoked by Francis' illness and death are informed by what we may call the rhetoric of tears.

Marguerite was not with Francis when he died. She was in the monastery at Tusson (in the province of Poitou), where she remained in seclusion for four months following his death. Most of the *Chansons spirituelles* are prayers or *complaintes* composed during Marguerite's stay at Tusson. Whereas the first *chanson*, written before the King's death, sounds the note of impending disaster, the second, which is entitled *Autres Pensees, faites un mois apres la mort du Roy. Sur le chant de, Jouyssance vous donneray* [Other thoughts, written a month after the King's death. To the tune of "I shall give you joy"], demonstrates Marguerite's reaction to the death of her brother:

> 1   Las, tant malheureuse je suis
> Que mon malheur dire ne puys,
> Sinon qu'il est sans espérance:
> Désespoir est desjà à l'huys,
> 5   Pour me jetter au fond du puits
> Où n'a d'en saillir apparence.
>
> Tant de larmes jettent mes yeux
> Qu'ilz ne voyent terre ne cieux:
> Telle est de leur pleur l'abondance.
> 10   Ma bouche se plaint en tous lieux,
> De mon coeur ne peult saillir mieux
> Que souspirs, sans nulle allegeance.

---

3. The word *souspir* echoes the musical motif in the word *chanson*. Cotgrave defines *souspir* thus: "a sigh; also, a short breath; also, a Minime rest in Musice."

Alas, so unhappy am I that I cannot express my unhappiness except to say that it is without hope. Despair is already at the door to throw me to the bottom of the pit, where there is no way to escape. My eyes are so filled with tears that they see neither earth nor heaven; such is the quantity of their tears. My mouth utters lamentations in every place; nothing better can come from my heart than sighs, without any relief.

Introducing a theme that will be developed in the longer poems she began to write during the spring and summer of 1547, Marguerite reflects on the utter difference between "absence" and "presence":

>   Je n'ay plus que la triste voix,
> 20   De laquelle crier m'en vois
>   En lamentant la dure absence.
>   Las, de celuy pour qui je vivois,
>   Que de si bon coeur je voyois,
>   J'ay perdu l'heureuse présence.

I no longer have any voice but a sad one; I see myself crying out, lamenting the cruel absence. Alas, him for whom I lived and whom I saw with such a light heart, I have lost his happy presence.

Feeling irreparably separated from him whom she considers part of herself (". . . mon corps est banny / Du sien, auquel il feut uny / Depuis le temps de nostre enfance," 37–39) [my body is banished from his, to which it has been united since the time of our childhood], she responds first by weeping:

> 46   Je crie par bois et par plains,
>   Au ciel et terre me complains;
>   A rien fors à mon dueil ne pense.

I cry out through the woods and through the plains; I mourn to heaven and to earth; I think about nothing except my sorrow.

The last four stanzas of the poem are an apostrophe to death, which Marguerite calls "tout mon refuge et ma défense" (51). With increasing urgency ("O mort, . . . / Vien donc," 61–62 [O death, come then]; "Viens donques, ne retarde pas; / Non: cours la poste à bien grands pas," 67–68 [Come then, do not delay; no; run the course with haste]), Marguerite entreats death to "transpercer la Soeur de ta lance" (63) [pierce the sister with your lance].

Seeking to resolve the absence/presence dilemma, she wishes to join Francis in a present that can be attained only by means of the absence provided by death. Claiming that her own death will signal the death of absence and the reign of presence, Marguerite invokes death in the third *chanson*,[4] called *Rondeau fait au mesme temps* [rondeau written at the same time]. She seeks to render present that whose essence is absence by appealing to the most primitive and visceral of our senses, i.e., taste and smell:

1   L'odeur de mort est de telle vigueur,
       Que désirer doit faire la liqueur
       De ce morceau, que ne veult avaller
       L'homme ignorant, lequel ne peut aller
5   Que par la Mort au lieu de tout honneur.

       La mort du Frère a changé dens la Soeur
       (En grand désir de mort) la crainte et peur,
       Et la rend prompte avec luy d'avaller
             L'odeur de mort.

The savor of death is of such vigor that it ought to arouse desire for the juice of this morsel, which the foolish man does not want to swallow, he who can go only by death to the place of all honor. The death of the brother has changed the sister's anxiety and fear, and makes her (who greatly desires death) ready to swallow with him the savor of death.

Realizing, however, that she has not yet "swallowed" death, Marguerite says that while waiting to die she will continue to talk about death ("En attendant, de la mort veut parler," 13) [While waiting, she (the sister) wishes to talk about death]. The linguistic constructs she now fashions reflect a reality that is non-verbal, for, as an event, death puts an end to speech. The paradox, of course—and Marguerite was aware of it—is that for the reader of her texts the non-verbal reality she seeks to communicate is real only in language. She says that she wishes to

4. This *chanson* is the third one in the 1547 edition. In the Dottin edition, it appears on p. 139.

attain presence (with Francis) by absenting herself from the body. What she actually does, though, is make her desire for absence present to the reader by embodying it in texts. We are thus dealing with ironic texts, that is to say, with texts that say what they mean through language that does not mean what it says.

During the period immediately following Francis' death, Marguerite wrote not only the *Chansons spirituelles* but also three long poems, the last two of which must be counted among her major poetic works: *La Comédie sur le trépas du roy* [The Play on the death of the king], *La Navire* [The Ship], and *Les Prisons*. All three are conspicuously allegorical. Furthermore, all three are deeply ironic. It is not surprising that irony permeates these texts, for, as theoreticians from Quintilian on have noted, allegory and irony are linked. In the rhetorical tradition, both allegory and irony are defined as saying one thing and meaning another. Discussing the relationship between allegory and ironic language, modern theorist Paul de Man comments that "this definition points to a structure shared by irony and allegory in that, in both cases, the relationship between sign and meaning is discontinuous. . . . In both cases, the sign points to something that differs from its literal meaning and has for its function the thematization of this difference."[5] Each of the three poems Marguerite wrote during the period of grief that followed Francis' death thematizes difference. Each is the product of Marguerite's meditation on the mystery of presence and absence (she lives on, Francis is dead) and, further, on the ability (or inability) of language to express and even alter the nature of this mystery. In a sense, this is true for most of Marguerite's poems. They thematize Marguerite's relationship with Christ in terms of presence and absence. Most of them are allegorical and ironic in the sense in which Quintilian used the word when he said that Socrates' whole life was ironic. In *La Comédie sur le trépas du roy*, *La Navire*, and *Les Prisons*, however, the thematization of difference in terms of presence and absence is given new impetus and greater specificity by Francis' death.

Owing much to medieval tradition, *La Comédie sur le trépas du roy* has many of the formal features of the pastoral elegy as prac-

5. "The Rhetoric of Temporality," in *Interpretation: Theory and Practice*, ed. Charles S. Singleton (Baltimore: The Johns Hopkins Press, 1969), p. 192.

ticed by a number of *grands rhétoriqueurs*.[6] It is composed of monologues and dialogues by four characters: Amarissime, i.e., Marguerite herself, Securus, i.e., Henri d'Albret, Agapy, i.e., Henri II, and Paraclesis, i.e., a feminine figure representing Christian consolation.[7] All express grief and various degrees of consolation on the occasion of the death of Pan, i.e., Francis I.[8] Consistent with the bucolic setting of *Le Trépas*, Pan is represented as a shepherd. Because Christ was often thought of as a shepherd (Briçonnet repeatedly called Christ "Le Berger"), there are instances in *Le Trépas* in which Francis seems to be identified with Christ. At the center of *Le Trépas* is Amarissime, whose opening monologue is a series of questions. Like so many of Marguerite's poems, *Le Trépas du roy* begins on a note of doubt and confusion:

1   Mais est-il vray, est-ce chose assurée
       Que Pan nous est osté de ces bas lieux?
       O la douleur voyre desmesurée!
       Mais est-il vray, est-il ravy aux cieulx?
5   C'est vérité.[9]

But is it true? Is it certain that Pan has been taken away from us and from these low places? O truly boundless grief! But is it true, has he been taken away to the heavens? It is true.

Elaborating on the immeasurability of her grief, Amarissime declares that she wishes to find a solitary place "Où ma douleur . . . / Puisse chanter" (20–21) [where my grief . . . can sing]. Like the Marguerite of the first *chanson spirituelle*, Amarissime announces that she has no rhetoric except that of grief and tears: "Chantez des vers de douleur seullement, / Qui composez sont sans entendement" (44–45) [Sing only verses of sorrow, which are composed without understanding]. Seeking to compensate

6. See Henry Guy, *Histoire de la poésie française de la Renaissance*, I, *L'Ecole des Rhétoriqueurs* (Paris: Champion, 1910), p. 121. Also C. M. Scollen, *The Birth of Elegy in France 1500-1550*, THR (Geneva: Droz, 1967).

7. Paraclete, in English, or *Paraclet*, in French (derived from the Greek *Parakletos*, meaning one who is invoked) was often used in ecclesiastical works to identify the Holy Spirit as an intercessor who comforts man.

8. Marot had already called Francis I "Pan" in his *Eglogue au roy sous les noms de Pan et Robin*.

9. I cite *Le Trépas* in Saulnier's edition of Marguerite's *Théâtre profane*.

for the inability of discourse to contain her pain, she begins to sing. Her song, which she sings to the tune of the hymn "Jouys-sance vous donneray" [Joy I will give you], is identical to the first stanza of the second *chanson spirituelle*. Throughout the course of the second scene (with Securus) and the third (with Securus and Agapy), Amarissime alternates spoken discourse with song, passing freely back and forth from speech, which incarnates *ratio*, to music, which embodies the absence of *ratio*. By the end of the third scene, Amarissime has in fact sung the first ten stanzas of the second *chanson spirituelle* (she does not sing the last two stanzas) as well as several other songs in which she is joined by Securus and Agapy.

In the fourth and final scene of the *Comédie*, Paraclesis informs the others that "Pan est vivant" (410) [Pan is alive]. "Pan n'est poinct mort," she announces, "mais plus que jamais vit" (404) [Pan is not dead, but is more alive than ever]. Expressing the Evangelical notion that the death of the body does not merit tears because it is the passageway to eternal life, Paraclesis exhorts Amarissime, Securus, and Agapy to be joyful:

470   Pan est, quoy qu'on die,
         Sain, sans maladie,
         Vif et immortel,
         Contant, satisfaict:
         (Comme esprit parfaict)
475   Croiez qu'il est tel.
         Or, soiez contens.

Pan is, whatever they say, healthy, without sickness, alive and immortal, content, satisfied; (like the perfect spirit). Believe that this is how he is. Therefore, be content.

Accepting intellectually Paraclesis' argument, Amarissime cannot, however, experience Francis' absence as a joyful occasion. When Securus and Agapy suggest that they all three sing a song of praise to God, "le grand Pasteur" (535), Amarissime replies:

         Ma pauvre voix vous accompaignera
542   En ceste joye, ainsi qu'en la tristesse.
         Mais toutesfois mon oeil se baignera.

My poor voice will accompany you in this joy as in sadness. Nevertheless, my eyes will weep.

The disjunctive "mais" qualifies Amarissime's assent. When Paraclesis says near the end of the *Comédie*, "Or, chantons donc tout d'un accord, / Puisque Pan est vivant, non mort" (549–550) [So, let us sing, all in harmony since Pan is alive, not dead], Amarissime sings along with the others; but she remains unreconciled to the absence of Pan.

The song that concludes *Le Trépas* is in Latin. As at the end of the *Petit Oeuvre*, French gives way to Latin, which, like music, is a paradigmatic or apocalyptic language that transcends *parole* and attains the status of *langue*. The transcendent nature of their song is further emphasized by the fact that the words are those of Job. Singing in unison, all four characters praise God: "Si bona suscepimus de manu Domini, mala autem quare non sustineamus, sicut Domino placuit? Ita factum est. Sit nomen Dei benedictium" [If we take happiness from God's hand, must we not take sorrow too? So it has come to pass. Blessed be the name of God." Job 2.10 and 1.21]. That Amarissime-Marguerite is unable to accept fully the point of view of Paraclesis is proved by the fact that the dilemma she sought to resolve in *Le Trépas* is expressed with even greater intensity in *La Navire*.

CLOSED SYSTEMS

Not until Abel Lefranc published *Les dernières poésies de Marguerite de Navarre* (1896) did *La Navire* appear in print. In the manuscript copy, the poem is untitled; nevertheless, the entire packet of manuscripts has an inscription that identifies the first work in the collection as *La Navire*: "Les dernieres oeuvres de la Royne de Navar [re] / lesquelles n'ont este imprimees / Premierement le livre que ladicte dame [the word *dame* is added between the lines by another hand] composa en / l'abbaye de Tusson dict le [sic] Navire" [The last works of the Queen of Navarre, which have not been printed. First, the book the aforesaid lady wrote in the monastery at Tusson, called "The Ship"].[10] Following

---

10. See *La Navire, ou Consolation du Roi François Ier à sa soeur Marguerite,* ed. Robert Marichal (Paris: Champion, 1956), p. 237. All quotations are from this edition.

common practice when dealing with an untitled work, the scribe who wrote this inscription no doubt took the first word of Marguerite's poem, which is "navire," and used it as the title.

Shortly after the publication of *Les dernières poésies*, Gaston Paris suggested that a suitable title for *La Navire* would be "Consolation de François Ier à sa soeur Marguerite."[11] The title proposed by Paris is not inappropriate. Marguerite's poem conforms to the general format of the *consolatio*, or consolatory poem, which was practiced both by pagan and Christian writers.[12] Like most *consolationes*, *La Navire*, on one level at least, seeks to console the bereaved and to extol the greatness of the departed. Recognizing the descriptive value of the title put forward by Paris, Robert Marichal, whose 1956 critical edition of the poem is the basis of all modern readings of the text, retained the title suggested on the manuscript copy but added Paris' proposed title as a subtitle. Thus, for the modern reader the title of Marguerite's poem as it is printed on the title page of Marichal's edition is *La Navire, ou Consolation du roy Francois Ier à sa soeur Marguerite.*

There are numerous similarities between *La Navire* and *Le Dialogue en forme de vision nocturne*, the poem Marguerite wrote more than twenty years earlier on the occasion of the death of her niece Charlotte. Less explicitly doctrinal than the *Dialogue*, *La Navire* illuminates the problematics of conversing with the dead and so sheds light on the early work, which comments far less self-consciously than does *La Navire* on the textual problems that inform both poems. Like the *Dialogue*, *La Navire* is a dream vision, or a *visio*, a genre that had special appeal to Marguerite for it allowed her to stress the importance of submission, self-effacement, and receptivity in the life of a Christian. In a *visio*, the dreamer is merely the vehicle of the experience he recalls; he is not the author of his dream. The fiction of a *visio* is that while the dreamer's rational faculties are asleep he becomes the passive page on which an Other writes. Such was the case in the *Comédie du désert*. While Mary slept, God sent her an apocalyptic vision that filled her with joy. In both the *Dialogue* and *La Navire*, the narrator, i.e., Marguerite,

---

11. Review of Lefranc's *Les dernières poésies* . . ., *Journal des Savants*, 61 (1896), 282.
12. See Curtius, *European Literature and the Latin Middle Ages*, op. cit., p. 80.

falls asleep. The text not only records Marguerite's words but also the words of an Other who speaks a language radically different from hers.

La Navire begins with an unidentified voice that comes out of the undifferentiated linguistic void that surrounds the text:

1   Navire loing du vray port assablee,
       Feuille agitee de l'impetueux vent,
       Ame qui est de douleur accablee,

       Tire toy hors de ton corps non sçavant,
5   Monte a l'espoir, laisse ta vielle masse,
       Sans regarder derriere viens avant.

Ship grounded far from the true port, leaf blown by the impetuous wind, soul that is overcome with sorrow, wrest yourself from your body, which has no understanding, rise up to hope, abandon your old mass; without looking behind, advance forward.

For five more stanzas, the voice speaks—now imploringly, now commandingly—to someone identified simply as "aveuglee" (13) [the blind woman]. In line 22, the "aveuglee" begins to stir, speaking timidly and hesitatingly at first and then with increasing firmness.

22   Que je devins, quant ceste voix j'ouys,
       Je ne le sçay, car soubdain de mon corps
       Furent mes sens d'estonnement fouys!

What I became when I heard this voice I do not know, for suddenly my senses had fled in astonishment from my body!

Soon the first-person narrator, the "aveuglee," recognizes the voice as that of her dead brother Francis. A conversation between the grieving Marguerite and the dead Francis ensues and continues for some 1400 lines, after which the sun comes up and Francis announces that he must leave. After a few parting words of advice, he vanishes, leaving Marguerite with the memory of his unexpected appearance. Bearing in mind the general configuration of the poem, we shall now take a closer look at the text.

In the opening lines of the poem, Francis compares Marguerite to a ship tossed about on a stormy sea and declares his intent
to console her. A conventional image,[13] the metaphor of a ship
assumes richer significance when we realize that the most primitive emblem of Christian faith was not the cross or the ichthyo-
graph but the anchor.[14] Inspired perhaps by Paul's epistle to the
Hebrews 6.19 ("Here we have an anchor for our soul, as sure as
it is firm"), the anchor appears on the earliest Christian funerary
monuments as a symbol of consolation and hope of God's promise of immortality in Christ.[15] Seeing Marguerite buffeted by
the turbulent sea of despair, Francis speaks to her, hoping that
his words will comfort her. His message is simple. "Quicte ton
corps, et lors, spirituelle, / Pourras sçavoir plus que n'as merité"
[Leave your body and then, spiritual, you will be able to understand more than you have merited], he says as early as lines
38–39. He repeats this message throughout the poem. As dawn
appears, he speaks for the last time: "Tue ta chair, afin que,
simple et vuide, / Du vray amour de Dieu tu soyes pleine"
(1393–94) [Kill your flesh so that, simple and empty, you will be
full of the true love of God]. Marguerite knows that Francis is
right; but she cannot literally abandon her body. Ostensibly the
bearer of consolation, Francis fails to comfort Marguerite. In
other words, *La Navire* does not do what it sets out to do, i.e.,
console.

The most obvious formal feature of the text is also the most
important one: the poem is a dialogue between the dead Francis
and the living Marguerite. The text is grounded on the premise
that language can serve as a mode of exchange between the living and the dead. But the reader, interpreting the text in terms
of his ordinary coded knowledge of the world, surely rejects
the notion that the text is a mimetic representation of a "real"
dialogue between Marguerite and Francis. Language, he knows,
cannot extend beyond the realm of time, with which it is consubstantial. Being outside time, the dead cannot communicate
with the living through words. The reader tends, therefore,

13. See Rosemond Tuve, *Allegorical Imagery* (Princeton: Princeton University Press,
1966), pp. 182, 196, 424, 427.
14. On the anchor as a Christian emblem, see Marjorie O'Rourke Boyle, *Erasmus on
Language and Method in Theology* (Toronto: University of Toronto Press, 1972), p. 60.
15. Louis Bréhier, *L'Art chrétien* (Paris: Renouard, 1928), p. 30.

to look for clues that will permit him to give a metaphorical reading to the text, which, claiming the impossible, purports to be a record of an unmediated dialogue between the living and the dead.

By drawing attention to its dialogic form, the text itself, however, seems to resist being metaphorized in this way. *La Navire* consists of alternating speeches by Marguerite and Francis. Every time one of the two speakers begins to talk, the text pointedly identifies him even though the context makes it clear who is speaking. At the end of a speech, the speaker is often identified once again. Each speech is introduced (and often concluded) with an expression such as "Encores dict" (31) [again he said], "Ainsi luy dis" (62) [Thus I said to him], "Il respondict" (63) [He answered], "Lors il me dict" (73) [Then he said to me], "Luy respondis" (116) [I answered him], "Cest voix . . . me dict" (175–76) [This voice said to me]. The apparatus of attributive discourse[16] keeps the reader conscious of the fact that he is reading what professes to be a genuine dialogue between the living (if sleeping) Marguerite and the dead (but speaking) Francis. But as he progresses through the poem, the reader senses increasingly that no real exchange occurs between Marguerite and Francis. Language simply does not function as a circuit of communication or as a cognitive channel between the two. Speech fails to facilitate communication. Neither speaker moves from his original position: Marguerite continues to mourn her loss and Francis continues to upbraid her for grieving. Thus the claim of dialogism, which is made by the *form* of the text, is undermined throughout the poem by the absence of exchange between the two speakers, each of whom seems to be locked within a closed system.

Although they use the same words, Marguerite and Francis do not really speak the same language. This point is made early in the poem when Francis rebukes Marguerite for misusing the word "love." Throughout the poem, Marguerite speaks of her "love" for Francis. Each time, Francis interrupts her angrily, telling her that what she calls love is a "faux amour, qui le mal nomme bien / Et le bien mal" (94–95) [false love, which evil

16. On attributive discourse, see Gerald Prince, "Le Discours attributif et le récit," *Poétique*, 35 (1978), pp. 305–13.

calls good and the good, evil]. Her "love" for him, Francis tells her, is nothing but a stubborn, odious attachment to carnal forms. "Love," as he uses the word, is synonymous with *caritas*. It "defait et deforme" (88) [undoes and deforms] man, transforming him into Christ (89–90). Marguerite agrees and says that Francis is no doubt correct. She does not, however, adopt his definition of the word and continues to speak of her "love" for him. Whenever Francis tells her that she must overcome her attachment to material forms, Marguerite answers, "Je crois, mais . . ." (705) [I believe you, but . . .]. If Marguerite and Charlotte spoke at cross purposes in the *Dialogue*, so do Marguerite and Francis in *La Navire*. Although the poem is formally a dialogue, the text denies that any exchange or intersubjective communication occurs between the two speakers; that is to say, it denies the reality of dialogue. In *La Navire*, attributive discourse is an ironic device that underscores the discontinuous frame of reference within which each speaker is enclosed. Francis and Marguerite cannot speak to each other, for he moves outside time, she, within.

At first, the poem seems to suggest the unfolding of narrative (Francis appears to Marguerite in a dream and tells her to . . .). Narrative is also suggested by the poem's metrical form, the *terza rima*, which *La Navire* shares with the *Dialogue* and the *Petit Oeuvre*. The *terza rima* establishes a forward, linear motion that, in the case of the *Divine Comedy* and the *Petit Oeuvre*, is reinforced by a firm narrative line in the poem itself. In *La Navire*, however, Marguerite rejects narrative because it moves forward in time and so reminds her of her future, which will be marked by the continued absence of her dead brother. Seeking to deny time, she excludes narrative as much as possible from the text. Instead of supporting narrative, the metrical form of the poem becomes an ironic statement on the absence of sustained narrative.

The two most obvious formal tendencies in the text—to be dialogic and to progress narratively along a temporal axis—are conspicuously frustrated. The discontinuity between form and content expresses at the level of discourse the irreconcilable difference between the living Marguerite and the dead Francis, between presence and absence.

Unwilling to move toward the future, which she envisions as

a void that everywhere proclaims the absence of her brother, Marguerite rejects the apocalyptic vision, which is the consolation provided by religion. Francis in fact reformulates the Christian apocalypse. In his attempt to draw Marguerite away from her preoccupation with the world of the flesh, he describes the joys he experiences in paradise: "Icy d'amour est la vraye clarté, / Icy se faict de charité le feu, / . . ." (421–22) [Here is the true light of love; here does fire turn itself into love]. "Icy . . ." is repeated four more times within the next few lines. Using anaphora, the main rhetorical figure by which Marguerite expresses the Christian paradigm throughout her poetry, Francis relies heavily on the repertory of images that we have noted in Marguerite's other representations of the apocalypse. Saying "heureux je suis" (472) [happy I am], Francis repeats the word "plaisir." "Ce plaisant jardin / Où il y a plaisir surnaturel" (557–58) [This pleasant garden where there is supernatural pleasure] is the *locus amoenus* where all desires are satisfied. Marguerite, however, rejects the paradise Francis describes. She tells Francis that she, too, seeks pleasure. But sorrow, she adds, resorting to oxymoronic formulation, is her pleasure: "Ma douleur m'est ung savoureux pain (247) . . . larmes, souspirs et cris / Seront mon boire et agreables mectz" (248–49) [My sorrow is for me a savory bread; tears, sighs, and sobs will be my drink and my delicious food]. Saying that her sole pleasure is to scratch her wound (334–36), she refuses to transcend concern for the body. As she did in the *Dialogue*, Marguerite, overcome with personal grief, rebels momentarily against the inhuman doctrine of the disembodied spirit that appears to her from the incorporeal world. Indeed, the text owes its existence to the fact that Marguerite refuses to abandon the body.

Hoping to "[la] destourner de la chair" (104) [turn her away from the flesh], Francis admonishes Marguerite to remember their past conversations in which they talked about the happiness of those whom "Charité" (109) burned and annihilated. Francis directs Marguerite's attention toward the past in the hope that it will serve as a springboard to propel her thought toward the future. But Francis' words have an unexpected effect. Unwilling to accept the future, Marguerite seizes upon the opportunity to embrace the past. Her immediate response to her brother is:

115   "Las! maintefoy il m'en est souvenu,
           Luy respondis, mais j'ay perdu ce bien
           Que plus tu n'es de moy entretenu.

121   O la presence a tous yeulx agreable,
           La plus parfaicte et la meilleure grace
           Qui fut jamais et la plus amyable!

Alas! often I have remembered it, I answered him, but I have lost this
treasure since I cannot converse with you any longer. O presence,
agreeable to all eyes, the most perfect and the best grace that ever was,
and the most lovable!

Throughout the rest of the poem, Marguerite, hearing but not
heeding her brother's injunction to think about the future, resur-
rects little by little the past. To escape an intolerable present, she
fixes her attention on the past. Memory is the tool she will use
to re-experience her absent brother's presence. In her memory
he lives not as a disembodied, scolding shade but as she knew
him when he was alive. "Amour le veult tousjours tenir," Marguerite exclaims, "non comme mort, mais comme plain de vie,
/ *Au temple heureux d'eternal souvenir*" (163–65, my emphasis)
[Love wants to hold him always, not as dead but as full of life, in
the happy temple of eternal memory]. Comparing her heart,
the *locus* of memory, to a written record of Francis' deeds and
virtues, Marguerite declares:

           J'ay faict mon cueur ung pappier d'inventaire
170   Depuis le temps de nostre jeune enfance
           Jusqu'a la fin de luy et son histoire.

I made my heart an inventory sheet since the time of our early child-
hood until the end of him and of his story.

Fashioning her text, Marguerite consciously constructs a monument, a pantheon designed to "contain" Francis. What the reader
witnesses throughout the course of the poem is the embodiment
of Marguerite's memory, or heart, in language. The absent
Francis is encoded into language, and thus becomes present to
the reader. In much the same way that the spirit becomes manifest in flesh, Marguerite's memory becomes manifest in a lin-

guistic construct that has the structure of a temple, fixing or containing time.

Concretizing her memory in language, Marguerite elaborates a text that is analogous to a fleshy body. Her concern from now on in the poem is with things fleshy and corporeal, as Francis immediately senses. "O vain et nul ton charnel pensement / Que tient ton cueur a la terre lié" (217–18) [O empty and worthless your carnal thinking, which keeps your heart bound to the earth], Francis exclaims, trying to divert Marguerite's attention away from the past and from language, the medium that structures memory. Polite but indifferent to his comments, Marguerite reaffirms her duty as she sees it: to erect a linguistic structure that will be an incarnation of her memory:

250   Tous les plaisirs du monde sont prescriptz
       Dedans mon cueur, ou tourmens et ennuys
       Sont paintz au vif, engravez et escriptz;

       Cours sont les jours, courtes me sont les nuictz
       Pour y penser et pour ramentevoir
255   Ce que oublier je ne veulx ny ne puis.

       Privee suis de l'ouyr et du veoir,
       Ou je trouvois toute felicité;
       Mais vraye amour n'en faict moings son debvoir,

       Car elle croist en ma necessité,
260   En reveillant sans cesse ma memoire
       Du tempz passé, tant loing d'adversité.

All the pleasures of the world are rejected in my heart, where torments and sorrows are painted from life, engraved and written; short are the days, short are my nights, to think about them and to remember what I cannot and do not wish to forget. Deprived am I of the sound and the sight of that in which I used to find all my happiness; but true love does not do its duty any the less because of that, for it grows in my need, awakening without ceasing my memory of past time, so far from adversity.

Because her memory cannot do justice to Francis, the text itself will become a new memory, richer and more vibrantly faithful than the old. Not only does Marguerite incarnate her memory in a text, but the text, in an act of perfect consubstantiality, re-creates her memory in a form that can be transmitted to a reader. For Marguerite, as for Augustine, writing and reading are essentially the same activity. The reader "rewrites," or translates, the text before him, seeing through the literal context to the significance it acquires in the light of a larger perspective. Marguerite's intent in *La Navire* is both to "read" the text engraved in her memory and to fashion a linguistic monument that will serve to commemorate Francis and to "translate" her memory of him into a structure that can be "read" by others.

With a persistence that exasperates Francis, Marguerite dwells on physicality. Declaring that she wishes to portray Francis as love painted him in the portrait she carries in her heart, Marguerite says:

766   Je voy tousjours ton visage et beau taint,
       Ton oeil joieulx, qui a tristesse ou joye,
       A tes amis ne pouvoit estre fainct.

I see always your face and fine coloring, your joyful eyes, which express sadness or joy, which could not be counterfeited for your friends.

Obsessively, Marguerite repeats words like "corps," "chair," "visage," "face," "bras," "piedz," "mains," "chef," "oz," "voix," and "yeux." [17] Francis tries in vain to obstruct this flow of words that evoke the flesh. "Laisse de moy tous ses charnelz recordz" [Set aside all these carnal testimonies], he says; "recorde toy de Celluy qui l'ouvrage / Faisoit en moy par ses divins accordz" (814–16) [bear testimony of Him who completed the work in me through His divine decrees]. But just as Francis' allusion to memory had produced an effect contrary to his intent (later Marguerite ironically accuses *him* of not remembering), so his admonition to think about Christ prompts Marguerite to contemplate Christ's crucified body. Instead of concentrating on

17. Relying on the Freudian concept of obsession-compulsion, Angus Fletcher, *Allegory: The Theory of a Symbolic Mode* (Ithaca: Cornell University Press, 1964), pp. 279–303, argues that the typical agent in an allegorical fiction exhibits the kind of obsessive behavior characteristic of the *compulsive syndrome*. Fletcher raises several issues that are pertinent to Marguerite's poetry. See especially his discussion of "compulsive ritual" and his comments on the absence of progress in allegory due to the repetitive nature of a compulsive's actions.

Christ's spiritual message, she focuses on the suffering body, on what she calls, in a phrase that retains an echo of the medieval *danse macabre*, "la dance / Du grand Helas" (940–41) [the dance of the great Alas].

Marguerite insists on the body not merely because she rebels against the effacement of her brother's physical presence. The textual enterprise she has set for herself is to construct an *embodiment* of Francis. Her project is to create the *literal* context, the pantheon that readers will translate back into spiritual significance. This point is illustrated graphically in the final third or so of the poem. Having erected a linguistic mausoleum in honor of Francis ("Je te vouldrois par escript honorer," 446) [I would like to honor you through writing], Marguerite invites, one after the other, three distinguished contemporaries to enter the edifice-text and pay their respects to the dead king. First, Eleonor, Francis' widow, is ushered in: "Eleonor, o noble Royne, approche, / Viens de tes yeulx son sepulcre honorer" (988–89) [Eleonor, O noble queen, approach; come honor with your eyes his sepulcher]. Throughout eight stanzas, Marguerite speaks to Eleonor. She then turns to Catherine, who, weeping, is led in. Finally, Henri II, "Roy, filz de Roy" (1091) [King, son of a King,] enters and listens to Marguerite as she speaks to him about his father. The presence of Eleonor, Catherine, and Henri gives a public and ceremonial dimension to the text. Ceremony is reflected, too, at the level of discourse, for the three apostrophes are rhetorical exercises that obey the rules laid down for epideictic eloquence by classical and medieval rhetoricians. Public pomp is increased when Marguerite recites Francis' most memorable deeds, fashioning linguistic frescoes (1170–1209) designed to decorate the walls of the mausoleum and to depict Francis' glory.

Beginning as a *complainte, La Navire* modulates into eulogistic discourse. Curtius tells us that "for eulogies of rulers epideixis had developed fixed schemata in Hellenistic times."[18] These schemata were adopted by medieval writers.[19] "Physical and

---

18. *European Literature and the Latin Middle Ages*, p. 180.

19. O. B. Hardison, Jr., *The Enduring Monument* (Chapel Hill: University of North Carolina Press, 1962), pp. 29–32, points out that the rules for epideictic oratory given in Scaliger's *Poetices Libri Septem* (1561) are almost identical with those given in the third century B.C. by Menander in his *Peri Epideiktikon*.

moral excellences," Curtius notes, "were arranged in series—
for example, beauty, nobility, manliness (*forma, genus, virtus*)."[20]
Physical beauty was particularly important, for it was interpreted as a sign of Nature's favor. By presenting Francis as an
exemplary work of Nature, handsome, noble, and manly, Marguerite seeks both to embody her memory in panegyrical language and to fashion a text that, displaying the formal features
of epideictic oratory, will have, perhaps, the durability of a classical eulogy. Manipulating the *topoi* of epideixis, Marguerite
constructs within the broader framework of her poem a series of
set-pieces in which her memory of Francis is transposed from a
private into a public register. Designed to serve as public monuments, they have, however, the remoteness, the inertness, the *ir-
relevance* of an ancient tomb, and so underscore the discontinuity
between the living Marguerite and the dead Francis. Formal eulogy fails to translate the "pappier d'inventaire" engraved in
Marguerite's heart.

This failure is symptomatic of the text's inability to do what
Marguerite would like it to do, i.e., resurrect the past and oblit-
erate absence. Furthermore, the text comments repeatedly on
the impossibility of accomplishing the task set for it. The central problem lies in the very structure of memory and language.
Early in the poem Marguerite discusses the essential role that
absence plays in memory:

> Je n'avois sceu ne bien penser ne croire
> Qu'amour eust sceu par mort prandre accroissance,
> Mais maintenant la chose m'est notoire:
>
> 265   Ainsi que l'oeil a parfaicte plaisance,
> Voiant le bien ou son desir repose,
> Amour le faict vivre par congnoissance,
>
> Rementevant jusqu'a la moindre chose
> Le temps passé de ce roy sans nul vice,
> 270   Au cueur duquel vertu fut tout enclose.

I had not known, nor really thought or believed, that love was able to
grow greater by death; but now this is obvious to me. As the eye has

---

20. Curtius, loc. cit.

perfect pleasure in seeing the good on which its desire has settled, so love makes him live through awareness, recalling in minute detail the past of this king, who had not the slightest vice, whose heart was completely enclosed in virtue.

Memory depends on absence, for we remember only what is past, other, not present. Without absence, or alterity, there is no memory. This point is illustrated at the beginning of the poem when Francis' voice comes to Marguerite as something Other, something absent from herself. Marguerite discovers that consciousness of Francis' absence permits her love for him to increase. Furthermore, absence plays the same role in language that it plays in memory. Language comes into being only when we are conscious of something Other, which we then designate with a word. The referent, or thing designated, is not contained in the word; it is absent. As Lacan observed, "the word is a presence made of absence."[21] Language, like memory, contains an absence that is immanent in it.

In *La Navire*, Marguerite fashions a linguistic construct by means of which she tries to place herself in a past that is alive in her memory, a past in which Francis still moves and talks. She discovers, however, that language is irremediably temporal. Every speech act is an affirmation of existence in the present. Seeking to deny the present through language, Marguerite succeeds only in situating her own existence in the hateful now. At the same time, the real absence of the referent (Francis) calls into the discourse the things this absence stands for: death, emptiness, silence.

Francis' absence from the text is expressed forcefully at the end of the poem. At the break of dawn, Francis announces that he must leave ("Voicy le jour, il m'en convient aller," 1399) [Here is dawn; I must depart]. Suddenly, Marguerite cries out in language we have not heard since the beginning of the poem:

> "O monseigneur, pas ainsy n'adviendra
> 1412   Te departir sy promptement d'icy,
> Dis je en criant, *ma main te retiendra!*"   (my emphasis)

O my lord, not so will it happen that you depart so promptly from here, I said crying out, my hand will hold you back!

21. Jacques Lacan, *Ecrits*, tr. Alan Sheridan, op. cit., p. 65.

These are the last words she addresses to Francis. As she speaks, he vanishes, seemingly disproving her claim that "ma main te retiendra!" Marguerite does, however, hold something in her hands: a linguistic cenotaph (*kenos*, empty, + *taphos*, tomb) that contains, or circumscribes, Francis' absence. The ending of the poem, with its overtones of an *aubade*, provides powerful poetic closure because it confirms the Otherness of Marguerite's relation to the text. *La Navire* set out to do what it cannot do (cannot be a consolation, cannot be a dialogue). The fact that the consolatory poem that ought to follow the title (*La Navire, ou Consolation du roy François Ier à sa soeur Marguerite*) is *not there* creates a gap or a silence in the text that duplicates with mimetic exactness the void in Marguerite's life.

We must now account for the last nine stanzas (1414–1440) of the poem. As Francis vanishes, Marguerite feels her heart pierced with love ("[le] cueur d'amour transy," 1414). Suddenly—and indeed for the first time in the poem—she is overcome with joy:

> 1432   Je n'uz sur moy os, chair, veine ny nerf,
> Qui ne sentist une joye amirable,
> Chassant dehors ennuy pesant et grief;

I did not have any bone, flesh, vein, or nerve that did not feel a wonderful joy, chasing away heavy sorrow and pain.

Looking at the rising sun, which often represents God in the mystical tradition, Marguerite, dazzled by its beauty, closes her eyes:

> 1435   Mais, regardant ce hault ciel desirable,
> L'ardant soleil vint esbloir ma vue,
> Me fermant l'eul par lumiere importable.

But, while I looked at this high, worthy sky, the burning sun dazzled my sight, making me close my eyes because of unbearable light.

Sight gives way to insight, light to a darkness that, as the Pseudo-Dionysius said of Divine Darkness, "is dark through excess of light" (*Div. Names* 32). Cessation of language at the end of the poem signals Marguerite's return to the undifferentiated state of unconsciousness—or, at least, unawareness of self—from which she was called in the first line of the poem by Francis' voice. Silence and Divine Darkness precede and follow the text, marking the unitive stage in which the Subject fuses with the All. In terms of the Saussurian distinction between *langue* and *parole*, the unitive stage is of the order of *langue*. The text, on the other hand, is always of the order of *parole* and so illustrates (in the classical sense of *illustratio*) the alterity inherent in language itself. *La Navire* demonstrates, above all, the relationship of Otherness.

Marguerite and Francis represent two distinct closed systems. A closed system is one that is independent of its context or that is defined as such (e.g., the solar system); an open system, on the other hand, is one that depends on its environment for its continuing existence and survival (e.g., an organism).[22] For the living Marguerite, Francis, who is dead, is the Other. Similarly, for Francis, Marguerite is the Other. Within the economy of the text, each "system" (Marguerite and Francis) is the "environment" or "context" of the other. Rejecting its "context," each system confirms its boundaries and remains closed. Each defines itself negatively by rejecting the injunctions of the other. Marguerite refuses to obey Francis, who says over and over: "*quicte ton corps*," "*tue ta chair*" [abandon your body, kill your flesh]. Francis' commands are paradoxical injunctions. Exhorting Marguerite to mortify the flesh, Francis would have her reject *la parole*, which, embodied in the text, is the means by which she mortifies the flesh. She must, in fact, resist his injunctions in order to obey them. Moreover, the reader shares in Marguerite's dilemma. Francis' injunctions have the pointedness of moral imperatives directed to him as well as to Marguerite. If he obeys them, he will cease attending to the text (flesh). Only by refusing to do what Francis commands can the reader continue to hear (read) the injunctions that he must disobey. Francis, too, disregards the injunction of the Other, for he rejects Marguerite's entreaties to remember their shared past. The lack of positive response on the part of both Marguerite and Francis to each other's appeals underscores (as does, for example, the music with which the *Ravie* answers the three uncomprehending ladies in *Mont-de-Marsan*) the monologism of a closed system.

22. Anthony Wilden, *System and Structure: Essays in Communication and Exchange* (1972; rpt. London: Tavistock Publications, 1980), p. xxxi.

The final irony of the text is that Marguerite can obey Francis' injunctions only when he ceases to make them. At the level of discourse, Francis' command that Marguerite abandon her body is tantamount to demanding that the text (*corpus verborum*) stop. However, Francis cannot make this injunction outside the textual body he would annihilate. His demands sustain and enflesh the body his injunctions seek to suppress. Only the *deus ex machina* at the end of the poem (*deus*, literally, for the sun represents God) can resolve the dilemma in which Marguerite finds herself. By compelling Francis to vanish from the text, by drying up his injunctions, the sun alters the "context" in which Marguerite operates. As the sun rises, Marguerite's heart is pierced with love. God's presence radiates throughout her being. The system represented by Marguerite, the only remaining system in the text, becomes (or, in Augustinian terms, is now rightly perceived as being) the ultimate closed system—ultimate because there is no "context" or "environment" beyond it.

The model for this kind of system is Cusanus' *machina mundi*. [23] In a celebrated passage from *De docta ignorantia*, Cusanus restates a medieval commonplace and defines the cosmos as "a *machina mundi* whose center, so to speak, is everywhere and whose circumference is nowhere, for God is its circumference and its center, and He is everywhere and nowhere." [24] Since the *machina mundi* comprises everything, there can be no "environment" that transcends its boundaries. It cannot open onto something else, for it is all (*Tout* is Marguerite's word). Because nothing (Marguerite's *Rien*) exists outside it, it is inexorably closed. Being *Tout*, God is the locus where there is coincidence of antitheses, concordance of differences.

Although within the economy of the text Francis represents the Other for Marguerite and Marguerite the Other for Francis, the text in its totality represents the Other for the reader. For him, Marguerite and Francis are sub-systems within the larger system that is the whole text. He sees in Francis and Marguerite symbols of a conflict between desire (for enclosure within Christ,

---

23. On Cusanus' model, see Anthony Wilden, "Changing Frames of Order: Cybernetics and the *Machina Mundi*," in *Communication and Control in Society*, ed. Klaus Krippendorff, pp. 9–29.

24. *Of Learned Ignorance* (New Haven: Yale University Press, 1954), Bk. II, Chap. 12. For a discussion of Cusanus' statement, see Koenigsberger, *Renaissance Man and Creative Thinking*, p. 133.

for atemporality) and experience (of doubt, despair, time), between what Marguerite (the author, not the "I" of the poem) *believes* and what she *knows* experientially. In other words, the author's ideology of self (Marguerite's view that the *moi* is infused with the presence of Christ) is in conflict with the actual phenomenology of the self represented in *La Navire*, indeed, in all her poetry. In a sense, each of Marguerite's poems could bear the title of the second poem in the *Marguerites*: *Discord estant en l'homme par la contrarieté de l'Esprit et de la Chair, et paix par vie spirituelle* [The Discord that is in man because of the opposition of spirit and flesh, and peace through spiritual life].

8
The Emblematic Mode

THE RITUAL OF CONFESSION

The poems in the *Marguerites* are all clearly religious poems. By contrast, those in the *Suyte des Marguerites* seem to be secular. Even the titles suggest worldliness and mundanity: *L'Histoire des satyres et nymphes de Dyane* [The Story of Satyrs and Diana's Nymphs], four *épîtres* addressed to Francis, *Les quatre dames, et les quatre gentilzhommes* [The Four Ladies and the Four Gentlemen], a *comédie* entitled *Deux filles, deux mariees, la vieille, le vieillard, et les quatre hommes* [Two Maidens, Two Married Women, an Old Woman, an Old Man, and Four Men], the *Farce de Trop, Prou, Peu, Moins* [The Farce of Too Much, Much, Little, Less] (which we have discussed), *La Coche* [The Coach], several short texts called *L'Ombre* [The Shadow], *La mort et resurrection d'amour* [The Death and Resurrection of Love], *Chanson faite à une dame* [Song Addressed to a Lady], *Les adieux des dames de chez la royne de Navarre allant en Gascongne à ma dame la princesse de Navarre* [The Farewells of the Ladies of the Court of the Queen of Navarre, Going to Gascony to My Lady the Princess of Navarre], and finally, two brief *énigmes*. Most of these poems belong to what Paul Zumthor has called "la tradition des 'genres dialogués.'"[25] Although none contains the word *débat* in its title, all prolong the medieval tradition of debate poetry, which had considerable attraction for early Renaissance Humanists and *grands rhétoriqueurs*.[26] With the possible exception of *Trop, Prou, Peu, Moins*, all the poems deal with love. Within the framework

25. Paul Zumthor, *Le Masque et la lumière: la poétique des Grands Rhétoriqueurs* (Paris: Seuil, 1978), p. 181.
26. In addition to Zumthor, ibid., see N. Dupire, *Jean Molinet: la vie, les oeuvres* (Paris: Droz, 1936), pp. 126–27 and Louis Marin, *Utopie: jeux d'espace* (Paris: Editions de Minuit, 1973), p. 60.

of a medieval *débat*, Marguerite blends courtly and Neoplatonic love themes.

In both the Neoplatonic tradition, especially as reinterpreted by Ficino, and the mystic Christian tradition, which relied heavily on the rhetoric of love, *eros* and *agape* were viewed as two manifestations of the divine principle of love, which is God Himself.[27] Whereas *eros* is the love that animates carnal forms, *agape* is that which infuses the spirit. Both the Neoplatonic and the mystic Christian traditions blur this distinction, however, by insisting that love is a continuum that begins in the flesh and then, in one continuous and inevitable movement, permeates the soul, raising it ever closer to God, its true locus and the place to which it must eventually return. In the fourth *épître*, which, like the others in the *Suyte*, is addressed to Francis, Marguerite allegorizes this continuum by presenting love as a Cupid who grows up and becomes Christ. "L'enfant leger, inconstant, et muable [devient] amour aymant, qui chacun fait aymer . . . car il est seul Verité, Vie et Voye" (p. 67)[28] [The lively child, inconstant and changeable, becomes love that loves and makes everyone love . . . for he is the only Truth, Life and the Way]. Christ is the mature form of Cupid. "C'est toujours luy toutesfois," Marguerite writes, "mais son [Cupid's] vice / Est converty en vertu, et justice" (p. 67) [It is still always he, but his vice has been converted into virtue and justice]. The fourth *épître* is a meditation on the process by which "l'homme de fange et terre" [the man of mud and earth] becomes "semblable à Dieu" (p. 71) [like God]. The agent that effects this "mutacion" is love, "qui a . . . / Premierement commencé en la chair" (p. 66) [which began first in the flesh]. Ultimately, love, the pulverizing fire of which Briçonnet had spoken, converts the flesh into spirit, "tant qu'en vivant d'un coeur deifié / [L'amant peut] jetter un cry à mon advis, / Disant, c'est CHRIST, et non pas moy qui vis" (p. 65) [so that while living with a deified heart, the lover can, I believe, cry out, saying, It is Christ and not I who lives]. Here *eros* and *agape* are indissolubly linked.

Most of the poems in the *Marguerites* deal with the absence or

---

27. The key Ficinian text is *Commentaire sur le Banquet de Platon*, trans. Raymond Marcel (Paris: Les Belles Lettres, 1956). On *eros* and *agape* in Christian thought, see Anders Nygren, *Agape and Eros: A Study of the Christian Idea of Love*, trans. P. S. Watson (Philadelphia: Westminster Press, 1953).

28. Page references to *La Suyte des Marguerites* (Johnson Reprint Corporation).

presence of *agape*; those in the *Suyte* deal with the absence or presence of *eros*. Although the problematic of absence informs both volumes, it is especially important in the *Suyte*. In none of the poems in the *Suyte* is the theme of absence more elaborately developed than in *La Coche*. One of the major poems in the *Suyte*, *La Coche* also illustrates how Marguerite adapted traditional modes of discourse (*débat* poetry and amatory verse) to her own ends and molded them until they became capable of expressing the concerns that are central to her entire corpus of poetry.

At the beginning of *La Coche*, the narrator, who is later identified as Marguerite, flees down a country lane. Distraught and grieved, she has left the court. In the opening lines of the poem, she identifies the two sources of her pain: the absence of love and an inability to write:

1	Ayant perdu de l'aveuglé vaincueur
	Non seullement le sentement du cueur,
	Mais de son nom, dictz et faictz la memoire,
	Ayant perdu le pouvoir et la gloire,
5	Et le plaisir de la doulce escripture,
	Où tant je fuz incline de nature. . . .[29]

Having lost not only the feeling of the heart associated with the blind conqueror [Cupid] but also the memory of his name, tales and deeds; having lost the power and the glory and the pleasure of sweet writing, to which I was so inclined by nature. . . .

Marguerite equates the loss of love with the loss of creative energy. The theme is not new, for in both the Neoplatonic and Christian traditions love is perceived as the energizing force in the world. Still, Marguerite's formulation of a direct link between the absence of love and an inability to write is striking. The problematics of writing is thematized in the opening lines of the text (Marguerite's flight may be read as a turning away from literary pursuits) and informs the whole poem. At one level, *La Coche* is "about" a writer's loss of inspiration, which is expressed in terms of a loss of love.

In order to avoid speaking to anyone, Marguerite chooses a

29. *La Coche*, ed. Robert Marichal (Geneva: Droz, 1971).

particularly solitary path. Throughout some dozen lines, she evokes the landscape through which she wanders. As Marichal points out, Marguerite's description consists mainly of *topoi* from medieval literature. It is derived largely from Alain Chartier, whom Marguerite names in the text (51), and Christine de Pisan.[30] The flowers, the trees, the brook, the sky that is reddened by the setting sun are all standard features in medieval descriptions. Coming upon a peasant, Marguerite stops and asks him about his crops and family. Suddenly, she sees three ladies dressed in black. All three are weeping. Recognizing them as ladies of the court, she urges them to tell her the cause of their despair. She wishes to see, she says, if their suffering is as great as hers.

The ladies tell Marguerite that they will disclose the cause of their grief only if she agrees to write down what they say. She consents, declaring: "Je reprendray la plume" (121) [I will take up the pen again]. The text we have before us is Marguerite's record of the ladies' words. It is a mirror not of *une âme pécheresse* but of three feminine souls that have suffered the effects of love. At the same time, it chronicles the return of Marguerite's creative energy, for by committing to paper the remarks of each lady, she rediscovers herself as a writer.

At first, the ladies are so overcome with grief they cannot speak. Tears are their sole language. Marguerite, however, reminds them that the text she has agreed to write must be composed of words, not tears. "Si ne parlez, je n'ay garde d'escrire" (130) [If you do not speak, I shall be unable to write]. "Pour Dieu tournez le pleur qui vous affolle / A descharger vostre ennuy par parolle" (131–132) [For pity's sake, instead of weeping, which is grieving you, unburden your sorrow by words]. The first lady explains in 214 lines (the meter is *terza rima*) that although her lover still professes to love her, she knows that his ardor has cooled. "Amour est en luy morte" (287) [Love is dead in him], she laments. As if that were not sufficient cause for despair, she suffers yet another humiliation. No longer loved by her *amy*, she is the object of the amorous attention of the second lady's lover, who has openly scorned his own lady and now pursues the first lady, importuning her with a love she rejects. She concludes the recital of her woes by entreating Marguerite to

30. Op. cit., pp. 6–17.

translate her pain into a text: "Or faites donc, ma Dame, le recueil / De mes douleurs" (345–46) [Now write, my lady, the
tale of my sorrows]. With these words, sobs stifle her speech.
Overcome with sorrow, she faints.

The sun is setting when the second lady begins to speak,
urged on by Marguerite who says that if the women continue to
weep she will never hear the accounts of the other two ladies and
so will never be able to determine "qui de vous troys seuffre plus
de martyre" (369) [which of you three suffers greater martyr-
dom]. Like her predecessor, the second lady speaks in triple
meter. Her stanzas, however, have a curiously halting appearance on the page; a line of four syllables is followed by two lines
of ten syllables. Each stanza has one rhyme (a-a-a, b-b-b, etc.).
The four-syllable line has the effect of disrupting the unity implied by the rhyme and by the two ten-syllable lines. Thus the
second lady's discourse has a graphic dimension that, metacommunicating rupture and discordance, renders visually a
message of broken unity, which is in fact the central theme of
her speech. Her discourse abounds in words like *destacher*
[detach], *couper* [cut], *rompre* [break] that evoke disjunction and
separation. For reasons she does not understand, her *amy* has
abandoned her and turned to her friend, the first lady. "Helas,
mon Dieu," she says, "comment s'est il fasché / De mon amour
et ainsi detaché?" (433–34) [Alas, my God, how did he get an-
gry with my love and so leave me?]. Grief overwhelms her and
she cannot go on speaking ("Et la doulleur sa parolle coupa,"
503) [And sorrow cut off her speech]. She, too, faints.

Unlike the speeches of the first two ladies, which have a triadic structure, the discourse of the third lady is organized into
quatrains. Her lines are decasyllabic (as are all the lines of the
poem except for the second lady's truncated line) and the rhyme
is the traditional one of a quatrain: a-b-b-a. The tetradic configuration of her discourse contrasts with the triadic configuration of the speeches of the first two ladies. Like the triad, the
tetrad had symbolic significance.[31] Since antiquity, it was thought
to be made up of contrary elements. Ancient, medieval, and
Renaissance cosmographers often represented the cosmos as a
tetradic structure whose dynamism is due to the attraction and
repulsion of two pairs of contrary elements, water/air and fire/

31. See Heninger, *The Cosmographical Glass*, op. cit., pp. 99–104.

water. Illustrating multiplicity in unity, mobility in stasis, and the reconciliation of opposites, the tetrad was inherently paradoxical.

The *rime embrassée* (a-b-b-a), which suggests enclosure or embrace, and the tetradic structure of the third lady's discourse both serve to express at a formal level the nature of the situation in which the speaker finds herself. Unlike the first two ladies, the third lady continues to be loved by her *amy*, whom she in turn loves ardently. The words *union*, *uny*, and *lien* appear repeatedly in her speech, defining the bond that links the lovers—a bond indicated at the level of discourse by meter and strophic form. Why, then, is she unhappy? Unable to bear the pain of seeing her friends suffer, she has voluntarily dismissed her own *amy* in order to share the sorrow of her two friends. She knows that her *amy* will die of grief, but, repeating the words *défaire* and *lien*, she explains that she must undo the bond that ties her to her lover in order to tighten the bond of friendship that links her with her two friends. Stressing the voluntarist nature of her decision, she says that she would like to divide her *amy* into three parts and give two of them to her friends. The numbers two, three, and four run through her discourse, giving a kind of arithmetic modeling to the shifting relationships evoked: the lady and her lover, her two friends, the three friends, the three ladies and the faithful *amy*.

603   Je le tiens tel, si parfait et si bon,
　　　　Que je vouldroys le mectre en troys parties
　　　　Et si serions toutes troys bien parties
　　　　Quand des deux pars je leur feroys le don.
　　　　. . .
621   Mon amy seul, qui en vault plus de troys,
　　　　Sera des troys amy. O quel lien
　　　　Qui quatre cueurs unira sans moyen
　　　　En ung voulloir!

I consider him to be so perfect and so good that I would like to divide him into three parts; and we would all three have a good share when I have made them a gift of two of the parts . . . My friend alone, who is worth more than three, will be the friend of all three. O what a bond, which will unite four hearts in one will, without anything separating them!

The first two ladies had ended their speeches by saying that they wished to die. The third lady does the same and, after affirming that death alone will bring release from her suffering, delivers an apostrophe to death, asking *la Mort* to unite the three friends in eternal rest:

647   Or venez donc et par compassion
           Mectez noz corps uniz en terre obscure
           Avant souffrir qu'au departir j'endure
           Si tresextreme et dure passion.

Come, then, and through compassion put our united bodies in the dark ground before I must endure the suffering of separation, so extreme and intense an emotion.

She, too, faints, and Marguerite, using the first person singular, tells us that she had to shake the lady and rub her hands to revive her.

The first lady, still believing that she suffers more than the other two, argues her case once again, using, of course, her characteristic meter, the *terza rima*. She is followed by the second lady and then the third lady, each of whom restates, in her own meter and strophic form, her reasons for believing that her sorrow is more intense than that of the other two. At the conclusion of the third lady's second speech, Marguerite notes that night has fallen, ending the *débat* for the time being. Tears, however, continue to flow, demonstrating a pain that is no longer expressed in words: "Et de lermes et souspirs feirent langues / Pour achever sans parler leurs harangues" (1011–12) [And they made languages of tears and sighs in order to conclude their speeches without speaking]. In fact, the flood of tears provokes a storm, and the ladies, "laissans au ciel achever leurs complaintes" (1032) [letting the sky finish their laments], seek shelter from the rain in Marguerite's coach, which has been standing nearby. During the ride back to Court, the ladies continue their discussion.

From the beginning of the debate, an epistemological current informs the text. The ostensible purpose of the debate is to permit Marguerite to determine which lady suffers the most. Epistemological concerns, which are expressed through repeated use of the word *congnoistre*, become increasingly important in the conversation that takes place in the coach. Marguerite herself introduces the word *congnoistre* in the discussion by saying that, although her talent is too weak to "réciter" satisfactorily "tous leurs propos" (1050–51) [recite all their words], she can "donner congnoissance / De leurs ennuyz comme leur ay promis, / Sans qu'un seul mot de leurs dicts soit obmis" (1052–54) [give knowledge of their sorrows, as I promised them, without omitting a single word of what they said]. The distinction Marguerite makes between "réciter / Tous leurs propos" and, on the other hand, "donner congnoissance / De leurs ennuyz" by recording everything the ladies say is part of the poetic fiction according to which she does not narrate or compose (*réciter*) the poem but simply writes down what she hears. A faithful representation of the words spoken will, however, permit the reader to *know* the suffering of the three unhappy women.

The ladies themselves seek a different kind of knowledge. Vying with each other for the honor of enduring the most pain, they confess to an Other on whom they depend to reveal the Truth to them. Indeed, in their lengthy discourses, the ladies enact in a secular mode a ritual like that performed in a confessional. The meadow, curtained off from the rest of the world by trees and flowers, and the darkened coach are enclosed areas in which the ladies, responding to Marguerite's injunction to declare their secret thoughts, confess ("privéement parler," 105) [tell in private] their suffering to the Other, who assumes the roles of judge, master, and superior.

The mechanics of confession informs most of Marguerite's texts, beginning with her first letter to Briçonnet. Michel Foucault has written about the profound effects of the Lateran Council's decision (1215) requiring all Christians to confess at least once a year and to probe their conscience and disclose to their confessor their most secret thoughts, feelings, and desires. In response to this decision, Western society developed complex confessional techniques and made confession one of the major rituals for the production of truth. Analyzing the process by which modern man has become "une bête d'aveu"[32] [a confessing animal] and Western society "une société singulièrement

---

32. Michel Foucault, *Histoire de la sexualité: La volonté de savoir* (Paris: Gallimard, 1976), p. 80. English translations of this work are taken from *The History of Sexuality*, trans. Robert Hurley (New York: Vintage Books, 1980), p. 59.

avouante"[33] [a singularly confessing society], Foucault makes the following observations about the nature of confessional discourse:

L'aveu est un rituel de discours où le sujet qui parle coïncide avec le sujet de l'énoncé; c'est aussi un rituel qui se déploie dans un rapport de pouvoir, car on n'avoue pas sans la présence au moins virtuelle d'un partenaire qui n'est pas simplement l'interlocuteur, mais l'instance qui requiert l'aveu, l'impose, l'apprécie et intervient pour juger, punir, pardonner, consoler, réconcilier; un rituel où la vérité s'authentifie de l'obstacle et des résistances qu'elle a eu à lever pour se formuler; un rituel enfin où la seule énonciation, indépendamment de ses consé-quences externes, produit, chez qui l'articule, des modifications intrin-sèques: elle l'innocente, elle le rachète, elle le purifie, elle le décharge de ses fautes, elle le libère, elle lui promet le salut.[34]

The confession is a ritual of discourse in which the speaking subject is also the subject of the statement; it is also a ritual that unfolds within a power relationship, for one does not confess without the presence (or virtual presence) of a partner who is not simply the interlocutor but the authority who requires the confession, prescribes and appreciates it, and intervenes in order to judge, punish, forgive, console, and rec-oncile; a ritual in which the truth is corroborated by the obstacles and resistances it has had to surmount in order to be formulated; and fi-nally, a ritual in which the expression alone, independently of its ex-ternal consequences, produces intrinsic modifications in the person who articulates it: it exonerates, redeems, and purifies him; it un-burdens him of his wrongs, liberates him, and promises him salvation.

Foucault's remarks shed light on the Briçonnet-Marguerite correspondence. The letters exchanged between the two corre-spondents record a *performance* in which each partner plays a part that is determined by the ritual of confession: she, the troubled penitent who confesses; he, the judge and dispenser of truth and pardon. Foucault's comments also apply to the *Miroir de l'âme pécheresse* and, indeed, to Marguerite's poetry as a whole. The *Miroir*, like the entire corpus of Marguerite's poetic produc-tion, is a confession to Christ, the supreme confessor. At the same time, the reflexive motifs that run through the *Miroir* trans-

---

33. Ibid., p. 79; English trans., Ibid., p. 59.
34. Ibid., pp. 82–83; English trans., Ibid., pp. 61–62.

form the text into a ritual in which the narrator confesses to her own reflected image. The "I" both confesses and absolves. A poem by Marguerite often modulates in such a way that the narrator, who, at the beginning of the poem, plays the part of the penitent, becomes the adjudicator as well.

There is a theological (some might say a specifically "Lutheran") basis for this assimilation of the confessing "I" with the judge; confession is, after all, the art of dissipating the cloudy elements that obscure the central core of self, which is Christ. The "I" of Marguerite's texts often comes to realize that, because Christ is immanent in creation and resides in the heart of man, it, too, partakes of divine authority. As the "I" moves from penitent to judge, the poem traces a shift away from voice to law, to decree, to text. The penitent eventually stops speaking and the "partenaire" (Foucault's word) to whom the confession has been addressed pronounces a judgment. In the final analysis, the partner who has heard the penitent's confession is the reader. In theological terms, this reader is Christ, for He reads man's heart; in terms of Marguerite's letters to Briçonnet, he is Briçonnet, the reader of her pleas for guidance; in terms of Marguerite's published work, the partner who hears her confession is the reading public. In each case, the reader, by interpreting and decoding the confession-text before him, becomes the author of a discourse in which truth is definitively revealed.

Their confessions completed, the three ladies seek an Other who will read the text that Marguerite, the narrator, has promised to write and that Marguerite, the poet, has in fact already written. Wishing to know the truth (the word *congnoistre* appears repeatedly in the discussion that takes place in the coach), they name three persons who could serve as readers, i.e., judges, of their confession. Because readers are invested with the power of determining what the truth is, the ladies are careful in their choices. They name King Francis as the most appropriate reader. The first lady praises Francis' *savoir*, *congnoissance*, and *grandeur*. Marguerite intervenes and says that she would not dare show her text, which she calls "un si tresbas et mal tyssu ouvrage" (1139) [such a lowly and badly woven work], to so august a personage. The second lady agrees that Francis is the ideal reader: "Luy seul congnoist l'estre et la subsistance / D'Amour, le bien, aussi la penitence / Qu'il peult donner" (1175–77) [He alone knows the essence and persistence of love, the good and also the

penitence it can give]. Nevertheless, because Marguerite refuses
to submit her text to the King, the second lady suggests that
Marguerite herself serve as reader and judge. Marguerite de-
clines, saying, first, that she had promised only "de les [voz en-
nuyz] escrire et dans ung livre mectre" (1213) [to write your
sorrows down and put them in a book], and, second, that at the
age of fifty, she, whose thoughts are now directed mainly toward death, is no longer capable of judging a debate that turns
on the casuistry of secular love. Having lost all memory (her
word) of love, she cannot be the informed reader the ladies seek.

The third lady then speaks and, after noting that Francis is indeed "l'abisme et source de sçavoir" (1230) [the abyss and source
of knowledge], suggests the Duchess of Etampes, the King's
mistress. All the ladies agree that the Duchess is the best choice.
Marguerite observes that if the Duchess finds the text to her lik-
ing she will no doubt show it to the King, who, "ayant le livre
ouvert / Regardera les poinctz où le lecteur / Se doit monstrer
advocat . . ." (1297–99) [having the open book will look at the
points where the reader must show himself to be an advocate].
Insisting that her text is an unworthy account of the debate that
actually took place, Marguerite summarizes the confessions of
the three ladies.

As Foucault points out, a confession is "un rituel qui se déploie dans un rapport de pouvoir" [a ritual that unfolds within
a power relationship]. In a Christian context, power (to judge,
punish, forgive) is concentrated in Christ. In a secular context,
which is that of *La Coche*, power resides not in the hands of
a spiritual master but in the hands of him who controls the political, social, and economic forces of society. For Marguerite,
Francis is the personification of this power. She assures the three
ladies that in due course the King, having been shown her account of their confessions, will pronounce a judgment that all
will recognize as just and equitable.

La Coche celebrates friendship. For Neoplatonists, friendship
was one of the loftiest and most ardent of passions. To formalize
their relationship, friends in the sixteenth century sometimes
exchanged vows of friendship; such bonds were called *alliances*.[35]
Not only did an *alliance d'amitié* signal a special link of friend-

---

35. See Emile V. Telle, *L'Oeuvre de Marguerite d'Angoulême, Reine de Navarre, et la
querelle des femmes* (Toulouse: Lion et Fils, 1937), pp. 307–308.

ship between two persons (occasionally, more than two); it also indicated, as Emile Telle has observed in his remarks concerning a link between sixteenth-century *alliances* and medieval bonds of fealty, a pledge in which each party promised to help the other party in every possible way. The three ladies in *La Coche* are bound together by such an *alliance*. Addressing the third lady, the first lady says: "Plaisir avez, gardant *la longue foy* / Que nous devez" (676–77), my emphasis [You have pleasure in keeping the long faith you owe us]. Even before the first lady's allusion to the pledge of friendship that compels the third lady to abandon her lover and join her two friends, Marguerite had referred to the three ladies as a trinity and had insisted on the inviolability of their union.

> Leur trinité, sans nulle difference,
> 85   Demonstroit bien par l'union des corps
> Qu'Amour leurs cueurs unist par doulx accords.

Their trinity, without any differences, demonstrated well, through the union of their bodies, that love united their hearts by sweet harmony.

The enclosed meadow and the coach are havens in which the ladies try to console each other for the loss of love. Unhappy in the world of men, they seek solace in the world of feminine *amytié*:

> Nous sommes troys dont le reconforter
> 145   Impossible est, car sans nostre amytié,
> Sans mort tel mal ne sçaurions supporter
>
> L'une de l'autre a egale pitié,
> Egale amour, egale fantaisie,
> Tant que l'une est de l'autre la moyctié.
>
> 150   Entre nous troys n'y eut onc jalouzie
> Oncques courroux, oncques diversité:
> Si l'une a mal, l'aultre en est tost saysie.
>
> Du bien, aussi de la foelicité
> L'une n'en a que l'autre n'y ait part,
> 155   Pareillement part en l'adversité.

Mort pourra bien des corps faire depart,
Mais nul malheur n'aura jamais puissance
De mectre ung cueur des deux autres à part.

We are three whom it is impossible to comfort; for without our friendship, we would not be able to bear such pain without dying. One has
equal pity for the other, equal love, equal affection, so that one is the
half of the other. Among the three of us there has never been jealousy,
never anger, never a quarrel. If one is ill, the other soon has the same
thing. One no sooner has riches or happiness than the other has a
share, similarly a share in misfortune. Death will certainly be able to
separate the bodies, but no unhappiness will ever have the power to
separate one heart from the other two.

The reader of Marguerite's text is never allowed to forget that
the friendship that links the ladies derives its peculiar intensity
from a shared sense of loss and deprivation. *La Coche* expresses
in a secular mode a concept that, in many of Marguerite's other
poems, is rendered in a sacred mode, namely, the concept of a
fall from grace and subsequent deprivation, which translates the
Christian's anguished sense of imperfection and separation from
Christ. By referring again and again to the lovers from whom
they are separated, the ladies each fashion a discourse that is, in a
fundamental way, structured around the notion of absence. Furthermore, it is the absence of the lovers that permits the ladies'
friendship to reach a pitch of incandescence. Metaphorically, the
lovers stand for love, plenitude, *unio*. At the same time, the real
absence of the referents (the lovers) calls into the discourse the
things this absence represents: deprivation, emptiness, separation. The ladies' *alliance d'amitié* is designed to supplant the union
of love they can no longer experience. In theory, at least, it consoles them for the absence of love.

Discourse, too, is supposed to bring consolation. At the beginning of the poem, Marguerite invites the ladies to "descharger votre ennuy par parolle" (132). The fact is, however,
that neither friendship nor discourse comforts the ladies. The
amytié and *union* of which they speak signify the absence of
amour and *unio*. For the reader, the ladies' insistence on friendship has an ironic dimension; it underscores the absence of the
consolation that *amytié* and *union* are supposed to provide. The
more the ladies affirm their mutual friendship, the more they

weep. Every time they declare their friendship they simultaneously confirm their separation from love, from "l'aveuglé vain-
queur" (1), who, in this text, stands for *unio*. To the extent that
La Coche is an allegorical text, it refers to the impossibility of
amytié replacing *amour*, of *union* substituting for *unio*.

Love or *unio* (as distinct from the *union d'amytié* of which the
ladies speak) is situated outside the text. Neither Francis nor the
lovers appear in the poem except as the absent Other. They bear
the same relation to the text that *langue* bears to *parole*. In *La
Navire*, *langue* (which is both immanent in, and transcendent to,
parole) is represented by the dead Francis, who is united with
Christ; in *La Coche*, it is represented by the lovers, the absent
Francis, and the Duchess of Etampes, who is an adjunct to Francis. The mechanics of signification in the two poems is the same.
Both texts locate paradise outside themselves, just as *parole* situates *langue* beyond actual speech. In discussing *La Navire*, I
pointed out that Marguerite's ideology of self, or the belief that
Christ resides in the heart, is in conflict with the phenomenology of self presented in the poem. *La Coche* illustrates the same
conflict with particular clarity. The assertion that friendship and
parole can fill the void created by the absence of love and *langue*
is constantly denied by the unremitting flow of tears. Even more
clearly than *La Navire*, *La Coche* depicts the confined, at times
almost claustrophobic, space characteristic of a closed system,
symbolized here by the meadow bordered by trees and the coach.
That the ladies' world is a closed system is illustrated at the level
of discourse by the way they repeat what they say. Again and
again they make the same points, describing a dilemma for
which there seems to be no solution. Only at the end of the
poem is there an indication that a resolution of the debate can be
reached. The resolution, however, is translinguistic and transtextual because it is situated beyond the discourse of the text.

GRAPHIC ENCODEMENT

In the 1547 edition of the *Suyte*, the most distinctive formal
feature of *La Coche* is a series of woodcuts illustrating the poem.
Interspersed throughout the ladies' lengthy *complaintes* are ten
miniature illustrations that give the poem a graphic dimension
far more explicit than that provided by the metaphors of sight
in, for example, the *Miroir*. *La Coche* is the only poem in the

1547 edition of the *Marguerites* and the *Suyte* that has illustrations, except for *L'Histoire des satyres, et nymphes de Dyane*, which has a single illustration. Of the five manuscript copies of *La Coche*, two are illustrated, three are not.[36] At the point in the text where the illustrated copies have a painted miniature, the unillustrated copies have a caption that describes the scene the reader is to visualize.[37] In his discussion of the manuscript copies, Marichal concludes that the captions, which are ten or twelve lines long, are by Marguerite and not by a scribe, and that Marguerite wrote them to specify what she wanted represented in the illustrations that were to accompany the text. The captions indicate the position of each lady in the pictorial composition, each lady's gestures, the color of the clothes they wear (black), and other details helpful to an illustrator. Marichal also points out that Bernard Salomon, the engraver responsible for the illustrations in the 1547 edition, was probably unfamiliar with the two illustrated manuscripts and followed the captions in making his woodcuts.

Although the woodcuts are distinct from the linguistic segment of the poem, they are obviously part of the text that the reader of the 1547 edition experiences. Jourda and Marichal, the principal commentators on *La Coche*, have both remarked that there are few descriptive passages in Marguerite's work as a whole. Noting the acuteness of her psychological penetration, the exactness of her evocations of states of mind, and the precision with which she indicates telling gestures, Jourda expresses surprise at "l'impossibilité où est la Reine de tenter le moindre portrait ou la description la moins développée"[38] [the Queen's inability to attempt the smallest portrait or the least developed description]. After observing that Marguerite does not take advantage of the numerous opportunities in her work to "esquisser un tableau champêtre" [sketch a rural scene], Marichal declares that "il est donc évident que la reine n'a pas une mémoire visuelle très exercée"[39] [It is evident that the queen does not have a very developed visual memory]. He points out that the description at the beginning of *La Coche*, which is the most extended

---

36. See *La Coche*, ed. Marichal, pp. 62–138.

37. Marichal gives the captions that are in the unillustrated manuscript copies but not the woodcuts that appeared in the 1547 edition of the *Suyte*. For the woodcuts, see the Johnson reprint edition.

38. Jourda, *Marguerite d'Angoulême*, p. 544.

39. Marichal edition, p. 15.

tableau champêtre in Marguerite's poetry, is copied from a descriptive passage in Alain Chartier's *Livre des quatre dames*.[40] Furthermore, it is likely that Marguerite wrote her captions while looking at an illuminated manuscript of *Quatre Dames*; details in the illustrations that accompany *La Coche* correspond to identical details in the miniatures that decorate the manuscript of *Quatre Dames*.

Marichal somewhat undermines his claim that the absence of descriptive passages in *La Coche* suggests a faulty "mémoire visuelle" when he points out the existence of other late fifteenth-century and early sixteenth-century works in which illustrations were considered an adequate substitute for verbal descriptions. He mentions a copy of *La Destruction de Troie la grant* in which the scribe simply omitted from an illuminated copy the passages being illustrated.[41] Graphic encodement made linguistic encodement superfluous. In itself, this does not necessarily indicate an absence of "mémoire visuelle." Furthermore, the medieval *descriptio*, which was a set-piece in which an author could display his mastery of rhetorical technique, had little appeal for Marguerite; she had no desire to impress readers with an exhibition of linguistic virtuosity. Nor was she interested in the more specifically Renaissance notion of *enargeia* (also known as *evidentia*, *demonstratio*, or *hypotyposis*), which, at least as Erasmus described it in *De copia*, refers to an abundance of surface decoration designed to make the scene described more visually present, more concrete.[42] Marguerite's poetry tends always toward a deconstruction of the visual, the concrete, the fleshy. Her landscapes are not of the outer but of the inner world. The ultimate decor in all her poetry is that of the human heart. In the case of *La Coche*, then, what role do the woodcuts play in the economy of the text? How do they help shape the reader's experience of the poem? These are the questions we must seek to answer.

The iterative nature of discourse in *La Coche* is due largely to the fact that the ladies' *complaintes* lack narrative thrust. Recounting the state in which they find themselves, the ladies each

40. Ibid., p. 14.

41. Ibid., p. 16.

42. See two articles by Terence Cave: "Copia and Cornucopia" in *French Renaissance Studies 1540–70*, ed. Peter Sharratt (Edinburgh: Edinburgh University Press, 1976), pp. 52–69, esp. p. 57 and "Enargeia: Erasmus and the Rhetoric of Presence in the Sixteenth Century," *L'Esprit Créateur*, 16 (1976), 5–19.

deliver a long lament that is marked by stasis. Because they en-
visage no solution to their grief (except death), they do not see
in the future anything different from the present. For them,
there is really no future, only a painful present that will be pro-
longed for the rest of their lives. The absence of a sense of future
time in the ladies' speeches is translated in the text as an absence
of sustained narrative. In other words, their discourse is essentially lyric in nature. Indeed, stasis is one of the distinctive features of lyric poetry. As Andrew Welsh has pointed out, "the
sense of time caught in space"[43] (the space of the text itself) is a
fundamental characteristic of the lyric mode. In *La Coche*, the
lyrical *complaintes*, which make up most of the body of the text,
are situated in a context that does, however, contain occasional
hints of narrative thrust. The beginning and end of *La Coche*
demonstrate, though rapidly and incompletely, forward motion
of the kind that marks narrative discourse. Furthermore, the
long *complaintes* are linked by brief comments by Marguerite,
who in fact narrates the entire poem.

The woodcuts appear at what we may call the narrative points
in the poem, that is to say, at the points of linkage between lyric
passages. They express graphically and explicitly a narrative content that is submerged by the tears that flow uninterruptedly
throughout the *complaintes*. The woodcuts are not simply illustrations of the text. They *tell* the story, tracing a syntagmatic
axis that propels the poem (and the reader) toward a conclusion,
which, however, is located outside the text. In the captions,
Marguerite refers to each of the illustrations as an "histoire."
Throughout the fourteenth and fifteenth centuries and well into
the Renaissance, the word *histoire* meant a graphic representation. According to Frédéric Godefroy, *histoire* had three meanings throughout the Middle Ages: picture, statue, and dramatic
presentation of the kind best exemplified by the royal *entrée*.[44]
Godefroy does not give a single instance of the word *histoire*
being used in the Middle Ages to mean linguistic construct or
recital of events. As for the sixteenth century, Edmond Huguet
notes that *les histoires* meant history or story but that the word
histoire in the singular meant image, design, painted picture,

43. Andrew Welsh, *Roots of Lyric* (Princeton: Princeton University Press, 1978),
p. 64.
44. *Dictionnaire de l'ancienne langue française*, IV (Paris: Vieweg, 1885), 478.

enamel, or statue.[45] The Greek and Latin words from which the French word *histoire* is derived did not, however, mean a pictorial representation but rather an account of events that had happened or a recital of imaginary events.[46] The concept of narrative is embedded in the etymological folds of *histoire*. If during the Middle Ages and the Renaissance a picture was called an *histoire*, it was because a picture was thought of as telling a story.

The relationship between narrative, or poetry in general, and the visual arts of painting and sculpture has been the subject of endless debate since antiquity. Simonides of Ceos, in a remark attributed to him by Plutarch, set the stage for these discussions when he observed that painting is silent poetry and poetry is speaking painting. Horace reformulated Simonides' insight in a phrase that was a commonplace in Renaissance aesthetics: *ut pictura poesis* (*Ars poetica* 361).[47] During the Renaissance, the link between poetry and painting was illustrated with particular force in the emblem, which consists of a picture, a motto, and an epigrammatic poem. Joining the concrete and the abstract, the emblem is a special case of metaphor. As Welsh notes: "The emblem is basically a metaphorical comparison juxtaposing two elements: one element, the more concrete one, exists in the visual medium; the other element, a more abstract one, exists in the verbal medium. The third element, the motto, is essentially an act of literary criticism directed toward the metaphor."[48] Quintilian's observation that if one extends a metaphor one gets an allegory is true for the emblem; if one extends an emblem one gets allegorical discourse, an essential element of which is narrative.

It is the progressive and sequential (that is to say, narrative) aspect of the woodcuts in *La Coche* that accounts for their allegorical dimension. The engraver who designed them emphasized temporality and sequentiality by showing the sun in different positions in the sky in succeeding pictures. In the fifth plate, the sun is situated in the center of the picture, immediately to

45. *Dictionnaire de la langue française du seizième siècle*, IV (Paris: Champion, 1925), 486.

46. A. Ernout and A. Meillet, *Dictionnaire étymologique de la langue latine*, 3rd ed. (Paris: Klincksieck, 1951), p. 296.

47. See R. W. Lee, "Ut Pictura Poesis: The Humanistic Theory of Painting," *Art Bulletin*, 22 (1940), pp. 197–269, and R. J. Clements, *Picta Poesis: Literary and Humanistic Theory in Renaissance Emblem Books* (Rome: Edizioni di Storia e letteratura, 1960).

48. Welsh, *Roots of Lyric*, p. 54.

the left of a mountain. Its beams radiate toward the top of the drawing and to both the left and right frames of the picture. In the following two drawings, the sun is no longer visible, having passed behind the mountain. Its rays, however, are visible, although they are no longer vertical but horizontal. The eighth plate shows a portion of the sun, which is now on the right side of the mountain and is cut off by the right frame of the picture. Its beams extend upward and toward the left of the drawing. As if to attract attention to the setting sun, Marguerite's right arm is raised and one finger points emphatically toward the sun and the right frame of the picture. The next scene depicts a rainstorm. The ladies move in single file toward the right side of the picture, where the coach waits for them. Throughout the entire sequence of images, the ladies have progressed from the extreme left frame of the picture, the side from which they entered the meadow, to the opposite frame.

The movement of the ladies and of the sun from the left side of the picture to the right is a pictorial representation of time. In accord with the poetics of paradox, to which she was attuned, Marguerite expresses time within spatial frames that, by their fixity, tend to deny temporality. Thus the abstract notion of time is immanent in the concrete part of the text, that is to say, in the visual component. On the other hand, the more abstract part of the text, i.e., the verbal medium (which, because of the sequentiality or linearity of language and the progression of words across the surface of the text, inevitably expresses time), seeks to duplicate the closed and atemporal spatial system of the drawings by resorting to iterative discourse in a series of *complaintes*. Throughout the course of the text, the drawings seek to reproduce the flowing time of the verses, whereas the words strive to attain the paradigmatic immobility of visual images. Both the verbal and the visual media tend to repudiate their most distinctive formal features. They endeavor to deny Self. The text represents the Self's submission to the Other.

The motto that concludes *La Coche* states clearly the theme of submission: "Plus vous que moy" [More you than I]. This motto was not printed in the 1547 edition of the *Suyte*. It does appear, however, in four of the five extant manuscript copies of *La Coche*. In the two manuscript copies that are illuminated, the motto is written in large letters not only at the end of the poem but also in the cartouches that form part of the frame for several of the illuminations. In emblematic literature, a motto is usually a statement of the general concept toward which both the picture and the verses work. I noted earlier that to the extent that *La Coche* is an allegory it refers to the impossibility of *amytié* replacing *amour* or *unio*. In other words, the Self (represented by the self-conscious bond of friendship established by the three ladies) cannot generate its own consolation. Nor can it perceive the Truth by means of its own limited powers. *Consolatio* and *veritas* are, like the *unio*, situated at the end of a road whose *terminus*, although it can be stated in the text ("Plus vous que moy"), must necessarily be located beyond the text itself.[49]

Submitting to Marguerite, the ladies submit to the power and authority of the text she promises to write. At the beginning of the poem, Marguerite is shown fleeing from the sterile, uncreative Self in which she felt entrapped. Yielding to the will of the Other, she rediscovers her creative impulse. The supreme *Vous* to whom the text addresses itself is the reader. At the literal level, the Duchess of Etampes and Francis are the readers of the text. At the allegorical level, we who read *La Coche* are the *Vous* to whom the text is directed. And at the anagogical level, Christ, He who reads the tablet of the living heart, is the reader. The text is a vehicle by means of which all four ladies move toward the reader(s).

The assumptions underlying *La Coche* inform all of Marguerite's poetry. The emblem method of linking the concrete and the abstract (the flesh and the spirit, in Christian terms), of fusing visual imagery and spatial form with the concepts of linearity and temporality, characterizes many Renaissance poems that are not, however, accompanied by actual pictures. Such texts may be read as emblems with the title taking the place of the picture.[50] Many of Marguerite's poems (especially those

---

49. Submission to the Other is the explicit theme of *L'Ombre*, the relatively brief poem that follows *La Coche* in the 1547 edition of the *Suyte*. Enfolded in "Amour," i.e., Christ, Marguerite denies the independent existence of Self, which she represents as His shadow: "Moy qui ne suis qu'une Ombre" (p. 323) [I who am only a shadow], she says early on in the poem; "ombre je suis de celuy qui m'ha faite" (p. 323) [I am a shadow of him who made me]. She denies the reality of her body and of all material forms. Throughout the poem, she works toward a total identity with Him. The poem concludes with a repudiation of "histoires" and "fables," i.e., texts, which necessarily unfold diachronically, and an affirmation that *unio*, which is of course transtextual, is the true paradise.

50. See Welsh, pp. 58–59.

with titles that evoke the emblematic tradition: *Le Miroir, La Navire*, and the work to which we turn next, *Les Prisons*) fall in this category. Within the economy of her poetry, *La Coche* occupies a unique place because, making explicit and graphic the emblematic union of body and spirit, it validates a way of seeing that translates into a way of reading—that is to say, a hermeneutics—applicable to all of Marguerite's poems.

9

"I Was in Prison and You Came to See Me"

THE METAPHORICS OF IMPRISONMENT

Of all of Marguerite's poems, none is nobler in concept or loftier in vision than *Les Prisons*. By far her longest poem, it consists of 4928 decasyllabic lines that are divided into three books. Book I contains 618 lines; Book II, 1906 lines; Book III, 3214 lines. An allegory of the soul's journey toward God, *Les Prisons*, though informed by a simple, even stark, vision of the *via Christi*, is complex in design and subtle in execution. Not only the *summa* of Marguerite's poetry, it is a *grand oeuvre* in the alchemistic sense; it incorporates into one work the themes, *topoi*, and strategies that characterize her poetry. Just as the Christian's "self" is finally submerged in the supreme, indivisible One, so the single texts that constitute Marguerite's poetry are, in a sense, contained within *Les Prisons*.[51]

Whereas the manuscript copies of several of Marguerite's poems are untitled, those of *Les Prisons* all bear the title of the work.[52] The prison image is so embedded in the text that surely Marguerite herself affixed the title to the poem. One of the oldest and most ubiquitous of images, the prison image appears

---

51. We do not know exactly when Marguerite wrote *Les Prisons*. At the end of Book III, she describes the final illness and death of Francis I. She was not with Francis when he died. The details of her account are derived from Pierre Du Châtel's *Oraison funèbre*, delivered on May 23, 1547. (Marichal published a lengthy extract from the *Oraison* in his edition of *La Navire*.) It is possible, however, that Marguerite read a manuscript copy of Du Châtel's *Oraison* prior to May 23. For Jourda (p. 583), the serenity and composure with which Marguerite speaks of Francis' absence suggests that the poem was written several months after the King's death. Like *La Navire*, the *Comédie sur le trépas du Roy*, and the last *Chansons spirituelles*, *Les Prisons* was probably written during Marguerite's extended stay in the monastery at Tusson.

52. On the manuscript copies of *Les Prisons*, see the edition of Simone Glasson, TLF (Geneva: Droz, 1978), pp. 59–66.

in two broad and interconnected traditions that have a bearing on Marguerite's poetry: first, the tradition of idealism that extends from Plato to Paul and Augustine and is central to Christianity; second, that of medieval love poetry. In both traditions, the prison image is ambiguous. Although it most readily evokes the undesirable state of forced incarceration, it is also able to suggest the mystical enfoldment of the self into the supreme Good. Plato declares that the soul is imprisoned in the body. When it encounters "a godlike face or bodily form that truly expresses beauty" (*Phaedrus* 251B), it recollects the world of Forms from which it came and, growing wings, flies back up to the realm of unity (249C) and indeterminateness, which for Plato is reality. Plato's soul/body antithesis was easily conflated with Paul's distinction between the spirit and the flesh, itself grounded on the Old Testament perception of a fundamental incompatibility between creation (the world of matter) and the creator (the divine spirit). Medieval mystics, to the extent that they considered their souls entrapped in matter, sought release from the prison of the flesh. On the other hand, to the extent that they sought union with Christ, they envisioned enfoldment or confinement in Him as the ultimate realization of their desires.

In both its negative and positive senses, the prison image appears often in Briçonnet's letters to Marguerite. Several of the letters are meditations on the paradox of imprisonment, or, and it amounts to the same thing, the paradox of freedom, for, in its "true," Christian sense, freedom can be experienced only by the soul that is firmly enclosed in Christ. Viewing the world of the flesh as a hindrance to the soul's progress, Briçonnet declares that "ce monde n'est que prison, en laquelle sommes liéz" (I.202) [this world is nothing but a prison in which we are bound]. In the consolatory letter he wrote to Marguerite after the death of Charlotte, he elaborated on the prison metaphor: "Ce monde est prison. Ceux qui demeurent doivent se consoler et esjouir quand voyent leurs compagnons dellivréz et les prier suggerer par prieres au Roy des Roys, qu'il luy plaise les getter hors de leur captivité, en laquelle, non innocens, mais comme pecheurs, sommes dettenuz, marriz quand entendons aucuns estre menéz au gibet" (II.265) [This world is a prison. Those who remain must console themselves and rejoice when they see their companions freed and beseech them to suggest to the King of Kings through prayers that he release them from their captivity, in which, not innocent but as sinners, we are held, vexed when we learn that others have been led to the gallows]. Throughout his correspondence, Briçonnet reminds Marguerite that "qui oublie Dieu pour plaire au monde et aux hommes est serf et prison-nier" (II.48)[53] [anyone who forgets God to please the world and other people is a servant and a prisoner].

In the same letter, however, he evokes the prison image to suggest a turning inward toward Christ, who is locked in the human heart. In the prison of God's love ("O desirée prison d'importable amour divine," II.48) [O desired prison of unbear-able divine love], the Christian experiences the ecstasy of spiri-tual escape from the limitations of the body and of time and space. The prison image is negative when it designates a closed system (such as the fleshy world of matter), whose perimeters serve as boundaries that delimit its space and mark off its area from an "outside" element, i.e., the spirit. Although the prison that is viewed as being coterminous with God's embrace is in one sense the ultimate closed system (it contains "everything"), it is also the ultimate open system, for, God being infinite, it has no boundaries and allows no distinction between flesh and spirit. Thus Briçonnet writes in one of his last letters to Marguerite that "prison d'amour est ouverte. S'en vad et vient qui veult. Amour est la portiere et clef de la prison d'amour . . . Il [le Tout-Puissant] tient en prison ceux qui l'ont prins prisonnier, se captivent et emprisonnet l'ung l'autre, disans chascun d'eux: 'J'ay trouvé ce que mon ame ayme. Je l'ay tenu, tiens et ne laisseray jamais'" (II.289) [the prison of love is open. One can come and go as one wishes. Love is the gatekeeper and the key to the prison of love. He keeps in prison those who have taken him as prisoner, holding each other captive and imprisoning each other, each one of them saying: "I have found what my soul loves. I have held it, am holding it, and will never let it go."].

Although language cannot describe directly the experience of him who lives in the "desired prison of unbearable divine love," it can in subtle ways reflect the paradox that "the prison of love

---

53. Throughout this letter, the metaphor of the prison is reinforced by that of the ship. Christine Martineau-Génieys, *Le thème de la mort dans la poésie française de 1450 à 1550*, op. cit., pp. 559–60, argues that this letter is the source of *La Navire*.

is open." In his letter of July 20, 1524 (II.213), and especially in that of September 26, 1524 (II.273, 288–90), Briçonnet explains the double significance of the Hebrew letter *mem*. Displaying a fondness for the kind of interpretative exercise characteristic of the Kabbalistic tradition, he notes that the thirteenth letter of the Hebrew alphabet, *mem*, can be written in two ways. When it appears in the middle of a word, it is open: מ; at the end of a word, however, it is closed: ם. Seeing in *mem*, which can be both "cloze et ouverte" (II.288) [closed and open], a sign of God's special relationship with man, Briçonnet explains that final *mem*, "par sa nature cloze" (II.289) [by its closed nature], is emblematic of God. "Divinité incomprehensible est encloze et comme prisonniere, mise au milieu de la diction, qui est nature humaine, pour la prandre, unir et estre prins: bonté au milieu de malice pour la bonnifier, lumiere au milieu de tenebres, pour les chasser et illuminer, paix en guerre pour appaiser et unyr, feu pour eschauffer la froideur mortelle, vie pour vivifier la mort et generallement incomprehensibilité et Tout en Rien pour le eslever et estre sublimé" (II.289–90) [Incomprehensible divinity is enclosed and, like a prisoner, put in the middle of speech, which is human nature, to take it, unite with it and be taken: goodness in the middle of malice in order to make it good, light in the middle of shadows in order to dissipate them and give them light, peace in war in order to pacify and unite, fire in order to warm mortal coldness, life in order to give life to death and general incomprehensibility, and All in Nothing in order to elevate it and make it sublime]. Final *mem* is "infinitude inserée et unye en finitude" (II.290) [infinity joined to and united with the finite]. Declaring that "Dieu est cloz en chascun de nous et que sommes membres des membres du corps du doux Jhesus" (II.290) [God is enclosed in each of us and that we are the limbs of the limbs of the body of sweet Jesus], Briçonnet notes that God's love is a prison that remains open during the course of a man's lifetime (during the course of the text), permitting him to enter at any moment. Ultimately, however, God embraces him with loving finality, enclosing him within the prison of love, "car l'on enferme songneusement ce que l'on ayme et selon l'amour est la sollicitude" (II.289) [for one locks up carefully what one loves and the care is proportionate to the love].

The prison image is equally complex and ambiguous in love

poetry of the Middle Ages.[54] Lovers both feared and desired the prison of love. Representing alternately the subjugation of Self by the Other and the apotheosis of Self in the Other, the prison image metaphorizes the displacement of the will from the center of being, a state deplored by Stoics and, generally, by Humanists but desired by mystics and lovers.

Reappearing often in Marguerite's work, the prison metaphor is especially rich and complex in *Les Prisons*. Each of the three Books in *Les Prisons* defines a particular prison: Book I depicts earthly love as a prison; Book II describes the thirst for worldly experience that leads to an imprisonment in material things; Book III reveals that human knowledge is a prison no less confining than earthly love and worldly experience. Our examination of Marguerite's text will take us through each of these three prisons.

THE TOWER OF LOVE

The first lines of *Les Prisons* tell the reader a number of crucial things about the poem: "Je vous confesse, Amye tant aymée . . ." (I. 1)[55] [I confess to you, beloved friend]. The poem is a first-person narrative by means of which the speaker, whom we soon learn is a man identified simply as *Amy*, "confesses" to a woman called *Amye*. From the point of view of classical rhetoric, the poem is cast in the form of a prosopopoeia, for Marguerite presents her text as being spoken by *Amy*. Although it was not uncommon for an author of a prosopopoeia to put his words in the mouth of a person of the opposite sex (in *La Parfaite Amye*, for example, Héroet speaks through the mouth of an *amye*), *Les Prisons* is unique in that it is the only one of Marguerite's allegorical texts in which the narrator is a man. In all of her other narrative texts, the narrator-pilgrim who travels along the *via Christi* is a woman, often explicitly identified in the work as Marguerite herself. Sorting out the deictics given at the beginning of *Les Prisons*, the reader realizes that in order to interpret the poem he must, contrary to everything Marguerite's poetry

---

54. See Roger Dragonetti, *La Technique poétique des trouvères dans la chanson courtoise* (Bruges: De Tempel, 1960), p. 107 ff.
55. I quote from Glasson's edition, indicating book and line.

has led him to expect, construct a first-person poetic persona who is male. Unanticipated within the economy of Marguerite's poetry as a whole, this reversal of sexual roles deserves closer scrutiny.

In a sense, all of Marguerite's major allegorical poems, including *Les Prisons*, are confessions. In none, however, is the confessional mode stated so pointedly, so formally, as in *Les Prisons* ("Je vous confesse, Amye . . ."). Whereas in the other texts the narrator confesses at first to no one in particular and then to Christ (behind whom stands, ultimately, the reader), in *Les Prisons* the recipient of the confession is incorporated into the formal narrative structure of the work. *Destinateur* and *destinataire* are formal categories within the narrative itself, the former being *Amy*, the Sender or Giver, the latter, *Amye*, the Receiver. However, in a confession the roles of *destinateur* and *destinataire* are problematic, indeed, reversible. The *destinateur* "gives" his confession to the *destinataire*, who, in the ritual of confession, is the guarantor of truth. The *destinataire*-confessor is the priest, the judge, the superior in whom authority resides. The ritual is completed when the *destinataire*-confessor responds to the revelations with which he has been entrusted by judging, by imposing punishment, and, finally, by extending pardon to the confessant. In other words, he who was initially the Receiver now assumes the role of *super-destinateur*, or super-Giver, and exercises his power by dispensing justice and consolation.

With the exception of *Les Prisons*, the "I" in all of Marguerite's allegorical texts is the humble, distraught Marguerite, who confesses her anguish and love to Christ, the *destinataire*. Christ, in turn, assumes His true majesty when, like all confessors, He dons the robe of judge-*destinateur* and, pronouncing a judgment, grants pardon and solace to the penitent. Marguerite, the poetic "I," is always at first the troubled Martha who entreats Christ. Christ's response is such that Marguerite, comforted and illuminated, tends to become the silent, adoring Mary, the exemplary *destinataire* and Receiver of His grace. In discourse that duplicates the ritual of confession, the *destinataire*-confessor-turned-*super-destinateur* is not only a projection of Christ but also of the father in the family and of the father-king in that larger family that is a national state. Within the economy of Marguerite's work, this role, which is, in other words, a projection of alterity, is always assumed by the male.

The seeming reversal of roles in *Les Prisons* is an illusion that disappears if we examine the functions that Marguerite assigns *Amy* and *Amye* within the text. *Amy*, the "I," confesses to *Amye* and is initially the *destinateur*, or Giver. Within the confessional mode, *Amye*, the *destinataire*, or Receiver, ought to be the controlling agent, the master. In a purely metaphorical sense, this is to some degree true. There is no doubt that Marguerite had Dante's *Divine Comedy* in mind when she composed *Les Prisons*. A new edition of Dante's poem, together with a preface by Maurice Scève, was published by Jean de Tournes in 1547 and may have provided Marguerite with an opportunity to renew her acquaintance with a work she had admired in her youth. Be that as it may, Marguerite alludes a number of times in *Les Prisons* to Dante and the *Divine Comedy*. *Amye* is a Beatrice, an incarnation of the principle of love that propels *Amy* on his spiritual journey. Reminding *Amye* that he used to read to her the story "de Beatrix et de Dante" (II.1042), *Amy* exhorts her to read the *Divine Comedy*: "Lisez ces chantz où tant de bien on trouve" (II.1046) [read these poems, in which one finds so much that is good]. As a metaphor for the compelling power of love, *Amye* has something of the authority of a *destinataire*-turned-*super-destinateur*.

The line just cited ("Lisez ces chantz . . .") makes it clear, however, that on the narrative level authority is vested in *Amy*, not in *Amye*. He, not she, is the dispenser of wisdom and truth. Marguerite has altered the functions of the narrator and narratee in *Les Prisons* so as to assure that power will continue to reside in the male character. The model of authority in *Les Prisons* conforms to the familial, religious, and political models underlying all of Marguerite's texts.

Representing authority, *Amy* is not a true penitent. Despite his opening words ("Je vous confesse, Amye . . ."), he does not really confess. Instead, he tells *Amye* how he arrived at truth and tries to draw her up to the higher state of consciousness he has already attained. In poems such as the *Dialogue*, the *Petit Oeuvre*, and *La Navire*, the reader accompanies the anguished "I" on her journey and shares her doubts and painful experience. In *Les Prisons*, he sides with *Amye*. Although *Amy* recounts his arduous journey, he speaks *ex cathedra* and presents his story as an *exemplum* designed to serve as a model for spiritual progress.

In accord with Neoplatonic principles, *Amy* first experienced beauty in the "godlike face and bodily form" (*Phaedrus* 251B) of *Amye*. Gradually, carnal forms became less attractive to him, and *Amy*, liberated from the prison of the flesh, moved up to the next rung on the Neoplatonic ladder of spiritual ascension. At this point, *Amy* revealed his ties with the courtly as well as the Neoplatonic tradition. Being the "parfait amant" [the perfect lover],[56] he cannot simply kick away the lower rung of the ladder, even though he no longer has any need for it. Motivated by a proselytizing spirit, by a desire to lead, guide, and direct, and by a sense of gratitude toward his former mistress, *Amy* charts the route he has followed and urges *Amye* to proceed quickly along the same path. The didactic impulse in *Les Prisons* is strong. At the beginning of Book III, *Amy* explains to *Amye*—that is to say, to the reader—why he is writing the text that she (we) is (are) reading:

III.1 Montant plus hault à la perfection,
     Plus je descendz à ceste affection
     Qui est de Dieu tresfort recommandée
     Et de l'Amour à l'amant demandée,
5   Et plus vertu rend mon esprit contant;
     Mon desir croist de trop plus ou autant
     Veoir par vertu contant le vostre esprit.
     C'est la raison qui me fait par escript
     Continuer de vous faire sçavoir
10   Tout le discours que au monde j'ay peu veoir.
     Or donc Amye, escoutez ce discours
     Dont les propoz ne pevent estre courtz.

As I rise higher toward perfection, the more I descend to this love which is strongly recommended by God and which Love demands of the lover, and the more virtue makes my heart content. My desire to see your spirit content through virtue grows even more or just as much. That is why I continue to inform you in writing of all the things I have managed to see in the world. Therefore, friend, listen to this account, which will not be brief.

56. As well as appearing several times in *Les Prisons*, the words "parfaict amant," along with "amytié parfaict" [sic], appear in Marguerite's last play, a brief courtly diversion of 186 lines written in 1549. Untitled in the manuscript copy, it was first published by Saulnier in his edition of Marguerite's *Théâtre profane*. Saulnier entitled the work *Comédie du parfait amant*.

As he continues his ascent to "la perfection," *Amy* becomes more and more *christiforme*. In the end, he is identified with the Spirit, with Christ, whom the *Ravie* in the *Comédie de Mont-de-Marsan* calls "mon amy," "mon amant," "mon grand mignon." Once *Amy* has been metaphorized into *esprit* and *Amye* into *corps* Marguerite describes Christian experience in textual terms. The text itself, although always separate from the spirit, is the incarnation of the spirit. "Par escript il [l'esprit] se fait reveler" (III.258) [Through writing He reveals himself], Marguerite says in the last book of *Les Prisons*.

The spirit's tender affection for the body is a distinctive feature of *Les Prisons*. Here, in the most mature and intricately elaborated statement of her religious beliefs, Marguerite generally avoids the words *aneantissement* and *pulverisacion*. No longer is the body represented as an enemy that deserves destruction; the *corps textuel* does not now seek to destroy itself. Throughout her poetry, Marguerite is attracted to the idea that the goal of the Christian life is the total abandonment of the body, a view held firmly only by a relatively small number of mystics. In *Les Prisons*, however, she moves closer to the more orthodox notion that the self is not "destroyed"; it is either damned in its damnable identity or fulfilled by salvation. *Les Prisons* is an allegory of fulfillment.

In his first letters to Marguerite, Briçonnet wrote at length about the need to pulverize and annihilate the self. However, in the long and richly textured letter of September 26, 1524, the last complete extant letter he wrote to Marguerite, he spoke not of destroying the self but of bringing the self into harmony with the divine will. This change of emphasis reflects less a change in belief than a change in the Church's attitude toward views ascribed to Luther. Luther was condemned by the Sorbonne on April 15, 1521. During the following two years, Briçonnet, who was suspected of harboring "Lutheran" sympathies, tried to separate himself as much as possible from views that bordered on heresy. The belief that man must immolate Self, that he must suppress every desire for independence, was not especially "Lutheran." It had long been held by mystics of pronounced otherworldly persuasion. Nevertheless, because of the increased dissension in the Church and the erosion of ecclesiastical authority, which was precipitated by the rapid spread of "Lutheranism," the Church tended to close ranks and reject as heretical all opinions that were not demonstrably orthodox. Whether Briçonnet deliberately purged his vocabulary of the words *aneantissement* and *pulverisacion* during 1523–24, we cannot be certain. The fact remains that in his letter of September 26, 1524, he expresses the orthodox view that God does not expect the impossible of man. God does not ask man to destroy his individual human will, for human faculties, which were created and are constantly being re-created by God, are the instruments by means of which man can express his love for God. What God requires of man is a genuine effort to achieve a measure of conformity with the divine will. This conformity can never be fully achieved in earthly life. God, however, in His love for man, takes the wish for the deed. As Juliana of Norwich wrote in 1373: "And thus was I learned to my understanding, that seeking is as good as beholding."[57] The mere impulse of the human will toward the love of God is sufficient for God to embrace man in mutual love.

Thus, ideally, the Christian's declarations of unworthiness are followed by expressions of love. Indeed, we have noted that in her poetry Marguerite, after denying any merit for herself, concludes with rapturous expressions of her love for God. The tendency of the will toward God is what redeems man, making him worthy after all. Briçonnet, expressing a Christian optimism that is grafted onto Neoplatonic optimism, tells Marguerite in his last complete letter that "l'ame fidelle trouve en toutes creatures, bonnes et mauvaises, eschelles d'assurection pour veoir la sapience divine cachée et partout gisant" (II.289) [the faithful soul finds in all creatures, good and bad, ladders of ascension to see divine wisdom lying hidden everywhere]. Declaring that God, though hidden, secretly accompanies the Christian and instills in him a yearning for *caritas* (which He then accepts as coming from man), Briçonnet continues with the following comment: "Il n'est si caché qui ne se trouve facilement venant au devant de ceux qui sentent et suivent l'esguillon divin, qui les stimule à le cercher. Il donne le desir de la queste, cerchant avec le questeur, se offrant en proye à qui la veult prendre" (II.289) [He is not so hidden that he cannot be easily found, coming as he does before those who feel and follow the divine goad, which

---

57. *Revelations of Divine Love Shewed to Mother Juliana of Norwich, 1373*, preface by George Tyrrell (London: Kegan Paul, Trench, Trübner & Co. Ltd., 1902), Ch. 10, p. 31.

incites them to look for him. He gives the desire for the quest, seeking with the seeker, offering himself as prey to him who wished to take it]. He concludes by citing Scripture: "Ego dilligentes me dilligo" ("I love those who love me; those who seek me eagerly shall find me." Proverbs 8.17).

Within the narrative framework of *Les Prisons*, *Amy* has completed his confession before he begins to speak at the beginning of the poem. He has already been forgiven before he says "Je vous confesse, Amye." The *now* that the narrative voice evokes in the first line of the poem by means of the present verb tense is not that of a separation from Christ that leads to confession but that of the joy that follows awareness of His forgiveness. It is identical with the *now* that, at the end of Book III, is defined not only by the present tense but more specifically by the present tense of the verb *être*, thus suggesting a state of perpetual presence. As he begins to speak in the opening line of the poem, *Amy* is already joyful, for he has attained the supreme state of "forte Amour" (III.3210) [strong Love], in which, as he says in the concluding lines of Book III, "l'Esprit est divin et vehement, / La liberté y est parfaictement" (III.3214) [the Spirit is divine and powerful, and freedom is absolute]. To the extent that *Amy* retraces the road he has traveled in order to arrive at that state, his account is exemplary.

For a Christian, the ultimate exemplar is Christ, often referred to by mystics and by Marguerite, as the *parfaict amant*. Seeing not the letter but the spirit, the reader can perceive in the word *parfaictement*, which is the last word of *Les Prisons*, a revelation of the identity of the *Je*, who, throughout the course of this long text, urges *Amye* to abandon her carnal ways and to move along the road that leads to true joy, to blissful repose with God. On one level of discourse, the *Je* is the *parfaict amant*. The poem begins and ends at the same point—in the *nowness* of Christ's presence. It does not really progress at all. Thus (in Augustinian terms) the reader, arriving at the end of Book III (*parfaictement/parfaict amant*) comes to a place where he was already; he comes to the *Je* that is the first word of the poem.

The anagogical nature of the *Je*, its true exemplarity, is revealed only gradually to the reader. Although the poem begins in a *now* that is eventually conflated with the timelessness of God, with the eternal present, the speaker no sooner enunciates *nowness* by means of the present verb tense than he slips into the past tense, that is to say, into the tense of narration: "Je vous confesse, Amye tant aymée, / Que j'ay longtemps quasi desestimée . . ." (I.1–2) [I confess to you, beloved friend, that I have for a long time almost regarded with disfavor . . .]. What follows is a narrative of *Amy*'s imprisonment in, and escape from, the Tower of Love. After having read all three books of *Les Prisons*, the reader can see that time, which is clearly articulated throughout Book I— and, indeed, throughout Books II and III—is enfolded or encircled within the timelessness that constitutes the frame (beginning and end) of the text. Like so many of Marguerite's poems, *Les Prisons* presents time within the context of timelessness, the human or finite within the framework of the divine or infinite, narrative within a structure that is basically circular and antiprogressive. The reader, like the Christian, is always called upon to operate simultaneously on both the fleshy (temporal) and the spiritual (atemporal) levels. He understands that flesh and spirit (or time and timelessness) are utterly different in one perceptual framework even though they are not only interdependent but essentially the same in another perceptual framework. Although the reader, like the Christian, may experience time as "real," the text conspires to force him to experience the unreality of time and narrative. It compels him to see in narrative flow a fiction.

Allegorically, the Tower of Love in which *Amy* is at first a happy captive is the text itself, within which the reader is confined. *Amy* finally realizes that the prison he thought was so solid and sturdy is an illusion: "O couverture, ô seure fiction! / O trop double dissimulation!" (537–38) [O mask, O certain fiction! O too cunning dissimulation], he cries out near the end of Book I. Looking back on the prison from which he has escaped, *Amy* marvels that he was ever so deluded as to mistake the *Tour d'Amour*, that "labirinthe estrange, / Là où j'estoys" (I.605–06) [strange labyrinth, there where I was], for reality. The reader, having finished Book I, looks back on the text and realizes that he, too, has been deluded. Whereas he at first saw in the text an allegory according to which the Tower of Love stands for the world of the flesh, he now understands that, although this view is correct on a surface (or fleshy) level, on a different perceptual level Book I is an allegorical text that refers to its own impossibility; that is to say, it demonstrates the inability of allegory to present anything but narrative, which, from the perspective of truth and timelessness, is always a "fiction."

Signs of the "fictitious" nature of the prison and of the text that represents it abound in Book I, although neither the reader nor *Amy* reads them correctly at first. Few works by Marguerite draw so strongly and so ostentatiously on literary tradition as does Book I of *Les Prisons*. The fiction of a hero-narrator imprisoned in a Tower of Love is conventional in medieval courtly literature. Throughout Book I, Petrarchan images and conceits appear over and over. *Amy* speaks repeatedly of the *lyens, chaines,* and *fers* that bind him. Antithetical formulations, a favorite device of Petrarchan poets, are common. To describe a state that he *now* knows to be illusory and odious but that he *then* thought was real and attractive beyond all measure, *Amy* resorts to oxymoron (e.g., "lumiere tenebreuse," I.8; "doulce poyson," I.426). Imprisoned in love, he was happy. Only now, in the light of subsequent revelations, does he realize that he was not free. Only now does he view his ensnarement with revulsion. He recalls that he used to believe that his tower was "ung plaisant terrestre paradis" (I.88) [a pleasant earthly paradise]. Marguerite portrays this "terrestre paradis" as a world of sensual delight. "Ouyr et veoir fut mon salut, ma vie" (I.89) [To hear and to see was my salvation], *Amy* says, stressing the noble senses. "Mon oeil, mon oreille et mon cueur" (I.85) [My eyes, my ears and my heart], he notes, were so thoroughly satisfied that he wished to remain forever in the earthly paradise in which he found himself. Here Marguerite seems to allude to the Ficinian canon, for *oeil, oreille,* and *cueur* represent the senses that, according to Ficino, are responsive to love.[58] (*Cueur,* roughly the equivalent of understanding, is not, strictly speaking, a sense, but it functions as one within the coordinates of Ficinian doctrine.) Marguerite gives particular importance to hearing, which is not surprising in the context of a theology that gives primary importance to the Word. Ecstatically, *Amy* declares that

> . . . oyant ung tel parler
> I.70 Je ne vouldroys jamais loing m'en aller.
> Je me moquoys de celluy qui s'aplique
> Et prent plaisir à la doulce musique;
> Vostre parler m'estoit toute armonie,

58. Marsile Ficin, *Commentaire sur le Banquet de Platon*, ed. Raymond Marcel (Paris: Belles-Lettres, 1956), I, 4, p. 144.

Qui ma prison rendoit si bien garnie
75   D'ung son en quoy gist ma felicité,
Que je n'avoys point de necessité
D'orgues, de lucz, de fifres, de violes:
Je trouvoys tout en voz doulces parolles.
Si ung bon mot ouyr de vous povoys,
80   Croyez pour vray que autre parolle ou voix
N'estoit, sinon ce mot qui revenoit
A mon oreille, là où il se tenoit.
Tout le parler que onques depuys ouy
Ne m'exemptoit, sinon ce doulx ouy.

. . . hearing such words, I would never want to go far away. I scoffed at
him who devotes himself to sweet music and takes pleasure in it. To
me your speech was all harmony; it furnished my prison so well with
a music that was the source of my happiness that I had no need for
organs, lutes, fifes, or viols. I found all of them in your sweet words. If
I heard a good word from you, you may be certain that no other word
or voice (except for this word that continued to sound in my ear) was
there where it was. No speech I have heard since then has ever freed
me, except for this sweet sound.

Ouyr, parolles, voix, oreille, musique, and *parler* resonate throughout the text, creating a paradise composed of words spoken by
a voice so caressing and melodious that no distinction can be
made between verbal artifact and music of a peculiarly intense
beauty. *Amye*'s harmonious *parler* ensnared *Amy*. He became entrapped in a prison of sweet sounding words: "Vostre parler que
souvent je recorde, / [Fut] mes durs fers et ma pesante chaisne"
(I. 52–53) [Your speech, which I often remember, fashioned my
cruel shackles and my heavy chain].

By representing *Amy*'s first prison as an edifice of "doulces
parolles," Marguerite has combined two motifs we have frequently seen (heard) in her work. In accord with the Johannine
principle that "In the beginning was the Word," Marguerite
gives special prominence to speech. *Amy*'s adventure begins
when he responds to language; it ends when he finds himself
face to face with Christ. Charmed by *Amye*'s speech, *Amy* suc-
cumbed to the "letter." He delighted in *parole,* the fleshy enve-
lope of *langue.* Only by breaking out of *parole* is he finally able
to perceive the *langue,* or *Tout-Verbe,* that is incarnated in *Verbe.*

The fact that *Amy* hears in his mistress' speech an exquisite music underscores his sensual response to language. But, as we have seen, music in Marguerite's work always signals something more than fleshy delight. As in the case of the *Ravie* (*Mont-de-Marsan*), it evokes the rapturous presence of Christ by virtue of the fact that, transcending *parole*, it discloses the spirit within the letter. In a paradoxical way, then, *Amy*, at the very beginning of his spiritual journey, is not far from his final destination. Or more precisely, he is really already there, although he does not know it because his perceptions are impaired. Love and music, which characterize his first prison, will eventually be signs of his liberation. At the end of Book III, he comes to the place where he was already. What he discovers is that Christ was with him always ("I am with you always; yes, to the end of time," Matthew 28.20). The love he thought he shared with *Amye* was in fact a sign of the love he shares with Christ. The music in which he delighted was really a sign of the translinguistic discourse by means of which *Amy* and Christ metacommunicate their love. But *Amy* read the signs incorrectly, mistaking the letter for reality. He was compelled to move away from the place where he found himself in the beginning in order to return to it with heightened perceptual powers in the end.

Amy found himself a prisoner because he failed to heed Augustine's distinction between things that are to be enjoyed and things that are to be used. As we saw in our discussion of the *Dialogue*, Augustine declares that "to enjoy something is to cling to it with love for its own sake. To use something," he continues, "is to employ it in obtaining that which you love, provided that it is worthy of love" (DDC I.4.9–10). Making it clear that the only things we can legitimately enjoy are the Father, the Son, and the Holy Spirit, Augustine explains that if we enjoy the amenities of the journey and take pleasure in those things we should use, we become entangled in "a perverse sweetness" (*perversa sauvitate*) that alienates us (*alienaremur*) from our homeland, a country of such "sweetness" that to reside there is to be blessed. *Amy* uses the word "aliené" to describe the state he was in. He notes that if anyone had seen him in the prison of love "il eust jugeé mon sens aliené" (I.98) [he would have considered me out of my senses], for he kissed the walls that confined him. In an act that borders on idolatry, he fell to his knees and worshiped his prison.

"O belle Tour, ô Paradis plaisant,
O clair Palais du soleil reluysant,
Où tout plaisir se voit en ung regard,
Las! qu'il me plaist d'estre icy seul à part
I.125   Pour contempler vostre perfection,
Vostre beaulté, vostre condition,
Par quel amour ne par quel artifice
Peult estre fait si parfaict edifice.
. . . .
"O digne Tour d'avoir toute louange,
Pour autre bien jamais je ne vous change!
Je vous requiers aussy ne me changer
I.140   Pour recevoir prisonnier estranger,
Et que jamais vostre porte ne s'ouvre
Qui le dedans de mon repoz descouvre.

O beautiful tower, O pleasant paradise, O bright palace radiant with sunlight where all pleasure may be seen in a glance; O how happy I am to be here alone to contemplate your perfection, your beauty, your qualities; through what love or what skill can such a perfect edifice be made . . . O tower worthy of all praise; I would never exchange you for anything else! I ask you not to exchange me to receive another prisoner, and may your gate never open and reveal the inside of my place of repose.

Using the vocabulary of spiritual experience, Marguerite portrays *Amy* as a man of religious temperament (clearly, he is not one of the "lukewarm" condemned in Revelations 3.16), who, however, misdirected his devotional impulse and so became an idolater.

Love and music, which are stressed in Book I, are signs that *Amy* was already close to the goal he would reach in Book III even though he did not know it, for, mistakenly, he saw with carnal rather than spiritual eyes. In the same way, prayer—more specifically, prayer for repose and stasis—is a sign that the prisoner/lover was indirectly seeking God, the only true repose, the guarantor of timelessness. *Amy*'s first prison is a negative image of definitive enfoldment in God. The Tower of Love in Book I is a fleshy and perishable model of the temple of love, spiritual and eternal, that will be revealed in Book III. Augustine had envisaged the *via Christi* as a spiritual cleansing. Purified and clean, the mind at last perceives the light that has been there from the beginning. "Let us consider this cleansing," Augustine advised, "to be as a journey or voyage home" (DDC I.10.13). Throughout *Les Prisons*, *Amy* undertakes a journey that, though it seems at first to take him away from his point of departure, is in fact a cleansing that permits him to focus more clearly on the truth and to see that he was right to love, wrong only in the object of his love; right to enjoy, wrong only in his choice of things to be enjoyed; right to worship, wrong only in adoring what was visible to the carnal eye.

Amy resembles the *Mondainne*, who, at the beginning of *Mont-de-Marsan*, declares: "J'ayme mon corps, voylà la fin: / C'est mon amy, c'est mon afin; / C'est mon tout, mon Dieu, mon idolle" (213–15) [I love my body; that is what I live for. It is my friend, it is my ally; it is my all, my God, my ïdol]. The *Mondainne*'s love is no doubt misplaced, but only partly so, for orthodox Christianity did not reject the body, which had been (and constantly is being) redeemed through the mystery of the Incarnation. In a fundamental way, the *Mondainne* is closer to the *Ravie*, who appears at the end of the play, than to the *Supersticieuse* and the *Sage*. The *Ravie* is a cleansed *Mondainne*. The *Mont-de-Marsan* traces a trajectory that circles back, linking beginning and end through a process of purification, or, to use the words mystics used to describe the soul's movement toward God, purgation and illumination.

If *Amy*'s entrapment in corporeality links him to the *Mondainne*, his experiences in Book II and most of Book III are close to those of the *Supersticieuse* and the *Sage*. Composed at approximately the same time, *Mont-de-Marsan* and *Les Prisons* complement each other. The *Mondainne*, the *Supersticieuse*, and the *Sage* are prisoners, each immured in an ideology that, although it contains an element of truth, distorts and disfigures Christ's law of love, the single, unique reality. Only the *Ravie*, singing a song that transcends verbal discourse, escapes imprisonment by being united with Christ ("A Mon amy, unie et joincte," 875) [united and joined with my friend], a union that guarantees perpetual existence in the ultimate closed-system, which is identical with the ultimate open-system. Both *Les Prisons* and *Mont-de-Marsan* trace out the clear evolutionary pattern of the *scala perfectionis*, each prison in the first work and each lady in the second representing a rung of the ladder that the Christian must negotiate before arriving at Christ.

Worshiping his prison, *Amy* prays for the cessation of time. He wishes to remain locked in his tower. He asks love to re-enforce the bars on the door and to tighten the chains that hold him. He wants the window securely fastened so that no sunlight can enter his cell. He is pleased to live exclusively by "la lumiere d'amour" (I.154) [the light of love]. *Amy*'s language is that of a Christian seeking to express the final, unitive stage of mystical experience. He says that, having attained the highest good conceivable to him at the time, he possessed what he believed constituted the *summum bonum*: "Je possedoys le seul bien que desire / Pour vivre heureux tout royaulme ou empire" (I.171–72) [I possessed the only wealth I desire in order to live happily, my whole realm or empire]. Possession is a sign of the heavenly bliss that marks the *unio*. Another sign is the effacement of difference and the emergence of resemblance as the essential mode of existence. Signaling *similitudo*, [59] the unitive stage is marked by man's awareness that Christ lives in the human heart and that the human is enfolded in the divine. *Amy* declares ecstatically that he and *Amye* are one. For a time, his experience of love resembles the Christian's experience of Christ. He seeks to assure himself that the love he and *Amye* bear each other is unchanging, for, in Augustinian terms, the only things man can truly enjoy are those that exist beyond time, "eternal and immutable" (DDC I.22.18). Using the vocabulary mystics used to signal their experience of atemporality, *Amy* tried to experience his love within the coordinates of the timeless *unio*.

That his experience of love is a reflection of his *desire* for *unio* rather than a representation of *unio* itself is first hinted at when *Amy* says that despite all his efforts to experience his love *unitively*, he often feared the effects of time:

> Crainte souvent disoit: "Ilz seront cours
> Ces grans plaisirs, et ne pourront durer!
> Pensez au mal qu'il vous fault endurer

---

59. In one of his sermons, Tauler contrasts *similitudo*, or that which comes from the spirit, with *dissimilitudo*, or that which comes from flesh. See Tauler, *Die Predigten Taulers*, ed. Ferdinand Vetter (Berlin: Weidmannsche Buchhandlung, 1910), p. 115.

I.185   Quand la prison sera par le vieulx Temps
              Mise à neant, et tous ses passetemps."
              Lors tout mon cueur se troubloit dedans moy.

Fear often said: "These great pleasures will be short, and they will not
last! Think of the pain you will suffer when the prison is leveled to
nothing by hoary Time and all its temporal delights." Then my heart
became troubled within me.

No further proof of the fictional nature of this pseudo-*unio* is
needed than *Amy*'s admission of his awareness of time, for an
essential feature of the experience of the *unio* is unawareness of
time. As Briçonnet wrote to Marguerite: "Qui bien est yvre et
endormy [en Dieu] ne pense de l'advenir. Il n'a que le present"
(II.164) [Anyone who is really intoxicated and asleep in God
does not think about the future. He has only the present].
Troubled by the thought of change, *Amy* realized that this
thought was itself a sign of his changing state of mind. Time
began to destroy his Tower of Love. Recalling the destruction of
his prison, *Amy* understands that time was the instrument God
used to draw him away from the fictional *unio* he himself had
constructed out of his own sensual desires.

    In her account of the destruction of *Amy*'s tower, Marguerite
stresses the idea that God, being immanent in the world, accomplishes His will through the flesh, that is to say, through time,
which is an attribute of the carnal world. In this sense, His will
was being accomplished from the very beginning, for all unfolding is in accord with divine will. As the Pseudo-Dionysius
observed, "God we must celebrate as both Eternity and Time"
(*Div. Names* 172). *Amy*'s recognition of the fact that God is
Time (He is also, of course, the opposite of Time, or Eternity) is
translated in the text by language that makes liberal use of temporal deictics ("Non en ung jour, ny en une sepmaine, / Mais
peu à peu . . . ," I.212) [Not in a day, nor in a week, but little by
little]). Deictics of time reintroduce narrative in the poem, for
narrative is the textual incarnation of time.

              Ung jour, ainsy ma prison regardant
              Comme le bien dont plus j'estoys ardant,
I.225   Le soleil viz entrer par la rompture

Que j'apperceuz dedans la couverture.   (my emphasis)
. . . .

I.235   *Le lendemain*, j'en viz encor autant. . . .   (my emphasis)

One day while looking at my prison, seeing in it the only thing that impassioned me, I saw the sun enter through an opening I noticed in the roof . . . The next day I saw the same thing again. . . .

Another deictic that signals the reappearance of narrative as the dominant textual axis is the past definite verb tense. The long prayer that *Amy* had addressed to his prison (I.121–66) was in the present tense. Concluding his prayer, *Amy* had continued to evoke his state of mind during his imprisonment by using the imperfect verb tense, which is the main tense in his account of his captivity in the prison of love. The present tense situates the prayer in a present time that is illusory because it is confined within the imperfect. The time rendered by the imperfect, however, is an unstable, "dependent" time,[60] a time *in posse*, that is to say, an indeterminate time that is fixed only by another verb.[61] Being incomplete (*imperfectus* = unfinished), the imperfect tense traces out an action whose beginning and end can be stated only in a "perfect" verb tense, i.e., in the preterit. To the extent that an immanent God accomplishes His will mysteriously and secretly through the instrumentality of time, the imperfect verb tense can convey *implicitly* the unfolding of divine design while expressing *explicitly* the essential incompleteness and untenability of *Amy*'s illusion of possession, joy, and finality.

But, as the Pseudo-Dionysius noted, if God is Time, He is also Timelessness, or Eternity. God's transcendence, His being-outside-time, is another idea that Marguerite stresses in the passage (I.203–15) that marks the beginning of the collapse of the Tower of Love and signals the narrator's realization that what he thought was a "real" paradise is nothing but fiction. *Amy* does not participate in his own liberation, which, in religious terms, is a conversion. Deliverance from the flesh cannot be effected within the coordinates of the flesh itself. It can come only from outside. In the case of *Amy*'s liberation from the prison of love,

60. Ferdinand Brunot and Charles Bruneau, *Précis de grammaire historique de la langue française* (Paris: Masson, 1949), p. 377: "L'imparfait est un temps 'dépendant'."
61. Gustave Guillaume, *Temps et verbe: théorie des aspects des modes et des temps* (Paris: Champion, 1929), pp. 9–10.

deliverance is a pure and unmerited gift that came to him in the form of light, which, streaming into his prison, permitted him one day to "see" that he was imprisoned. The otherness of this gift is translated by the sudden shift from the imperfect verb tense to the preterit.

At first, *Amy* tried to reenforce his crumbling prison, seeking against all evidence to "la rendre eternelle" (I.252) [make it eternal]. Becoming brighter and brighter, the light changed into a purifying fire. As the clothes he was wearing began to burn, *Amy* caught sight of his mistress, who, instead of pitying him, laughed at his distress. He then understood that the love he had thought existed between *Amye* and himself was illusory. He had not been a prisoner of love at all, but rather a prisoner of self: ". . . prisonnier de moymesmes j'estoys" (I.321) [I was a prisoner of myself]. Looking back on his experience, *Amy* realizes that the prison, now reduced to ashes, was of his own making.

In Lacanian terms, the prison in Book I is that of a self grounded in the Imaginary. *Amye* is the *imago* that *Amy* appropriates in accord with the identificatory process operative in the Imaginary structuration of self. *Amy* appropriates for himself the completeness and perfection he perceives *imaginairement* in the other. His first "self" is constituted as an other; that other is, as in the mirror stage, a reflection of himself. Furthermore, the *imago*, as Lacan stressed, is a persecutory agent, for it is a domineering *alter ego* that provokes feelings of inadequacy and humiliation in the self. *Amy* experiences the humiliation that the *imago* can inflict when he asks *Amye* to help in putting out the fire that has started to burn down the tower, and she, instead of coming to his rescue, throws firebrands down on his head.

The *difference* (*dissimilitudo*) between *Amy* and *Amye* marks a progression away from the Imaginary. This shift is signaled by self-accusatory language that reflects the experience of *mortificatio*. "Le feu estrange" (I.362) [the strange fire] that liberates *Amy* by compelling him to abandon his imaginary prison (or the prison of the Imaginary) is the purifying agent whose function, in Briçonnet's terms, is to pulverize self, or at least the self that is constructed in the order of the Imaginary. Before advancing to a "higher" order (the business of Books II and III), *Amy* looks back with distaste on where he was and what he was: "Fy! qu'elle est layde et salle la prison / Que j'aymoys tant, par sa doulce poyson" (I.425–26) [Fie! how ugly and dirty is the prison

I loved so much, through her sweet poison]. "Je ne devoys donc pas edifier / Sur ce où nul ne se doit confier" (I.433–34) [I ought therefore not to have built on that which no one can rely on], he says, reflecting on the "labirinthe estrange, / Là où j'estoys" (I.605–06) [strange labyrinth, there where I was].

The reader may legitimately see in the text itself a "labirinthe estrange." Looking at the ruins of his tower, *Amy* himself metaphorizes his demolished prison into a linguistic construct. It occurs to him that the very material he used to erect his prison/text, that is to say, language, was flawed:

> Ma servitude estoit si voluntaire,
> Que incessamment je ne me povoys taire;
> I.445　*Par mes sermons, dont faisoys ceste boue,*
> *Je m'enfermoys. . . .*　(my emphasis)

My servitude was so self-imposed, for I could not keep silent at all. By my words, with which I made this mud, I imprisoned myself. . . .

In light of the higher truth that is represented by the sun, *Amy* calls the declarations of love he addressed to *Amye* "sermons," meaning, on the most literal level, speech, discourse, or, as he himself suggests, an incessant babble of words. "Sermon," however, has etymological resonances that give Marguerite's text a richer meaning. Derived from *serare* (to sow, beget), Latin *sermo* designated ordinary speech, talking, the language of conversation as distinct from formal discourse.[62] When used to define literary texts, the word meant satiric verses written in a conversational style, as in Horace. Because *sermo* designated common talk, it was used as a synonym for rumor or gossip and so, by extension, slander and calumny. During the fourth century, *sermo* became the Christian term for preaching, including catechesis and exegesis.[63] Seeing his tower, which is now reduced to rubble, *Amy* understands that his "sermons," the matter with

---

62. See "sermo," *A Latin Dictionary*, ed. Charleton F. Lewis and Charles Short (Oxford: Clarendon Press, 1879), p. 1679; see also "sermo," *Dictionnaire étymologique de la langue latine*, ed. A. Ernout and A. Meillet, 4th ed. (Paris: Klincksieck, 1959), p. 617.

63. See Christine Mohrmann, "Praedicare-tractare-sermo," in *Etude sur le latin des chrétiens* (Rome: Storia e Letteratura, 1958–1965), II, 71. On the controversy surrounding Erasmus' translation of the Johannine prologue as "In principio erat sermo," see Marjorie O'Rourke Boyle, *Erasmus on Language and Method in Theology* (Toronto: University of Toronto Press, 1977), pp. 3–31.

which he fashioned his prison, belong to the category of *parole*, not, as he had thought, to the category of *langue*. His tower was, he now declares, a "fiction" (I. 537), a "dissimulation" (I. 538). "En mille part mainctenant je vous voy," he says; "plus n'estes rien" (I. 541–42) [I now see you in a thousand fragments; you are no longer anything]. Just as *Amy*, in accord with the identificatory process operative in the Imaginary, appropriated the perfection of *Amye*, so language, conforming to the same process, appropriated the wholeness and immutability of *langue*. Like the self confined in the tower of carnal love, the "sermons" that constitute the textual labyrinth from which *Amy* now escapes belong to the order of the Imaginary. The "foible plume" (I. 575) [feeble pen] that recorded the Imaginary throughout Book I will be set to other tasks in Books II and III. Resorting to anaphoric formulation of the kind that, in Marguerite's texts, usually signals a displacement of the syntagmatic axis by the paradigmatic axis, *Amy* takes leave of his tower:

	Or adieu donc, ma prison et ma Tour
I.610	Où je ne veulx jamais faire retour!
	Adieu l'abisme où j'estoys englouty!
	Adieu le feu où souvent fuz rosty!
	Adieu la glace où maincte nuict tremblay!
	Adieu le lac de larmes assemblé!
615	Adieu le mont pour moy inaccessible!
	D'y retourner il ne m'est plus possible
	Par vous: de vous plus compte je ne faiz,
	Adieu vous dy pour la seconde foys!

Farewell, then, my prison and my tower, to which I wish never to return! Farewell abyss in which I was swallowed up! Farewell fire in which I was often burned! Farewell icy cold in which I shivered many a night! Farewell lake of tears that formed! Farewell summit, inaccessible to me! It is no longer possible for me to return to it through you. I no longer count on you. Farewell I say to you a second time.

Although he realizes that he can never return to the order of the Imaginary, he looks back on his experience in the prison of love as an inevitable and necessary first step in his pilgrimage toward "parfaicte amour" (I. 566).

IN THINGS CONFINED

If the relationship *Amy* established between himself and his narrow world in Book I may be said to belong to the order of the Imaginary, the bond he forms between himself and the broader worlds he enters in Book II and the first part of Book III belong to the order of the Symbolic. Being a preexisting order, impersonal, or, more precisely, superpersonal, the Symbolic is structured like a language. The self that is grounded in the Symbolic is a signifier whose being is determined by its position within a system of symbolic (linguistic) exchange in human society.

Liberated from his prison, *Amy* discovers the external world. He marvels at the beauty and order of God's great Book of Nature, which he calls "ung oeuvre parfaict" (II.64) [a perfect work]. Being both within, and yet superior to, the natural world, man is the reader of the *liber naturae*, the witness who attests to the beauty of God's handiwork. He is the signifier who, in a sense, makes God's creation beautiful by calling it so. His function is to see and to praise. *Amy*'s attention, however, soon focuses on man and his activities. He views man as master of all other creatures and is astonished at human ingenuity in dominating and manipulating the natural world. Admiring man's cunning and skill, he takes "grant plaisir" (II.106) [great pleasure] in learning "les façons, les usaiges / Dont les veneurs sçavent les bestes prendre" (II.100–101) [the ways, the means by which hunters can capture animals]. As he continues to observe the *theatrum mundi*, *Amy* is astounded by man's incessant activity, by the changes man has effected in the world as a result of agriculture, industry, exploration, construction, and trade. Everywhere he looks, both on land and on the sea, he discerns signs of human energy and enterprise. Overcome by the desire to share man's labor and his pleasures, *Amy*, thinking of the "voyaiges / Que ont fait les preuz" (II.141–42) [voyages that courageous men went on], decides to participate in human activity so that he, like the heroes of old, can "aquerir le bruyt des vertueux" (II.144) [acquire the reputation of the valiant].

Up to this point, Marguerite's text is in no way a condemnation of human enterprise and commerce. On the contrary, the fifty or so lines that describe man's apparently endless capacity to alter the world around him are informed with a sense of wonder and excitement comparable to that which informs numerous other Renaissance texts that extol the power of man. Indeed, *Amy*'s exhilaration seems to echo the *exhilaratio voluntatis* that Augustine discerned in mankind's first agricultural activity, which, Augustine tells us, was not thought of as labor but as a joyful and voluntary participation in divine creativity.[64] Emboldened by something like the Augustinian *exhilaratio voluntatis*, *Amy* strides eagerly into the world.

No sooner does *Amy* enter man's cities, however, than a discordant note is sounded in Marguerite's praise of human industry. Debarking from the ship he had been examining, *Amy* heads inland "pour aller veoir et villes et chasteaux, / Palais, jardins, paradis de delices / *Dont les beaultez font ignorer les vices*" (II.146–48, my emphasis) [to go to see cities and castles, palaces, gardens, paradises of delight, whose beauties make one unaware of the corruption]. Unfamiliar with architecture (except for his prison, whose walls had been unadorned), he is now delighted by the "dorure" [gilding] and "paincture" (II.150) [painting] he sees all around him. Suddenly, he is overcome by a consuming desire to amass wealth.

II.155   Mais delivré de ma prison antique,
          Ambition, dont le feu brulle et pique,
          Me vint saisir, par desir de bastir
          Mille maisons, et de les assortir,
          Et d'aquerir possessions et terres,
160   Dont souvent sort procès, debatz et guerres.

But after I was freed from my old prison, ambition, whose fire burns and pierces, came and seized me through a desire to build many houses and to furnish them, and to acquire land and possessions, which are often the source of lawsuits, quarrels and wars.

He finds the glitter of gold irresistible and decides "de faire mon effort / De ces grans biens par estatz aquerir, / Et les tresors amasser et querir" (II.174–76) [to make an effort to acquire great riches through holding public office and to amass and seek wealth]. He throws himself into worldly affairs and seeks to "le gain multiplier" (II.165) [make his profits multiply]. Once his

---

64. See Terry Comito, *The Idea of the Garden in the Renaissance*, p. 37.

desire for "biens" (II.185) has been thoroughly aroused, *Amy* becomes insatiable, motivated by "Ambition" and "Avarice, / Qui si tresbien sçavait couvrir son vice" (II.184–85) [Avarice, which knew very well how to cover up its corruption].

The emergence of "Ambition" and "Avarice" as the forces that motivate *Amy* marks a subversion, or rather, perversion of the Augustinian *exhilaratio voluntatis*. Marguerite tries to maintain a distinction between the *possession* of riches and honor, which in itself she does not explicitly condemn, and the impulse that compels *Amy* to seek them in the carnal world. Worldly riches and honor can be attained only by yielding to the impulses of "Ambition," "Avarice," and, significantly, "Madame Hypocrisie" (II.232), who, *Amy* declares, ". . . bien tost dedans ma fantasie / Se vint loger" (II.231–32) [soon came to dwell in my imagination]. In short, *Amy*'s desire for wealth and fame leads him to exclusive concern with the surface of things, "le dehors" (II.212) [the outside], *le paraître*; with, as Lacan put it,[65] *le par-être, l'être para* (the Greek prefix *para* means "beside"), the being-that-is-next-to-being, the substitute being, the covering that conceals being from eyes capable of discerning only what is outside and on the surface. That *Amy* moves in the world of *paraître* is illustrated pointedly when he speaks of churches, stressing their physical beauty and the sensual responses aroused in him by the music, the candles, the chimes:

> Rien je n'y ouy que chantz melodieux,
> Orgues sonnant pour resjouyr les dieux;
> II.215 Je n'y entendz sinon parolles sainctes,
> Prebstres devotz, predications mainctes
> Pour consoller tous les devotz espritz,
> Et ramener à bon port les periz.
> Les sacrementz je y viz administrer,
> 220 Et les petis en evesques mistrer,
> Brief, je viz tout ce que font les prelatz
> Officiant. . . .[66]

I hear nothing but beautiful songs, organs resounding to delight the gods. I hear nothing here but holy words, devout priests, many ser-

---

65. *Séminaire XX* (Paris: Seuil, 1975), p. 44.
66. Glasson points out (p. 259) that this is the only passage in Marguerite's poetry that alludes to liturgical ceremonies.

mons that console all the devout spirits and bring safely to port those
who have perished. I saw the Sacraments administered here and little
ones serve as bishops—in brief, I saw everything that officiating prel-
ates do. . . .

Exclaiming "c'est Paradis icy" (II.211) [it is paradise here], *Amy*
admires worldly pomp and splendor; he believes that he has attained "le but et fin de [son] pelerinage" (II.228) [the goal and
end of his pilgrimage].

The "mistake" *Amy* makes in Book I and again in Book II (he
will repeat this "error" at the beginning of Book III) is to confuse *par-être* with *être*, "le dehors" with "le dedans" (II.212) [the
inside]. Throughout the first part of Book I, *Amy* sees his prison
as a defense from the outside world, a protective covering, a
vestment wrapped comfortably around him. The word "couverture" (I.242), which is one of *Amy*'s metaphors for his first
prison, suggests that the Tower of Love belongs to the category
of *par-être*. "Couverture" means both "garment" and "the art of
covering with a garment," both *vêtement* and *vestissement*, or,
to cite Cotgrave's translation, both "apparell, rayment, attire"
and "an arraying, cloathing, cladding, attiring." As Micheline
Besnard-Coursodon observes in a study on Huysmans, *couverture*, or *vestissement*, "fonde le paraître"[67] [is the basis of appear-
ing]. She notes that "tout vestissement, en quoi se décèle un in-
vestissement, se supporte d'une réparation symbolique, et par là
confère à l'objet (être ou chose) l'investiture de son rôle dans le
cérémonial"[68] [all putting on of garments, in which one can
discern a covering, is supported by a symbolic reparation, and
thereby confers on the object (being or thing) the investiture of
its role in the ritual]. *Amy* is captivated by Church liturgy and
the solemnity of the decor, by ritual and ceremony. Unable to
distinguish between *le dehors* and *le dedans*, between the letter
and the spirit, he believes that reality is structured in accord
with the principles of formalization, ritualization, and theatri-
calization that mark liturgy. He enters a world governed by a
preexisting and superpersonal order, a world in which the self is
a signifier whose being is defined by the place it occupies within
a system of ceremonial exchange. He enters a world that belongs to the order of the Symbolic.

67. "A rebours: le corps parlé," *Revue des sciences humaines*, 43 (1978), 53.
68. Ibid.

As soon as *Amy* identifies reality with ritual and exteriority, "Madame Hypocrisie . . . se vint loger . . . dedans [sa] fantasie" (II.231–32) [Madame Hypocrisy came to dwell in his imagination]. From the Pauline-Augustinian perspective, the order of the Symbolic is the world of the letter, of *para*-reality, a world whose system of exchange, ritualistic and ceremonial, is a product of human fantasy. In *Les Prisons*, Marguerite obliquely associates ritual and ceremony with hypocrisy. This link between Church ceremony and hypocrisy suggests that she, like other Evangelicals, saw in the rites of the Church not, of course, hypocrisy but a form of Christian expression that, because it appealed to the senses and the imagination, was imperfect. In any case, *Amy* enters fully into the Symbolic order when, having noted the rules that govern the world in which he now wishes to distinguish himself, he decides hypocritically that "j'aquerroys honneur / Si à l'Eglise estoys devot donneur" (II.233–34) [I would acquire honor if I were a devout donor to the Church].

Ambition, avarice, and now hypocrisy propel *Amy* toward the court, the center of worldly power. "J'ouvriz mes yeulz pour myeulx veoir que c'estoit" (II.255) [I opened my eyes to see better what it was], he declares. What he sees is a "teatre" (II.291) in which human activity is organized into "masques, mommons, farces et comedies" (II.287) [masks, mummeries, farces and comedies]. So completely enthralled is *Amy* by the glitter of the court that he embraces the principles governing this world, seeking to define self within the coordinates of an order distinctly different from that which prevailed in the Tower of Love. Although *Amy* does not realize it at first, submission to this order is tantamount to enslavement, for the court is ruled by three implacable tyrants: *plaisir*, *honneur*, and *richesse* (II.522). In her description of the court, which represents human activity unilluminated by an awareness of Christ's presence in the world, Marguerite draws once again on I John 2.16: "The love of the Father cannot be in any man who loves the world, because nothing the world has to offer—the sensual body, the lustful eye, pride in possessions—could ever come from the Father but only from the world." Referring explicitly to this biblical passage ("Voyez Sainct Jehan," II.1058) [See Saint Jean], Marguerite appropriates the language of Scripture to identify the ". . . troys /Cruelz tyrantz" (II.1021–22) [three cruel tyrants] whose authority determines the course of worldly affairs:

II.1025   Gardez vous bien, de toutes voz puyssances,
           Des deux premiers qui sont concupiscences,
           L'ung de la chair, remply d'ordure et vice,
           L'autre des yeulx, apportant avarice;
           Le tiers, orgueil de vie, et le plus faulx
1030   De tous les troys, engendrant plus de maulx
           Que cueur ne peult penser, ne bouche dire.

Protect yourself well, with all your power, from the first two, which
are lustful desires, one being of the flesh, filled with corruption and
vice, the other being of the eyes, causing avarice; the third, pride of life
and the falsest of all three, producing more evil than the heart can
think or the mouth say.

Despite a slight confusion in Marguerite's initial identification
of the three members of this triumvirate (at first they seem to be
Ambition, Hypocrisy, and Carnal Pleasure; but Avarice, which
is initially an adjunct of Ambition, soon becomes autonomous,
whereas Hypocrisy is downgraded to the status of an attendant
on Ambition), all belong to that category of passions tradition-
ally designated as concupiscible.[69] These are the *passions vitieuses*
that Briçonnet had pointed out in an early letter to Marguerite.
He had explained that the prominence of these vicious (vitiat-
ing) passions in the contemporary world was the cause of the
deplorable spiritual barrenness of the Church. "La challeur d'avarice, ambicion et voluptueuse vie a deseché son eaue de vie, doctrine et exemplarité" (I.85) [The heat of avarice, ambition, and
carnal living has dried up the water of life, doctrine, and ex-
emplarity], he had written in 1521. In his letters, Briçonnet
condemned these vices, often citing I John 2.16. "Orguoeul, avarice et luxure" (I.167) [Pride, avarice and lust], he notes, were
sown in the human heart by the "prince de tenebres" [the prince
of shadows]. So rank are they that they stifle all other growth,
making it impossible for "la semance divine" [the divine seed]

69. In the *Republic* (IV, 441A), Plato distinguishes between rational, courageous, and
appetitive parts of the soul. Plato's terms—*Logistikon, Thumoeides, Epithumetikon*—were
rendered by Ficino as *ratio, iracundia*, and *concupiscentia*. Aristotle (*De anima*, 414b, Book
2, Chapter 3) divided the passions into two basic categories, the irascible and the concupiscible. By and large, the distinction between the irascible appetite and the concupiscible appetite was maintained in medieval and Renaissance theories of the passions. See
Anthony Levi, *French Moralists: The Theory of the Passions, 1585 to 1649* (Oxford: Clarendon Press, 1964), pp. 8–21.

to germinate and flourish in a soul given over to *concupiscentia*.

Throughout her poetry, Marguerite contends that the world dances to a tune called by the concupiscible passions. In her early *Dialogue en forme de vision nocturne*, Marguerite, manipulating the images and *topoi* that Briçonnet had provided in his first long letters, represented godlessness as the reign of "plaisir, richesse, honneur" (221), a sinister triad that later in the same poem is identified as "plaisir, honneur, proffit" (1157) and again as "plaisir, bien, honneur" (1171). Although this theme reappears in nearly all of her major poems,[70] it is elaborated more extensively in Book II of *Les Prisons* than elsewhere. Emphasizing the extent to which the concupiscible appetite determines behavior at court, Marguerite stresses first the ritual of festive dining:

II.280   J'entray au lieu où ung tresgrand festin
          L'on prepara, si plain de friandises
          Qu'il incittoit gourmandz à gourmandises,
          Et le bon vin, tant delicat et souef,
          Et puys je viz sortir de l'habundance
285   Les enyvrez, et commancer la danse. . . .

I entered a place where a great banquet was being prepared, so full of special dishes that it incited gluttons to gluttony; and good wine, so delicate and smooth; and then I saw them, drunk, leave the table of plenty and begin to dance. . . .

Surrounded by beautiful women, *Amy* decided that he would "des femmes user . . . ainsy comme fait une beste, / Sans passion" (II.311–14) [use women as an animal does, without affection]. Promising himself never to marry or be bound to another woman, neither wife nor mistress, he says "je useray de toutes à loysir, / Sans nul travail, pour y prendre plaisir" (II.337–38) [I will use them all leisurely, without any concern, so that I can take my pleasure]. He then gives a lengthy description of the training he must undergo in order to learn the part he intends to play in the *theatrum mundi*:

70. See Glasson's edition of *Les Prisons* (p. 26) for a partial listing of the passages in Marguerite's poetry in which the theme appears.

II.340

> Je m'essayray de farder mon visaige,
> Et d'accoustrer et pollir mon langaige,
> De deviser nouveaulx habillemens,
> De bien danser, de jouer d'instrumens,
> De manier chevaualx et porter armes,
> De feindre avoir souvent aux yeulx les larmes. . . .

I shall try to paint my face and to adorn and polish my language, to make up new ways of dressing, to dance well, to play musical instruments, to handle horses and carry arms, to pretend often to have tears in my eyes. . . .

Amy realizes that to succeed he must modulate his performance in such a way that his persona conforms in every particular to the codes that transmit value in the society he wishes to enter. Further, he understands that signification is embodied in both linguistic and nonlinguistic signs. Marguerite's depiction of the *theatrum mundi* in *Les Prisons* is a duplication of her representation of the world of matter (of the letter) in *L'Inquisiteur* and *Trop, Prou, Peu, Moins*. Here again Marguerite describes a world in which the pleasure principle has been displaced by the reality principle. Moreover, here, as in the two *comédies*, the reality principle is rendered in terms of an economic system that valorizes the active pursuit of profit. Even more than in the earlier works, Marguerite now stresses the dynamics of work. By giving special prominence to the performative aspect of *Amy*'s behavior, she demonstrates more clearly in *Les Prisons* than elsewhere what Herbert Marcuse, elaborating on Freud, calls the performance principle, which he defines as the prevailing historical form of the reality principle.[71] The acquisition of wealth is the goal that determines every detail of *Amy*'s performance; power and honor depend on the possession of "des biens" (II.377). Acquisition and performance can occur, of course, only within a temporal framework. As we saw in *L'Inquisiteur* and *Trop, Prou, Peu, Moins*, time is the constitutive element in a world ruled by the reality principle. Since narrative is the linguistic mode especially suited to translate the concept of temporality, *Amy*'s account of his experiences along the *via mundi*

---

71. Herbert Marcuse, *Eros and Civilization* (New York: Vintage Books, 1955), p. 32.

("Lors m'advisay et le chemin cherchay / Duquel pensoys avoir meilleur marché," I.397–98) [Then I deliberated and looked for the road I thought would have the best business] is expressed in a narrative whose unfolding is marked by temporal deictics: "Et me trouvay à ce commancement / Bien recuillez de tous humainement" (II.399–400) [And, at this beginning, I found myself greeted very courteously by all]; "Et peu à peu, et degré à degré, / Montay tousjours . . ." (II.405–406) [And little by little and step by step I continued to climb]; "J'aquis honneur par travail, et fuz riche / Soudainement" (II.407–408) [I acquired honor by work and was suddenly rich]. He worked tirelessly to increase his wealth:

> Tant me brulloit ceste concupiscence
> II.410 Que je n'avoys moyen, force ou puyssance
> De vivre en paix, ne de me reposer,
> Mais sans dormir ne cessoys d'exposer
> Mon temps, mon corps, ma vie et ma santé,
> Pour avoir biens et honneurs à planté.
> 415 Plaisir m'estoit d'endurer froit et chault
> Pour aquerir chose qui trop myeulx vault;
> De çà, de là, je couroys sans cesser;
> Importuner sçavoys bien et presser,
> Tant qu'à la fin j'emportoys quelque plume!

This lust burned in me so much that I had no way, no strength or power to live in peace or to rest; but without sleeping I constantly sacrificed time, my body, my life and my health to have riches and honors in abundance. For me it was a pleasure to endure cold and heat to acquire something of much value; hither and yon I ran ceaselessly; I knew well how to importune and press so that in the end I would carry off some feather!

Amy's acquisitive spirit soon prompted him to collect books. His attitude toward books is similar to his attitude toward women: they are tools he can use. From books he learns how to manipulate language in ways that allow him to dominate society. His persona is above all a linguistic construct, a point he stresses in a significant passage that, despite its length, deserves to be cited in full.

Cela me fist des livres assembler
II.435 Pour myeulx sçavoir racompter leurs histoires
Dont les escriptz ramentent les memoyres,
Pour myeulx *parler* des sciences exquises
Pour bien sçavoir prononcer toutes langues,
440 Affin de faire en tous pays harangues:
Car à tous ceulx qui font de longs voyaiges,
Est bien requis de sçavoir tous langaiges;
Et l'on a veu, par estre embassadeur
Et bien *parler*, parvenir à grandeur.
445 Des advocatz chanceliers ont esté
Par leur *parler* bien propre et affetté;
D'embassadeurs cardinaulx on a faictz,
De cardinaulx, papes sainctz et parfaictz;
Faictz ont esté empereurs et vaincueurs
450 Ceulx qui ont sceu gaigner hommes et cueurs
Par bien *parler*, par vives oraisons,
Par art subtil, par tresfortes raisons.
Donques je veulx avoir doresnavant
Le bruyt d'estre ung homme sage et sçavant:
455 Par ce sçavoir, du prince on a l'oreille,
Par bien *parler*, au conseil on conseille,
Le bien *parlant* trouve assez qui l'escoute,
Du bien *parlant* nul ignorant n'a doubte.
Je *parleray* myeulx que tous, si je puys:
460 Les livres j'ay qui sont la porte et l'huys
Par où l'on va à l'honneur de science.
Repoz n'auray, ny paix, ny passience
Que à bien *parler* ne soye parvenu.   (my emphasis)

That made me collect books; to know better how to tell their stories, the written accounts of which recall the past; to talk more knowledgeably about the excellent learning that is so much sought after by the curious; to know how to speak all languages in order to deliver orations in every country; because for all those who go on long voyages it is quite necessary to know all languages; and there have been cases in which, by being an ambassador and speaking well, one has arrived at greatness. Judges have been considered able and crafty because of their speech; cardinals have been made from ambassadors; from cardinals, holy and perfect popes; emperors and conquerors have been made from those who managed to persuade men and hearts by speaking well, by lively speeches, by subtle art, by very strong arguments. Therefore I want from now on to have the reputation of being a wise and learned man; by this learning, one has the ear of the prince; by speaking well, one gives counsel to the council; he who speaks well easily finds people who will listen to him; no unlearned person suspects someone who speaks well. I shall speak better than everyone, if I can. I have books, which are the door and gateway through which one goes toward a reputation for learning. I shall have no rest, no peace, no patience until I succeed in speaking well.

The key element in the *par-être Amy* constructs is *parole*. The association of *par-être* and *parole* is not accidental. The two words are linked etymologically, for *parole* is composed of the prefix *para* and the Greek verb *ballein*, meaning "to throw." In Marguerite's text, the *couverture* or *vestissement* that (repeating Besnard-Coursodon's phrase) "fonde le paraître" is mainly *parole*. Once more Marguerite allegorizes the Pauline duality of letter and spirit. The letter is *parole* or *paraître* (in Briçonnet's terminology, *Verbe*), whereas the spirit, which is identical with *être*, transcends language. *Amy*'s error in Book II is basically the same as his error in Book I: he confuses *paraître* with *être* and, failing to see in the letter a sign of the spirit, becomes, in Augustine's words, "entangled in a perverse sweetness." There he will remain until, compelled by a force outside himself, he begins to recognize his mistake. Only after his eyes are cleansed will he learn to read correctly—that is to say, will he learn to distinguish between *par-être* and *être* and then, eventually, to discern the presence of the *Tout-Verbe* in the *Verbe*.

As in the *Petit Oeuvre*, the outside force in Book II of *Les Prisons* is incarnated in the figure of an old man. In a harangue that extends over 457 lines, an old man tells *Amy* that, instead of being free, he is in fact more securely imprisoned than when he was in the Tower of Love. Moreover, continues the old man, it is better to be a captive in the Tower of Love than to submit to the "troys tyrans" (II.502) who now control *Amy*'s life. Revealing himself little by little to be a defender of Neoplatonic ideals, the old man notes that *Amy*'s love for *Amye* remained carnal. *Amy*'s error was not in loving *Amye* but in failing to use, in the Augustinian sense, this love to propel himself toward a "higher" goal. In other words, his love became idolatrous (". . . cest amour se peult dire ydolatre," II.563) [one can call this love idolatrous],

and *Amy*, instead of moving toward the paradise for which he
yearned, found himself on a false course, "so that," in Augustine's words, "[he was] retarded in obtaining those things which
are to be enjoyed, or even prevented altogether, shackled by an
inferior love" (DDC I.3.9).

At the end of Book I, the sunlight that streams into the tower
permits *Amy* to "see" that he has mistaken fiction ("o seure fiction . . . o trop double dissimulation") for reality, *par-être* for
être. Similarly, the old man's harangue in Book II allows *Amy* to
understand that his incessant activity is motivated by "ung desir
de vertueux *paraistre*" (II.595, my emphasis) [a desire to appear
courageous] and not by a desire to *be* courageous. The old man
does not of course condemn desire. Rather he condemns *Amy*'s
refusal to distinguish between the outside and the inside, between, as he puts it, the word and the thing.

> Ambition de si mauvais renom
> Vous embrassez, ayant d'honneur le nom,
> II.625   Mais si elle estoit devant voz yeulx desclose,
> Vous trouveriez que le nom et la chose
> Sont differentz. . . .

You embrace ambition with its very bad reputation as having the name
of honor; but if it were revealed before your eyes, you would find that
the name and the thing are different. . . .

By expressing the difference between *par-être* and *être* in terms
of the difference between word and thing, the text invites both
an intertextual and a metatextual reading. Ever since Cicero
fixed the distinction between *verba* and *res*, discussions of reality
and the linguistic constructs designed to represent reality focused
on these two terms.[72] Examined by many writers, including Augustine and Erasmus, the polarity of words and things was a
convention derived from parts one and three of the five parts of
rhetoric. To *inventio* belonged the function of generating *res*
(ideas, concepts, topics) and to *elocutio* that of verbal elaboration. Erasmus, however, in his handbook *De duplici copia verborum ac rerum* (1514), a work that in many ways reflects the

---

72. On Cicero's distinction between *res* and *verba*, see Alain Michel, *Rhétorique et philosophie chez Cicéron* (Paris: Presses universitaires de France, 1960), pp. 278–79.

Renaissance attitude toward language, blurred the distinction
between the two by insisting that linguistic plenitude is attained
only when *verba* are informed by, or "filled with," *res*.[73] Since
"things" cannot become apparent except through language (in
this sense, language creates reality), *res* and *verba* are not two
distinct domains but rather aspects of a single domain—that of
language. When Marguerite's text is read in light of Erasmus'
text, it is apparent that Marguerite holds to an "older," more
medieval view. Like Erasmus, she was acutely aware of the generative power of language, but unlike him, she doubted that language had the power to generate anything but artifice and façade. Words, the old man reminds *Amy*, are the favorite tool of
"l'Ennemy" (II.648).

But Marguerite's poem is itself composed of "words." Is it
therefore artifice and façade? This question is implicit in the
text, which, by posing the problem of its own "reality," invites
a metatextual interpretation. On the narrative level, the function
of the old man is the same as that of Charlotte in the *Dialogue*, of
the mysterious figure in the *Petit Oeuvre*, of the angels in the
Comédie du désért, of Francis I in *La Navire*, indeed of Briçonnet
in Marguerite's poetic corpus as a whole. He is the intercessor
whose *parole* (*Verbe*) mediates *langue* (*Tout-Verbe*). He reveals to
the narrator the difference between *par-être* and *être*. In Marguerite's texts, this revelation is signaled first of all by an interruption of narrative flow. The syntagmatic axis of narrative, clearly
defined by temporal deictics that indicate succession within
a past time, is interrupted by an intercessor's discourse, which is
invariably marked by a preponderance of verbs that, being in
the present tense, trace a paradigmatic axis. "Je viens à vous"
(II.489) [I come to you], declares the old man as he appears before *Amy*, echoing the words of all the intercessors throughout
Marguerite's poetry. To convince the young man that what he
takes for "reality" is nothing but "masques" (II.613) and "couverture" (II.609), the "vieillart / Blanc et chenu, mais dispost et
gaillart" (II.473–74) [old man, white-headed, but lively and
cheerful] undermines *Amy*'s faith in the referentiality of language. There is, the old man says, an ontological gap between

73. See Terence Cave, "Enargeia: Erasmus and the Rhetoric of Presence in the Sixteenth Century," *L'Esprit Créateur* and his "Copia and Cornucopia," in *French Renaissance Studies 1540–70*, ed. Peter Sharratt. Both articles have been incorporated into Cave's
The Cornucopian Text: Problems of Writing in the French Renaissance.

what is (*res*) and the signs that mediate that which is. The fundamental question, then, comes down to reading the signs "correctly." *Amy*, "povre aveugle" (II.537) [poor blind man], had looked around him and interpreted the signs ("honneurs, / Plaisirs et biens," II.746–47) as a representation of reality. He had read the text (i.e., the *liber mundi*) on a purely mimetic level.

By its referential language and its stress on temporal evolution, the text encourages us to see *Amy*'s account of his successive "performances" in the world as a mimesis of the *theatrum mundi*. Michael Riffaterre has pointed out that "variation and multiplicity," that is to say movement, are essential to mimetic representation:

Now the basic characteristic of mimesis is that it produces a continuously changing semantic sequence, for representation is founded upon the referentiality of language, that is, upon a direct relationship of words to things. It is immaterial whether or not this relationship is a delusion of those who speak the language or of readers. What matters is that the text multiplies details and continually shifts its focus to achieve an acceptable likeness of reality, since reality is normally complex. Mimesis is thus variation and multiplicity.[74]

Riffaterre's distinction between heuristic reading and hermeneutic reading helps us to understand the semiotic process whereby both the reader of Marguerite's poem and *Amy*, who is a reader of the *liber mundi*, "hurdle the mimesis"[75] and effect a transfer of signs from the mimetic level to a higher level of discourse in which the unit of significance is the text in its entirety. *Heuristic* reading, which is the initial or "simple" reading of the text, is "where the first interpretation takes place"[76] and is grounded on the assumption that language is referential, i.e., that words relate to things. Furthermore, this first interpretation, which results in the perception of mimesis, is coextensive with the decoding of the poem that begins as the reader follows the syntagmatic unfolding of the text, reading line after line and page after page in a linear, predetermined fashion. *Hermeneutic* reading, which for Augustine is "correct" reading, is a second (Riffaterre

74. Michael Riffaterre, *Semiotics of Poetry* (Bloomington, Ind.: Indiana University Press, 1978), p. 2.
75. Ibid., p. 5.
76. Loc. cit.

calls it a "retroactive") reading in which the reader, remembering what he has just read, modifies his understanding of the text in light of what he is deciphering. Riffaterre notes that the integration of signs from the mimetic level into the higher level of significance, which is the semiotic process, "really takes place in the reader's mind, and it results from a second reading."[77] Revising and composing backwards, the reader surmounts mimesis and performs a structural decoding that allows him to integrate all the seemingly disparate or deviant elements of the poem. Thus hermeneutic reading produces significance that extends across the whole text, whose beginning and end are now perceived as related.

When the old man in Book II tells *Amy* that words and things are different (II.626–27), he denies the referentiality of language and discredits mimesis, which is dependent on the perception of language as referential. What he tries to do, in effect, is persuade *Amy* to move from one level of reading to another. His statement that "le nom et la chose / Sont differentz" expresses a truth that *Amy*, in a sense, understood dimly from the moment he entered the world, for he perceived at once that dissimulation governs relationships in society. And yet, such was *Amy*'s passionate commitment to the world that he persisted in his heuristic reading of the *liber mundi*. By reminding *Amy* of the difference between word and thing, the old man seeks to encourage him to perform a structural decoding of the *liber mundi* in order to arrive at a significance that, in Augustinian terms, has always been there (truth is always present everywhere) but that was obscured by a "faulty" reading of the text. In other words, he encourages *Amy* to read the text hermeneutically.

To this end, he points out that time, identical with the syntagmatic flow on which mimesis depends, brings nothing but loss, illness, decay, and dissolution to all material things, including, of course, the text itself to the extent that it is a *corps charnel*. The surmounting of time will be a sign that *Amy* has "hurdled the mimesis" and reached the second stage of reading. This moment comes when *Amy*, heeding the old man's advice to read and reread classical texts and Scripture until the virtues "qui dedans sont encloses / Devant vos yeux soient du tout descloses" (II.895–96) [which are enclosed within will open up before your

77. Ibid., p. 4.

eyes], decides to abandon the incessant activity that had characterized his life in the world and resolves *to sit down*. "En l'escoutant ma veue n'espergnay, / Et pour le veoir, myeulx à mon gré m'assis" (II.946–47) [Listening to him I did not spare my sight, and in order to see him better I made up my mind to sit down], *Amy* says, marking the point at which the syntagmatic axis, which is dominant in heuristic reading, is displaced by the paradigmatic axis, along which hermeneutic reading is organized.

The shift from syntagmatic to paradigmatic flow had been prepared by the old man, who had advised *Amy* to study books until he could discern in them paradigms that would serve as models for his own conduct. In effect, the old man had told *Amy* to stop reading the *liber mundi* and to devote his energies to a concentrated study of Greek and Roman texts and, above all, Scripture, for it is in Scripture that *Amy* will find the supreme paradigmatic figure of Christ ("Et Jesuchrist y est mys pour exemple," II.922) [And Jesus Christ is put there as a model]. Giving up the constant activity that made him resemble Martha, *Amy* sits down and, in the state of physical if not spiritual repose that characterizes Mary, begins to read "livres de toutes sortes" (II.1033) [books of all kinds]. Two books, however, are of special importance: "le discours de Dante" (II.1055) and I John, particularly Chapter Two, in which the "trois puyssans" (II.1060) [three powerful ones] that govern the world of matter are identified and condemned.

Even as he tells how the chains of ambition and hypocrisy fell from him while he read books that were "rempliz de . . . saige parler" (II.975) [full of wise speaking], *Amy* is *already* at the end of his spiritual adventure. The conclusion of Book II, like that of Book I, is addressed to *Amye*, who, being the reader of *Amy*'s account, is the fictional incarnation of the reader of Marguerite's text. Exhorting *Amye* to follow his example and to read "de l'oeil interieur" (II.993) [with an inner eye], *Amy* urges the reader to "hurdle the mimesis" and perform a structural decoding that will generate significance. Such a decoding, which is synonymous with hermeneutic reading, can be accomplished, however, only by a second reading. Marguerite's text never lets the reader forget that *Amy*, even at the beginning of the poem, has already completed the experiences he relates. Thus his account constitutes for him a kind of second reading in which all textual elements relate to each other in such a way that significance can be produced. Like Christ, who is the custodian and guarantor of a truth the Christian can see clearly only after he has completed his earthly life, *Amy* is the custodian and guarantor of a significance that the reader can perceive only after he has read the text in its entirety. *Amy*'s exhortations at the end of Books I and II serve to remind the readers (both *Amye* and the reader of Marguerite's text) that they are not yet in a position to discover the full significance of the text. They must continue to read, being mindful of the fact that only by transcending mimesis, or the letter, can they reach the goal of all reading, which is the discovery of significance, or perception of the spirit.

BOUND BY BOOKS

Like matter that awaits the illuminating grace of spirit, Book III, which is nearly twice the length of Books I and II combined, is massive and, in parts, opaque. Central to the poetics of the text is a *technè* capable of animating (from *anima*, "soul") this dense textual mass. The first lines of Book III announce the thematics of movement, more specifically, of ascent. Reminding *Amye* that he is relating the process whereby he reached "perfection" (or, as a reader, the process whereby he perceived—or produced—significance in the text before him), *Amy* begins Book III by saying that he was not content to climb higher and higher himself but wanted to help *Amye* ascend too. The opening lines of Book III trace a circuit of communication between high and low, soul and matter, spirit and letter, that expresses in a thematic register the dynamism, or *enargeia*, that both animates the text and informs our reading of the poem, a reading that culminates in the production of significance. To clarify the nature of this *enargeia*, which runs through the whole of *Les Prisons*, indeed, through the whole of Marguerite's poetry, is the central concern in our discussion of Book III.

Near the end of Book II, the old man had identified himself as an *amateur de science* ("Amy, j'ay nom de Science Amateur," II.937). Analogous to the *Sage* in *Mont-de-Marsan*, he embodies the *exhilaratio voluntatis* and the aspirations of Renaissance Humanism. Like the *Sage*, he represents human learning, one of the most persistent temptations in Marguerite's poetry. Entering the world of books at the end of Book II, *Amy* believed that he had escaped from the closed world of ambition and avarice.

With a sense of liberation, he began to read books, which seemed to him to define an open system of limitless space and infinitely expanding horizons. The first few pages of Book III make it plain, however, that *Amy* did not find in books the freedom he sought. Once again he was guilty of idolatry. Worshiping *sçavoir*, he built around himself another prison. Books are pillars that sustain the edifice in which he finds himself entrapped throughout the first part of Book III.

Amy's liberation from the Tower of Love and his entry into the world of nature and of human society can be related, as we have seen, to Lacanian categories. Having first defined self in the order of the Imaginary, *Amy* restructured self in the order of the Symbolic when he left the Tower of Love and moved into society. The world of books he entered at the end of Book II and in which he feels entrapped at the beginning of Book III is a further manifestation of the Symbolic. Indeed, the prison in which *Amy* is now confined is a more exact representation of the Lacanian order of the Symbolic than the prison of worldly ambition had been; for the prison of *sçavoir* is a prison-house of language, and language, for Lacan, is the mark of the Symbolic order.

Like the first two prisons, the prison of learning is the product of a misdirected will. Each of the prisons in Marguerite's text is built by a willful self that "enjoys" (". . . mes pilliers de beaulx livres / Dont je receuz mainctz plaisirs," III.35–36) [my pillars of beautiful books, from which I received much pleasure] what ought to be "used." Describing the *prison de science*, *Amy* names the nine pillars, or branches of learning, that support the edifice in which he is confined. Simone Glasson has pointed out that there seems to be a hierarchical modeling in *Amy*'s description of his prison.[78] With only two exceptions, *Amy* devotes an increasing number of lines to his description of succeeding pillars.

Philosophy	ll.37–48	total lines 12
Poetry	ll.49–64	total lines 16
Law	ll.65–84	total lines 20
Mathematics	ll.85–108	total lines 24
Music	ll.109–114	total lines 6
Medicine	ll.115–168	total lines 54

---

78. *Les Prisons*, ed. Glasson, p. 30.

History   ll. 169–198   total lines 30
Rhetoric   ll. 199–228   total lines 30
Theology   ll. 229–328   total lines 100

Although music, one of the exceptions, appears as a separate pillar, it follows mathematics, from which it is derived and to which it is appended in Marguerite's text as a kind of afterthought. Line 109, which is the first line devoted to the evocation of music as a branch of learning, does not even begin a sentence but serves to continue *Amy*'s praise of geometrical shapes and numbers. Music appears in the text only as an illustration of one of the functions to which mathematics can be put. If *Amy* devotes only a few lines to music (we have seen that for Marguerite music symbolizes the nonlinguistic circuit of communication that signifies *unio* and, as such, would not figure prominently in an emblem of human knowledge), he gives considerable attention to medicine, which, as Ferdinand Brunot notes,[79] was viewed throughout the Renaissance as one of the most important branches of learning. Marguerite obviously attached importance to the number nine, for after describing the ninth pillar, that of theology, *Amy* discussed two additional branches of learning, grammar and cosmography, without, however, identifying them as the tenth and eleventh pillars. In addition to being the square of three, the number nine is "almost complete" by virtue of its nearness to the perfect number, ten.[80] Number nine is, then, a sign that perfection, or the end, is at hand.

Because of the hierarchical pattern formed by the nine pillars, Marguerite's emblematic representation of the prison of knowl-

79. Ferdinand Brunot, *Histoire de la langue française des origines à nos jours* (Paris: Colin, 1966), II, 36. Cf. Robert Mandrou, *Introduction à la France moderne*, pp. 258–59. In the speech he delivered at Marguerite's funeral, Sainte-Marthe commented on Marguerite's interest in medicine: "Elle devisoit donc, à son disner et souper, . . . de Medecine, comme des viandes mal saines ou salubres au corps humain, et des choses naturelles, avec les sieurs Schyron, Cormier, Esterpin, ses medecins très experts et très doctes, qui soigneusement la regardaient boire et menger, comme l'on observe en cela les Princes" [She talked, then, at dinner and supper about medicine—discussing things such as foods that are harmful or wholesome for the human body, and natural things— with the gentlemen Schyron, Cormier, and Esterpin, her very skilled and very learned doctors, who carefully watched her eat and drink, as one observes princes at the table]. *Oraison funèbre de Marguerite de Navarre*, published in *L'Heptaméron*, ed. Le Roux de Lincy and Montaiglon (Paris: Auguste Eudes, 1880), I, p. 69.

80. Hopper, *Medieval Number Symbolism*, p. 10; see also pp. 60, 43–44, 102, 106.

edge resembles a late medieval or Renaissance *scala intellectualis*, many of which depicted nine steps leading from lower to higher levels of understanding.[81] Often the *scala intellectualis* leads up to the "castle of knowledge."[82] Furthermore, the notion of an orderly ascent leading from discrete branches of learning to an *intellectus conjunctus*, or an "integrated understanding" of all human knowledge, appeared frequently in the literature of the period. Representations of the *scala intellectualis* and of the castle of knowledge are graphic reminders of Humanistic aspirations. *Amy*'s initial exhilaration and passion for learning surely reflect Marguerite's own respect for Humanistic goals. And yet Marguerite's whole point is that human knowledge, i.e., knowledge that can be contained in language, is infinitely removed from the knowledge the Christian seeks. Unlike those of her contemporaries who delighted in man's ability to construct the temple of knowledge, Marguerite, after fashioning the edifice of learning in the first part of Book III, demonstrates the inadequacy, the emptiness or vanity, of human knowledge. Like Montaigne, who, in his *Apologie de Raymond Sebond*, casts doubt on man's power to arrive at certain and absolute truth, Marguerite doubts man's ability to attain knowledge of Christ through the human instrument of language.

The last three pillars, in particular, are described as linguistic constructs. History is a series of "exemples" (III. 183) and "proverbes" (III. 190) that are bound together in "beaulx livres . . . [qui] sont à ouvrir bien faciles" (III. 188–91) [beautiful books that are easy to open]. Repeating the Ciceronian dictum of *historia magistra vitae*[83] ("Les faictz passez sont maistres des presens," III. 187) [Past deeds are the masters of present ones], Marguerite introduces into *Amy*'s discourse an intertextual element that, by calling attention to literary tradition, underscores the notion of linguistic artifact. Moving from the pillar of history to that of rhetoric, *Amy* points out the verbal nature of the castle of

81. For a discussion of the *scala intellectualis*, see S. K. Heninger, Jr., *The Cosmographical Glass*, pp. 160–63.

82. Robert Recorde used the expression as the title of his textbook, *The Castle of Knowledge*, published in London in 1556.

83. Cicero, *De Oratore*, Loeb Classical Library (Cambridge: Harvard University Press, 1959–60), II.9.36. For a discussion of Cicero's dictum as it applies to Montaigne, see Karlhinz Stierle, "L'Histoire comme exemple, l'exemple comme histoire," *Poétique*, 10 (1972), pp. 176–98.

knowledge by stressing the purely linguistic composition of the eighth pillar (rhetoric). Consisting of books "de tous pays et langues" (III.201) [of all countries and languages], the pillar of rhetoric is composed of "parolles" (III.218 and 220) ". . . [qui] sont doulcement portées aux oreilles" (III.222) [which are carried gently to the ears]. The pillar of theology, too, is made up of *parolles*, for it consists of countless numbers of exegetical texts designed to interpret Scripture—glosses, translations, paraphrases. Discouraged by contradictions in these books, *Amy* sensed dimly that *différence* is a sign of error, of misreading ("Leur different en herreur me tenoit," III.266) [their difference kept me in error]. He continued to read, however, aware that the "Saint Esprit," ever identical to Itself, is incarnated in the imperfect and fragmented "esprit" that circulates through every individual text.

To build the pillar of theology, *Amy* first moved into place the heavier, more opaque volumes, which form the base of the column. At the top of the pillar, he placed "la Bible admirable / Comme le but où tous les autres tendent" (III.272–73) [the wonderful Bible, as the goal to which all the others tend]. The Bible is the model text that all other texts seek to imitate; indeed, a work's "worth" is determined by the degree to which it duplicates Scripture. All texts are mimetic in the sense that they are all imperfect representations of a model text. At the same time, however, the model text is itself a human (and therefore flawed) representation of primary reality, which, although immanent in language, cannot be contained in human speech and in time. The centrality of time (or, in a purely textual register, allegory) in Marguerite's work is a consequence of her use of what Joseph Mazzeo, speaking of Augustine, calls "mimetic dialectic,"[84] which he defines as a progression from sense to thought, from flesh to spirit, from "a lower 'imitation' to a more real archetype which may in turn be 'mimetic' relative to something still higher."[85] The dialectical nature of the particular kind of mimesis presented in Marguerite's text is demonstrated in the hierarchical modeling not only of the pillars themselves but in the composition of individual pillars, especially that of theology (exegesis at

84. "St. Augustine's Rhetoric of Silence: Truth vs. Eloquence and Things vs. Signs," in *Renaissance and Seventeenth-Century Studies* (New York: Columbia University Press, 1964), p. 23.
85. Ibid., p. 27.

the bottom, Scripture at the top), which, incidentally, follows the pillar of rhetoric just as divine eloquence follows and transcends human eloquence. This modeling serves as a graphic illustration of one of the notions underlying mimetic dialectic: all thought, Augustine wrote, moves "from the exterior to the interior, from the lower to the higher" (*ab exterioribus ad interiora, ab inferioribus ad suprema*—*Enarr. in Ps.*, 14.5; PL 27, col. 1887). Stating a concept of reading similar to Augustine's concept of "correct reading," *Amy* says that for the man who is "du Saint Esprit apris" (III.284) [instructed by the Holy Spirit] reading is an interpretative exercise, the purpose of which is to discover the signs that point to an indivisible and higher reality, i.e., Christ the Word.

Confined in the Tower of Knowledge he had built, *Amy* did not at first read "correctly." He saw "la lettre et la figure" (III.295) [the letter and the image] of the texts before him but not the spirit immanent in them. He was, as he puts it, "enfermé dans la lettre" (III.329) [enclosed in the letter]. "Je n'avoys laisse nulle fenestre / Pour veoir dehors" (III.348–49) [I had not left any window through which I could see outside], he notes. Although *Amy* remained motionless in his prison, his mind was not at rest. With great insistence, he speaks of his intellectual and spiritual agitation. Prompted by "le desir d'aprendre" (III.375) [the desire to learn] and "le cuyder de sçavoir" (III.376) [the presumptuous ambition to know], he pursued every question, searching for answers, reasons, explanations. Again and again he stresses activity and movement: "Faisoit mon cueur courir de grand ardeur" (III.366) [Made my heart beat quickly with great ardor]; "Sans cesser couroys par fantasie" (III.368) [Ceaselessly, I ran where my imagination took me]; "Me proumenant en mille questions" (III.373) [Examining a thousand questions]. Within the economy of Book III, *Amy*'s incessant intellectual activity is analogous to his constant physical movement in Book II. In both cases, he is driven by a desire that at first leads him into error but that keeps him looking for the locus of true joy, which is Christ.

Recalling his third prison, *Amy* realizes that his infatuation with books was a manifestation of *cuyder*, from which God sought to protect man by forbidding Adam to eat the fruit of the tree of knowledge. Like Adam, *Amy*, however, could not resist temptation: "Je desiroys le plaisant fruit manger / De tout sçavoir" (III.385–86) [I wanted to eat the pleasing fruit of all

knowledge]. At this point in the text, Marguerite begins to asso-
ciate *Amy* with Adam. *Amy* becomes a symbol of mankind, who
fell into error but will be redeemed through Christ. Narrating the
story of *Amy*/Adam, Marguerite's text imitates Scripture, the
model text, which, for a Christian, relates the only story there is
to tell. Seeing in the text a "copy" of the model text, which is
itself the embodiment of a still "higher," invisible text, the reader
of *Les Prisons* is led by degrees to the realization that he is being
asked to give a metatextual interpretation to the work he is reading. The unfolding of this metatextual interpretation is coextensive with the reader's understanding of the text's significance.

   Amy mistook the prison of knowledge for the paradise he had
longed for. He would have stayed there indefinitely had God not
chosen to show him his error. In Marguerite's works, awareness
of the true way is always an unmerited gift that comes from God.
As *Amy* puts it:

> Ung tel estat jamais n'eusse laissé
> Si le Treshault ne se fust abessé,
> Ainsy qu'il fist, quand Adam regarda
> III.420   Qui au beau fruict sa main trop hazarda.
> Et me voyant au milieu des delices
> D'ung paradis (ce sembloit) loing de vices,
> Dont ne vouloys ny ne povoys vuyder,
> Pris et lyé finement d'ung cuyder
> Faulx et menteur, contraire à verité.

I would never have left such a state if the most High had not lowered
Himself, as He did when He looked at Adam, who rashly moved his
hand toward the beautiful fruit. And He saw me in the middle of the
delights of a paradise (so it seemed) far from vices, which I neither
wanted to nor was able to leave, caught and bound cunningly by a false
and lying presumptuousness contrary to truth.

The "Tres Hault," being the Word, reveals Himself in the only
way He can—through the word, that is to say, through the text,
which is synonymous with His creation or His incarnation. "Par
un seul mot" (III.466) [By a single word], *Amy* says ecstatically,
God showed him his error and the vanity, or emptiness, of knowledge. Using anaphora, a rhetorical device that appears in Marguerite's texts to mark the transcendence of a lower order by a
higher order that subsumes the first, *Amy* repeats the word *mot*:

Mot prononcé et digne d'estre ouy,
Mot par qui est tout le ciel resjouy,
Mot apportant aux mortz vie eternelle,
III.470   Innominable à la bouche charnelle,
Mis sur la terre et pour nous abregé;
Mot par qui est le monde soulagé,
L'enfer rompu, peché mort, et mort morte. . . .

Word, spoken and worthy of being heard; word, through which the whole heaven rejoices; word, carrying eternal life to the dead, unnameable by the carnal mouth, put on earth and for us reduced to its essential element; word, through which the world is consoled, hell torn apart, sin dead, and death dead. . . .

He then recounts the moment of *illuminatio*:

Et la façon fut en lisant ung texte
Où Jesuchrist sa bonté manifeste,
III.485   Disant à Dieu: "Pere, je te rendz graces,
Qui aux petis et à personnes basses
As revelé les tresors et secretz,
Et aux sçavans, gentz doctes et discretz,
Les as cachez; tel est ton bon plaisir."
490   Lisant ce mot, soudain me vint saisir
Une clarté plaisante à veoir et belle;
Mais sa lumiere et vertu estoit telle
Que l'oeil charnel la trouva importable,
Pour estre trop luysante et agreable.
495   Ce feu par qui tout mal est consummé,
Pour mon oeil cloz ne fut moins alumé
Dedans mon cueur, qui de luy fut espris
Avant que l'oeil l'eust conceu ne compris.

And it occurred while I was reading a text in which Jesus Christ manifests his goodness, saying to God: "Father, I am grateful to you for having revealed riches and secrets to the humble and to persons of low birth, and for having hidden them from the learned, from wise and prudent people; such is your good pleasure." As I was reading this passage, suddenly a light, pleasant to see and beautiful, came and took possession of me; but its brightness and strength was such that the carnal eye found it unbearable, for it was too dazzling and gracious. Although my eye was closed, this fire by which all evil is destroyed, was nevertheless lighted in my heart, which was enthralled by it before the eye had apprehended or understood it.

Condemnation of the reader's tendency to see texts as "things" rather than as "signs" of the reign of charity comes from Scripture. Marguerite's own text not only imitates the Bible but incorporates Scripture into its own folds, for *Amy* cites (485–89 above) the Scriptural passage that permitted him to perceive the unsubstantiality of the castle of knowledge: "I bless you, Father, Lord of heaven and of earth, for hiding these things from the learned and the clever and revealing them to mere children. Yes, Father, for that is what it pleased you to do" (Matthew 11.25–26).

Few ideas are more common in Marguerite's work than the notion that the humble and the weak are ultimately elevated above the wise and the powerful. Frequent in Paul's Epistles, attacks on human knowledge, or, more precisely, on the *cuyder* or presumption that inevitably attends it, appear often in the works of writers sympathetic to the *Devotio moderna*. Jacques Lefèvre d'Etaples defended his translation of the New Testament by citing in his *Epistre exhortatoire*[86] the passage from Matthew that "stopped" (III.499) *Amy* (stopped him from reading further, stopped the flow of narrative in the text) and illuminates a central feature of Christian faith. The children in *L'Inquisiteur* and the *Ravie* in *Mont-de-Marsan* both illustrate the Scriptural dictum that truth is hidden from the "wise," who are proud of their knowledge, but revealed to those who are "wrapped in humility" (I Peter 5.5), for, in the words of Jesus: "The one who makes himself as little as this little child is the greatest in the kingdom of heaven" (Matthew 18.4).

Like the sun that broke into the Tower of Love at the end of Book II, the *illuminatio* that *Amy* experiences in Book III pierces the wall of the prison (the wall of flesh) and touches his heart. But the prison does not immediately collapse. Just as in Book I, *Amy* at first resists the truth.

> Bien longuement ceste luicte dura
> Entre nous deux, dont mon cueur endura
> Par maincte année et longue experience,

---

86. See *Les Prisons*, ed. Glasson, p. 305.

Par mainct tourment et maincte impassience,
III.515   Tant de douleurs, qu'à la fin se rendit,
Quand dans ce feu une voix entendit.   (my emphasis)

For a very long time this struggle between the two of us lasted; for many years and through long trials, through much anguish and much agitation, my heart suffered so much sorrow that it finally surrendered when it heard a voice in this fire.

He resisted until he heard a voice that spoke to him from the fire that burned in his heart, "ce feu par qui tout mal est consummé" (III.495) [this fire by which all evil is destroyed]. Coming to him out of the purifying element of fire, the voice is a response to *Amy*'s dissatisfaction with the multiplicity of words that veil the truth. It "answers" *Amy*'s growing desire for Christ the Word.

"I AM WHO I AM"

The voice *Amy* heard was the voice of God as reported in Exodus 3.14: "And God said to Moses, 'I Am who I Am [*EGO SUM QUI SUM*]. This,' he added, 'is what you must say to the sons of Israel: I Am has sent me to you.'"

C'est ceste voix qui au buysson ardant
Fist au pasteur, qui estoit attendant,
De son Sainct Nom la verité sçavoir:
III.520   "Je suys qui suys, que oeil vivant ne peult veoir."
Ceste voix là, ceste parolle vive,
Où nostre chair ne congnoist fondz ne rive,
Me print, mua et changea si soudain,
Que je perdis mon cuyder faulx et vain.
525   Car en disant: "Je suys qui suys", tel maistre
M'aprint alors lequel estoit mon estre:
S'il est qui est, hors de luy je ne puys
Dire de moy, sinon que je ne suys;
Si rien ne suys, las! où est ma fiance,
530   Vertu, bonté et droicte conscience?
Or suys je riens, s'il est Celluy qui est!

It is this voice that, in the burning bush, revealed to the shepherd who was waiting, the truth of his Holy Name: "I am who I am, which no living eye can see." That voice, that living word, in which our flesh discerns no bottom or shore, seized me, altered and changed me so suddenly that I lost my false and empty presumptuousness. For by saying "I am who I am," such a master taught me what my being was. If he is what is, outside of him I cannot say of myself anything except that I am not; if I am nothing, alas, where is my confidence, strength, goodness and firm conscience? Then I am nothing if He is the one who is!

The exultant line "Or suys je riens, s'il est Celluy qui est!" expresses *Amy*'s understanding that if God *is*, that is to say, if all that exists is enfolded in Him, then he, *Amy*, has no existence outside God. Because God is coterminous with everything, we cannot even speak of something existing outside God. I Am negates *Amy*'s *has been*. By saying I Am, "Verité . . . sçait cuyder abattre" (III. 534) [Truth . . . succeeds in crushing presumptuousness] and frees *Amy* from the prison of knowledge.

At the same time, I Am frees *Amy* from self. When *Amy* says that he is *riens*, he is observing that he has moved out of the Lacanian category of the Symbolic and into what I have called the category of the Iconic. *Amy* does not now distinguish between "self" and "other." The Christian who has understood the significance of the words I Am *is* in fact an other. Seeking to represent this perception (and striving to compel the reader to share it), the text conspires to become iconic in just the way the *Miroir de l'âme pécheresse*, relating the same experience, sought to become an iconic text. The nowness of I Am makes narrative and allegory untenable because God, being a denial of time, is also a denial of narrative. Diachrony, the medium in which the castle of knowledge was constructed, is now viewed as an illusion, a misreading that resulted from excessive attention to the letter and neglect of significance.

Once again Marguerite uses anaphora to signal the cessation of temporal flow. The words *je suis* and *mot* are repeated over and over, stilling time and effacing from the text all traces of progression. The present tense of the verb displaces the past tense. To the extent that *Amy* relates a revelation that came to him at a particular moment (this he does, however, less and less throughout the rest of the poem), he continues to use the preterite. But to the degree that he moves out of narrative time and meditates on what *is* (this he does more and more), he uses the present tense. *Amy* soon ceases altogether to recount what happened to him and begins to meditate on what he sees before him, that is to say, reality, which, of course, is Christ and the reign of charity. That alone is. Furthermore, that is the only reality there has ever been. What *is* is in fact what was. Illuminated by this perception ("Viz la lumiere et entendiz ce mot / 'Je suys qui suys,'" III.640–61) [I saw the light and heard these words: "I Am who I Am"], *Amy* begins to understand that reading "correctly" means discerning Christ everywhere. To the eye that sees spiritually, Christian reality, which, being beyond time and space, is reflected rather than narrated, is everywhere present. The Christian's task is to discover in the multiple texts before him the iconic figure of Christ, which has to be there. Thus *Amy*, continuing to read, now sees I Am in the texts of Hermes Trismegistus (III.677), in the Book of Job (III.689), in the figure of Socrates (III.699), in the works of Plato (III.711).

Recounting his rereading of texts, *Amy* would seem to be reintroducing the notion of narrative, or time, into the work. In a sense, this is true, but the important point is that the narrative fragments that now appear in the poem are not only discontinuous but also circumscribed by the notions of atemporality and a-spatiality that inform the text. The idea of circumscription is expressed powerfully in the lines in which *Amy*, "tout [son] travail . . . tourné en repoz" (III.789) [all his work changed into rest], discovers that all texts contain the same identical discourse, which is the word of God ("ce beau mot," III.790) [this beautiful word], emblematized, here as in the *Miroir*, as a circle. Lines 791 to 826 are Marguerite's linguistic representation of the *Tout-Verbe*, of God's speech, which seeks to define Itself in terms comprehensible to man.

> "Je suys qui suys, fin et commancement,
> Le seul motif d'ung chascun element,
> Auquel tout est, et a vie, et se meult.
> Celluy qui est fait du tout ce qu'il veult:
> III.795 Du sercle rond sans la circunference,
> Par tous costez egal, sans difference,
> Commencement ne fin ne s'y retrouve,
> Et n'y a chose estant ou vieille ou neufve
> Qui de ce rond n'ayt pris creation
> 800 Et nourriture et conservation.
> Du monde tiens multitude et grandeur
> Dans ma divine eternelle rondeur.

La ligne suys, le chemin et la voye,
Par qui nully jamais ne se forvoye;
805   D'exterieur en l'interieur entre
Qui va par moy, et au milieu du centre
Me trouvera, qui suys le poinct unique,
La fin, le but de la Mathematique.
Le cercle suys dont toute chose vient,
810   Le poinct où tout retourne et se mainctient.
Je suys qui suys, triangle tresparfaict,
Le Tout Puyssant saige et bon en effaict,
Qui fuz, qui suys et seray à jamais,
L'eternel Dieu où n'y a si ne mais:
815   Pere puyssant du monde Createur,
Tressaige Filz du monde Redempteur,
Esprit Tressainct le monde illuminant,
Divinité les troys en ung tenant.
Brief, au neuf cieulx ne se voit nul aspect
820   Qui n'ayt à moy sa fin et son respect.
En ces papiers et livres n'a figure
Où ne soit veu, trop myeulx qu'en l'Escripture,
"Je suys qui suys", mais que l'espesse toille
De l'ignorent et trop aveugle voille
825   Soit mys à rien, aveques son venin,
Par mon clair feu et mon Esprit divin."

"I Am who I Am, end and beginning, the single cause of every element, that by which everything is and has life and moves, he who is made of everything he wishes; who is a round circle without circumference, the same from all sides, without difference; there is no beginning or end there; and nothing exists, either old or new, that has not been created by, and taken its nourishment and sustenance from, this circle. I hold the whole world and its grandeur within my divine and eternal roundness. I am the line, the road and the way by which no one ever goes astray; he who goes through me enters the interior from the exterior and will find me in the middle of the center, for I am the single point, the end, the ultimate of Mathematics. I am the circle from which everything comes, the point to which everything returns and in which everything is sustained. I Am who I Am, perfect triangle, the All Powerful, wise and good in action, who was, am, and ever will be, the eternal God in which there is no "if" or "but," the powerful Father, Creator of the world, the very wise Son, Redeemer of the world, the Very Holy Spirit illuminating the world, the Divinity, the three together in one. In short, throughout the nine heavens there can be seen no element that does not have in me its end and its cause. In these papers and books there is no image in which one cannot see, better than in scripture, "I Am who I Am"; but let the thick cloth of unknowing and the veil that blinds, and its poison, be reduced to nothing by my bright fire and my divine Spirit."

This speech is composed almost entirely of commonplaces drawn from older, authoritative texts.[87] That God's discourse is represented by commonplaces is appropriate, for He is literally a common place, a point of convergence.[88] The speech begins

87. We may here indicate some of the more obvious allusions in III.791–826. Line 791 is composed of two biblical quotations: Exodus 3.14 ("I Am who I Am") and Revelations 1.8 ("I am the Alpha and the Omega"). Line 813 comes from the second half of the same verse in Revelations (". . . says the Lord God, who is, who was, and who is to come, the Almighty."). The image of a circle whose center is everywhere and circumference nowhere had great appeal to the Renaissance mind and was used by many authors, including Nicholas of Cusa. On this image, see *Oeuvres complètes du Pseudo-Denys l'Aréopagite*, p. 40, Dorothy Koenigsberger, *Renaissance Man and Creative Thinking*, p. 125, and Anthony Wilden, "Changing Frames of Order: Cybernetics and the *Machina Mundi*," in *Communication and Control in Society*, ed. Klaus Krippendorff (New York: Gordon and Breach Science Publishers, 1979), pp. 9–29. The use of mathematics to support theological speculation was a feature of Cusanus' thought. The reference in line 807 to God as "le point unique" may also suggest Cusanus, who offered a mathematical explanation of God as a point; see Glori Cappello, "Nicolò Cusano nella corrispondenza di Briconnet con Margherita di Navarra," in *Medioevo*, I (1975), 118–19. However, this concept predates Cusa. In *Revelations of Divine Love*, which dates from 1373, or twenty-eight years before Cusanus' birth, Juliana of Norwich wrote: "And after this, I saw God in a point; that is to say, in my understanding: by which sight I saw that he is in all things" (ch. 26, p. 67). The idea that God could be represented as a triangle (811) was common, for a triangle served to emblematize the Trinity. The juxtaposition of triangle and circle had appeared in the *Roman de la rose*: "Cest le cercle triangulier / Et le triangle cerculier" (II.19.510) [It is the triangular circle and the circular triangle]. Lines 823–24 are derived from II Corinthians 3.14–15: "And anyway their minds had been dulled; indeed, to this very day, that same veil is still there when the old covenant is being read, a veil never lifted, since Christ alone can remove it. Yes, even today, whenever Moses is read, the veil is over their minds." The comment in line 794 that in God the will and the act are identical reminds us of Romans 7.15, in which Paul laments that man fails to do what he wants to do and does the very things he hates. On the allusion to "neuf cieulx" (819) [nine heavens], see note 79 above.

88. On the commonplace in Renaissance thought, see Rosalie L. Colie, *The Resources of Kind: Genre-Theory in the Renaissance* (Berkeley: University of California Press, 1973), p. 33, Eugene F. Rice, *The Renaissance Idea of Wisdom*, op. cit., and Walter J. Ong, "Commonplace Rhapsody: Ravisius Textor, Zwinger and Shakespeare," in *Classical Influences on European Culture A.D. 1500–1700*, ed. R. R. Bolgar (Cambridge: Cambridge University Press, 1976), pp. 91–126. One of the major themes in Marc Fumaroli's *L'Age de l'éloquence: rhétorique et "res literaria" de la Renaissance au seuil de l'époque classique* (Geneva: Droz, 1980) is the establishment in the Renaissance of a "rhétorique des citations," a form of chastened, anti-aesthetic eloquence that embodies the Humanistic reverence for antique sources. Marguerite's Scriptural citations, illustrating the same severe, "pu-

by duplicating the words God spoke to Moses from the burning bush. The image of fire in the last line returns the reader to the Scriptural source that was the point of departure, tracing in this way a circular movement that makes of the text a linguistic equivalent of the perfect O, which stands for God. Effacing narrative and avoiding the past verb tense, Marguerite's representation of God's discourse aspires to the fixity and timelessness of the icon. It takes the reader back to the beginning and invites him to see a whole in it. When the reader sees (as Frye put it in a phrase we have used in our discussion of the *Miroir*) not only *the* whole *of* the text but *a* whole *in* it, he perceives a Oneness in which all multiplicity is dissolved. For many Christian mystics, this perception was the essential element in their experience of God's presence.

What Marguerite is here stressing is God's immanence. The corollary of HE ALONE IS is that things *are* only to the extent that they participate in Him; they *are* only to the degree that they signify Him. The truth *Amy* perceives while listening to God's voice is that "to the healthy and pure internal eye He is everywhere present" (DDC I.12.13). This means that the healthy and pure internal eye sees correctly insofar as it produces interpretations that contribute to the reign of charity. Returning to his books, which he had rejected when he read Jesus' comment that the truth is revealed not to the learned but to the humble, *Amy* discovers that all texts, if they are read correctly, contain a reflection of Him who informs all things. "La fiction faicte subtilement / Ne donnoit plus du vray l'empeschement" (III.847–48) [The fiction, subtly done, no longer was a real hindrance], he observes. He sees in history not a progression of events along a syntagmatic axis but an unfolding of God's pres-

---

rified" eloquence, incarnate humility, the word's reverence for the Word. Fumaroli traces the decline of authorial humility in the latter part of the sixteenth century and the quotation's gradual loss of status as a revered citation of authority glossed by a self-effacing commentator. Marie Comeau, *La Rhétorique de Saint Augustin d'après les Tractatus In Ioannem* (Paris: Boivin, 1930), remarks: "Pour l'orateur chrétien, l'unique source d'inspiration est la Bible, l'unique ou presque unique forme du discours est l'homélie, c'est-à-dire l'explication d'une partie plus ou moins considérable du texte sacré" (p. 73) [For the Christian orator, the only source of inspiration is the Bible, the only, or almost only, form of discourse is homily, that is to say, the explication of a section, more or less lengthy, of the sacred text]. In the introduction to his edition of the *Chansons spirituelles*, Georges Dottin examines the influence of the Bible on Marguerite's style (pp. LII–LXVI).

ence in a changeless "now." The interpreter who is inspired by faith and the law of love, the one great principle to which all the rules of exegesis are subordinated, "[retrouve] ce seul Ung / En chascun livre" (III.998) [rediscovers this single One in every book]. *Amy* equates this perception of Oneness with the repose that attends the apocalyptic vision: "Mais l'oeil qui est par la foy inspiré / . . . Ne regardant que Ung seul en toute chose, / Aura repoz et desjà se repose" (III.1069–72) [But the eye that is inspired by faith, seeing only the One in everything, will have rest and is already resting].

Because God is a circle in which all things are enclosed, the reader of Marguerite's text may be inclined to see in Him a prison reminiscent of the circular Tower of Love in Book I. This view is not entirely wrong. The text, folding back on itself so that the ending joins the beginning, is a creation that, like all of creation, reflects the Creator. Then, too, as Briçonnet repeated to Marguerite, God *is* a prison of love. In this sense, however, *prison* means something different from what it meant in Book I. A prisoner in the Tower of Love, *Amy* did not realize he was imprisoned until he saw *Amye* looking at him from outside the tower. Only when he understood that there was an outside did he comprehend that, being excluded from the world beyond his tower, he was in fact a captive within the walls of a prison. In the case of God, there is no outside and, consequently, no inside. Here the transcendent is immanent, a fact that is signified by the circle whose center is everywhere and circumference nowhere. To be contained in God's love is to be free, not imprisoned. Looking back on his captivity in the Tower of Love and seeing in God's commandment of love the supreme law of Christian faith, *Amy* "reads" the situation in which he found himself in Book I and finds that his love for *Amye* was in fact a reflection of the love that is Christ.

> Brief il n'y a d'amour nulle figure
> Où je ne trouve au vif la proutraicture
> Du vray Amant et seul Amour parfaict,
III.900   Par qui tout est pensé et dit et faict.

In brief, there is no image of love in which I do not find, painted from life, the portrait of the true Lover and only perfect Love, through which everything is conceived and said and done.

Just as the *Ravie* at the end of *Mont-de-Marsan* is a cleansed form of the *Mondainne* who appeared at the beginning of the play, so the *Amy* of Book III, the reader who understands that his function is to scrutinize texts until he discerns a relationship between them and the reign of charity (which he knows they must signify), is a purified form of the lover in Book I. We recall that the composition of *Les Prisons* was an act of love that *Amy* undertook in an effort to reflect a truth he now possesses (or, and this amounts to the same thing, that possesses him) and that will permit *Amye* to join him in that perfect love, that "rightful knitting" and "endless oneing"[89] which is the *unio*. Love of the creator can only be expressed as love of the creatures and "things" that constitute His creation.

Like every Christian, *Amy* is an author as well as a reader. He produces interpretations of God's texts consonant with the law of love. In fact, reading and writing are a single, continuous act; writing is the process of committing to paper an interpretation that the reader produces while scrutinizing the text before him. The imagery of reading, which dominated the first thousand lines of Book III, is followed by that of writing, the metaphorics of reading and writing being the same. The writer is first of all a reader of the truth immanent in himself and in all of creation, which was "inscribed by the finger of God" (Exodus 31.18). Every writer, the most frivolous as well as the most profound, is "du Sainct Esprit l'instrument imparfaict / Sans lequel n'est ung seul bon livre fait" (III.1219–20) [the imperfect instrument of the Holy Ghost, without which not a single good book is written]. Some writers are of course better than others. The criterion by which a work is judged is the degree to which a reader "qui a l'experience / Du Sainct Esprit" (III.1221–22) [who has experienced the Holy Ghost] can discern in it "Celluy qui est" (III.1224) [the One who is]. Just as every creature is imperfect to the extent that he seeks to be autonomous (this desire is the essence of *Cuyder*), so every text is imperfect to the degree that the reader whose internal eye is cleansed sees in it "un cuyder haultain / De trop sçavoir, conduysant plume et main" (III.1227–28) [a proud presumptuousness of too much knowledge guiding pen and hand]. Texts are judged by the degree to which they are informed by God, or, which is another way of saying the same

---

89. *Revelations of Divine Love Shewed to Mother Juliana of Norwich*, Ch. 53, p. 143.

thing, by the degree to which they reflect, duplicate and imitate the Bible. Marguerite is explicit on this point:

> Mais pour juger des mauvais et des bons
> III.1230 Ce qui en est, fault que nous regardons
> Qui le plus près de l'Escripture touche,
> Car l'Evangile est la pierre de touche
> Où du bon or se congnoist la valeur,
> Et du plus bas la foiblesse et paleur.

But to judge which are the bad ones and which are the good ones, we must look at which ones are closest to Scripture, for the Gospels are the touchstone by which the value of good gold is recognized and the weakness and paleness of what is inferior.

Accepting the common opinion that Scripture is plain, humble, unadorned,[90] Marguerite condemns rhetorical beauty, which, she suggests, expresses *cuyder* rather than the Holy Spirit. "Ces escriptz là," she observes, ". . . bien painctz, bien dictz, et rempliz de beaulx motz, / Ils sont suspects, leurs doctrines aussy" (III.1289–91)[91] [Those writings, well done, well spoken, and full of fine words, are suspect, their doctrines, too]. As an illustration of a text that is animated by "cest Esprit divin qui est aucteur / De verité" (III.1311–12) [this divine Spirit which is the author of truth], Marguerite mentions the work "d'une femme, / Depuys cent ans escript" (III.1315–16) [of a woman, written a hundred years ago], a text in which the sole argument, from beginning to end, is love. Marguerite does not name the writer or the book. Abel Lefranc suggested that the author was Catherine of Siena, although he admitted that his "longues recherches"[92] had failed to reveal any specific link between Catherine and Marguerite. In an article published in 1963,[93] Jean Dagens argues convincingly that Marguerite was referring to *Le Miroir des simples âmes*, an anonymous work now

---

90. On prose style in the Bible, see Joseph Anthony Mazzeo, "St. Augustine's Rhetoric of Silence," p. 14. See also Marie Comeau, op. cit., pp. 72–73, Fumaroli, op. cit., pp. 70–75, and especially Henri Marrou, *Saint Augustin et la fin de la culture antique* (Paris: E. de Boccard, 1958).

91. In the *Imitation*, Thomas à Kempis warned: "Let not the beautiful and subtle sayings of men affect thee," III, 43, p. 148.

92. *Les dernières poésies de Marguerite de Navarre*, ed. Abel Lefranc, p. 230.

93. Jean Dagens, "*Le Miroir des Simples Ames* et Marguerite de Navarre," in *La Mystique rhénane* (Paris: Presses universitaires de France, 1963), 281–289.

attributed to Marguerite Porète, who lived in Valenciennes at
the end of the thirteenth century and was burned at the stake as a
heretic in 1310.[94] The manuscript of the French version of *Le
Miroir des simples âmes* was prepared by an unknown scribe between 1450 and 1530 and was in the library of the convent of the
Madeleine-lès-Orléans.[95] Since Marguerite maintained friendly
relations with this convent, it is likely that she read the manuscript there.

Marguerite Porète's *Miroir* is a *débat*. Although an occasional
poem appears in the text, the work is mainly in prose. The principal speaker is *Ame*, who, aided and encouraged by *Amour*, relates her spiritual ascension, which is marked by encounters and
discussions with allegorical figures such as *Entendement de raison*,
Entendement de haultesse d'amour, *Entendement de divine lumière*,
Lumière de foi, *Tentation*, *Discrétion*, *Crainte*, *Sainte Eglise la petite*
(governed by reason), and *Sainte Eglise la grande* (governed by
love), among others. The work belongs to the anti-intellectual
tradition of the *Devotio moderna*. Much of it is an ecstatic evocation of the state that the *âme enfranchie* [freed soul], or *âme anean-
tie* [annihilated soul], attains when, stripped of self, it contemplates the Trinity. United with the Trinity, which Porète calls "le
Loingprés" [the Farnear], the soul dwells in a region above
virtue, above even love. It is released from ritual and dogma, freed
from the Church itself.

Porète was probably a Beguine. Suspicious of the Beguines
and of the current of otherworldly mysticism that marked the
thirteenth and early fourteenth centuries, the Church cautioned
against a faith so "pure," so detached from the world that it denies the sanctity of matter (a heresy, for Christ's coming redeemed matter). Porète's radical mysticism attracted Marguerite, who was tempted to experience Christ as a rejection of the
world. In the eighty or so lines that extend from line 1324 to line
1400, Marguerite, inspired by Porète, contemplates the figure
of Christ, "le vray Amy" (III.1328) [the true friend], "le Gentil
Loing Près" (III.1329) [the Gracious Far Near]. Repeating the

----

94. Romana Guarnieri published an edition of *Le Miroir des Simples Ames*. See her *Il
Movimento del libero spirito* (Rome: Edizioni di storia e letteratura, 1965). Part I of Guar-
nieri's book is devoted to "testi e documenti"; Part II (pp. 513–635) is her edition of the
French version of Porète's work.

95. Guarnieri, p. 400.

words *gentil*, *loing*, and *près*, Marguerite combines them in various ways and writes a litany that is a gloss on Porète's text.

Despite the attraction Porète's mysticism had for her, Marguerite, however, was basically too orthodox and too committed to the Renaissance spirit of inquiry to accept it wholeheartedly. Whereas Porète strives ultimately to efface all distinction between man and Christ, Marguerite, more theologically cautious, perhaps, but certainly more conscious of the mechanics of discourse and of the dialogic structures of language, maintains a separateness between what is *loing* and what is *près*, marvelling all the while that the two are joined in a continuous and unbreakable circuit of communication. The change Marguerite made in the term Porète used for Christ and the Trinity is significant. In Marguerite's text, Porète's *Loingprés* becomes *Loing Près*. This modification is symptomatic of the theological difference between the two writers. Marguerite's *Loing Près* designates a transcendent God who is immanent in, but not identical with, creation. Porète's *Loingprés*, which eliminates all distance between the Far and the Near, designates a God who is identical with creation. *Loing Près* is orthodox; *Loingprés* borders on heresy.

Marguerite alters Porète's term in order to be able to see in *Le Miroir des simples âmes* an image of the Christ she discerns in Scripture. Her reading of Porète's text illustrates her claim that books are good insofar as they can be read as a duplicate of Scripture. Furthermore, it shows that for Marguerite duplication, or imitation, does not mean necessarily a repetition of the narrative line of the model text. It means, rather, an iconic reading of the paradigmatic text, i.e., a reading that permits the reader to see a whole in the text before him. That whole is always Christ. The reader-turned-writer produces a text that redefines Christ in language that is necessarily more opaque than that of Scripture but that nevertheless incarnates the same reality. The concept of *Loing Près*, identified by Marguerite as "fin et commancement" (III.1396) [end and beginning], is a reformulation of the God who is "Alpha and Omega" (Revelations 1.8) and who is emblematized in *Les Prisons* as a circle. All texts, Marguerite says, "tendent de declairer la Bible" (III.1426); they are circular, the end being always inscribed in the beginning. The task of the reader (and every Christian is a reader) is to dis-

cern the circular pattern inscribed in the text before him, to discover (or produce) the whole.

Having understood that a reader deconstructs the armature of
words until the text breaks open and reveals its inner unity,
which is a duplication of the Oneness of God, *Amy* is on the
threshold of insight. He sits down and prepares to perform a
hermeneutic exercise that will result in the reconciliation of the
Old and New Testaments, of beginning and end. He seeks to
"accorder leur different langaige / A monstrer ung Seul bon,
puyssant et saige" (III. 1601–02) [to reconcile their different languages, to reveal a single One, good, powerful and wise]. As he
studies the signs before him, *Amy* hears a voice, "ung parler
d'Esprit et de feu plain" (III. 1613) [a voice full of Spirit and fire].
Coming to him out of the wind, the voice tells him that he will
never be able to capture in language the experience of wholeness
and signification, which, being the experience of divinity itself,
always transcends the text in which it is inscribed. The most that
Marguerite's text can do is duplicate Scripture by recounting
biblical scenes in which God spoke to man. Her text reflects the
Tout-Verbe by repeating what God said to Adam, Noah, Moses,
Abraham, David, John, Jesus. By linking together in an uninterrupted sequence those biblical passages in which God spoke directly to man, Marguerite's text stresses the continuity of God's
voice across the discontinuities of Scriptural discourse. For some
four hundred lines (1591–2000), *Amy* seeks to convey the experience of *unio*, using oxymoronic formulations to express the
bond between man and God, letter and spirit, *Rien* and *Tout*: "O
petit grand! ô Rien en Tout fondu! / O Tout gaigné par Rien en
toy perdu!" (III. 1931–32) [O small great One! O Nothing dissolved into All! O All, won by Nothing lost in you!]. Antiprogressive and antinarrative, the language that seeks to signify
the *unio* effaces difference, striving for a similitude that erases
distinctions and articulates "ceste union dedans la multitude"
(III. 1969) [this oneness in the many].

Les Prisons could very well end with the soul singing God's
praises (". . . ses louanges chantant," III. 2000; music once again
marks the *unio*). *Le Miroir de l'âme pécheresse* and *Mont-de-Marsan*
ended on such a note. *Les Prisons*, however, is presented as a description of an experience the narrator has already had but that
Amye, the reader, has yet to undergo. *Amy* must fall back into

language if he wishes to accompany *Amye*, for she has yet to work her way through the *Verbe* toward the *Tout-Verbe*; she has yet to move from language toward the trans-linguistic speech of God, which, as the Pseudo-Dionysius maintained, must be thought of as silence, an opinion shared by Marguerite Porète, who wrote that "tout ce que l'en peut de Dieu dire ne escrire, ne que l'en en peut penser, qui plus est que n'est dire, est assez mieulx mentir que ce n'est vray dire"[96] [everything that one can say or write about God, or that one can think about Him, which is more than one can say, is more like lying than telling the truth]. *Amy*, too, concludes that "le povoir . . . deffault / A declairer ce qui n'est pas licitte / De prononcer" (III.1945−47) [the power is lacking to state that which we are not allowed to say].

Still, human speech cannot be denied, for language is the incarnation of the *Tout-Verbe* and has been redeemed by Christ. Man, who cannot know God except through Christ, cannot know the *Tout-Verbe* (silence) except through *Verbe* (speech). With a touch of weariness in his voice, *Amy* says:

> Mais parler fault ça bas comme les hommes,
> Vivant comme eulx tant qu'avec eulx nous sommes,
> III.2005 Non pas suyvans leurs oeuvres et couraiges,
> Mais ouy bien, sans peché, leurs langaiges.

But one must speak down here like men, living like them since we are with them, not following their works and thoughts but hearing very well, without sin, their languages.

Accepting the necessity of speaking in a human tongue, *Amy* declares that "il n'est possible / De traverser ce desert espineux / Sans se piquer ou estre bien peneux" (III.2010−12) [it is not possible to cross this thorny desert without being pricked or being very dejected]. "Ce desert espineux"[97] is another formulation of the *via Christi*, metaphorized, in a context of reading, as a text the Christian reader must cross. The text being a "desert espineux," the reader is a penitent whose experience of significance (the textual equivalent of *illuminatio* and *unio*) is coextensive with his experience of *mortificatio* (the process of reading),

96. Ibid., p. 614.
97. Briçonnet developed the image of thorns at great length in a letter to Marguerite (I.165−76).

for, as we noted in our discussion of *Le Miroir de l'âme pécheresse*, *mortificatio* does not lead sequentially to *illuminatio* but rather *signifies* union with Christ (*Loing Près*). The *Tout* can be discovered (significance can be produced) only by crossing this thorny desert. As *Amy* puts it:

> Et qui vouldra les Escriptures lire,
> III.2040   Il trouvera que au milieu du martyre,
> Ce tout estoit si à clair advisé,
> Qu'il n'y avoit nul tant martirisé
> Qui ne sentist plus de joye certaine
> Dedans l'esprit que de tourment et peyne
> 2045   Au corps, sachant ne leur estre donné
> Rien qui ne fust par le Tout ordonné.

And anyone who wishes to read the Scriptures will find that in the middle of martyrdom this "all" was so clearly perceptible that there was no one, however martyred, who did not feel more certain joy in spirit than anguish and pain in the body, knowing that nothing was being done to them that had not been ordered by the All.

Leading *Amye* across "ce desert espineux," *Amy* recounts the death of numerous martyrs. He then states once again that love is the force that compels him to write the text by means of which *Amye* will be led to discover Christ. "Tout le but" (III.2152) [the whole purpose] of *Les Prisons*, he says, is to show *Amye* that "qui ce Tout en tout peult veoir et croyre, / Il est en paix et liberté" (III.2154–55) [anyone who can see All in all, and believe, that person is in peace and freedom].

As an immediate consequence of *Amy*'s assertion that his purpose is to demonstrate that the reader who sees a whole in the text discovers significance and peace, *Amy* recounts in leisurely fashion the death of four persons particularly close to Marguerite: Marguerite de Lorraine, mother of the Duke of Alençon, Marguerite's first husband; the Duke of Alençon; Louise de Savoie, Marguerite's mother; and Francis I. Extending over nearly seven hundred lines (III.2167–2865), these four successive *tombeaux* are *exempla* designed to illustrate the power of faith, for each exemplary figure, crossing the thorny desert of death, abandoned himself to Christ and died joyously. Furthermore, because the Evangelicals tended to view a man's comportment at the time of his death as a mirror of his past life, Marguerite, by recounting the edifying death scenes of Marguerite de Lorraine, the Duke of Alençon, Louise de Savoie, and Francis I, is bearing witness to the greatness of four persons whose lives were intimately associated with her own.[98] The *tombeaux* are set-pieces in which Marguerite uses the devices of classical rhetoric, especially prosopopoeia, to impart to her text both monumentality and immediacy. At the same time, they serve a precise function in the economy of *Amye*'s spiritual experience. *Amy* introduces them by saying that he intends to demonstrate "par parolle ou histoire" (III.2152) [by word and story] a truth he wishes *Amye* to understand. The four *tombeaux* are the "histoires" *Amy* promised. They are designed to serve *Amye* as objects of "meditation," which is the first level of religious experience and depends heavily on images and inspiring scenes. Meditation in turn leads to contemplation, the true mystical experience.[99]

In one sense, these four elaborately fashioned *tombeaux* are external to *Amy*'s account of his liberation from the various prisons in which he was a captive. They provide *Amye*, however, with opportunities to meditate on death. Furthermore, they develop the common medieval *topos* of death as the great liberator who frees the spirit from its fleshy prison. With his last breath, Francis announces ". . . la deffaicte / De la prison de ce vieil corps charnel" (III.2589) [the defeat of the prison of this old carnal body].

Like Marguerite de Lorraine, the Duke of Alençon, and Louise de Savoie, Francis yearns for the dissolution of the flesh and restates the Pauline theme of *cupio dissolvi*. Briçonnet had glossed the key Pauline passage in a letter to Marguerite dated January 1523: "Tout vray chrestien est ou doibt estre mort, non comme la statue dont j'ay cy devant parlé, mais en Jesus Christ, et sa vie

---

98. Marguerite was present at the deaths of Marguerite de Lorraine, the Duke of Alençon, and Louise de Savoie but not at the death of Francis.

99. Contemplation is usually divided into the three stages we have frequently referred to: purgation, illumination, union. Briçonnet and Marguerite often mention these three stages as if they were clear-cut steps. For some mystics, however, contemplation is a continuum that cannot be subdivided so neatly. See Dom David Knowles, *The English Mystical Tradition* (New York: Harper & Row, 1966), p. 91, and Joseph E. Milosh, *The Scale of Perfection*, p. 38. On the distinction between meditation and contemplation, see Henri Delacroix, *Etudes d'histoire et de psychologie du mysticisme* (Paris: Alcan, 1908), pp. 359–60.

en luy cachée et, par ce, incensible (car Dieu n'est susceptible de sensibilité exteriore) et toutesfois languissant et comme malade desirant estre absoubz de l'union corporelle, pour le commuer à la spirituelle. A cest cause disoit sainct Pol: 'Cupio dissolvi et esse cum Christo'" (II.23) [Every true Christian is or ought to be dead, not like the statue I spoke of above, but in Jesus Christ, and his life hidden in him and, because of this, insensible (for God is not responsive to the exterior senses) and yet languishing and like a sick person wishing to be freed from the corporeal union and to exchange it for the spiritual union. For this reason Saint Paul said: "I wish to be dissolved and to be with Christ"]. By taking the words "Cupio dissolvi et esse cum Christo" (Philippians 1.23) out of the context that gives them the meaning Paul intended, Briçonnet distorts Paul's thought. He seems to suggest that Paul rejected creation for the world of I Am. In truth, Paul's thought expresses not rejection of the creature in favor of the Creator, not condemnation of the flesh (or the letter) in favor of the soul (or the spirit) but rather awareness of the fact that the creator cannot be known except through the creature, from whom He remains, however, distinct. Paul may have wished "to be gone" (*cupio dissolvi*) but, as he wrote to the Philippians, he wished even more to "stay alive in this body" and to help others read aright the signs of God in His creation:

My one hope and trust is that I shall never have to admit defeat, but that now as always I shall have the courage for Christ to be glorified in my body, whether by my life or by my death. Life to me, of course, is Christ, but then death would bring me something more; but then again, if living in this body means doing work which is having good results—I do not know what I should choose. I am caught in this dilemma: I want to be gone and be with Christ, which would be very much the better, but for me to stay alive in this body is a more urgent need for your sake. This weighs with me so much that I feel sure I shall survive and stay with you all, and help you to progress in the faith and even increase your joy in it. (Philippians 1.20–25)

The metaphorics of textuality is so pervasive in *Les Prisons* that when Marguerite's text alludes to this passage from Philippians we may see in Paul's dilemma a metaphor of the text's own dilemma. Marguerite's text is "caught" between two modes of discourse, one of which we may call imitative, the other autonomous or autoreflexive.[100] Because a text is "good" to the extent that it effaces self and yields to the authority of the Bible, *Les Prisons*, especially the second half of Book III, imitates or "cites" Scripture again and again. The text effaces itself in favor of Scripture, becoming *Rien*. The reader, however, knowing that he is reading Scripture, sees the text as *Tout*. In this way, *Rien* becomes *Tout*, a text that fixes its identity in Christ the Text, whom it reflects endlessly.

And yet, what Marguerite's text demonstrates is not actual identity with Christ the Text but rather the *desire* for identity with Him. When Paul said, "I live now not with my own life but with the life of Christ who lives in me" (Galatians 2.20), he did not deny his existence as a visible form. On the contrary, he affirmed the existence of the visible as a habitation for the invisible.[101] The textual equivalent of Paul's "I live now not with my own life but with the life of Christ who lives in me" is the imitative mode of discourse whereby the text "repeats" Scripture. Imitative discourse, however, is constantly subverted by self-referentiality, from which no text can escape. Every text, unless it is *identical* in every detail with the model text (in which case it is not a "text" at all) creates a universe of signs that, even while they refer to an anterior *logos*, also refer back to the work itself as to an autonomous world. The conflict between composing autonomous texts while maintaining a Christian submission to authority informs the problematics of writing in Marguerite's poetry and reflects a tension between love for the creature and love for the Creator. The self-assertive nature of a text clashes with the purported authorial impulse that generates Marguerite's discourse, that is to say, with the desire to proclaim and demonstrate submission to the Word.

Following the conclusion of the fourth *tombeau*, the first-person narrator speaks again. He apologizes for the interruption in his account of *Rien*, who is the desiring subject that seeks to attain *Tout*, the object of desire: "A ce Rien donq, que long temps j'ay laissé, / Retourner fault" (III.2865–66) [To this Noth-

---

100. See John Freccero, "The Fig Tree and the Laurel: Petrarch's Poetics," op. cit., p. 38, for a discussion of a text as "an autonomous universe of autoreflexive signs."

101. Marcia L. Colish, *The Mirror of Language*, makes this point in her discussion of "Augustine's Incarnational theology" (p. 49). Even as he moves from earth to heaven, the Christian never leaves the Incarnation behind him.

ing, then, which I abandoned for a long time, I must return].
Presumably, the "I" that speaks is still *Amy*. And yet, the voice
we now hear is distinctly different from the one we heard prior
to the four death scenes. Narrative has been utterly effaced from
the text. The concluding three-hundred-odd lines of the poem
are marked by discourse whose phraseology (present verb tense
and a profusion of anaphoric formulations) precludes narrative,
excluding from the text any event other than the "event" of language. Indeed, the "I" who speaks after the *tombeaux* passages is
the omniscient "I," the author herself, who, like the reader,
stands outside the text and interrogates *Verbe* (*Rien*), searching
still for *Tout-Verbe*, or significance (*Tout*), which is inscribed in
it. She reads *Verbe*, the signifier, seeking by a hermeneutic
exercise to attain the signified, the *Tout-Verbe*. "O leger Rien"
(III.2956), she says, "que trouves tu . . . / En maladie, en injure,
en excès, / Prisons, gibetz, lances, canons, espée, / Dont la vie
est avant son but couppée?" (III.2996–98) [O light Nothing,
what do you find in sickness, in injuries, in intemperance, prisons, gallows, spears, cannons, swords, with which life is cut
off before its end?]. Provoked by *Rien*'s silence, she says: "Ne
voys tu pas en ung Dieu troys Personnes? / Racomptes m'en!"
(III.3095–96) [Do you not see in a God three persons? Tell me
about it!]. When *Rien* still does not answer, Marguerite exclaims, "Mais quoy, mot tu ne sonnes!" (III.3096) [What, you do
not say a word!]. Suddenly, she understands that *Rien* will speak
no more, for it has been engulfed in the Word, in the silence that
subtends reality, grounding both desire and language, which, in
Augustine's theology of the Word, are the same.[102] As John Freccero notes in his discussion of the Word as the central metaphor
in Christianity, God the Word is the end of all desire and the in-
terpretant of all discourse: "Like the intentionality of a sentence
that preexists its utterance and emerges concretely, in retrospect,
from that utterance, the uncreated Word produces its signifier
and is in turn made manifest by it. Like language, itself, the redemptive process is tautology, ending where it began."[103]

---

102. In the first chapters of the *Confessions*, Augustine represents language and desire
as indistinguishable, even coextensive, both beginning in consciousness. Hence the importance he attaches in *On Christian Doctrine* to enjoyment and the distinction between
what is to be enjoyed and what is to be used.

103. Freccero, op. cit., p. 35.

As a result of its absorption into *Tout*, *Rien* is now indistinguishable from *Tout*. Thus *Rien* itself is divine:

> O divin Rien, divinement mys bas,
> Divinement monté au vray soulas,
> III.3175 Au vray plaisir, à la joye indicible. . . .
> III.3194 Car ce grant Tout fait de Rien son chef d'oeuvre.

O divine Nothing, divinely brought down low, divinely raised up to
true solace, to true pleasure, to ineffable joy . . . For this great All
makes of Nothing its masterpiece.

In the long verbal rite that concludes the poem (III.2866–3214),
the language of the text *dis*-scribes *Rien*, de-emphasizes the self
until the whole fiction of *Amy*'s love for *Amye* becomes a me-
tonomy for the process of poetic productivity itself. Like all signifiers, the words *Loing Près* and *Tout*, signaling Marguerite's
desire for Christ, for love, mark an absence. Traversing the inert
circle of the written text, they denote the writer's experience of a
lack. However, as the text exercises its autonomy and achieves a
distinctive attractiveness, in short, as it imposes its own presence, it asserts itself as a rival in the fulfillment of desire, displac-
ing the *unio* that the poet purports to invoke. Manifesting its
own charm, the text interposes itself as a negative mediator between the desiring subject and the object that it desires.[104] The
astonishingly self-aware conclusion of *Les Prisons* demonstrates
that the text eventually intervenes between the spoken signifier
and its signified, dispossessing both into a centerless and unfail-
ing productivity that is properly textual.

> III.3210 O forte Amour, à qui tout est soubzmys
> De recevoir ce Rien par ton mistere!
> *Ceste voix là ne puys ny ne doy taire:*
> Que où l'Esprit est divin et vehement,
> La liberté y est parfaictement.   (my emphasis)

O strong Love, to which everything submits in order to receive this
Nothing through your mystery! I cannot and ought not silence that

---

104. Cf. Eugene Vance, "Love's Concordance: The Poetics of Desire and the Joy of
the Text," *Diacritics*, 5, No. 1 (1975), pp. 40–52.

voice; for there where the Spirit is divine and powerful, there is perfect freedom.

Here, in the final lines of the poem, Marguerite commits herself to an unending production of texts, which refuse, however, to be simple vehicles by which signs are exchanged between writer and reader. As her texts participate in an order of discourse, the signifiers in them point less and less to a referential context; instead, they point with increasing insistence to the discourse in which they begin and end. Discourse itself becomes the signified, that is to say, reality, which in Christian typology as codified by Augustine, is God's Book, having Him for both its Author and subject matter. In Book III of *Les Prisons*, the superimposition of a quadruple model (the four *tombeaux*), recalling as it does the Pythagorean tetrad, the symbol of created matter, on the triadic configurations so deliberately stressed throughout much of the work ("Je suys qui suys triangle très parfaict," III.811 [I am who I am, the perfect triangle], God declares) may be read as a textual ritual whereby the indivisibility of Author and (subject) matter is experienced anew.

Near the end of *Les Prisons*, Marguerite draws close to the mystical view of Porète and speaks of man, who is a product of God's "speech," as being deified by virtue of his identity with Christ on the cross: ". . . il est deifié,/ Uny au Tout et au souverain Bien / Pour estre fait aveques Jesus Rien" (III.3204–3206) [he is deified, united with the All and the sovereign Good to be made Nothing with Jesus]. In the same way, we can speak of the "I am" of the text as being identical with the I Am of Scripture. As a fulfillment of desire, "I am" displaces I Am. Like all of Marguerite's poetry, *Les Prisons* solemnizes timeless (and therefore silent) presence. It is a text, an *unio* whose "I am" incarnates and celebrates, across the discontinuity of human speech, the unending and ceaselessly productive I Am.

Conclusion

The mystical tradition on which Marguerite's poetry is based elevated the contemplative life, represented by Mary, above the active life, represented by Martha. At the same time, it defined a third kind of life, called the "mixed life," that permitted "active" people to experience, however partially, the spiritual insights that result from contemplation. Although mystics invariably professed the superiority of the contemplative life over the other two, those who were close to the religious handbook tradition and who wrote with an intent to help their readers achieve a richer spiritual life, were careful not to scorn the mixed life. Saint Teresa of Avila, for example, warned her sisters against the danger of elevating Mary too far above Martha: "Believe me, Martha and Mary must work together when they offer the Lord lodging, and must have Him ever with them, and they must not entertain Him badly and give Him nothing to eat. And how can Mary give Him anything, seated as she is at His feet, unless her sister helps her?"[1]

St. Teresa's question underlies much of Marguerite's poetry. Mary is concerned with reality, with the Truth, with the Word, which, because it is transcendent and eternal, cannot be uttered in human speech and so must be thought of as silence. Martha, on the other hand, is concerned with appearances, with phenomena, with "fallen" speech, which, though it may retain a trace of the primal Word, is irremediably separated from the paradigm that was in the beginning. In the Christian tradition within which Marguerite wrote, the Incarnation, however, re-

---

1. *The Complete Works of Saint Teresa of Jesus* (the "Seventh Mansion" of the *Interior Castle*), trans. and ed. E. Allison Peers (New York: Sheed & Ward, 1946), p. 348.

deemed human languages. As the Pseudo-Dionysius stressed, the Word is both transcendent and immanent. It is transcendent because "It is Absolute Perfection and possesseth in Itself and from Itself distinctive Uniformity of Its existence and is wholly perfect in Its whole Essence" (*Div. Names* 184). It is immanent in all of creation because "It penetrates to all things." As a result of the Incarnation, the world of "things" participates in the "Absolute Perfection" of the divine *logos*. The Christian's task is to see *through* words and things and to perceive the divine, creative Silence that existed before language came into being.

Marguerite's texts are allegories of the Christian's search for the Word, i.e., the Silence, the "Uniformity," which, Augustine says, is "our native country" (DDC I.4.10). Exiled for a time from our homeland, we move forward, wishing—in Augustine's words—to "return" to the country where "we may comprehend the eternal and the spiritual."

Marguerite's poems are also allegories of the Word's operation in human language. In the temporality of its unfolding along the syntagmatic axis of metonymic succession, allegorical narrative actualizes the paradigm whose loss is the origin of speech. In their own wholeness and "uniformity," Marguerite's poems end up embodying and signifying the *unio*, the "native country" toward which all words "wish to return." Seeking to recover Silence, that is to say, the primal metaphor that antedates the signifying chain of narrative time, each of Marguerite's texts is a discourse whose structurality, or metaphoricity, holds out the promise of a final—though perpetually deferred—return to the "Absolute Perfection" of the Word.

Bibliography

EDITIONS OF MARGUERITE'S WORKS

L'Art et usage du souverain mirouer du chrestien. Paris: Guillaume le Noir, 1556.

Chansons spirituelles. Ed. Georges Dottin. Geneva: Droz (TLF), 1971.

La Coche. Ed. Robert Marichal. Geneva: Droz (TLF), 1971.

La Coche. Ed. Robert Marichal. *Humanisme et Renaissance,* 5 (1938), 37–99, 247–96.

La Coche. Ed. Edouard Scheegans. Strasbourg: Heitz, 1936.

Comédie de la nativité de Jésus Christ. Ed. Pierre Jourda. Paris: Boivin, 1939.

Guillaume Briçonnet-Marguerite d'Angoulême Correspondance (1521–1524). Eds. Christine Martineau, Michel Veissière, Henry Heller. 2 vols. Geneva: Droz (THR), I, 1975; II, 1979.

Les Dernières Poésies de Marguerite de Navarre. Ed. Abel Lefranc. Paris: Colin, 1896.

Dialogue en forme de vision nocturne. Ed. Pierre Jourda. *Revue du seizième siècle,* 13 (1926), 1–49.

Epîtres et comédies inédites. Ed. Pierre Jourda. *Revue du seizième siècle,* 13 (1926), 177–204.

L'Heptaméron des Nouvelles de très haute et très illustre princesse Marguerite d'Angoulême. Eds. Le Roux de Lincy and A. de Montaiglon. 4 vols. Paris: Auguste Eudes, 1880 (rpt. Geneva: Slatkine, 1969).

L'Heptaméron. Ed. Michel François. Paris: Garnier, n.d.

L'Heptaméron. Ed. Pierre Jourda. In *Conteurs français du XVIe siècle.* Paris: Gallimard (Bibliothèque de la Pléiade), pp. 701–1131.

Nouvelles (L'Heptaméron). Ed. Yves Le Hir. Paris: Presses universitaires de France, 1967.

"Jugendgedichte Margaretes aus einer Wiener Handschrift." Ed. Auguste Becker. *Archiv für das Studium der neueren Sprachen und Literaturen,* 131 (1913), pp. 341–59.

Lettres de Marguerite d'Angoulême. Ed. François Génin. Paris: Jules Renouard, 1841.

Marguerites de la marguerite des princesses, très illustre Royne de Navarre. Lyon: Jean de Tournes, 1547 (facsimile rpt., ed. Ruth Thomas, The Hague: Johnson Reprint Corporation, Mouton, 1970).

Les Marguerites de la marguerite des princesses. Ed. Félix Frank. 4 vols. Paris; Jouaust, 1873 (rpt. Geneva: Slatkine, 1970).

Le Miroir de l'âme pécheresse. Ed. Joseph L. Allaire. Munich: Fink, 1972.

Le Miroir de l'âme pécheresse. Ed. Renja Slaminen. Suomalaisen Tiedeakate-
mian Toimituksia Annales Academiae Scientiarum Fennicae. Helsinki: Suo-
malainen Tiedeakatemia, 1979.
La Navire, ou Consolation du Roi François Iᵉʳ à sa soeur Marguerite. Ed. Robert
Marichal. *Bibliothèque de l'école pratique des hautes études. Sciences philologiques
et historiques,* 306. Paris: Champion, 1956, pp. 235–303.
Nouvelles lettres de la Reine de Navarre adressées au roi François Iᵉʳ. Ed. François
Génin. Paris: Jules Renouard, 1842.
Oeuvres Choisies. Ed. H. P. Clive. 2 vols. New York: Appleton-Century-
Crofts, 1968.
Oraison a nostre Seigneur Jésus Christ. Ed. Renja Salminen. Suomalaisen Tiedea-
katemian Toimituksia Annales Academiae Scientiarum Fennicae. Helsinki:
Suomalainen Tiedeakatemia, 1981.
Le Pater Noster faict en translation et dyalogue par la Royne de Navarre. Ed. Eugène
Parturier. *Revue de la Renaissance,* 5 (1904), 108–114; 178–90; 273–80.
Le Pater Noster de Marguerite de Navarre. Ed. W. G. Moore. In *La Réforme alle-
mande et la littérature française.* Strasbourg: Publications de la Faculté des Let-
tres, 1930, pp. 432–41.
Petit Oeuvre dévot et contemplatif. Ed. Hans Sckommodau. *Analecta Romanica,*
H. 9. Frankfurt am Main: Klostermann, 1960.
Poésies inédites. Ed. Pierre Jourda. *Revue du seizième siècle,* 17 (1930), pp.
42–63.
Les Prisons. Ed. Simone Glasson. Geneva: Droz (TLF), 1978.
Suyte des Marguerites de la marguerite des princesses, très illustre Royne de Navarre.
Lyon: Jean de Tournes, 1547 (facsimile rpt., ed. Ruth Thomas, The Hague:
Johnson Reprint Corporation, Mouton, 1970).
Théâtre profane. Ed. V. L. Saulnier. Geneva: Droz (TLF), 1946.

WORKS ON MARGUERITE DE NAVARRE

Andon, James. "Contribution à l'établissement d'un tableau social du peuple
français dans la première moitié du XVIᵉ siècle. Portrait des devisants dans
l'*Heptaméron* de Marguerite de Navarre." *Bulletin de l'Association Guillaume
Budé,* 26 (1967), 293–301.
Arathoon, Leigh A. "The 'Compte en viel langaige' behind *Heptaméron,*
LXX." *Romance Philology,* 30 (1976), 192–99.
Argus, Elisabeth. *Clémont Marot und Margarete von Valois, Herzogin von Alençon, Königin von Navarra.* Munich: Borna-Leipzig, 1918.
Atance, Félix R. "Les Comédies profanes de Marguerite de Navarre. Aspects
de la satire religieuse en France au XVIᵉ siècle." *Revue d'histoire et de phi-
losophie religieuses,* 66 (1976), 289–313.
———. "Marguerite de Navarre et ses activités en faveur des novateurs." *Neo-
philologus,* 60 (1976), pp. 505–24.
———. "Les Religieux de l'*Heptaméron*: Marguerite de Navarre et les novateurs." *Archiv für Reformationsgeschichte,* 64 (1974), pp. 185–210.
Auld, Louis E. "Music as Dramatic Device in the Secular Theatre of Marguerite de Navarre." *Renaissance Drama,* 7 (1976), pp. 192–217.
Baker, M. J. "The Role of the Moral Lesson in Heptaméron No. 30." *French
Studies,* 31 (1977), pp. 18–25.

Bambeck, Manfred. "Religiöse Skepsis bei Margarete von Navarra?" *Zeitschrift für französische Sprache und Literatur*, 72 (1967), pp. 12–22.

Bataillon, Marcel. "Autour de l'*Heptaméron*: à propos du livre de Lucien Febvre." *Bibliothèque d'Humanisme et Renaissance*, 7 (1946), pp. 245–53.

Becker, Philip-August. "Marguerite, duchesse d'Alençon, et Guillaume Briçonnet, évêque de Meaux, d'après leur correspondance inédite (1521–1524)." *Bulletin de la Société de l'histoire du protestantisme français*, 49 (1900), pp. 393–477, pp. 661–67.

Benson, Edward. "Marriage Ancestral and Conjugal in the *Heptaméron*." *Journal of Medieval and Renaissance Studies*, 9 (1979), pp. 261–75.

Brockmeier, Peter. "Limiti della critica sociale nella novellistica: Decameron—Heptaméron—Novelas ejemplares." In *Il Boccaccio nelle culture e letterature nazionali*. Ed. Francesco Mazzoni. Florence: Olschki, 1978.

————. *Lust und Herrschaft: Studien über gesellschaftliche Aspekte der Novellistik: Boccaccio, Sacchetti, Margarete von Navarra, Cervantes*. Stuttgart: Metzler, 1972.

Cazauran, Nicole. *L'Heptaméron de Marguerite de Navarre: Histoires piteuses ou plaisantes*. Paris: CDU & SEDES, 1978.

————. "La Trentième Nouvelle de l'*Heptaméron*, ou la méditation d'un 'exemple'." In *Mélanges de littérature: du moyen âge au XXe siècle. Offerts à Mademoiselle Jeanne Lods*. Paris: Ecole Normale Supérieure de Jeunes Filles 10, 1977, pp. 617–52.

Certi, Marie. *Marguerite de Navarre*. Paris: Sorbier, 1981.

Clements, Robert J. "Marguerite de Navarre and Dante." *Italica*, 18 (1941), pp. 37–50. Also in his *Peregrine Muse: Studies in Comparative Renaissance Literature*. Chapel Hill: University of North Carolina Press, 1969, pp. 125–40.

Clive, H. P. *Marguerite de Navarre: An Annotated Bibliography*. London: Grant & Cutler, 1983.

Comte, Charles. "Le Texte de Marguerite de Navarre." *Revue de métrique et de versification*, 1 (1894–95), pp. 97–128.

Costra, Jean. "Sentiment et humanisme dans les *Chansons spirituelles* de Marguerite de Navarre." *Revue de l'Université de Laval*, 2 (1966), pp. 767–74.

Courteault, Paul. "Les Dernières Poésies de Marguerite de Navarre." *Revue Critique*, 41 (1896), pp. 505–13.

————. "Marguerite de Navarre, d'après ses dernières poésies et ses derniers historiens." *Revue du Béarn et du Pays-Basque*, 1904, 49–70, 116–73.

Dagens, Jean. "Le 'Miroir des simples âmes' et Marguerite de Navarre." *La Mystique rhénane*, Colloque de Strasbourg 16–19 mai 1961. Paris: Presses universitaires de France, 1963, pp. 281–89.

Dassonville, Michel. "Le Testament spirituel de Marguerite de Navarre." In *From Marot to Montaigne. Essays on French Renaissance Literature*. Ed. Raymond C. La Charité. *Kentucky Romance Quarterly*, 19, Suppl. 1 (1972), pp. 109–24.

Davis, Betty J. *The Storytellers in Marguerite de Navarre's Heptaméron*. Lexington, Ky.: French Forum Publishers, 1978.

Delègue, Yves. "Autour de deux prologues: l'*Heptaméron* est-il un anti-Boccace?" *Travaux de linguistique et de littérature romanes de l'Université de Strasbourg*, 4 (1966), pp. 23–37.

Doumic, René. "Marguerite de Navarre d'après ses dernières poésies." *Revue des Deux Mondes*, 3 (1896), pp. 934–45.

Dudon, Paul. "La Marguerite des Marguerites." *Etudes*, 3 (1931), pp. 688–707.

Ely, Gladys. "The Limits of Realism in the *Heptaméron* de Marguerite de Navarre." *Romanic Review*, 43 (1952), pp. 3–11.

Farinelli, Arturo. "Dante e Margherita di Navarra." *Rivista d'Italia*, 1902, pp. 274–301. Rpt. in his *Dante e la Francia dall'eta media al secolo di Voltaire*. Milan: Hoepli, 1908, pp. 328–59.

Febvre, Lucien. *Amour sacré, amour profane: autour de l'Heptaméron*. Paris: Gallimard, 1944.

Fontanella, Lucia. "Per una edizione del *Miroir de Jesus Christ Crucifié* di Margherita di Navarra." *Le Moyen français*, 3 (1978), pp. 107–19.

Gelernt, Jules. *World of Many Loves: The Heptaméron of Marguerite de Navarre*. Chapel Hill: University of North Carolina Press, 1966.

Hauser, Henri. "Les Dernières Poésies de Marguerite de Navarre." *Revue Critique*, 41 (1896), pp. 510–13.

Heller, Henry. "Marguerite de Navarre and the Reformers of Meaux." *Bibliothèque d'Humanisme et Renaissance*, 33 (1971), pp. 271–310.

Jourda, Pierre. *Marguerite d'Angoulême, Duchesse d'Alençon, Reine de Navarre (1492–1549): Etude biographique et littéraire*. 2 vols. Paris: Champion, 1930.

———. "Le Mécénat de Marguerite de Navarre." *Revue du seizième siècle*, 18 (1931), pp. 253–71.

———. "Notes sur la versification de Marguerite de Navarre." *Revue de philologie française*, 42 (1930), pp. 89–105.

———. "Récents écrits italiens sur Marguerite de Navarre." *Revue du seizième siècle*, 11 (1924), pp. 273–88.

———. *Répertoire analytique et chronologique de la correspondance de Marguerite d'Angoulême*. Paris: Champion, 1930.

———. "Tableau chronologique des publications de Marguerite de Navarre." *Revue du seizième siècle*, 12 (1925), pp. 209–55.

Kaspryzk, Krystyna. "L'Amour dans l'*Heptaméron*. De l'idéal à la réalité." In *Mélanges d'histoire littéraire (XVIe–XVIIe) siècle offerts à Raymond Lebègue par ses collègues, ses élèves et ses amis*. Paris: Nizet, 1969, pp. 51–57.

Krailsheimer, A. J. "The *Heptaméron* Reconsidered." In *The French Renaissance and Its Heritage: Essays Presented to Alan M. Boase by Colleagues, Pupils and Friends*. London: Methuen, 1968, pp. 75–92.

Kraus, Claudia. *Der religiöse Lyrismus Margaretes von Navarra*. Munich: Wilhelm Fink Verlag (Münchener Romanistische Arbeiten, 53), 1981.

Krömer, Wolfram. "Die Struktur der Novelle in Margaretes *Heptaméron*." *Romanistisches Jahrbuch*, 18 (1967), pp. 67–88.

Kupisz, Kazimierz. "La Mal Mariée et l'*Heptaméron*: Contribution à l'histoire d'un thème littéraire." *Zagadnienia Rodzajow Literackich*, 21 (1978), pp. 23–40.

———. "Modernité de la poétique de Marguerite de Navarre." *Bérénice*, 1 (1980), pp. 65–76.

La Ferrière, H. de. *Marguerite d'Angoulême, soeur de François Ier. Son livre de dépense (1540–49)*. Paris: Aubry, 1862.

La Garanderie, Marie-Madeleine de. *Le Dialogue des romanciers: une nouvelle lecture de l'Heptaméron.* Paris: Minard, 1976.

Lajarte, Philippe de. "L'*Heptaméron* et le ficinisme." *Revue des sciences humaines,* 147 (1972), pp. 339–71.

———. "L'*Heptaméron* et la naissance du récit moderne." *Littérature,* 17 (1975), pp. 31–42.

———. "Le Prologue de *l'Heptaméron* et le processus de production de l'oeuvre." In *La Nouvelle française à la Renaissance.* Eds. Lionello Sozzi and V. L. Saulnier. Geneva: Slatkin, 1981, pp. 397–423.

Lanson, Gustave. "Les Dernières Poésies de Marguerite de Navarre." *Revue d'histoire littéraire de la France,* 3 (1896), pp. 292–98.

Lebègue, Raymond. "Marguerite de Navarre et le théâtre." *Humanisme et Renaissance,* 5 (1938), pp. 330–33.

———. "Le Second Miroir de Marguerite de Navarre." *Comptes rendus des séances de l'Académie des Inscriptions et Belles-Lettres,* 1963, pp. 46–56.

———. "Les Sources de l'*Heptaméron* et la pensée de Marguerite de Navarre." *Comptes rendus des séances de l'Académie des Inscriptions et Belles-Lettres,* 1958, pp. 466–72.

Leckman, Hannah Hone. *Mysticism in the Poetry of Marguerite de Navarre.* Diss. Washington: The Catholic University of America, 1982.

Lefranc, Abel and Jacques Boulenger. *Comptes de Louise de Savoie et de Marguerite d'Angoulême.* Paris: Champion, 1905.

Lefranc, Abel. "Les Idées religieuses de Marguerite de Navarre d'après son oeuvre poétique." *Bulletin de la Société de l'histoire du protestantisme français,* 46 (1897), pp. 7–30, 72–84, 137–48, 295–311, 418–42.

———. "Marguerite de Navarre et le Platonisme de la Renaissance." *Bibliothèque de l'Ecole des chartes,* 58 (1897), pp. 259–92; 59 (1898), pp. 712–57. Rpt. in his *Grands Ecrivains de la Renaissance.* Paris: Champion, 1914, pp. 139–249.

Le Hir, Yves. "L'Inspiration biblique dans le *Triomphe de l'agneau* de Marguerite de Navarre." In *Mélanges d'histoire littéraire de la Renaissance offerts à Henri Chamard.* Paris: Nizet, 1951, pp. 43–61.

———. "Sur des *Epîtres* de Marguerite de Navarre corrigées par Jean Favre." *Travaux de linguistique et de littérature,* 16 (1978), pp. 317–22.

Marichal, Robert. "La Coche de Marguerite de Navarre." *Humanisme et Renaissance,* 5 (1938), pp. 37–99, 247–96.

Martineau-Génieys, Christine. "Le Platonisme de Marguerite de Navarre." *Réforme, Humanisme, Renaissance,* 83 (1978), pp. 12–35.

Martineau, Christine and Christian Grouselle. "La Source première et directe du 'Dialogue en forme de vision nocturne': la lettre de Guillaume Briçonnet à Marguerite de Navarre, du 15 septembre 1524. Publication et commentaire." *Bibliothèque d'Humanisme et Renaissance,* 32 (1970), pp. 559–77.

Masters, G. Mallary. "Structured Prisons, Imprisoned Structures: Marguerite de Navarre's *Prisons.*" *Renaissance Papers,* 1973, pp. 11–22.

Meijer, Marianne. "The *Heptaméron*: Feminism with a Smile." *Regionalism and the Female Imagination,* 3 (1977–78), pp. 1–10.

Meylan, Edward F. "La Date de 'l'Oraison de l'âme fidèle' et son importance pour la biographie morale de Marguerite de Navarre." *Modern Language Notes,* 52 (1937), pp. 562–68.

Neubert, Fritz. "Zur Problematik der Briefe der Marguerite von Navarre." *Zeitschrift für romanische Philologie*, 79 (1963), pp. 117–72.

Norton, Glyn P. "The Emilio Ferretti Letter: A Critical Preface for Marguerite de Navarre." *Journal of Medieval and Renaissance Studies*, 4 (1974), pp. 287–300.

———. "Narrative function in the *Heptaméron* Frame-story." In *La Nouvelle française à la Renaissance*. Eds. Lionello Sozzi and V. L. Saulnier. Geneva: Slatkin, 1981, pp. 435–47.

Palmero, Joseph. "L'Historicité des devisants de l'*Heptaméron*." *Revue d'histoire littéraire de la France*, 69 (1969), pp. 193–202.

Paris, Gaston. "Les dernières poésies de Marguerite de Navarre, publiées par Abel Lefranc." *Journal des savants*, 1896, pp. 273–88, 346–68.

Parturier, Emile. "Les Sources du mysticisme de Marguerite de Navarre." *Revue de la renaissance*, 5 (1904), pp. 108–14; 178–90; 273–80.

Pellegrini, Carlo. *La prima opera di Margherita di Navarra e la terza rima in Francia*. Catania: Battiato, 1920.

———. "Reflessi di cultura italiana in Margherita di Navarra." In *Tradizione italiana e cultura europea*. Messina: Anna, 1947.

Picot, Emile. *Les Français italianisants au XVIᵉ siècle*. Paris: Champion, 1906, Vol. 1, pp. 41–50.

Phillips, M. Mann. "Marguerite de Navarre et Erasme: une reconsidération." *Revue de littérature comparée*, 52 (1978), pp. 194–201.

Renaudet, Augustin. "Marguerite de Navarre. A propos d'un ouvrage récent." *Revue du seizième siècle*, 18 (1931), pp. 175–78.

Reynolds, Regine. *Les Devisants de l'Heptaméron: dix personnages en quête d'audience*. Washington: University Press of America, 1977.

Ritter, Raymond. *Lettres de Marguerite de Valois-Angoulême*. Paris: Champion, 1927.

———. *"Les Solitudes de la Reine de Navarre*. Paris: Champion, 1953.

Rossi, Daniela. "*Honneur* e *conscience* nella lingua e nella cultura di Margherita di Navarra." *Journal of Medieval and Renaissance Studies*, 5 (1975), pp. 63–87.

Sage, Pierre. "Le Platonisme de Marguerite de Navarre." *Travaux de linguistique et de littérature*, 7 (1969), pp. 65–82.

———. "La Sainte Vierge dans l'oeuvre de Marguerite de Navarre." *Bulletin des Facultés catholiques de Lyon*, January–June (1954), pp. 17–27.

Sainte-Marthe, Charles de. *Oraison funèbre de la Mort de l'Incomparable Marguerite, Royne de Navarre et Duchesse d'Alençon, composée en latin par Charles de Sainte-Marthe et traduite par luy en langue françoise*. In *L'Heptaméron*, Vol. 1. Eds. Le Roux de Lincy and Montaiglon. Paris: Eudes, 1880, Rpt. Geneva: Slatkine, 1969.

San Miguel, Angel. "Die Comédie jouée au Mont de Marsan von Margarete von Navarra." *Literaturwissenschaftliches Jahrbuch*, 23 (1982), pp. 71–80.

Saulnier, V. L. "La Correspondance de Marguerite de Navarre." *Bibliothèque d'Humanisme et Renaissance*, 33, No. 3 (1971), pp. 571–605.

———. "Etudes critiques sur les Comédies profanes de Marguerite de Navarre." *Bibliothèque d'Humanisme et Renaissance*, 9 (1947), pp. 36–77.

———. "Intrigues pour un évêché: Marguerite de Navarre et le siège de Sarlat (1530)." *Kwartalnik Neofilologiczny* (Warsaw), 23 (1976), pp. 209–16.

————. "Marguerite de Navarre, art médiéval et pensée nouvelle." *Revue universitaire*, May-June (1954), pp. 154–62.

————. "Marguerite de Navarre au temps de Briçonnet: étude de la correspondance générale (1521–22), première partie." *Bibliothèque d'Humanisme et Renaissance*, 39 (1976), pp. 437–78.

————. "Marguerite de Navarre au temps de Briçonnet: étude de la correspondance générale (1521–22)." *Bibliothèque d'Humanisme et Renaissance*, 40 (1978), 7–47.

————. "Marguerite de Navarre, Catherine de Médicis et les psaumes de Marot: autour de la lettre dite de Villemandon." *Bibliothèque d'Humanisme et Renaissance*, 37 (1975), 349–76.

————. "Marguerite de Navarre en ses derniers temps. Sur les lettres de 1547–49." *Bibliothèque d'Humanisme et Renaissance*, 36 (1974), pp. 533–73.

————. "Marguerite loin du roi blessé: sur la correspondance de Marguerite d'Angoulême aux lendemains de Pavie." In *Missions et démarches de la critique: mélanges offerts au Professeur J. A. Vier*. Paris: Klincksieck, 1973, pp. 435–53.

————. "Sur des lettres de Marguerite d'Angoulême aux temps d'Espagne." *Travaux de linguistique et de littérature publiés par le Centre de philologie et de littératures romanes de l'Université de Strasbourg*, 13 (1975), pp. 31–45.

————. "Troubles au couvent de Tarascon (Marguerite de Navarre, Guillaume du Maine, Claude de Bectoz et Denys Faucher)." In *Renaissance Studies in Honor of Isidore Silver*. Ed. Frieda S. Brown. *Kentucky Romance Quarterly*, 21, Suppl. 2 (1974), pp. 309–17.

Schneegans, Edouard. "Le Poème des *Prisons* de Marguerite de Navarre." *Bulletin de la Faculté des lettres de Strasbourg*, 24 (1945–46), 53–59.

Sckommodau, Hans. *Galanterie und vollkommene Liebe in L'Heptaméron*. Munich: W. Fink, 1977.

————. *Die religiösen Dichtungen Margaretes von Navarra*. Cologne: Westdeutscher Verlag, 1955.

————. *Die spätfeudalistische Novelle bei Margarete von Navarra*. Wiesbaden: Steiner, 1977.

Stone, Donald. "Narrative Technique in *L'Heptaméron*. *Studi francesi*, 11 (1967), pp. 473–76.

Strohl, Henri. *De Marguerite de Navarre à Louise Scheppler. Quelques étapes de la pensée protestante en France*. Strasbourg: Etudes d'histoire et de philosophie religieuses, 1924.

Telle, Emile V. "Un Document sur le mécénat de Marguerite d'Angoulême, reine de Navarre." *Bibliothèque d'Humanisme et Renaissance*, 34 (1972), pp. 279–81.

————. *L'Oeuvre de Marguerite d'Angoulême, Reine de Navarre, et la querelle des femmes*. Toulouse: Lion, 1937.

Tetel, Marcel. "Marguerite de Navarre et Montaigne: relativisme et paradoxe." In *From Marot to Montaigne. Essays on French Renaissance Literature*. Ed. Raymond C. La Charité. *Kentucky Romance Quarterly*, 19, Suppl. 1 (1972), pp. 125–35.

————. *Marguerite de Navarre's Heptaméron: Themes, Language, and Structure*. Durham, N.C.: Duke University Press, 1973.

Toussaint du Waast, Nicole. *Marguerite de Navarre. La Perle des Valois*. Paris: Max-Fourny, 1976.

Vernay, Henri. *Les Divers Sens du mot Raison autour de l'oeuvre de Marguerite d'Angoulême, reine de Navarre (1492–1549).* Heidelberg: Carl Winter. 1962.

Wagner, Nicolas. "Le Sentiment religieux et le refus de l'utopie dans les *Nouvelles* de Marguerite." *Réforme, Humanisme, Renaissance,* 5 (1977), pp. 4–8.

Wiley, William L. "The Complexities of Marguerite de Navarre's Secular Theatre." In *Renaissance Studies in Honor of Isidore Silver.* Ed. Frieda S. Brown. *Kentucky Romance Quarterly,* 21, Suppl. 2 (1974), pp. 319–330.

Winandy, André. "Piety and Humanistic Symbolism in the Works of Marguerite d'Angoulême, Queen of Navarra." *Image and Symbol in the Renaissance.* *Yale French Studies,* 47 (1972), 145–69.

———. "Piété et symbolique humaniste dans l'oeuvre de Marguerite de Navarre." In *L'Humanisme français au début de la renaissance.* Paris: Vrin, 1973, pp. 225–39. (A French translation of his article in English.)

Zamparelli, Thomas L. "Duality in the *Comédies profanes* of Marguerite de Navarre," *South Central Bulletin,* 38 (1978), pp. 166–69.

OTHER WORKS

Apel, Karl. *Die Idee der Sprache in der Tradition des Humanismus von Dante bis Vico.* Bonn: Archiv für Begriffsgeschichte, 1963.

Arbor amoris. Der Minnebaum. Ein pseudo-Bonaventura-Traktat. Ed. Urs Kamber. Berlin: E. Schmidt, 1964.

Armstrong, Christopher. "The Dialectical Road to Truth: The Dialogue." *French Renaissance Studies 1540–70.* Ed. Peter Sharratt. Edinburgh: Edinburgh University Press, 1965, pp. 36–51.

Aubin, Paul. "L'*Image* dans l'oeuvre de Plotin." *Recherches de science religieuse,* 41 (1953), pp. 348–79.

Audin, Maurice. *Histoire de l'imprimerie.* Paris: A. et J. Picard, 1972.

Augustine, Saint. *Confessions.* Trans. R. S. Pine-Coffin. London: Penguin Books, 1961.

———. *De doctrina christiana; De vera.* Ed. Josephus Martin and K. D. Daur. *Corpus christianorum,* series latina, 32. Turnholti: Typographi Brepols Editoris Pontifici, 1962.

———. *De doctrina christiana.* Ed. J. P. Migne. *Patrologia latina cursus completus,* 34. Paris: Garnier, 1845.

———. *Enarrationes in Psalmos.* Ed. D. Eligius Dekkers and Ioannes Fraipont. *Corpus christianorum,* series latina, pp. 38–40. Turnholti: Typographi Brepols Editoris Pontifici, 1956.

———. *De trinitate.* Ed. J. P. Migne. *Patrologia latina cursus completus,* 42. Paris: Garnier, 1845.

———. *De trinitate.* Trans. Stephen McKenna. Washington: The Catholic University of America Press, 1963.

———. *On Christian Doctrine.* Trans. D. W. Robertson, Jr. Indianapolis: Bobbs-Merrill Company, Inc. (The Library of Liberal Arts), 1958.

Baldwin, Charles Sears. *Medieval Rhetoric and Poetic (to 1400) Interpreted from Representative Works.* New York: Macmillan, 1928.

Becker, Philip-August. "Les Idées religieuses de Briçonnet." *Revue de Théologie,* 1900, pp. 318–58, 377–416.

Bedouelle, Guy. *Lefèvre d'Etaples et l'intelligence des Ecritures.* Geneva: Droz (THR), 1976.

Benveniste, Emile. "Le Langage et l'expérience humaine." In *Problèmes de linguistique générale.* Paris: Gallimard, 1966, pp. 3–13.

Besnard-Coursodon, Micheline. "A rebours: le corps parlé." *Revue des sciences humaines,* 43 (1978), pp. 52–58.

Billanovich, G. *I primi umanisti e le tradizioni dei classici latini.* Freiburg: Edizione universitarie, 1953.

Bloch, Oscar and W. von Wartburg. *Dictionnaire étymologique de la langue française.* Paris: Presses universitaires de France, 1964.

Bloomfield, Morton. "Joachim of Flora." *Traditio,* 13 (1957), pp. 249–311.

Boyle, Marjorie O'Rourke. *Erasmus on Language and Method in Theology.* Toronto: University of Toronto Press, 1977.

Bradley, Sister Ritamary. "Backgrounds of the Title *Speculum* in Mediaeval Literature." *Speculum,* 29 (1954), pp. 100–115.

Bréhier, Louis. *L'Art chrétien.* Paris: Renouard, 1928.

Bretonneau, Guy. *Histoire généalogique de la maison des Briçonnet.* Paris: J. Daumalle, 1620.

Brunot, Ferdinand. *Histoire de la langue française des origines à nos jours.* Paris: Colin, 1966.

Brunot, Ferdinand and Charles Bruneau. *Précis de grammaire historique de la langue française.* Paris: Masson, 1949.

Butler, Dom Cuthbert. *Western Mysticism: The Teaching of SS. Augustine, Gregory and Bernard on Contemplation and the Contemplative Life.* London: rpt. E. P. Dutton, 1951.

Calvin, John. *On God and Political Duty.* Ed. John T. McNeill. Indianapolis: Bobbs-Merrill, 1956.

Cappello, Glori. "Neoplatonismo e reforma in Francia: dall'epistolario tra Guglielmo Briçonnet e Margherita di Navarra." In *Logica e semantica ed altri saggi.* Ed. Carlo Giacon. Padova: Antenore, 1975.

———. "Nicolò Cusano nella corrispondenza di Briçonnet con Margherita di Navarra." *Medioevo,* 1 (1975), pp. 97–128.

———. "Per la storia dell'ermeneutica biblica nel 1500: Guglielmo Briçonnet." In *Storiografia ed ermeneutica.* Padova: Editrice Gregoriana, 1975, pp. 293–304.

Carré, Meyrick Heath. *Realists and Nominalists.* London: Oxford University Press, 1961.

Cartier, Albert. *Bibliographie des éditions des de Tournes.* 2 vols. Paris: Editions des Bibliothèques Nationales de France, 1937.

Catherine, Saint. *Libro della divina dottrina.* Bari: Laterza, 1912.

Cave, Terence. "Copia and Cornucopia." In *French Renaissance Studies 1540–70.* Ed. Peter Sharratt. Edinburgh: Edinburgh University Press, 1976, pp. 52–69.

———. *The Cornucopian Text: Problems of Writing in the French Renaissance.* Oxford: Clarendon Press, 1979.

———. *Devotional Poetry in France c. 1570–1613.* Cambridge: Cambridge University Press, 1969.

———. "Enargeia: Erasmus and the Rhetoric of Presence in the Sixteenth Century." *L'Esprit Créateur,* 16 (1976), pp. 5–19.

Chapman, Emmanuel. *Saint Augustine's Philosophy of Beauty*. New York: Sheed & Ward, 1939.

Cicero. *De oratore*. Cambridge: Harvard University Press (Loeb Classical Library), 1959–60.

Clements, Robert J. *Picta Poesis: Literary and Humanistic Theory in Renaissance Emblem Books*. Rome: Edizioni di storia e letteratura, 1960.

Colet, John. *De sacramentis ecclesiae super opera Dionysii*. Ed. and trans. J. H. Lupton. London, 1867. rpt. Gregg International Publishers, 1966.

Colie, Rosalie L. *Paradoxia Epidemica: The Renaissance Tradition of Paradox*. Princeton: Princeton University Press, 1966.

———. *The Resources of Kind: Genre-Theory in the Renaissance*. Berkeley: University of California Press, 1973.

Colish, Marcia L. *The Mirror of Language: A Study in the Medieval Theory of Knowledge*. New Haven: Yale University Press, 1968.

Comeau, Marie. *La Rhétorique de Saint Augustin d'après les Tractatus In Ioannem*. Paris: Boivin, 1930.

Comito, Terry. *The Idea of the Garden in the Renaissance*. New Brunswick, N.J.: Rutgers University Press, 1978.

Congar, Yves. "Langage des spirituels et langage des théologiens." In *La Mystique rhénane*. Colloque de Strasbourg, 16–19 mai 1961. Paris: Presses universitaires de France, 1963, pp. 15–34.

Cotgrave, Randle. *Dictionarie of the French and English Tongues* (1611). Rpt. Columbia, South Carolina: University of South Carolina Press, 1950.

Culler, Jonathan. *Structuralist Poetics*. Ithaca: Cornell University Press, 1975.

Curtius, Ernst Robert. *European Literature and the Latin Middle Ages*. Princeton: Princeton University Press, 1952.

Cusanus. *Idiota*. English trans. London, 1650. Rpt. San Francisco: Sturo Branch of California State Library, 1940.

———. *Of Learned Ignorance*. Trans. Germain Heron. New Haven: Yale University Press and London: Routledge & Paul, 1954.

———. *Opera*. Paris: Jod. Badium Asc., 1514. Rpt. Frankfurt am Main: Minerva, 1962.

Dagens, J. "Humanisme et évangélisme chez J. Lefèvre d'Etaples." In *Courants religieux et humanisme*. Paris: Presses universitaires de France, 1959, pp. 121–34.

Dauzot, Albert. *Dictionnaire étymologique de la langue française*. Paris: Larousse, 1938.

Dauzot, Albert and Jean Dubois, Henri Mitterand. *Nouveau dictionnaire étymologique et historique*. Paris: Larousse, 1964.

Da Vinci, Leonardo. *Literary Works*. Ed. J. P. Richter. Oxford: Oxford University Press, 1939.

Delacroix, Henri. *Etudes d'histoire et de psychologie du mysticisme*. Paris: Alcan, 1908.

Dieckmann, Liselotte. *Hieroglyphics: The History of a Literary Symbol*. St. Louis: Washington University Press, 1970.

Dionysius the Areopagite. *Oeuvres complètes du Pseudo-Denys l'Aréopagite*. Paris: Aubier Editions Montaigne, 1943.

———. *On Divine Names and the Mystical Theology*. Ed. C. E. Rolt. New York: Macmillan Company, 1920. Rpt. 1951.

Dragonetti, Roger. *La Technique poétique des trouvères dans la chanson courtoise*. Bruges: De Tempel, 1960.

————. *La Vie de la lettre au Moyen Age*. Paris: Seuil, 1980.

Dubois, Claude-Gilbert. *La Conception de l'histoire en France au XVIe siècle (1560–1610)*. Paris: Nizet, 1977.

————. "Corps de la lettre et sexe des nombres: l'imagination de la forme dans le traité de Geoffroy Tory sur la *Vraye proportion des lettres*." *Revue des sciences humaines*, 170 (1980), pp. 77–91.

————. *Mythe et langage au seizième siècle*. Bordeaux: Ducros, 1970.

Dupire, N. *Jean Molinet: la vie, les oeuvres*. Paris: Droz, 1936.

Du Plessis, T. *Histoire de l'église de Meaux*. Paris: J.-M. Gandouin and P.-F. Giffart, 1731.

Eckhart. *Meister Eckhart*. Trans. Raymond B. Blakney. New York: Harper & Brothers, 1941.

Edelstein, Ludwig. *Studies in Intellectual History*. Baltimore: The Johns Hopkins Press, 1953.

Ellel, Jacques. *L'Apocalypse: architecture en mouvement*. Brussels: Desclée, 1975.

Erasmus. *On Copia of Words and Ideas (De Utraque Verborum ac Rerum Copia)*. Trans. Donald B. King and H. David Rix. Milwaukee, Wis.: Marquette University Press, 1963.

————. *Handbook of the Militant Christian (Enchiridion Militis Christiani)*. Trans. John P. Dolan. Notre Dame, Ind.: Fides Publishers, Inc., 1962.

————. *Opus Epistolarum*. Ed. H. N. Allen. Oxford: Oxford University Press, 1926–28.

————. *Opera omnia*. Ed. J. Clericus. Leiden, 1703–1706.

Ernout, A. and A. Meillet. *Dictionnaire étymologique de la langue latine*. 3rd ed. Paris: Klincksieck, 1951.

Eymard, Julien. *Le Thème du miroir dans la poésie française, 1540–1815*. Lille: Service de reproduction des thèses, Université de Lille III, 1975.

Farinelli, Arturo. *Dante e la Francia dall'eta media al secolo di Voltaire*. Milan: Hoepli, 1908.

Febvre, Lucien and Henri-Jean Martin. *L'Apparition du livre*. Paris: Michel, 1958.

Febvre, Lucien. "L'Idée d'une recherche d'histoire comparée: le cas Briçonnet." *Au coeur religieux du XVIe siècle*. Paris: SEVPEN, 1957, pp. 145–66.

Ferguson, Wallace K. *The Renaissance in Historical Thought*. Cambridge: Houghton Mifflin Co., 1948.

Ficin, Marsile. *Commentaire sur le Banquet de Platon*. Ed. Raymond Marcel. Paris: Belles-Lettres, 1956.

Finaert, Joseph. *L'Evolution littéraire de Saint Augustin*. Paris: Belles Lettres, 1939.

Fish, Stanley E. *Self-Consuming Artifacts: The Experience of Seventeenth-Century Literature*. Berkeley: University of California Press, 1972.

Fletcher, Angus. *Allegory: The Theory of a Symbolic Mode*. Ithaca: Cornell University Press, 1964.

Foucault, Michel. *Histoire de la sexualité: la volonté de savoir*. Paris: Gallimard, 1976. *The History of Sexuality*, trans. Robert Hurley. New York: Vintage Books, 1980.

———. *Les Mots et les choses.* Paris: Gallimard, 1966. *The Order of Things,* n. trans. New York: Pantheon, 1970.

Freccero, John. "The Fig Tree and the Laurel: Petrarch's Poetics." *Diacritics,* 5, No. 1 (1975), pp. 34–40.

Freeman, Rosemary. *English Emblem Books.* London: Chatto & Windus, 1948.

Frye, Northrop. *Anatomy of Criticism.* Princeton: Princeton University Press, 1957.

Fumaroli, Marc. *L'Age de l'éloquence: Rhétorique et "res literaria" de la Renaissance au seuil de l'époque classique.* Geneva: Droz, 1980.

Gamillscheg, Ernst. *Etymologisches Wörterbuch der Französischen Sprache.* Heidelberg: Carl Winter's Universitätsbuchhandlung, 1928.

Gandillac, Maurice de. *Le Soleil à la Renaissance.* Brussels: Presses universitaires de Bruxelles, 1965.

Gardner, Helen. "Walter Hilton and the Mystical Tradition in England." *Essays and Studies,* 22 (1937), pp. 11–30.

Geiger, Louis-B. *Le Problème de l'amour chez Saint Thomas d'Aquin.* Paris: Vrin, 1952.

Giamatti, A. Bartlett. *The Earthly Paradise and the Renaissance Epic.* Princeton: Princeton University Press, 1966.

Glatstein, Irwin Lee. "Semantics, too, Has a Past." *The Quarterly Journal of Speech,* 32 (1946), pp. 48–51.

Godefroy, Frédéric. *Dictionnaire de l'ancienne langue française.* Paris: Vieweg, 1885.

Goldin, Frederick. *The Mirror of Narcissus in the Courtly Love Lyric.* Ithaca: Cornell University Press, 1967.

Goldschmidt, E. P. *The Printed Book of the Renaissance.* Cambridge: Cambridge University Press, 1950.

Graf, Charles-Henri. *Essais sur la vie et les écrits de Jacques Lefèvre d'Etaples.* Geneva: Slatkine Reprints, 1970. Original publication date, 1842.

Graf, Karl-Heinrich. "Jacobus Faber Stapulensis: ein Beitrag zur Geschichte der Reformation in Frankreich." *Zeitschrift für die Historische Theologie,* 3 (1852), pp. 3–86, 165–237.

Guarnieri, Romana. *Il Movimento del libero spirito.* Rome: Edizioni di storia e letteratura, 1965.

Guillaume, Gustave. *Temps et verbe: théorie des aspects des modes et des temps.* Paris: Champion, 1929.

Guy, Henry. *Histoire de la poésie française de la Renaissance.* 2 vols. Paris: Champion, 1910.

Hardison, Jr., O. B. *The Enduring Monument.* Chapel Hill: University of North Carolina Press, 1962.

Hauser, Henri. *Les Débuts du capitalisme moderne en France.* Paris: F. Alcan, 1902. Rpt. 1931.

Hauvette, Henri. "Dante dans la poésie française de la Renaissance." In *Etudes sur la Divine comédie.* Paris: Champion, 1922.

Heller, Henry. "The Briçonnet Case Reconsidered." *The Journal of Medieval and Renaissance Studies,* 2 (1972), pp. 223–58.

———. "The Evangelism of Lefèvre d'Etaples: 1525." *Studies in the Renaissance,* 19 (1972), pp. 42–77.

Heninger, Jr., S. K. *The Cosmographical Glass: Renaissance Diagrams of the Universe.* San Marino, Calif.: Huntington Library, 1977.

Henkel, Arthur and Albrecht Schöne. *Emblemata. Handbuch zur Sinnbildkunst des XVI and XVII Jahrhunderts.* Stuttgart: Im Auftrage der Göttinger Akademie der Wissenschaften, 1967.

Henle, Paul. *Language, Thought, and Culture.* Ann Arbor: University of Michigan Press, 1958.

Herminjard, A.-L. *Correspondance des réformateurs dans les pays de langue française.* 9 vols. Geneva: Georg; Paris: Lévy, 1866–97. Rpt. Nieuwkoop: B. De Graff, 1965.

Hilton, Walter. *Minor Works of Walter Hilton.* Ed. Dorothy Jones. New York: Benziger Brothers, 1929.

———. *The Scale of Perfection.* Ed. Evelyn Underhill. London: J. M. Watkins, 1923. Rpt. 1948.

———. *The Scale of Perfection.* Introduction by Dom. M. Noetinger. New York: Benziger Brothers, 1927.

Hopper, Vincent Foster. *Medieval Number Symbolism.* New York: Cooper Square, 1932.

Hugedé, Norbert. *La Métaphore du miroir dans les épîtres de Saint Paul aux Corinthiens.* Neuchâtel: Delachaux et Niestlé, 1957.

Huguet, Edmond. *Dictionnaire de la langue française du seizième siècle.* Paris: Champion, 1925.

Hyma, Albert. *The Christian Renaissance. A History of the "Devotio Moderna."* New York and London: The Century Co., 1924.

Imbart de la Tour, Pierre. *Les Origines de la Réforme.* Paris: Hachette, 1914.

Inge, William Ralph. *Christian Mysticism.* London: Methuen & Co., 1899. Rpt. 1948.

Jackson, Darrell B. "The Theory of Signs in St. Augustine's De Doctrina Christiana." *Revue des études augustiniennes,* 15 (1969), pp. 9–49.

Javelet, R. "Psychologie des auteurs spirituels du XIIᵉ siècle." *Revue des sciences religieuses,* 33, No. 1, 2, 3 (1959), pp. 18–64, 97–164, 209–268.

Jeanroy, Alfred. *La Poésie lyrique des Troubadours.* Paris: Didier, 1934.

Juliana of Norwich. *Revelations of Divine Love.* London: Kegan Paul, Trench, Trübner & Co., 1902.

Kaiser, Walter. *Praisers of Folly: Erasmus, Rabelais, Shakespeare.* Cambridge: Harvard University Press, 1963.

Kastner, L. E. "History of the terza rima in France." *Zeitschrift für französische Sprache und Literatur,* 26 (1904), pp. 241–53.

Katsaros, Thomas and Nathaniel Kaplan. *The Western Mystical Tradition.* New Haven: College and University Press, 1969.

Kierkegaard, S. *Repetition: An Essay in Experimental Psychology.* Trans. Walter Lowrie. Princeton: Princeton University Press, 1946.

Knowles, Dom David. *The English Mystical Tradition.* New York: Harper & Row, 1966.

Koenigsberger, Dorothy. *Renaissance Man and Creative Thinking. A History of Concepts of Harmony 1400-1700.* Hassocks, Sussex: Harvester Press, 1979.

Lacan, Jacques. *Ecrits.* Trans. Alan Sheridan. London: Tavistock Publications, 1977.

————. *Séminaire XX*. Paris: Seuil, 1975.

Laplanche, J. and J.-B. Pontalis. *Vocabulaire de la psychanalyse*. Paris: Presses universitaires de France, 1967.

Lebègue, Raymond. "Le Cuyder avant Montaigne et dans les Essais." *Cahiers de l'association internationale des études françaises*, 14 (1962), pp. 275–84.

————. *La Tragédie française de la Renaissance*. Brussels: Office de Publicité, 1954.

Lee, R. W. "*Ut Pictura Poesis*: The Humanistic Theory of Painting." *Art Bulletin*, 22 (1940), pp. 197–269.

Levasti, Arrigo. Ed. *Mistici del duecento e del trecento*. Milan: Ziaaoli, 1960.

Levi, Anthony. *French Moralists: The Theory of the Passions, 1585 to 1649*. Oxford: Clarendon Press, 1964.

Levin, Samuel R. *Linguistic Structures in Poetry*. The Hague: Mouton, 1962.

Lewalski, Barbara Kiefer. *Protestant Poetics and the Seventeenth-Century Religious Lyric*. Princeton: Princeton University Press, 1979.

Lohmann, Johannes. "Das Verhältnis des abendländischen Menschen zur Sprache." *Lexis*, 3 (1953), pp. 5–49.

Lovejoy, A. O. *The Great Chain of Being*. Cambridge: Harvard University Press, 1936.

Loyola. *The Spiritual Exercises of Saint Ignatius of Loyola*. Ed. W. H. Longridge. London: A. R. Mowbray, 1919.

McFarlane, I. D. *A Literary History of France*. London: Ernest Benn, 1974.

McKeon, Richard. "Rhetoric in the Middle Ages." In *Critics and Criticism*, ed. R. C. Crane. Chicago: University of Chicago Press, 1952, pp. 260–96.

Man, Paul de. "The Rhetoric of Temporality." In *Interpretation: Theory and Practice*. Ed. Charles S. Singleton. Baltimore: The Johns Hopkins Press, 1969, pp. 173–209.

Mandrou, Robert. *Introduction à la France moderne: essai de psychologie historique 1500–1640*. Paris: Albin Michel, 1961.

Marcuse, Herbert. *Eros and Civilization*. New York: Vintage Books, 1955.

Marin, Louis. *Etudes sémiologiques*. Paris: Klincksieck, 1971.

————. *Utopie: jeux d'espace*. Paris: Editions de Minuit, 1973.

Margolin, Jean Claude. *Erasme et la musique*. Paris: Vrin, 1965.

Markus, R. A. Ed. *Augustine: A Collection of Critical Essays*. New York: Doubleday Anchor, 1972.

————. "St. Augustine on Signs." *Phronesis*, 2 (1957), pp. 60–83.

Marrou, Henri-Irénée. *Saint Augustin et la fin de la culture antique*. Paris: Boccard, 1958.

Martin, Victor. *Les Origines du gallicanisme*. Paris: Bloud & Gas, 1939.

Martineau-Génieys, Christine. *Le Thème de la mort dans la poésie française de 1450 à 1550*. Paris: Champion, 1978.

Maulde de la Clavière, R. *La Diplomatie au temps de Machiavel*. Geneva: Rpt. Slatkine, 1970.

Mayer, C. P., O.S.A. *Die Zeichen in der geistigen Entwicklung und in der Theologie des jungen Augustinus*. Würzburg: Augustinus Verlag, 1968.

Mazzeo, Joseph Anthony. "St. Augustine's Rhetoric of Silence: Truth vs. Eloquence and Things vs. Signs." In *Renaissance and Seventeenth-Century Studies*. New York: Columbia University Press, 1964, pp. 1–28.

————. *Structure and Thought in the Paradiso*. Ithaca: Cornell University Press, 1948.

Medieval Handbook of Penance. Eds. John T. McNeill and Helen M. Gardner. New York: Columbia University Press, 1938.

Michel, Alain. *Rhétorique et philosophie chez Cicéron*. Paris: Presses universitaires de France, 1960.

Michelet, Jules. *Histoire de France (Réforme)*. In *Oeuvres complètes*. Paris: Flammarion, 1978.

Milosh, Joseph E. *The Scale of Perfection and the English Mystical Tradition*. Madison, Wisc.: University of Wisconsin Press, 1966.

Mohrmann, Christine. *Etude sur le latin des chrétiens*. Rome: Storia e letteratura, 1958–65.

Moore, W. G. *La Réforme allemande et la littérature française: recherches sur la notoriété de Luther en France*. Strasbourg: Publications de la Faculté des Lettres, 1930.

Munteano, B. "Humanisme et rhétorique: la survie littéraire des rhéteurs anciens." *Revue d'histoire littéraire de la France*, 58 (1959), pp. 145–56.

Nygren, Anders. *Agape and Eros: A Study of the Christian Idea of Love*. Trans. P. S. Watson. Philadelphia: Westminster Press, 1953.

Olivier, Pierre. *Le Mirouer du chrestien et moyen de cognoistre Dieu et soimesme*. Paris: Guillaume le Noir, 1556.

Ong, Walter J. "Commonplace Rhapsody: Ravisius Textor, Zwinger and Shakespeare." In *Classical Influence on European Culture A.D. 1500–1700*. Ed. R. R. Bolgar. Cambridge: Cambridge University Press, 1976, pp. 91–126.

————. *Ramus, Method, and the Decay of Dialogue*. Cambridge: Harvard University Press, 1958.

Paris, Jean. *Rabelais au futur*. Paris: Seuil, 1970.

Peirce, Charles S. *Collected Papers*. Cambridge: Harvard University Press, 1933.

Pellegrini, Giuliano. "Introduzione alla letteratura degli emblemi." *Revista di letterature moderne e comparate*, 29 (1976), pp. 5–98.

Perella, N. J. *The Kiss, Sacred and Profane*. Berkeley: University of California Press, 1969.

Picoche, Jacqueline. *Nouveau dictionnaire étymologique du français*. Paris: Hachette-Tchou, 1971.

Pike, Robert. "The Blason in French Literature of the XVIth Century." *Romanic Review*, 27 (1936), pp. 223–42.

Pinborg, J. *Die Entwicklung der Sprachtheorie im Mittelalter*. Copenhagen: Münster/West f. Aschendorff in Verbindung mit dem Verlag Arne Forst-Hansen, 1967.

Plato. *The Republic*. Cambridge: Harvard University Press (Loeb Classical Library), 1935.

————. *Timaeus*. Cambridge: Harvard University Press (Loeb Classical Library), 1935.

Plotinus. *Enneads*. Cambridge: Harvard University Press (Loeb Classical Library), 1966.

Porète, Marguerite. *Le Miroir des simples ames*. In Romana Guarnieri, *Il Movimento del libero spirito*. Rome: Edizioni di storia e letteratura, 1965.

Prince, Gerald. "Le discours attributif et le récit." *Poétique*, 35 (1978), pp. 305–13.

Quinones, Ricardo J. *The Renaissance Discovery of Time.* Cambridge: Harvard University Press, 1972.

Rabelais. *Tiers Livre.* Ed. Michael Screech. Geneva: Droz (TLF), 1974.

Renaudet, Augustin. "Un Problème historique: la pensée religieuse de J. Lefèvre d'Etaples." In *Medioevo e Rinascimento. Studi in onore di Bruno Nardi.* Florence: Sansoni, 1955, pp. 623–50.

———. *Préréforme et humanisme à Paris pendant les premières guerres d'Italie, 1494–1517.* Paris: Rpt. Librairie d'Argences, 1953.

Rewar, Walter. "The Cybernetic Modeling of Performance." *Language and Style* (Spring 1980), pp. 282–93.

Rigolot, François. *Poétique et onomastique: l'exemple de la Renaissance.* Geneva: Droz, 1977.

Rice, Eugene. Ed. *The Prefatory Epistles of Jacques Lefèvre d'Etaples and Related Texts.* New York: Columbia University Press, 1972.

———. *The Renaissance Idea of Wisdom.* Cambridge: Harvard University Press, 1958.

Ricoeur, Paul. *The Rule of Metaphor.* Trans. Robert Czerny. Toronto: University of Toronto Press, 1977.

Riffaterre, Michael. *Essais de stylistique structurale.* Paris: Flammarion, 1971.

———. *Semiotics of Poetry.* Bloomington, Ind.: Indiana University Press, 1978.

Roelker, Nancy Lymann. *Queen of Navarre, Jeanne d'Albert, 1528–1572.* Cambridge: Harvard University Press, 1968.

Santinello, G. "*Materia prima* e Lefèvre d'Etaples." In *Studi sull'umanesimo europeo.* Padova: Antenore, 1969, pp. 45–73.

Sckommodau, Hans. "Vortridentinische Klima in der französischen Renaissance-Literatur." *Romanische Forschungen*, 65 (1954), pp. 69–93.

Shapiro, Marianne. "Mirror and Portrait: The Structure of Il Libro del Cortegiano." *The Journal of Medieval and Renaissance Studies*, 5 (1975), pp. 37–61.

Shearman, John. *Mannerism.* London: Penguin Books, 1967.

Siegel, J. E. *Rhetoric and Philosophy in Renaissance Humanism.* Princeton: Princeton University Press, 1968.

Sombart, Werner. *Der Bourgeois: zur Geistesgeschichte des modernen Wirtschaftsmenschen.* Munich: Duncher & Humbolt, 1913.

Spitzer, Leo. *Classical and Christian Ideas of World Harmony. Prolegomena to an Interpretation of the Word "Stimmung."* Ed. Anna Granville Hatcher. Baltimore: The Johns Hopkins Press, 1963.

Spont, Alfred. *Semblançay. La Bourgeoisie financière au début du XVIᵉ siècle.* Paris: Hachette, 1895.

Stierle, Karlhinz. "L'Histoire comme exemple, l'exemple comme histoire." *Poétique*, 10 (1972), pp. 176–98.

Struever, Nancy S. *The Language of History in the Renaissance: Rhetorical and Historical Consciousness in Florentine Humanism.* Princeton: Princeton University Press, 1970.

Tawney, Richard H. *Religion and the Rise of Capitalism.* London: Marray, 1929.

Tomarken, Annette and Edward. "The Rise and Fall of the Sixteenth-Century French Blason." *Symposium*, 29 (1975), pp. 139–63.

Tory, Geoffroy. *Champ fleuri* (1529). Rpt. The Hague: Johnson Reprint Corporation, 1970.

Trapp, J. B. "John Colet, His Manuscripts and the Ps.-Dionysius." In *Classical Influences on European Culture A.D. 1500–1700*. Ed. R. R. Bolgar. Cambridge: Cambridge University Press, 1976.

Tuve, Rosemond. *Allegorical Imagery*. Princeton: Princeton University Press, 1966.

Vance, Eugene. "Augustine's Confessions and the Grammar of Selfhood." *Genre*, 6 (1973), pp. 1–28.

———. "Love's Concordance: The Poetics of Desire and the Joy of the Text." *Diacritics*, 5, No. 1 (1975), pp. 40–52.

———. "Saint Augustine: Language as Temporality." *In Mimesis: From Mirror to Method, Augustine to Descartes*. Eds. John D. Lyons and Stephen G. Nichols, Jr. Hanover and London: University Press of New England, 1982.

Veissière, Michel. "Le Groupe évangélique de Meaux à la lumière de quelques travaux récents." *Bulletin de la Société d'Histoire et d'Art du diocèse de Meaux*, 1973.

———. "Guillaume Briçonnet, abbé rénovateur de Saint-Germain-des-Prés (1507–1534)." *Revue d'Histoire de l'Eglise de France*, 40, No. 164 (1974), pp. 65–84.

Victor, Joseph M. *Charles de Bovelles 1479-1533: An Intellectual Biography*. Geneva: Droz (THR), 1978.

Vignaux, Paul. *Nominalisme au XIVᵉ siècle*. Paris: Vrin, 1948.

Villain, M. "Le Message biblique de Lefèvre d'Etaples." *Recherches de science religieuse*, 40 (1952), pp. 234–59.

Walker, D. P. *The Ancient Theology. Studies in Christian Platonism from the Fifteenth to the Eighteenth Century*. Ithaca: Cornell University Press, 1972.

Weber, Henri. *La Création poétique au XVIᵉ siècle en France*. 2 vols. Paris: Nizet, 1955.

Welsh, Andrew. *Roots of Lyric*. Princeton: Princeton University Press, 1978.

Welter, J. Thomas. *L'Exemplum dans la littérature religieuse et didactique du moyen âge*. Paris: Guitard, 1927.

Wilden, Anthony. "Changing Frames of Order: Cybernetics and the *Machina Mundi*," In *Communication and Control in Society*. Ed. Klaus Krippendorff. New York: Gordon and Breach, 1979, pp. 9–29.

———. "Montaigne on the Paradoxes of Individualism: A Communication about Communication." In *System and Structure: Essays in Communication and Exchange*. London: Tavistock Publications, 1972.

Wimsatt, W. K. *The Verbal Icon*. Lexington, Ky.: University of Kentucky Press, 1954.

Zumthor, Paul. *Le Masque et la lumière: la poétique des Grands Rhétoriqueurs*. Paris: Seuil, 1978.

Index